The Shoe and Canoe

Village of St Paul.

THE SHOE AND CANOE

OR

PICTURES OF TRAVEL

IN

THE CANADAS.

ILLUSTRATIVE OF

THEIR SCENERY AND OF COLONIAL LIFE;

WITH FACTS AND OPINIONS ON EMIGRATION,
STATE POLICY, AND OTHER POINTS OF PUBLIC INTEREST.

With Numerous Plates and Maps.

By JOHN J. BIGSBY, M.D.

HON. MEM. AMERICAN GEOLOGICAL SOC., LATE SECRETARY TO THE BOUNDARY
COMMISSION UNDER ART. VI. AND VII. TREATY OF GHENT.

IN TWO VOLUMES.

VOL. I.

LONDON:
PUBLISHED BY CHAPMAN AND HALL.

MDCCCL.

"There He setteth the poor on high from affliction; and maketh him families like a flock. The righteous shall see it and rejoice."—*Ps.* cvii.

"Make my grave on the banks of the St. Lawrence."—LORD SYDENHAM, *late Governor-Gen. of British North America.*

PREFACE.

Having in comparative leisure, for a period of six happy years, wandered, pencil and pen in hand, over the greater portion of the Canadas, I purpose, in the following pages, to present to the reader a group of popular pictures of their scenery and social condition.

Through the medium of a series of excursions, it is intended to pourtray the objects which fill the traveller's eye, the life he leads, and the company he meets with, in this romantic and fertile part of North America.

A ready opportunity will thus be afforded

of noticing many important topics: such as emigration, colonial policy, Christian missions, the late Boundary Commission, the Hudson's Bay Company, and of placing on record some new topographical details.

My humble but earnest wish is (and most disinterestedly) to show my fellow-countrymen that Western Canada in particular is a pleasant land; that it presents a variety of enjoyments—sport to the sportsman, inspiration to the poet, excitement to the brave, and health to the delicate; while, at the same time, it offers unfailing abundance to the destitute, and a haven to the homeless.

Many who go thither for a year choose to stay all their lives; and not a few, having left it, are sad and ill at ease until they once more stand upon the breezy shores of Lake Ontario.

Like all who possess personal information on the subject, from the late Lord Metcalf downwards, I beg to recommend and urge a large planned emigration, under the auspices, though not altogether at the expense, of Government.

With the most complete and gratifying success of previous efforts at colonisation, with the full consciousness of wide-prevailing distress at home, and well aware of the millions of rich acres in our American dependencies ready for occupation, the continued apathy of the British people and their rulers seems to call for the expression of no common indignation.

Let us then leave for a brief space the miseries we do not solace, the tears and crimes of our towns and villages, for the great lakes of Canada, reservoirs of crystal waters and wholesome airs, for the broad forest streams which pour into them, whose banks are peopled and peopling with our own energetic race.

Let us contemplate the diligent stirs and

exhaustless plenty of the new world. We shall find much to interest us in the august and singular features of the country, in its natural history, and in its population; among whom, besides the solemn Indian, the stereotyped French Canadian, and the enterprising New Englander, we shall meet with many originals from Europe; some hiding in woody nooks, others standing openly in the sight of a community too busy to bestow upon them more than a passing glance.

As my pages are meant to chronicle with fidelity actual incidents, feelings, and facts, they will tell of few extraordinary adventures, and of neither miracles nor monsters.

I deal not with the perishing things of the hour—with statistics, which (good in their place) are, in Canada, a kind of "dissolving view," so fugitive,—that truth to-day is falsehood almost on the morrow. Who can cope with the statistics of a great country like Canada West, whose population and capital sometimes double in eight years?*

My object is, I repeat, to delineate, not the evanescent, but some of the fixed aspects of this noble colony—in its waters and forests, in its red and white inhabitants, their manners and prospects; and this from notes carefully made on the spot, with frequent corrections up to the present day.

Both my duty and my pleasure took me out of the common track,—into Lakes Simcoe Huron, Superior, &c.; into a portion of South Hudson's Bay, and up the River Ottawa, into Lake Nipissing, as well as to the rarely-visited Highlands of the St. Lawrence below Quebec.

Mine is a personal narrative. The reader's indulgence is, therefore, requested for the egotism which is unavoidable. The impersonal is unreadable: it is the current incident of the day which gives transpa-

* As in 1822–28, according to Sir F. Head and others.

rency and life. Some may say, that I gossip a little. This possibly may be so. It has happened to the wisest of men when beguiled by an agreeable theme. The cheerful get-along style which I desire to adopt is now acknowledged to be the true descriptive; and the stately and sonorous circumlocution of our forefathers is happily out of fashion.

But I must not abuse the great modern privilege of paper and ink in abundance, with the best of pens. A preface should be a title-page developed—a short letter of introduction, prophetic of the coming story, and no more.

Cicero, too, it is well to remember, somewhere lays it down that an auctioneer is to be allowed one puffer; but he does not say the same of an author.

P.S.—The public may be congratulated on the possession, at a moderate cost, of the two charming volumes of "Canadian Scenery," by Mr. Bartlett. His views are equally beautiful and true: mine represent places which that gentleman did not visit, and were selected less for the extremely picturesque than for the characteristic.

London, May 1850.

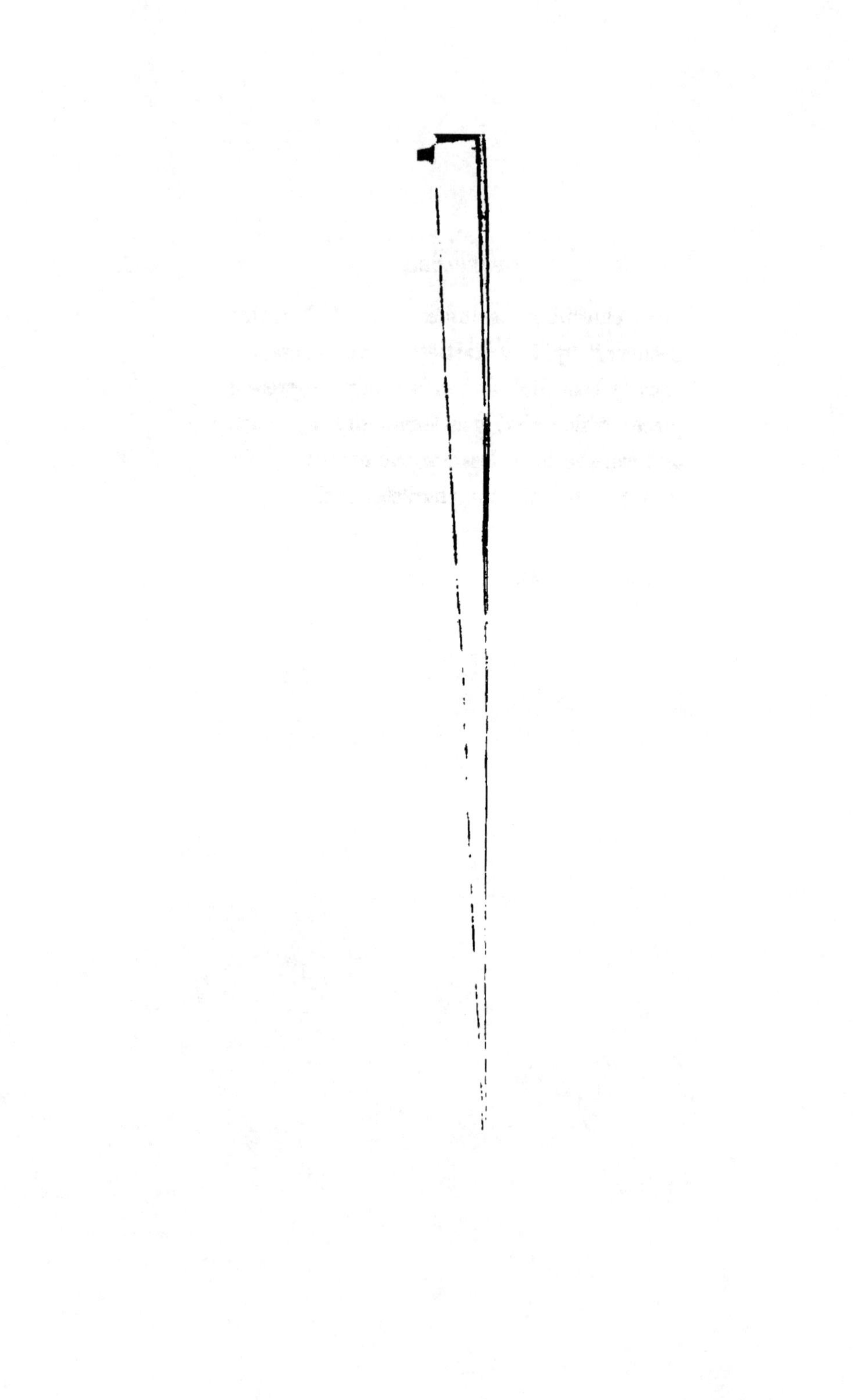

CONTENTS

OF

THE FIRST VOLUME.

EXCURSION THE SECOND.

MONTREAL, THE OTTAWA, ETC.

EXCURSION THE THIRD.

THE ST. LAWRENCE BELOW QUEBEC.

EXCURSION THE FOURTH.

KAMOURASKA AND MALBAY.

EXCURSION THE FIFTH.

PART I.

LAKE ERIE AND THE RIVER DÉTROIT.

EXCURSION THE FIFTH.

PART II.

THE WATERS OF THE ST. CLAIR, ETC.

DIRECTIONS TO THE BINDER.

MAPS.

PLATES.

THE

VOYAGE TO QUEBEC.

VOYAGES across the Atlantic are such every-day events that I shall say but little of mine. They seldom have pleasant reminiscences; and the exploits of young gentlemen in shooting gulls and petrels, or in catching to their cost the stinging medusæ, have ceased to interest.

Steamboats have now converted such passages into mere courses of good eating in good company for prescribed periods, except for ambassadors, governors of colonies, and such-like, who must still submit to the honours and head-winds of the Queen's frigates.

I embarked as the medical officer to a large detachment of a German Rifle Regiment in the English service, amounting, together with a few emigrant families, to the number of three hundred and forty souls.

I think it was inconsiderate in our worthy

sea-captain to direct his course so near the pleasant coasts of Hampshire, Dorset, and Devon, that, as we left our native isle, we could see the slow wain and the gay chariot journeying on the high-roads—the country-seats and farmsteads surrounded by luxuriant crops, in large chequers of yellow, green, and white. Lovely did they look, and hard to leave. A wistful, regretful expression, was strong in every face on board; and when the night closed in, dark, raw, and showery, a young emigrant leaped into the sea, and was lost.

It may seem culinary and mean; but so it was;—much of our comfort came from the cooking talents of a worthy Major, who regulated our mess. He is now a Major-general, and knighted for his services. I shall never forget the felicity with which he daily added to our soup two powders, pinch by pinch; the one a bright orange, and the other of a chocolate colour. Their nature I know not; but their effects on the soup were very gratifying.*

Except a few frights among the ladies, which ended in nothing serious, we had no mishaps

* A very elegant poet and accomplished man, who had spent a day for the first time at Newstead Abbey, was asked, when he returned to the house where he was staying, what he had enjoyed most. His answer was, "I think, my dinner." This, of course, was half a joke; but only half.

worth relating but one. It forms what may be called "the doctor's story."

We had had four or five days' dirty weather, contrary winds and high, with rain,—the seas sweeping over the deck so freely and often that the main-hatchway was usually closed, to the great detriment of the air between decks.

The sky being still dark and squally, I proceeded to fumigate this place, the fetid abode of at least two hundred persons, with sulphuric acid and the nitrate of potass.

The sentinel stood, as usual, over the hatchway, with drawn cutlass, to transmit messages below and to maintain order. He was a fair-haired young German, with the mild, simple look so frequent among his countrymen. I gave him my bottle of strong acid to hold while I descended by the unsteady ladder, so that he had both hands full. At that moment a heavy sea struck the ship, threw the poor German upon the deck, and scattered over him nearly the whole two ounces of burning liquid. Down came his cutlass upon me. He fell bellowing and rolling on the slushy deck like a madman. I thought he would have pushed through the loose flap of the bulwark into the sea. His shrieks and contortions were dreadful.

I took off the upper parts of his dress, and saw that the vitriol had burnt off large strips of skin and flesh from the face, all down the back and breast. I dashed magnesia water over him, and, laying myself down by the poor fellow (as the only means of making him drink), I contrived to pour down his throat, in spite of his convulsive throes, an hundred drops of laudanum.

This produced a lull. I repeated the dose twice at small intervals, until he was pretty well stupified. As the hot, stifling berth in the hold would do harm, I allowed him to lie in the rain on the wet deck for three or four hours, and only padded his sores with fine cotton—giving from time to time a little more laudanum.

As he was then becoming cold, we placed him in a berth below; and he was very grateful for some warm tea.

On stripping him further, we found his legs, too, were peeled. For three days he was in great torment; and a month elapsed before he was convalescent.

I remember but few cases where my feelings were so painfully drawn upon as in this of the amiable and patient German. The rolling, greasy deck, the sheets of drenching spray, the falling rain, and the crowding of affrighted spectators—

together with the agony of the young soldier (caused by myself), made out a scene of gloom and misery which quite overwhelmed me.

During his medical treatment, the doctor and patient became great friends. Many were the tit-bits begged from the officers' mess; and books were supplied, to give pleasure and profit to the weary hour.

As we lay becalmed on the banks of Newfoundland, fishing for cod was a great treat to all ranks on board; both in the catching with hook and line, and in the eating.

The fog was so penetrating as to soak with moisture the blankets in our state-cabins: and yet no one caught cold; and so dense was it, that sometimes we could not see the length of our small vessel.

Not being certain of our position, a boat, into which I jumped, was sent out to sound. The sailors soon learnt where they were from the nature of the bottom.

During our absence, kettles, bells, and bugles, were kept sounding terrifically on board the good ship, or we never should have found it again; for at twenty yards' distance we lost sight of her. I shall never forget the vast magnifying effect of the mist on the ship, her spread sails, shrouds, and cordage. She loomed into sight an immense white mass, filling half the heavens. Young travellers should, on principle, be always placing themselves within reach of new impressions.

Our German soldiers were remarkably docile and good-humoured. Every tolerable evening, a party of them sat in the forecastle, upon the beam which carries the ship's bell, and sang in parts the beautiful airs of their fatherland.

We sailed close past the Isle of St. Paul in the Gulf of St. Lawrence, and thence onwards, very favourably. One fine morning, looking through the porthole of my little cabin, with joy and surprise I saw a pretty shore about half a mile off—a crescent beach of bright yellow sand, with low rocks and woods behind. It was a bight on the coast of Labrador, where we had anchored during the night in a fog.

We soon set sail again, and in due time anchored off Apple Island, sixty or seventy miles below Quebec.

While waiting for a favourable tide we went on shore, and found the island loaded with ripe bilberries (*Vaccinium Canadense*), and in its centre a spring of pure fresh water, bubbling up from beneath a smooth brown rock. The sugar-loaf mountains of New Brunswick were on the south-east in the remote distance, and a low, rugged wilderness on our north, with a few fishermen's huts on the margin of the water.

Only those who have been pent up among the evil scents and dissonant noises of a ship can estimate the pleasure of a wash, a fragrant stroll, and a banquet upon the juicy fruit of America for the first time.

Awaking early next morning, we found the anchor raised and our ship driving rapidly up a magnificent but slowly narrowing gulf, twenty to thirty miles broad. On our north were mountainous forests, dimpled and cut through by populous valleys (Eboulements. St. Paul); while on the south shore we saw gentle uplands, for the most part cultivated, with the white dwellings of the peasantry picturesquely beading the edge of the river St. Lawrence.

By this time we had a first-rate river-hurricane. Two sails were blown to rags. Tide assisting, we drove on under bare poles, at the rate of seventeen to eighteen miles an hour. The winds tore off the sharp white crests of the waves, and dashed them in our faces. Two or three of those sportive fish called "thrashers," a kind of whale, of a shining white colour, were not far off, rushing about in uproarious pastime, and occasionally flinging themselves out of the sea bodily. It was a most animating scene.

We soon came abreast of the large islan
Orleans, and pursued a narrow channel bet
it and the south shore for ten or twelve
when a most splendid panorama burst upo
sight, as we began to cross a basin in fro
Quebec, more than a league broad.

To the left we had the pine-clad rocks,
tered white houses, and trim churches of
Levi; to the right, the lengthy village of
port, and the graceful cascade of Montmo
screened by purple mountains. Before
front, was the fine city of Quebec, crow
lofty promontory, and alternately in gloo
gleam with the scud of the tempest; wh
battlements of Cape Diamond, overlook
city, were seen to extend out of sight
now contracted river. Some vessels of w
crowds of merchant-ships and steamers,
the shore.* Imagination had no diff
placing this noble and varied picture i
propriate frame, "the amplitudes of sa
solitary nature" all around, and reachin
Arctic circle.

* Among other vessels was one which left Portsm
same day that we did, and arrived three hours befor
our having once seen each other on the voyage.

'D ITS ENVIRONS.

' AND SOCIETY.

.ter — The Irish Poor — Society, its
Charivari — Public Institutions — The

r. I landed on one of the
›wn, and found myself amid
ıeavy-built houses and ware-
›y very high, perpendicular
eets, and bearing on their
›uld see from hence, princi-
ıde of the Château St. Louis,
Governor-general.

: the water's edge, Mountain
ıd up a cleft in the precipice

way up I looked down Break-
; flight of steps leading down
›icturesque Champlain Street.

ficer having ridden down them without

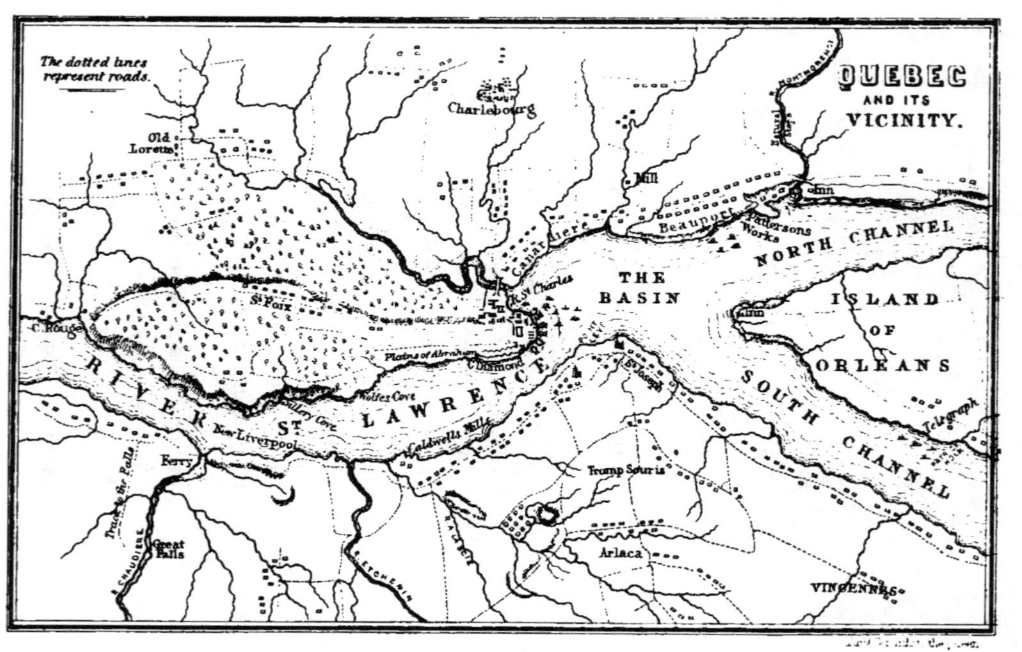
QUEBEC
AND ITS
VICINITY.
The dotted lines
represent roads.
Old
Lorette
Charlebourg
Mill
Inn
Beauport
Patersons
Works
Canardiere
R. St Charles
THE
BASIN
NORTH CHANNEL
ISLAND
OF
ORLEANS
Inn
SOUTH CHANNEL
Telegraph
St Foix
C. Rouge
Plains of Abraham
C. Diamond
Wolfes Cove
Sillery Cove
RIVER ST LAWRENCE
New Liverpool
Caldwells Mills
St Joseph
Ferry
Tramp Souris
Arlaca
VINCENNES
Great
Falls
R. CHAUDIERE
R. ETCHEMIN
Track to the Falls

QUEBEC AND ITS ENVIRONS.

SCENERY AND SOCIETY.

Walk round Quebec — Winter — The Irish Poor — Society, its Materials — Anecdotes — Charivari — Public Institutions — The Vicinity, &c.

We soon cast anchor. I landed on one of the quays of the lower town, and found myself amid a jumble of dingy, heavy-built houses and warehouses, overhung by very high, perpendicular rocks in smooth sheets, and bearing on their brow, so far as I could see from hence, principally, the broad façade of the Château St. Louis, the residence of the Governor-general.

A little way from the water's edge, Mountain Street begins to wind up a cleft in the precipice laboriously steep.

One-third of the way up I looked down Breakneck Stairs,* a long flight of steps leading down to the narrow and picturesque Champlain Street.

* So called from an officer having ridden down them without breaking his neck.

Continuing my upward course, I at length thankfully found level ground on the terrace of the House of Assembly, from whence, sitting on a shotted cannon, my sailor friends and the whole river scene could be espied.

A few stone steps and the turning of a corner or two soon brought me to the Albion Hotel, in the Place d'Armes, the open space near the English church, where I found my military fellow voyagers refreshing themselves right merrily.

This having been done to our complete satisfaction we determined upon a ramble, and thought it best to make for the highest point first; from thence to master the principal bearings and features of our new home, for such to most of us was Quebec to be.

We soon stand upon one of the summits of Cape Diamond, 347 feet above the river.

Of the fortress itself we may only prudently say that it is, externally, an assemblage of low, thick, stone walls, pierced with portholes, running here and there according to the form of the ground and the rules of art. Walled ditches are without, and low barracks, storehouses, and magazines within; and everywhere officers, soldiers, and artificers, are moving about in their different vocations.

From this commanding elevation the eye delights itself in a scene unrivalled in the western world for grandeur, variety, and picturesque beauty. There is nothing comparable, either at New York, Boston, or Philadelphia.

South-westwards (up the river) we have, rising in woody steeps, about 300 feet above the St. Lawrence, the battle-plain of Abraham, now a stony pasture and race-course, but for ever memorable as the spot where died Wolfe and Montcalm, —men of views, and aims, and qualities far in advance of their age. The plain is shut in by pine-woods, which hide several pretty villas and all the country beyond.

Behind me, as I now stand, and far below, the tide runs roughly and swiftly up the river.* Immediately at our feet lies the dusky and dense city of Quebec, with its houses, churches, convents, barracks, and other public edifices, all gloomy and heavy roofed, stretching away into the gradually vanishing suburbs of St. John and St. Roque.

* The river channel was not worn down and formed by itself, but left after some great convulsion, which raised the promontory of Quebec to its present height. Its rocks have been upheaved and torn violently from the adjacent and continuous horizontal strata of limestone. The black limestone of Quebec is perpendicular, or at a very high angle, while its kindred rock all over Canada and the state of New York is horizontal, lying now as it was deposited.

We observe that the city is completely girt with military defences, with occasionally a massive gate, and empty spaces within the walls, either for promenades or markets.

We hear a regimental band playing on the esplanade, near the St. Louis gate, before a crowd of soldiers and spectators.

Passing the eye northwards over the city, it crosses seven miles or more of a rough, partially-cultivated country, dotted with houses, to rest upon a range of steep wooded mountains, which strike the St. Lawrence at Cape Tourment; a black headland, remote, but still high and imposing.

Looking now easterly, we have below us the ample basin of Quebec, alive with ships; and the placid island of Orleans on the far side, twenty miles long, and almost filling up the river.

The immediate south shore, we perceive, is rugged and high, occupied with dwellings, and farms near at hand, while the more distant region, the valley of the Chaudière chiefly, is a sea of undulating forests, extending within sight, I verily believe, of the frontiers of the United States.*

* In winter this whole scene is most splendid, but in a different way. With the exception of the high-pitched roofs of the houses in the town beneath, whose smooth metallic coverings will not allow the snow to rest, the hues of summer are gone. The whole region—the city, suburbs, environs, the plains and slopes, with

Let us now descend into the town. It is a strange place to the mere English. In its architecture it is French, or perhaps it resembles yet more the semi-palatial massiveness of Augsburg.

Standing aloft in the air, swept in winter by Siberian blasts, thick walls and double windows are indispensable at Quebec.

the farm fences—lie asleep, as it were, under a vast envelope of snow, crystalline and dazzling white, while the steeper parts of the sugar-loaf mountains are of a glowing purple.

The St. Lawrence looks dull and leaden, full of ice-fields, with here and there an up-torn tree, the sport of the incessant tides, forming a singular contrast by its drear aspect with the glittering snow and sapphire sky.

Every morning during winter, while at breakfast, I had before me the animating sight of hundreds of the peasantry crossing with laden canoes the boisterous strait between Point Levi and Quebec, at one time pushing their canoes across the floes, and at another paddling through clear water. About every third winter these wandering sheets of ice become fixed, jammed up by a strong wind, and cemented together by two or three sharp nights. This is an event of public interest, and very useful.

A couple of hundred soldiers are sent to mark out the road, by planting young pines at short distances, and winding among high mounds of upheaved sheets and blocks of ice.

A very picturesque scene it is. We are in a deep trough or chasm: on the one side are the Lauzon Precipices (Point Levi continued), fringed with pines; and on the other the city, with its roofs and spires sparkling under a cloudless sun. Indeed the skies are here perfectly Italian, except during the snow-storms, which, by the way, for violence must be seen to be appreciated.

I have repeatedly observed, in severe frosts, the singular fact,—that when the snow has been hard packed it rings on being struck, or clinks, like basalt or greenstone.

This elevation, however, has its advantages also, particularly in the heats of summer; and there is scarcely a turn or opening in any of the streets which does not present to the surprised and charmed sight an exquisite picture of bright waters and mountains, framed in the time-stained rampart or mouldering convent wall. My friend, Mr. Adams, C. E., made a beautiful series of coloured sketches of these peeps, which I greatly coveted.

As I am not writing topography, I shall simply say that we soon found ourselves in a grotesque old market-place, admirably delineated by Bartlett, with a blackened Jesuits' college, now a barrack, on one side, and a large unsightly Roman Catholic church opposite; the two other sides being filled up with antique dwellings, their roofs pierced with windows.

From the market-place there diverge a number of streets with stiff, beetle-browed houses, and some sleepy retail shops, leading either into the country by some sentinelled gateway, or down to the Lower Town.

East of the market-place is St. Louis Street, long, broad, and handsome, the residence of many officials. It has the esplanade, already alluded to, at its south-west end; the English church, the Place d'Armes, and, until lately, the Château

St. Louis, at its north-east end. The château was burnt down not long ago, and its site converted into a promenade of extreme beauty.

There is at the head of Mountain Street a convenient House of Assembly, overlooking the St. Lawrence Basin, and an extensive pile of buildings used as a Catholic seminary.

Having mentioned the respectable Court of Justice and the Albion Hotel, now converted into public offices, I do not leave unnoticed any very prominent structure.

The suburbs of St. Louis, St. John, and St. Roque, although large, are mere rectangular streets, of wooden houses, for the most part unpaved, and only with an edging on the side-walks, of squared logs, to keep the pedestrian out of the deep quagmire which six months out of the twelve reigns triumphant in the carriage-way. Near St. Roque is a spacious and handsome hospital, built under the French *régime*. It is in full employ.

Near St. Roque, also, the River St. Charles passes from the mountains to join the St. Lawrence. Around its slimy embouchure are various breweries and ship-building establishments, which with the timber trade form the staple occupations of Quebec.

We were never allowed to forget that we were

in a military stronghold, especially when we approached the outskirts, bristling and defiant with its covered ways, walls, and bastions, its cannon and pyramids of iron balls guarded by jealous sentries innumerable. We meet not only the French shopkeeper, the active and somewhat assuming English merchant, the sea-captain and his ruddy, whiskered sailors, but everywhere and continually, military of all arms, palpably forming an important portion of the general population.

The French physiognomy and manners everywhere prevail. The young have usually slight figures, short faces, and dark, quick eyes; the old are very wrinkled, but the step is firm, the fire of the bright eye unquenched, and many a mouth is made happy by a short pipe.

I was surprised to find pigtails lingering among the old men, among other relics of the days of Louis XV., and therefore did not wonder in 1837 on being told that a grenadier of Austerlitz and Friedland finds himself at home as beadle of the large church of St. Mark on the banks of the Richelieu.

All the native Canadians of the working class are dressed in a coarse grey cloth of their own manufacture, with the warm hooded capote in winter, of the same colour, bound close to the body by a worsted sash of many gay hues.

The women of the lower orders, dressed in purple and red, as in Normandy, are noisy and brisk. They have the easy, elastic walk, and the amiable look, of their sisters in France, the same neatly-clad feet, the same ready ability and self-confidence. You may see some few charming faces and figures among the very young; but the climate, the stoves, the hard work, and especially the early loss of teeth, destroy all this before the attainment of their thirtieth year.

We do not go far into the streets without meeting an Indian or two, squalid and abject, not revelling in vermillion and feathered finery, like their brethren of the far interior. In the course of the ensuing winter I soon found out, that if we hear the multitudinous barking of curs in the street, it is caused by their besetting and snapping at Indians, who have come from the woods, or from their village of Lorette, to beg, or to sell game and baskets.

The extreme antipathy of town-bred dogs to Indians partly arises from their peculiar odour, which is perceptible at some distance, but to me is not disagreeable.* The Indians take little more

* A short time ago the Indians of the Red River settlement memorialised the Church Missionary Society to send them a missionary—not a new one, but the Rev. Mr. Cockran, who, said they, "was accustomed to their stink."

notice of this annoyance than an occasional lunge with a stick at any dog who comes too forward. The troops of large wolfish dogs which rush upon the traveller, riding or on foot, as he enters any Canadian village, is a great nuisance. They accompany him, as he traverses the place, with open mouth and loud cries, beyond the very last house.

It is high time to put an end to this our first and very gratifying walk round Quebec. On our return to the hotel, our affable landlady surprised us at supper with some prime beaver-tail, which gave rise to much talk and many opinions as to its merits; and the next day, dining at a regimental mess, I partook of a sparerib of bear, and found it excellent.

In common with several of my ship companions I wintered in this city, and collected the desultory observations which now follow.

I scarcely know of anything more interesting to a man of an active and inquiring spirit than a winter residence at Quebec.

If it be pleasant to dwell among an intelligent and proverbially social community; if, taking higher ground, it be pleasant to be a sympathising observer amid a people educating for great destinies, busily working out their material prosperity by means of their great river, and its mediterraneans of fresh water (gifts inestimable), planting and fostering the institutions of science, charity, and religion; then Quebec is an eminently desirable abode and watch-tower.

At Quebec we have all the singularities and novelties of Tobolsk, without a Russian governor, his fiery beard, and fetters.

The town stands so high that all the atmospheric changes of a Siberian climate, so gloomy and so brilliant by turns, are in full display. Many of the houses look directly upon the wilderness, its mountains and floods, so that from your double-windowed drawing-room you can witness in their birth and explosion either the black-grey, blinding, choking snow-storm of the cold season, or the almost unequalled electric tempests of the warm. To gaze upon the aurora borealis of this region is worth a long voyage.

In the streets we walk, with spikes in our shoes, upon ice three and six feet thick, in heavy fur caps and wrappers. We meet with milk for sale, carried about in cabbage-nets; frozen fish, which come to life again; we see stout little horses pinned, or all but pinned, to the ground by icicles hanging from their noses, sometimes three feet long.

Twice within five minutes I have informed persons that their nose or ear was frost-bitten.

Sunshine and the heavens are usually as bright as in Italy.

It is then that you daily hear in the streets a concert of musical horsebells, giving notice that one or other of the numerous cavalcades of elegant sledges are in motion, filled with beauty and fashion, lying warm in a profusion of furs. They are on their way, in long lines, to some well-known place of resort, as Lake Charles or Montmorenci, or are merely parading the town, as the wont is; and it is a charming sight.

The sportsman has free scope for his skill and endurance in the neighbourhood of Quebec. Elks, bears, and deer, may be found in their native woods at no great distance, but fifty or sixty miles off they are always to be encountered, with the assistance of the Lorette Indians. Snipe, wild duck, &c. &c. are abundant much nearer.*

It is true that Quebec, in north latitude 47°, has the winter of St. Petersburgh in north lati-

* To see a sportsman, as you may here occasionally do, drifting slowly down a wintry river in a white boat, disguised by an ice-like pile of white calico, towards, and finally into, a flock of wild ducks peacefully feeding, is a painfully interesting sight. The discharge takes place. Up rise the affrighted birds; ten or twenty are struggling, wounded, in the water; and the exulting fowler collects his prey.

Fred. Tolfray On this subject I know no book so life-like and entertaining as Tolfrey's "Sportsman in Canada." To this inexpensive work I refer the reader altogether for information on this head.

tude 60°, and, at the same time, a summer more oppressively hot than Paris.

Its mean annual temperature is 37° 5′ Fahr., that of London being 49°. There is perhaps no part of the world where the annual range of the thermometer is greater than at Quebec; it is here 128°. In the course of a day I have seen a descent of from 37° Fahr. to 28° below zero.

Three principal reasons have been adduced by Dr. Rolph of Toronto to explain the fact of North America being much colder than Europe in the higher corresponding latitudes.

They are, first, the greater proximity of the vast body of ice and snow stretching southwards from the Arctic regions; secondly, the multitudes of frozen lakes in Hudson's Bay; and thirdly, the absence of a mountain barrier to screen the Canadas from the cold winds of the north-west and west.

These, I may add, are the prevailing winds, and bring to the Atlantic coasts not only the Arctic temperature, but the extreme cold of the Rocky Mountains, and the bare and lofty plains on their east.

Lower Canada is, in fact, placed in the zone of transition between the polar and temperate climates, and would have been probably far colder than it is, were it not for the admirable provision

* of nature, that water, in freezing, liberates a large amount of heat which had been latent, and so raises the general temperature.

It is remarkable that the longer the European remains in Lower Canada the more susceptible he becomes of cold. For the first two or three winters he scarcely feels it; but afterwards his wrappings gradually increase, till at last he is buried in furs and woollens. So it is with the heats of India.

Dr. Kelly, in an excellent paper published in the third volume of the "Literary and Historical Society of Quebec," mentions that the average mortality of Canadian towns is nearly double that of the country. He accounts for this by stating, that at Quebec, &c. (I know it too well) there is no regular system of cleaning the streets; that the public sewers are in such a state that some of the houses in one of the principal streets are scarcely habitable at times from stench. He adds, that the sewers open into the lower town most offensively. The suburbs, with few exceptions, have neither paving nor sewers. After the melting of the snow, in April and May, the streets of the flat suburb of St. Roche become ponds or sloughs of ice, melting and mixing with the accumulated putridities of the whole winter.

* This statement is paradoxical. The "latent heat" does not make it warmer but, as a consequence, the water does not freeze so fast.

I hope there are few towns in Christendom where such an amount of disease and destitution exists as in Quebec. There are still fewer, I am sure, where it is met by a charity so untiring by the various Christian denominations. I shall not record the names of those who were most conspicuous in this holy labour; they have no wish to be known beyond the sphere they adorn and bless. This misery does not touch the native poor, but the fever-stricken, naked, and friendless Irish — a people truly "scattered and peeled" — who year after year are thrown in shoals upon the wharfs of Quebec * from ships which ought to be called "itinerant pest-houses."

These unwelcome outcasts are crowded, without proper provision, into vessels fitted up almost slave-ship fashion, by the agents of impoverished and unprincipled landlords, who rely on the public and private commiseration of the western world; and it has been taxed beyond endurance. Much of the guilt, certainly, lies upon the Irish Government, who do little or nothing to prevent so frightful a state of things. Thus matters continue to the present hour, I believe; worse rather than better.

These poor creatures, on landing, creep into any hovel they can, with all their foul things

* About the time of the famine in Ireland?

about them. When they are so numerous as to figure in the streets, they are put, I believe by the Colonial Government, into dilapidated houses, with something like rations, of which latter the worthier portion of the emigrants are apt to see but little: they are clutched by the clamorous.

The filthy and crowded state of the houses, the disgusting scenes going on in them, can only be guessed by a very bold imagination. I have trod the floor of one of such houses, almost over shoes in churned and sodden garbage, animal and vegetable. It required dissecting-room nerves to bear it.

After starving about Quebec for months, the helpless Irishman and his family begin to creep up the country on charity or government aid, and thus strew the colony with beggary and disease. A Quebec winter does not allow of lazzaronism. Some perish, some are absorbed into the general population, and many more go into the United States.

For six winter months I was medical officer to the emigrants at Quebec, whether in hospital or in forlorn lodgings; until, in fact, I nearly lost my life by typhus and dysentery. While so employed, I have often been deeply interested in the history of individual families, in their misfortunes from villany, inexperience, sickness, and the like.

The resignation manifested by young and old has been marvellous; and more than once have I had the pleasure of seeing my poor friends led on, in the course of time, even to prosperity.

Many of the beds in the low lodging-houses of Quebec are in recesses made in the walls. Not unfrequently, when I have entered on duty a dark and crowded apartment, containing several of these impure holes, I have seen a large black mass of clothes half thrust into one of them. It was the present excellent Bishop of Montreal (Dr. Mountain), in his bulky winter dress, administering religious instruction to the sick, utterly regardless of the poison he was breathing, and anxious only to console and succour.

His lordship reads the service of Common Prayer in a very singular manner, no doubt unconsciously. On my first hearing him, and not being acquainted with his apostolic character, I could not help smiling; but when I found out whose faithful disciple and servant he was, I smiled no more.

The remedies for the miseries I have been briefly describing lie in a well-paid and well-organised system at home for the licensing and inspection of emigrant ships; and another in the colonies for the reception and distribution of the new comers, especially during the present transition state of Ireland.

Society at Quebec, in the usual accepted meaning of the word, as formed of people of talent, acquirements, good income, and good temper, is of a very superior and varied kind; not, however, in summer, because then every one is either absent or extremely busy.

The materials for this good society are furnished by the vice-regal court, the ministers of religion, the numerous members of the Colonial Legislatures, the courts of law, the French gentry coming in from their seigniories, the professions, the large garrison. I am sorry to place (accidentally) last in this list the truly respectable and hospitable class of resident merchants and their families, who, although overworked in summer, are permitted in winter to indulge in a well-earned repose. During this season the Canadian capital exhibits a perpetual flow of dinners, balls, concerts, governor's receptions, pic-nic parties, &c. &c., for men of good income. For the poor soldier, and the labouring class generally, the only recreation is, or was, that of the dram-shop and canteen.

I served under two governors-general, the late Duke of Richmond and the late Earl of

Dalhousie,—two men, though both Scotchmen I think, as dissimilar as could well be found.

The Duke was Irish all over, frank, benevolent, sanguine, expensive, a lover of sporting men, and of an occasional gentlemanly carouse.

In the exercise of his public functions he was most probably bound hand and foot to the narrow policy of the Castlereagh ministry.

The Duke of Richmond died of hydrophobia very distressingly in the backwoods of the River Ottawa. A Plantagenet dying thus in a hovel in a Canadian wild might be made a very searching text. He was popular and much lamented.

Lord Dalhousie was a very favourable specimen of the Scottish mind. He was a quiet, studious, domestic man, faithful to his word, and kind, but rather dry. He spoke and acted by measure, as if he were in an enemy's land; and so, in truth, he was, because, in the face of the most powerful and determined opposition, he was honestly carrying out, as well as he could, the instructions of ill-informed men residing three thousand miles away.

Both these noblemen exercised a generous hospitality.

Lady Dalhousie was a pattern of every virtue to the whole colony, an accomplished and highly educated person. She received her company with a quiet, self-possessed grace, which, while it encouraged the timid, repelled the undue familiarity of her promiscuous visitors. She had the precious art of making the right people talk, and to some agreeable or useful purpose. She herself excelled in miniature-painting and botany.

I have little to say respecting the Quebec clergy. They were personally amiable. They worked the outward machinery of the Church of England with professional accuracy, but I fear they did little more than visit and relieve the sick when called upon. The archdeacon, Dr. Mountain, however, of whom mention has already been made, was a priest after another and a better order.

How beautiful it is to watch the effects upon a congregation of an earnest ministry—to see how the little, secret lamps of love and service light up, one after another—how they brighten, enlarge, and multiply under the teaching, until suddenly they burst into one great and beneficent illumination, which cannot be hid, and which manifests itself in painstaking labours for the souls and bodies of men.

A congregation thus becomes one compact spiritual host, prepared to work for their Master's glory in a thousand ways,—as a refuge for the sinful and miserable, a training-school for the young, a support to the feeble and aged, and a buckler to the oppressed.

But what is a congregation now, too frequently? Its members know nothing of each other; and often sit as coldly and unconcernedly in a church as in a railway waiting-room.

Quebec always had a well-conducted garrison, men and officers in a high state of efficiency and discipline.

I recollect well that we had the dashing and dressy ensign, the more prudent lieutenant, the sententious field-officer, and the thoughtful and reserved general in command, with his high-bred aides-du-camp,—the latter, frivolous as they may occasionally seem at his excellency's table, when the pinch comes usually shew that they are gallant and capable men.

There were here in the army a few fast men—some of them full of misapplied talent—fountains of fun and laughter which never failed. I think it hardly possible to excel the mimic and pantomime of two gentlemen in particular, whom to describe more nearly would not be fair, as they are yet among the living, and not noted for gravity.

I shall never forget the [illegible] pronounced and acted by one of those merry sprites, of an old original Dugald Dalgetty (a German colonel), being canted out of a sledge into a snow-wreath—the torrent of abuse in bad English—the grimacings, the flight of passions across his face, the groom's explanations, and the final settling of the storm into the good colonel's usual stiff and silent complacency.

Of course the fast men were often in difficulties. There was in the garrison a very handsome lieutenant (now dead). He was an universal favourite for his various social qualities; but he had little or no private fortune, and good society requires a full purse. He therefore got into arrears with his tailor and others.

At this time there resided at Quebec a man of immense wealth and much generosity. The lieutenant one morning boldly laid his case before this Crœsus, as many other respectable persons had done theirs, and successfully. He instantly received a cheque for the required amount. Six months afterwards the young officer returned with a similar tale. The rich man looked very blue upon him, and saying, "Sir, I am sorry to perceive that your indebtedness is not an accident, but a habit," he retired into his bedroom. After waiting for his return in vain for a quarter of an hour, Lieutenant W. retired.

Mr. N. was a plain, quiet man, of about fifty years of age, and occupied a parlour and bedroom at a hair-dresser's in Mountain Street. His charities were very large, and at the same time judicious. He had been very poor at Quebec a year or two previous to succeeding to a fortune of from 15,000*l.* to 20,000*l.* per annum, about the year 1822, and was then glad to accept an occasional dinner from a little schoolmaster in the Lower Town. Upon him Mr. N. settled an annuity of 200*l.*

The whole history of this gentleman is a romance — his agreement with the schoolfellow who left him his fortune that the survivor should take all; their separation for life; the shipwreck and other misfortunes of Mr. N.; his cultivating a little barren patch in Labrador when advertised for as the owner of a princely property; his subsequently living on one of the lonely but beautiful Hero Islands in Lake Champlain, made celebrated in Cooper's "Last of the Mohicans;" and his final removal to one of the less frequented cantons of Switzerland, where he became naturalised, and not long after died.

Among the great variety of capacities and dispositions afforded by the other portions of general society there was ample room for selection, from grave to gay, from the scientific to the elegant and accomplished. In the days I speak of, a man fond of discussion, full of wit, anecdote, and startling notions—not always the soundest—the highly-gifted son of the most popular of our law-writers (Judge Blackstone), was always happy to descant over a moderate wine-cup with a kindred spirit until sunrise.

Another son of the law, a district judge, was quite as remarkable a personage. He was a large pale-faced man, odd, absent, unequal, ingenious far beyond ordinary men, learned and eloquent, abounding in all knowledge save that which might profit himself. He was as artless as a child, ever in perplexity, but ever ready to serve others (Judge Fletcher). He fancied he had been bitten by a mad dog, and sat all day long (for a time) on his door-steps in colonial simplicity, calling out to the passer-by that the poison was ripening, and that he should explode soon in hydrophobic rage. He was mistaken, and lived several years after to lose his office by some blunder or other. He died in the Eastern townships. He possessed a very large and excellent library.

Any one fond of politics might interest himself, but not mingle, in the fierce and unceasing struggle going on between the Governor-general with his officials and the House of Assembly;

both parties ardent and able, the foremost on each side trained by an European and legal education, as well as thoroughly well informed in everything relating to the personages and transactions of the mother-country.

In Lower Canada there is a very considerable number of ancient French families, worthily bearing the high-sounding names of Old France, such as Du Plessis, De Salaberry, and Montizambert. Some possess a good deal of landed property; others hold secondary official situations. From one reason or another—the late dinner-hour or the stiff manners of the English—they seldom appear out of their own national coteries, save from time to time at the Château St. Louis. This is to be lamented.

The French families are very sociable among themselves, and together with the French figure and general appearance display in their gestures and tones the same vivacity and eager interest in trifles we see in them at Paris. They are attentive to their religious duties, and keep up many old observances which elsewhere are dying away. The Continental custom of visiting all acquaintances on New-Year's day, so useful and laudable, is practised at Quebec with great spirit, and not only by the French gentry, but by the English of all classes. I believe that many a rising enmity has been dissipated by the kind words and small presents which on this day are exchanged.

The French children are very interesting little creatures. When arrived at their teens they have an exceedingly pretty dance, called " La Ronde," which, from great ignorance of the saltatory art perhaps, I never saw before. It is accompanied by an air and words of its own, both lively and musical.

The French Canadian has brought from his dear France one remarkable custom,—the charivari, and has improved upon it. It is intended to reach delinquents not amenable to the common process of law—offenders against propriety and the public sense of honour. Ill-assorted marriages are its especial objects. I need not say that a charivari is an unpleasant incident in an honeymoon—itself perhaps none of the sweetest. It is a procession on a large scale by torchlight in the evening. In many cases the attack is met courteously, with lighted halls and a cold collation to the principal actors, when the din and hubbub cease, and the thing ends. But it is not always so ;—not in the charivari I witnessed.

I fear that these celebrations are sometimes unjust. It perhaps was unfairly applied in the instance which I am about to sketch.

Here a stout, high-spirited young adjutant of a marching regiment, thought well to marry the widow—still handsome and but little past her prime—of an opulent brewer. She was of a good French family, and resembled the famous widow of Kent in having a most agreeable annual income. For aught I know she may have thrown off her weeds too soon, or was thought to have made a *mésalliance.* Be these things as they may, there was a charivari.

I was at home, in one of the principal streets, when my ears were assailed with loud, dissonant, and altogether incomprehensible noises, gradually drawing nearer and nearer. A broad red light soon began to glare upon the houses and fill the street. The throng slowly arrived and slowly passed my door. I will try to describe some parts of the show.

First came a strange figure, masked, with a cocked hat and sword—he was very like the grotesque beadle we see in French churches; then came strutting a little hump-backed creature in brown, red, and yellow, with beak and tail, to represent the Gallic cock. Fifteen or sixteen people followed in the garb of Indians, some wearing cows'-horns on their heads. Then came two men in white sheets, bearing a paper coffin of great size, lighted from within, and

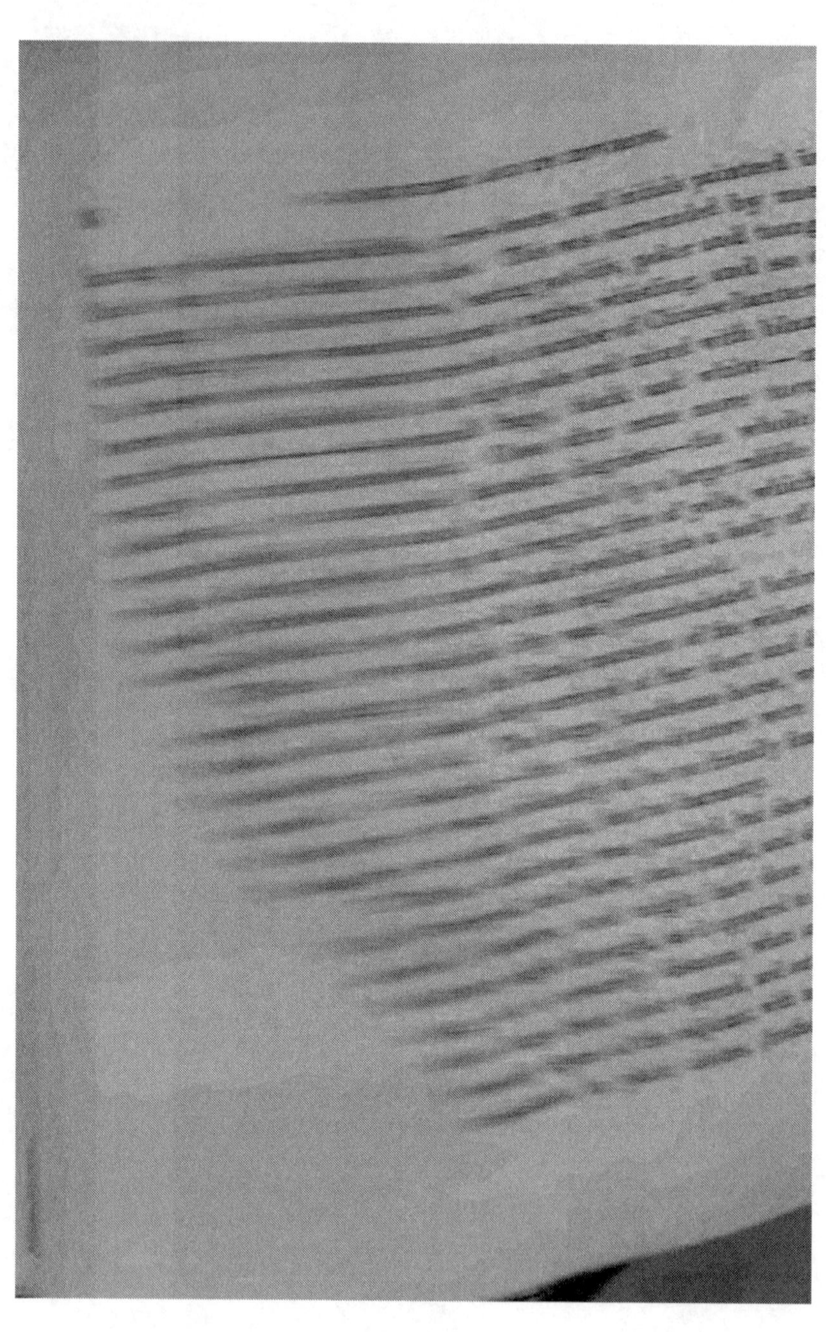

fear), and armed with cudgels. To work they went upon the defenceless crowd, and especially among the masquers, where the torches gave useful light. The whole attack and flight was an affair of a few moments—the fun-loving crowd, actors and spectators, fled amain—and gone in an incredibly short space of time were torches, lanterns, coffin, kettles, buffaloes' heads, &c.

One unhappy little hunch-back, in the disguise of a Gallic cock, the bridegroom seized and began to belabour, but he most piteously confessed himself to be the well-known editor of a local paper, and was dismissed with a shake, and told that in future cripples crowing in charivaris would always be treated as able-bodied men. I cannot but think, with the insulted lady, that the mummers were well served.

The philanthropic institutions, supported by private or public funds, are very numerous. Among the principal may be mentioned several hospitals, a lunatic asylum, dispensary, emigrants' friend society, savings' bank. The same Bible and Missionary associations which are to be found throughout the British dominions also flourish here, and are the fairest ornaments of our times and nation.

There is an exceedingly good library, for the use principally of the military; another as good belonging to the House of Assembly; and several private collections of great value. Booksellers' shops in my day were few and poorly provided. Monsieur Rousseau, a dealer in French books, shewed me many copies of a "History of Canada,"* in 2 vols. octavo, written with great talent and research by the Hon. R. Smith [William? Smith], late Chief Justice of Canada, the author of a "History of the late Province of New York." This work, as far as I am aware, has never been put into circulation, on account of some strictures it contains on the conduct of a late Governor-general. (It has been published since.) The "History of Canada" I do not intermeddle with; but I know of no war-story so interesting, so full of vicissitudes, gallantry, and heroism in suffering, although it extends over but a brief space of time. This has arisen out of the remarkable qualities of the three races, the English, the French, and the Indian, who have contended for the mastery in a country abounding in hazards from climate, from woods and waters. I cite the spirited history of the "Conquest of Canada," by Captain Warburton, R.A., in proof of this assertion.

There are few cities in any quarter of the globe so rich as Quebec in attractive spots for summer excursions; its whole environs are very lovely—

* This History now (1917) sells for a great price.

there is nothing plain or ordinary about them; and each has its own new charm—from the sweet dingle of Sillery to the Natural Steps and Cascade of Montmorency.

They have been so often described that I shall pass rapidly over them. The principal are Lakes St. Charles and Beauport, and the Falls of the Chaudière, Etchemin, and Montmorency, the woods and cliffs of Carouge, and the Bridge of Jacques Cartier, Lorette and Point Levi. (*Vide* diagram.)

It will take a whole summer's day to visit the Indian Village and Lake St. Charles. They lie on the same road. In the first we see, in his neglected dwelling and ill-cultivated field, how unequal at present the Indian is to continuous labour. In his own face, at once a history and a prophecy, we read much that is Pagan, notwithstanding the large silver cross slung across his wife's back, and the Roman Catholic church on the village green. At the same time I am persuaded that the ministers of that church are largely the poor Indian's benefactors.

But descend into yonder chasm—deep, dark, and fringed with elegant foliage. It contains the River St. Charles. The painter will rejoice in its torn, uplifted rocks, and fierce billows, while the geologist will be rewarded by some rare fossils.

Lake Charles is a small but picturesque body of water, divided into two unequal parts by a long headland; it is twelve miles from Quebec, among the nearer mountains, and is well worth a visit.

The Bridge of Jacques Cartier, thirty-three miles from Quebec, is well sketched both by Dr. Beattie and Mr. Tolfrey. The Jacques Cartier is an impetuous and rocky stream in a pine forest, abundant in fine fish.

Few visitors will fail to spend a day at the Falls of Montmorency, nine miles from Quebec; it is the first cascade with which the traveller from Europe by the St. Lawrence makes acquaintance. It has been described and sketched times innumerable, and is well worthy of its reputation. Its dress and appearance are very novel in winter; the surrounding pines loaded with masses of snow, and the rocks hung with rows of large icicles; but the cove below is the most remarkable winter feature. "When the St. Lawrence is frozen below the falls the level ice becomes a support, on which the freezing spray descends as a sleet; it there remains, and gradually enlarges its base and its height, assuming an irregular conical form: its dimensions, thus continually increasing, become, towards the close of winter, stupendous. Its height varies each season; it has not been observed higher than one hundred and twenty-six feet (1829): the whole of the preceding season had been unusually humid. The face of the cone next the falls presents a stalactitic structure not seen elsewhere; sometimes it is tinged with a slight earthy hue."—(MR. GREEN, *Quebec Historical Society Transactions*, vol. ii. 218.)

The so-called "Natural Steps" are rather more than half a-mile above the Falls of Montmorenci. I do not think Dr. Beattie has succeeded in his delineation so well as usual—the wildness is well given, but not so the artificial look of the rock. Their ascent, in many parts, from the water is by regular ledges, or steps of horizontal rock. It is a singular spot. The river has been wandering over gently undulating meadows for a few miles, when on a sudden it enters and rushes through a trough, twenty to thirty feet broad and eight hundred to one thousand yards long, cut through a barrier of rock, and thus makes its way to the St. Lawrence.

The Fall of La Puce is also very graceful, and should be seen,—it is seven miles beyond the Fall of Montmorenci. I should be ungrateful did I not add, that there is a clean and comfortable inn near the latter fall, where the guest will meet also with that cheerful civility and the moderate charges we so often experience at the inns of French Canada.

The falls of the rivers Etchemin and Chaudière, respectively, about seven and nine miles from Quebec, must not be forgotten. They, too, with a little diligence, may be seen on the same day, being southern affluents of the St. Lawrence.

Both are very effective combinations of pine-woods, falling waters, and rocky heights; that of the Chaudière especially, which has no need to retire in shamefacedness before any of the cataracts of Canada—a very few excepted.

They have been so often described, that I shall pass on to relate a few circumstances which occurred at one of my visits to these rivers, as illustrative of a Canadian holiday.

I had two officers for my companions, equipped in the stiff, hot military dress, cocked hat and feathers, enjoined in almost every climate by general orders. Our nags were brought out into a parade-ground full of soldiery. Being of varying qualities, external and internal, we cast lots for choice. A very sorry beast fell to my share; but I mounted, and was suffered there to remain. My friend of the Royal Engineers, while in the act of alighting in the saddle, was pitched by a sudden elevation from behind some feet over, and before the horse's nose, on the soft sand—hat and whip also. Some brother-officers came up, and gave them to him with a sort of quizzical solemnity.

Off we set at length, rode through the town with great decorum, and crossed the river by the horseferry to Point Levi. Scarcely, however, had we set foot on the south shore of the St. Lawrence, when the horse of my second companion rushed up the steep road close by at a gallop. We followed pretty fast; but, on gaining the summit, we saw our commissariat friend, an old Spanish campaigner, far away on the road, flying at full speed. Every now and then we caught a glimpse of him, pushing on in the same involuntary haste. He rode well; so that we were only amused, not alarmed, and quietly jogged after him. We came upon him suddenly, after a ride of four miles, sitting upon a low fence, in front of a decent house, with a stable in the rear. His features were discomposed, and not very clean. He looked shaken, too, and one side of his dress was plastered with the mud of an adjacent ditch. In fact, he told us that the horse, in spite of all he could do, continued at high-pressure speed until he came to this place, where dwelt an old master of his, and where, turning suddenly and unexpectedly to the left, he landed our friend in the ditch, and himself at the stable-door—and not for the first time, as his former owner told us. Being an indifferent horseman, I was glad my animal was of a mild disposition. We were pleased with both the Etchemin and the Chaudière; and towards evening we all, three abreast, slowly returned to Quebec and our duties.*

The scenery along the road is worth all the journey. It passes by a line of farms on the high grounds skirting the St. Lawrence. The dwellings of the peasantry, in some parts, formed quite a street; in others, we rode through fields and copses. At the mouth of the Etchemin, where the road descends to the tide-level, we found myriads of logs from the Ottawa, stranded at low water; and many rafts lying out in the St. Lawrence, waiting to be received into harbour at New Liverpool, as some houses and a timber establishment here are called.

We all agreed that the most solemn and captivating view of Quebec anywhere to be met with is obtained from the high grounds we were then riding over, near the Etchemin River. The spectator here stands on a lofty cliff, and is master of a large horizon; in the centre of which, with

* Gold in dust and grains has been found on the River Famine, a tributary to the Chaudière. Sir James Alexander, in his pleasant "L'Acadie," says he has seen some.

many a domestic bower unseen, in those thick woods on the west, stands the great escarped rock on which is enthroned the first-class fortress of Cape Diamond, its vast buttresses, bastions, and batteries encircling, in prolonged curves, the nearly hidden city, with its steeples and spires; overhanging, too, the restless St. Lawrence, and the battle-plain of Abraham, while from this point of vantage we take in fully the glorious framework of grey mountains and dark green woods in which it is set.

The evening had toned down all discordant tints. None of the disenchanting details of ordinary life met the eye. We irresistibly felt ourselves in the presence of the Ehrenbreitstein of the West, or rather of a great war palace of Odin, guarding the Scandinavia of America.

It is to be regretted that Mr. Bartlett did not transmit this view to Europe. His other views of this neighbourhood are admirably selected.

EXCURSION THE FIRST.

TO HAWKSBURY, ON THE RIVER OTTAWA.

Typhus Fever at the Hawksbury Settlement—The Seigniory of St. Anne de la Perade—Steam Voyage to Montreal—The company on Board—Montreal—Baggage Lost—Irish Emigrants at Point Fortune—Local Politics—Hamilton Mills — Settlers in comfort —Colonial Department—Emigration—Walk to Montreal—Insane lady.

In the month of August, after a hot summer, typhus fever appeared, both extensively and fatally, in a portion of the township of Hawksbury, on the River Ottawa, 260 miles from Quebec, and recently settled by a large party of Irish. As it continued with undiminished severity throughout September, Government determined to send a military medical officer to take charge of the sick, and to report on the causes and nature of the pestilence.

I was selected for this errand of mercy, and now present to the reader a non-professional sketch of the excursion.

Although I did not embark at Quebec, it will be well to premise that the River St. Lawrence, for thirty or forty miles above that city, is eminently picturesque, being for the most part bounded on both sides by woody steeps, or dusky red cliffs, of which the most prominent are Carouge, Point des Trembles, and Cape Santé. It is then ascended for 140 miles through a level country, with little change of feature, save at Lake St. Peter.

Above Cape Santé the visible population begins to thicken; and from this point, the north shore especially, seldom exceeding ten or twenty feet in height, is embellished with a pleasing line of white houses and churches, extending, with few interruptions, for 800 miles westward. The high-road runs close to the river. The traveller, on horseback or in a calash, is within view of us for miles, not seldom beset by a train of clamorous dogs.

The strong rapids of the Richelieu occur forty-five miles above Quebec, and are caused by a contraction of the river's breadth to half a mile, and its obstruction by reefs and rolled blocks.

Having a couple of days to spare, on account

of certain official credentials not yet ready, and the fitting up of a medicine chest, I made my way by calash to the Seigniory of St. Anne de la Perade, sixty miles above Quebec, and six miles below the large River Batiscan, a northern affluent of the St. Lawrence, and once famous for its bog ore and ironfoundry.

The excellent Seignior, the Honourable Colonel Hale,* had invited me to pay him a visit at St. Anne. I gladly embraced the opportunity thus afforded of observing the position of a proprietor in Lower Canada, which, with a little tact, firmness, and moderation, is far from being an uncomfortable one. Kindness goes far with the Canadian *habitans*, as the rural population are called.

My friend had a roomy, lightsome house, built mansion-like, one hundred yards from a trout-stream, the St. Anne de la Perade, on the upper edge of a large park-like meadow, which runs down to the St. Lawrence. From the house we saw the river, a woody islet or two, close in shore, and had between them a momentary glimpse of the passing steamers.

The Seignior had at this time 300 acres in his

* The modest but sufficient prosperity which has attended me through life began in the disinterested kindness of this eminent person. I am glad of this opportunity of acknowledging it.

own hands, partly for profit, and partly as a model farm for his tenants. The remainder of the cleared portion was held under peculiar French tenures, and divided into about 500 holdings. But still the greater part of the seigniory was in a state of nature, and was altogether about 70,000 acres.

For the most part, the tenants had clustered round the church in the form of a very rural-looking village, with a comfortable little inn. As the proprietor spoke French excellently, was affable and obliging, and was extending and improving the roads in the back settlements, a walk through the village with him was a very agreeable thing. It was a promenade of unconstrained greetings and pleasant looks. Red worsted caps and uncouth hats were doffed at every turn.

The revenues of a Canadian seigniory are derived from several sources. There is a rent of a dollar a-year from every tenement having a fire-place; a considerable fine upon every transfer of the numerous small tenancies, or rather properties; and the profits of the seigniorial flour-mill—the law compelling all the *habitans* to grind their corn there. There are other dues of less importance. A satisfactory interest is derived from the usual amount of purchase-money laid out upon an estate of this kind.

We embarked at St. Anne's for Batiscan in a canoe, and, after a pleasant row of six miles, mounted the deck of one of the great steamers going to Montreal, which makes Batiscan a stopping-place.

Glancing at the scene in the steamer, we were a good deal dismayed. The whole of the fore deck was crowded by horses, cows, pigs, carriages, and furniture, as well as by dirty and destitute Irish emigrants, one of whom was fighting drunk. Having been, and continuing to be, extremely troublesome, he was forcibly set on shore, ignorant both of the people and the language. As we paddled off, I saw him, shillelah in hand, —for it had been thrown to him,—vapouring away alone on the beach, by the side of his little bundle.

We counted thirty-two cabin passengers of various qualities; some of them were of great eminence, and would have become so in any country. A chance gathering like this is quite different from the company on board of an European pleasure-steamer. There were no coronetted families and their liveried domestics—not a single English snob, or bearded French *flaneur*, in his white-jane boots. Most of the passengers were on business.

We did not make acquaintances at first. The

heat was extreme; so that most of us remained on deck to catch the slender but refreshing breeze. For myself, I went below to finish a letter.

Sitting down, I espy the eyes of a little fat steward lazily twinkling on me from a square compartment full of spirit-bottles, called the bar. Close to me on my right sits, reading with a consequential air, a young American, dressed in the Burgershaft style—his broad shirt-collar descending over his coat-collar, and tied by a black riband; while his luxuriant hair falls over his shoulders in long tresses. Before me are parties playing at picquet, and refreshing themselves with London porter. Several are dozing as comfortably as Prince Aldebaronti himself.

After a time I mount the companion-ladder, and find that we are in the middle of the majestic St. Lawrence, making good way, with the two handsome spires of Varennes Church some distance a-head of us, among trees; over which, in the south-west, I see the storm approaching, of which the sultry heats had given us notice. There is not much to attract the eye beyond a few moments. We see, however, that we are on an American river of the first order, fed by innumerable streams, whose sources are often a thousand miles and more apart.

We meet a tall steamer coming from Montreal,

or a fleet of rafts, the same in form, but larger than those of the Rhine. A wind-bound vessel from Europe is overtaken, or a steam-tug labouring up the current, with a reluctant merchant-ship on each side, and another at its stern. Few words suffice to describe either the Orinoco or the St. Lawrence for a hundred miles together.

In an hour we were in the midst of the storm, in all the usual forms of lightning, thunder, hail, and rain—sweeping the decks of all who could crowd below, fore and aft. The cabin was so full during its continuance that we began to get familiar, and converse.

I soon found by my side a young man of coarse, heavy look and build, not well clad, and indifferently schooled. He was the son of a Scotch peer, sent into the woods of Canada under the charge of an agent, for having married a stout dairymaid, to his lady-mother's great disgust. The poor lad certainly had not his full share of brains. The young wife looked far more respectable and intelligent than himself. A farm had been purchased for them in Glengarry, Upper Canada. And yet the Honourable Mr. C—— had his cogitations. In the course of the voyage a clerical acquaintance of mine observed to me, directing my attention to Mr. C——: "That fat, dense Scotchman has been puzzling himself,

Presbyterian-like, upon an odd subject. Perhaps he thinks he is Adam going to Eden. Noticing my ecclesiastical dress, he entered just now into talk with me; and among other things, he put this question to me: 'Sir,' said he, 'after Eve had eaten the apple, she offered another to Adam. Now, I wish to know what would have become of Eve if Adam had refused to eat; and what would have been the upshot of the whole matter?' I told him his question was unprofitable, and not worth an answer."

When the grey darkness of the storm had passed away, leaving a clear sky and cool air, much of the cabin company dispersed. Then there came out of a small state-room a foreign lady, of elegant and commanding presence. She was accompanied by her younger brother, a Genevese, like herself. He was an officer of one of our Rifle corps, slight in figure, precise in his dress, with a coat by Stultz, close-fitting pantaloons, strapped to the foreign-made boot. His features were small and gentlemanly, but motionless and resigned, as I have often seen in those who live with clever women.

But I do not wish to forget the lady, Madame de M——. She took an arm-chair near the doorway of the magnificent cabin, with the officer by her side. A circle soon formed round her;

for she was well known, and was returning to Montreal from a visit to her native land.

When I first saw her, I thought of Madame de Staël and the charms of Coppet, and stuck myself in a corner near her, on an uneasy camp-stool. I had time to examine her while waiting to hear what a lady so gifted and gallant might say.

I had before me a tall lady, of graceful carriage, a trifle too stout, and not now to be called young, —no fault of hers. Her fine features had become somewhat too marked, but were instinct with that superior intelligence which successful culture of a rich soil alone can give. Let me remember. She had an oval pale face, darkened a little by the stoves of her youth; a high nose, exactly chiselled; smooth, round, full forehead, and a kindling dark eye.

After the usual congratulations and mutual inquiries, there was silence for a few moments, when she broke out in the true rhythmical tones of a high-class Genevese *réunion*, with a full, ringing, musical voice, and all the gentle fearlessness of practice in good society—enforcing her words with such pretty cadences, and such an eloquent, but scarcely perceptible, play of feature, eye, and neck, as I never expected to see in western Christendom.

She did not speak of regret at leaving Switzerland,—the social circles of Geneva (hard to relinquish), for the inferior civilisation of a colony; but she said:

"I have been in Canada again for a week, and am anew delighted with my adopted country. I have infinitely enjoyed its natural grandeurs—its splendid suns, wide waters—amid the fragrance of its fine forests I have wandered already. I find an exceeding beauty here—not Swiss, not French, nor Scottish, but Canadian, perfectly distinct, and unspeakably charming."

"Yes," says my friend Col. H——, "you may well be happy here; because, as soon as the steamer draws alongside the quay of Montreal, you will see leaning over the long balcony of a many-windowed mansion overhanging the St. Lawrence, a delighted, expecting group of bright young faces, waving their little kerchiefs, with their *bonnes* and their aunts, while the father is on the pier awaiting you."

"Yes," she replied, "a large measure of good has been bestowed on me. May I be sufficiently thankful!

"I have been rambling over my old Swiss mountains. I had not quite my usual interest in them. I was surprised to see how rapturously those alpine pictures were enjoyed by my companion, old Professor Pictet, for the hundredth time. And I do feel that there is no comparison between the scientific apprehension of the works of creation and that which is within the reach of the common observer like myself. In the same way, I can conceive somewhat of the prophetic triumph with which the enlightened statesman can look upon the broad and fertile lands among which we are now moving, and rejoice in their splendid and populous, and I trust, happy future."

Madame de M—— had been playing, Staël-like, with a little well-worn magazine, such as are seen everywhere in America, and said,—

"By the bye, I have met in my cabin with a little monthly miscellany, which contains some beautiful ideas. How greatly indebted, under Providence, is the new world to the old! Not only has Europe formed and arranged her daily comforts, filled her libraries with undying wisdom, paid in blood and anguish the price of her present political blessings—having driven the ploughshare of truth through the clods of despotic ignorance—but she goes on to fill the American mind with just and lofty thoughts.

"These little magazines exist chiefly upon the

genius of England. Permit me to read the passage which has given rise to these remarks. It is from Coleridge:—

"'In the middle ages, there was in Europe a continued succession of individual intellects—the golden chain was never wholly broken. A dark cloud, like another sky, covered the entire cope of heaven; but in this place it thinned away, and white stains of light shewed a half-eclipsed star behind it: in that place it was rent asunder, *and a star passed across the opening in all its brightness, and then vanished.* Such stars exhibited themselves only; surrounding objects did not partake of their light. There were deep wells of knowledge, but no fertilising rills.'

"Is not this an astronomical metaphor of extreme magnificence? How else bring into the light of day the vast darkness of the middle ages? From this, modern North America has been spared. In its dispersion, my own townsmen of Geneva have performed a noble part, both now, and at the time when Erasmus read by moonlight, because he could not afford a torch, and begged a penny, not for the love of charity, but for the love of learning."

And thus she went on, with many a friendly questioning from her circle of admirers, giving utterance to her full heart as freely and melodiously as ever musician scattered sweet sounds from flute or harp.

She was about to tell us of the delight with which she had witnessed in London the operations of an infant-school, then unknown in Canada,* and not many years ago commenced by Wilderspin, a singular person, who might almost be said never to have attained to actual manhood, but was arrested in a state of perpetual babyhood —an aged and wise baby; and the very individual for his important mission.

She was about to say that she must have an infant-school near her place, when a young physician came and told me that a poor female emigrant had been frightened into premature labour by the storm, and had given birth to a girl, but that she had nothing prepared, and no money. We immediately collected, among the cabin passengers, nearly four pounds, to the no small surprise and gratitude of the sufferer when it was given her in a little bag.

The eloquent Genevese contributed liberally, and greatly encouraged the subscription.

How valuable are such persons in a colony, with their love of order and cleanliness, their finished education and enlarged views!

After leaving the steamboat I never heard

* There are now several in Montreal.

more of this accomplished lady. I suppose she is the light of her quiet home, not far from Mount Belœil, and a winter resident at Montreal.

We passed Three Rivers, the third or fourth town in the lower province during the storm. Here the influence of the tides of the ocean ceases. I shall say little about this place, as I was only five minutes in it once; but it is little better than a large village. It is near the three mouths of the St. Maurice, an important river, with the iron works of the Messrs. Bell on it, and abounding in fine scenery and good land. A very large tract of fertile country ranges from the middle and upper parts of the St. Maurice north-eastwards towards Quebec, and embraces the valleys of the St. Maurice, Batiscan, St. Anne, and Jacques Cartier, more than sixty miles across. But who will face its Siberian climate?

From this time to our arrival at Montreal, most of the passengers were on deck enjoying the tempered breezes, and that homogeneity of atmosphere which brings distant objects so wonderfully near, and gives to the whole landscape a delicious purity, softness, and precision of outline.

I was leaning over the bulwark of the steamer, examining a fragment of rock, with an oblong note-book peeping out of a side-pocket, when M. Papineau, the Speaker (at the time) of the House of Assembly, came blandly up and entered into conversation with me.

He was then the most distinguished and popular person in Canada; and he has since become still more noted for his share in the late insurrection.

M. Papineau was a well-dressed, handsome man, standing erect, and a little above the middle size, with the black hair and eyes of France, his features regular, rather long, fine, but not ingenuous. He appeared to me subtle, persuasive, confident, and eager for information. He questioned me on the subject of my rock specimen, and on geology. I told him I was only a learner. "True: that may be," said he, "but *un borgne* is king among the blind."

In a short time I had given him the titles and merits of all the best books on the subject, and the way to procure from London labelled cabinets of mineralogical and rock specimens.

He left me high and dry. I had nothing more to tell. I wished to talk political economy with him, and perhaps a little politics; but no, there was to be nothing given in exchange. I was left courteously, but before I had received my reward, which was unpleasant.

Some are surprised that M. Papineau did not fight in the insurrection, but without reason. I am sure that he values life and limb at no higher rate than other people; but it is not fair to expect the same man to be the slashing hussar and the astute parliamentary tactician.*

He has taken advantage of the amnesty so wisely proclaimed by the British Government, and is again a leader in the House of Assembly.

The rebellion which M. Papineau at all events stimulated, was sanctioned in heart by the great majority of the Lower Canadians; but it was mainly defeated by the Roman Catholic clergy, who are salaried by the British Government, and have little faith in the mercies of the cabinet of Washington. If it had been successful, M. Papineau would probably have been the first president of a new people, and an historical character.

As far as Lake St. Peter, a few miles above Three Rivers, we were passing up broad waters, with distant shores, and here and there a tributary stream, the banks of the St. Lawrence occasionally running out into points, marked by a church, a windmill, or a line of tall poplars. Once or twice, soon after the storm, all these objects,

* Since writing the above I have had reason to believe that M. Papineau was not for trying it out in arms, and took no share in the late insurrection. As long as he confined himself to constitutional measures, M. Papineau was a freeman contending against despotism. Nearly all that was sought has since been conceded.

while distant, were raised picturesquely high above the river by a thin haze, and later in the evening steeped in the ruby glow of the setting sun.

We found Lake St. Peter to be a shallow expansion of the St. Lawrence, nine or ten miles broad and twenty-five miles long, with many islands at its upper end, used as pasturage by the farmers on the densely-peopled mainland.

Being a zealous geologist, I longed to jump ashore on one of these islands to examine their stony beaches, which we were successively grazing,—a propensity which had nigh cost me dear at Sorel, a village-town on the south shore, forty-five miles below Montreal, at the mouth of the large river Richelieu, the outlet of Lake Champlain, and remarkable for being much smaller at its mouth than at its head.

The steamboat having stopped here to take in wood, I stepped on shore (contrary to rule) to gather a specimen of a rock I saw in the river bank. While thus employed the steamer started. Seeing this, I jumped into a canoe with a little boy in it, and paddled after, urging and screaming to the top of my powers, when the owner and captain, worthy Mr. Molson, kindly backed ship and took me in.

When I had cooled after my exertions sufficiently to cast a glance around, I observed a group deeply interested in the explanations of an athletic American in the garb of a master-mechanic. He was exhibiting the model of a bridge invented by himself, of wood, cheap, strong, and durable. It was formed by a simple but very ingenious interlacement of bars of wood, the longitudinal being about eight feet long, and the cross-bars about five. Besides having the qualities just stated, it had the important one of an equally diffused strain under burthens. It was particularly adapted to rapid rivers and such as are liable to floods. He had built one in Canada and several in the United States. The bars having been put together, one end of the framework thus formed was fixed to the side of a river, then directed across, and the other end pressed down to the opposite bank by heavy weights, and there retained. While standing upon the raised end of a bridge which he was placing in the United States, the weight slipped off, and he was hurled to an immense distance and taken up dead, while the bridge floated away in fragments.

From hence to Montreal is a continuation of the same scenery as below St. Peter's—a wide stream with occasional islets, low cleared shores with an endless street of houses, their very roofs whitewashed. Here and there is the mouth of a river hid in reeds and trees. One of these I think I am correct in naming the Recollet, a river coming from the Ottawa, and with another branch forming the northern boundaries of the islands of Jesus and Montreal. Few pass by the mouth of this stream as it flows into the St. Lawrence without admiring its antique church, two or three old-fashioned high-roofed houses, the cleanly little inn, and its elm-trees.

To reach Montreal, the steamer has to breast for the last mile the powerful Rapid of St. Mary, such as only a strong wind can enable a sailing vessel to surmount. It is occasioned by shallows and the small island of St. Helen's, a locality of much military importance, and occupied by fortifications and store-houses, at present half hid in woods.*

In due season the steamer discharged her varied burthen, and we separated, each on his own business.

It was my duty to pass through Montreal as rapidly as possible, but as I had to receive from the military depôt some additional medicines, I went thither, leaving my portmanteau within the doorway of Pomeroy's Hotel. I had scarcely left the house, when a stage-coach for Albany in the

* A whale was killed near Montreal in Sept. 1823, 220 miles above salt water. Seals are not very uncommon there.

State of New York, 300 miles off, drove up to the door. Seeing my portmanteau close by, directed "Albany Barracks," an old English direction unerased, the driver placed it upon the coach and drove off, leaving me with such clothes as I stood in, and nearly moneyless, in a strange place. I received my property again some weeks afterwards; meanwhile I borrowed a very scanty outfit from a brother-officer.*

One of the calashes of the country soon transported me to La Chine, a village nine miles from Montreal, at the foot of Lake St. Louis; a splendid body of still water, with fine islands here and there, and elevated lands in the north. It is, of course, a part of the St. Lawrence.

I then embarked in a large heavy boat manned by three Canadians, and successively passed village after village to the pretty ruins of the French fort, Château-brillant, in the midst of charming lake and hill scenery.

We had left Lake St. Louis behind us. In our front was the broad and tumultuous meeting

* This gentleman I had seen labouring under severe spitting of blood in the Isle of Wight. For this he was ordered to the West Indies; but in the confusion of a dark night and of a crowd of transports he got on board of a ship for Canada by mistake, and thus, I am convinced, saved his life. His is not the only case of hæmoptysis in which I have known the dry Canadian climate beneficial.

of the two giant streams, the St. Lawrence and the Ottawa—waters of equal magnitude, but not mixing for many miles downwards, as we see from the chocolate colour of the latter. In our rear were the fine wooded heights of "The Two Mountains," with a pilgrim's oratory at mid-height.*

We now sped up the succeeding tranquil portion of the Ottawa, and arrived late at Point Fortune. We only landed once, a couple of miles below the Point, to rest, and look at a party of two hundred Irish emigrants, staying for the night in a wood, under a few loose boards and bushes, pushed carelessly together.

They consisted of the very aged, those in middle life, and the babe at the breast. Their faces wore an anxious but resigned look. The country was strange to them. Good-natured friends had painted freely the privations of the coming winter in their allotment, seventy-eight miles above Point Fortune. Some oatmeal and potatoes, with a limited stock of clothes (like my own), was all they possessed. I did not despise, but encouraged them, as I sat by the women washing their clouts in the stream. I remembered that a little man's all is great in the sight of God.

* All given with great truth and spirit by Mr. Bartlett.

Although extremely poor, and, to their honour, laden with their grandsires, I afterwards heard that they prospered, and are now comfortable.

Point Fortune is a cluster of houses, inns, and stores, on the west bank of the Ottawa, at the foot of the Long Sault Rapid, which is nine miles long, very violent, full of narrow passes, rocky bars, and tall fir-clad islets, delightful to the painter. Their whole descent is fifty-six feet—commencing at Hamilton Mills, the place of my destination.

I found an uneasy bed and a suffocating room at the principal tavern—boarded off from a club-room, full of tobacco-smoke, whisky-fumes, and a crowd of the chief inhabitants of the west bank of the river. They had met to assess themselves for the formation of a road along the river side, in opposition to one on the east bank. I heard and suffered all during the tedious orgies of a hot night. It was a fine exhibition of drunken shrewdness. Personal dislikes and ill-will gave way after a few skirmishes. They resolved that, without the road, their lands would be worthless—that trade and transport would fix on the opposite bank—and that they would be ruined.

The matter was plentifully *spoken*, and I believe it was afterwards well *done;* for they soon had a road—a good road; and not such an one as the next morning I passed over, mostly through woods, in a cart—first descending at a leap ledges a yard high, then wading in a slough up to the horse's belly, and often foot-fast in a net-work of tree-roots far below.

Hamilton Mills is a large establishment for sawing up the timber which the lumberer rafts down from the higher parts of the Ottawa;—the adjacent rapids furnishing the motive power. I was afterwards astonished at the quantity of logs I saw floating in a back water—at the easy manner in which each was presented and held to the saw—and the number and vast force of the saws.

The immediate vicinity of the mills was all but in a state of nature. The mill, that is, the building containing the saws, was merely a large oblong wooden shed:—the proprietor's dwelling-house (barely comfortable) was surrounded by offices, forges, workmen's dwellings, and stables. A kitchen-garden there certainly was, with little patches of wheat here and there; but the eye saw little else than the charred stumps of trees, clumps of young beech and alder on a rugged surface, covered with rocks, stones, and sand, and hemmed in by the virgin forest. Around the mills for half a mile the accumulation of foreign loose rocks is so enormous and so various that almost every known rock formation has its representative. Many of the blocks of granite are from twenty to thirty feet long. They have been left here by an ancient still-water at the point of obstruction, created by a sudden narrowing of the river, when at a higher level.

I felt not a little awkward in presenting myself to Mr. and Mrs. Hamilton of the mills, at whose house, as the principal person in the settlement, it was arranged that I should reside—not only from the extreme slenderness of my personal effects, but for want of my introductory letter and public credentials, then somewhere on the banks of the river Hudson.

I explained my situation in a few words, shewed my stock of galenicals, and observed that few evil and designing persons would travel as I had done, sixty miles into a wilderness to catch the typhus fever gratuitously. They had been surprised, but were easily satisfied.

I passed a pleasant and busy month at their hospitable dwelling, and hope never to forget their united kindness.

A very few years after this visit, their four children requiring education, Mr. and Mrs.

Hamilton embarked in a stout boat for Montreal, as is done every day.

While descending the Long Sault Rapids, which are close to the mills, the boat upset, and every soul perished, boatmen included, except the father and one child. He lived only a year or two after, a broken man.

The Hawksbury settlement, now called Hawksbury West, is an oblong block of heavily-timbered land, of variable fertility. Its exact dimensions I do not know. There are many swamps and sand-hills; but in places I noticed many excellent crops of wheat growing among the tree-stumps. It now contains about two thousand inhabitants, and on the whole is healthy.

Mr. Hamilton furnished me with a horse, and was so good as to accompany me to my scattered patients on the first day: otherwise most certainly I should not have found my way, along primitive bye-paths, over crazy bridges, through morasses and woods, whose pines were of a size and height I never saw equalled elsewhere.

As very often happens, the fever had nearly spent itself before the greatly-needed aid arrived. During my stay the sick became rapidly convalescent, and no new cases occurred; but it was thought best to detain me a week or two longer than absolutely necessary.

My duties lay among a young colony of Irish planted apart in the woods, and were pleasant, because the people were truly grateful. I was much pleased by the universal cheerfulness (except in the houses of the sick), the friendly feeling, the great readiness to assist each other which prevailed. Several times did I meet hearty, smiling young Irishwomen on horseback, laden with dainties for distant sick acquaintances.

I had a young single man under my care, exceedingly reduced, living alone in a one-roomed hut. He had a fine crop of wheat on a patch of ground close to his house; but he was totally unable to reap it. This his neighbours did for him; doubtless expecting that on some emergency he would do the like for them. I have the merry scene, only lasting a few hours, before my eyes now. Such a working party is called a "Bee," and extends to every in-door or out-door operation requiring numbers.

Hawksbury is not in the far-off wilds: there are settlements all around; too much severed by bad roads, except where the Ottawa offers easy transport, and especially to the good market at Montreal. These emigrants, therefore, were not beyond human help, like the solitary squatting families. These people had placed their rude but warm log-huts either in the form of a straggling street, or else each on his own land, according to temper or circumstances.

The advantages of public worship and of schools were within their reach. The comfort and security which they either had, or saw that with the blessing of Providence they should attain, had a striking effect on the expression of their countenances, which was happy, friendly, open, and intelligent.

I was much pleased with an Irishman's place who had been three or four years on the spot, with a large family of sons and daughters—he himself still in the full force of manhood. He lived in the social street, his farm of twenty or thirty acres cleared, being in the bush. He had built a log-house, thirty-five feet long by twenty, in the clear. The ground-floor still remained a single apartment, save that a thick green curtain screened the female sleeping-place, while the young men found their lair in the roof by a ladder. The walls were lined with bags of flour, Indian corn, pumpkins, onions, mutton or pork hams, flitches of bacon, and agricultural tools.

The sick daughter on whom I attended sat often in the fresh air before the door, much interested in the visit of the Government doctor sent from Quebec "to her and her likes." I have little fear but that by this time the green baize curtain is replaced by a strong partition of boards —or rather, I feel pretty sure that the house is a stable, and the family are occupying a new one, with sash windows and green shutters. The good looks of every member of this Irish family, their activity, the interest they took in their little world, bespoke satisfaction and rough plenty.

Two or three days before my first visit, one of the lads, about thirteen years of age, was chopping fire-wood in the bush, with a much younger boy, when a large bear came out of the wood and put a fierce foot on the very log he was working at. The boy faced the animal with uplifted axe, and drove him away.

I have very strong convictions on the subject of emigration from Great Britain and Ireland, and shall here place nearly all I have to say upon the subject.

Deriving all I know from personal investigation on the spot, I desire to be literally "*vox clamantis è deserto.*"

I declare in all sincerity that one of the most distressing thoughts of my whole life has been called forth by seeing millions and millions of acres of fertile land, in a healthy climate, lying waste, while my countrymen, in multitudes at home, are left in profound misery, and under the strongest temptations to crime.

There is a field in Canada alone open to capital and to labour which it will take a busy century to occupy, opening new lands and giving additional value to those already in use; while the systematic developement of the resources of British North America, so far from being a drain on the mother-country, will be of immediate and signal advantage to her.

Not to press forwards emigration is to partake of the guilt and sin brought on by the crowded state and the social inequalities of Great Britain.*

* The following painfully instructive statement leads us to believe that misery has been the lot of the bulk of our fellow-countrymen from early times. The condition of the poor has sensibly improved, but not so much as that of the easier classes:—

"By a survey of Sheffield, made Jan. 2, 1615, by twenty-four of its most sufficient inhabitants, it appeareth that there are in the town of Sheffield 2207 people, of which there are,

725 who are not able to live without the charity of their neighbours. These are all begging poor.

100 householders who relieve others. These (though the best sort) are but poor artificers: amongst them there is not one who can keep a team on his own land, and not above ten who have grounds of their own that will keep a cow.

160 householders not able to relieve others. These are such (though they beg not) as are not able to abide the storm of fourteen days' sickness, but would be drawn thereby to beggary.

1222 children and servants of the said householders, the greater part of which are such as live of small wages, and are constrained to work sore to provide themselves necessaries."

——

2207

HUNTER'S *Hallamshire*, p. 118.

But it must ever be remembered that emigration is only one of many remedies. The mere removal of surplus population does but little, happy as the change may be for the individuals. The gap is filled up almost immediately.

The British people must do their own work, stirringly and earnestly.

I have little hope in any ministry in the present inefficient state of the Colonial Office. Until a costly and bloody revolt takes place, carrying desolation to the hearths of hundreds, or thousands perhaps (as in Ceylon, Canada, Ireland, South Wales), Government will allow almost any grievance to pursue its melancholy course. The wretchedness, which the official eye seeth not, goes for nothing; and this, not from any inhumanity inherent in the man, but from the immense amount and distracting variety of his labours.

Emigration is too expensive, it is said; but let there be a whisper only of war, and millions are at once squandered on every imaginable engine of devastation. The arsenals of the Tower, of Woolwich, and Portsmouth, shake with the preparations.

All our ministries are alike. The air of office is soporific. I really think that the higher officers of the Colonial department may be fairly likened to certain curious shell-fish in the British seas.

During the first half of their existence (out of office) they swim freely about, and have eyes, ears, and feelers, which they use as freely; but as soon as their great instinctive want is supplied —that of finding a berth, a mooring-place, on a rock or on a fish, these important organs, one by one, successively drop off, and they perform but one act—that of feeding. They descend into a lower rank of animal life, and become what are called barnacles. So it seems to be in the Colonial Office. It appears to be comparatively deaf and sightless.

I am immeasurably astonished that men of undoubted conscientiousness and talent, of high birth and ample fortune, like Earl Grey, will undertake impossible duties, and thus consent to injure their fellow-subjects, through unavoidable oversights, misinformation, and crude views. And yet, seeing all this, they are the last to call out for a remedy, when in the sight of all thinking persons they are themselves equally sufferers.

The fact is, that through the lapse of time the Colonial Office requires to be reconstituted. The whole responsibility of governing forty-three most dissimilar colonies should not be thrown, as it truly is, upon one man, whose tenure of office is but, upon an average, two years.

As Mr. Scott stated in Parliament, in the spring

of 1840, "the duties of the Colonial Secretary are of the most varied and embarrassing nature. They are legal, judicial, political, naval, and military. They are connected with the ordnance, the church, the state, with convicts, with old and new colonies, to preserve ancient possessions, and establish fresh settlements."

Earl Grey, then Lord Howick, in 1845, stated himself that it was not possible for any man, be his powers what they may, adequately to administer the complicated affairs of the British colonies.

The work of the Colonial Office ought to be immediately distributed into three or more departments, separate, or conjoint in the form of a Board. Let one principal Secretary, with an adequate staff, preside over (and be responsible in Parliament for) our North American colonies; another for those in the West Indies, Africa, and South America; and a third for our Australian and other dependencies in the South Seas. Our possessions in the Mediterranean may be otherwise attended to. If we confide to this board, or to these three secretaries, the superintendence of emigration, in addition to the ordinary business of the colonies, there will be plenty to do.

When Sir George Murray was Secretary of the Colonies, with Mr. Wilmot Horton as one of the

Under-secretaries, it was proposed to form a Colonial Board; but the project unfortunately fell through, like many other good things in which neither party nor personal interests were concerned.

Diligent and enlightened men to undertake these important departments abound; their salaries would be repaid to the country a thousand-fold.

The work of emigration is eminently government work, says Mill, the political economist. It is called upon to remove, or rather re-distribute supernumeraries (not as a cure, but as a relief), by its being the great colonial landowner, by its capital and credit, by its possession of various public depôts (buildings, &c.) both at home and abroad, and likewise of experienced agents.

It might feel itself urged to assist emigration by a decent sense of the duty it owes to its distressed constituents, by the facility and certain success of the task (would there were a working will!), and by the sure gratitude of a delivered people.

There is no occasion at this time of day to argue about the advantages of emigration, both to the mother-country and to the new colonist. These have long been known to be great, but especially to the latter. Mill and Malthus, common sense and ample experience, all speak the same language upon this subject.

As long as a man can obtain a fair day's wages for a fair day's work there is no occasion for him to leave his birth-place on the score of subsistence; but when he cannot, and has no reasonable prospect of doing so, like the labourers of Wilts and Dorset at all times, and like the artisans of Yorkshire, &c. but too often, it is high time to emigrate to some more generous land. The labour-market at home is permanently overstocked.

For myself, if I belonged to either of these classes—if I found my country profitless and hard—if I had here to linger a portionless man—if I were daily growing more wan under privation—with no other prospect than that of a workhouse at last—then I certainly should look around for a soil less ungrateful—for a future more cheering—and towards some corner of the earth where my spade and axe would yield me a manna less scanty. There are hundreds of thousands in Britain thus circumstanced, and they know it bitterly.

The true remedy for this state of things lies deep in the moral nature of man, and will be mainly found there; all others are only secondary. We need the diffusion among our people of such an industrial and religious training as shall direct aright their abundant energies, enable them to maintain themselves without excessive anxiety, create a desire for, and a hope of, the comforts of life, teach them to appreciate the pleasures of the mind, to postpone present gratifications for a greater future good, and finally to bring them under the easy yoke of Christianity. Then, and not till then, shall we make much impression on the accumulated dissatisfaction and sorrow which prey upon one-half of our fellow-countrymen. But this is a slow process, and must have the aid of emigration and other agencies of like tendency.

I shall now, once for all, put together a few practical observations, as derived from my wanderings among the settlers; but it must be remembered that I am not writing an emigrant's guide.

Emigration by single individuals or solitary families is often unwise, always full of anxiety, and not seldom disastrous;* but the case is altered if the party go out to friends, or to an already selected spot, or be skilled in some much needed handicraft.

Emigration should be prosecuted systematically—such should be the rule. People should

* It may be said that the poor emigrant may apply to the agent at Liverpool, London, Quebec, or elsewhere; but having no pleasing recollections of officials, he is shy of approaching them abroad.

leave these shores in such organised bodies, so selected and so led, from the first step to the last, that as little as possible should be left to chance.

This is the *great desideratum*. Having provided a district of country—with due regard to health, markets, fertility, and a few other points—thither *direct* should be taken, in the month of May, one, two, or three ship-loads of emigrants, assorted according to age and sex, as well as to trades and occupations, adapted to supply the wants of the whole emigrating community. How excellent is the German plan of emigration—that of the whole village (or its greater part) going, and taking with them their clergyman. One or more superintendents (medical men,* if possible), with assistants accustomed to the colony, should remain on the settlement for some time to keep the people together, encourage them, direct their exertions, persuade them to assist each other in hut-building and other heavy operations, and even for a period to work for the common good. Associated labour in the commencement is of especial im-

* A class of medical men, experienced in the superintendence of large emigrant parties, and constantly employed, should be created and encouraged by fair remuneration. The profession contains a large number of men of administrative ability, medical skill, and philanthropic views, who would gladly embrace this mode of life for twenty years or so.

portance, and is almost sure to lead to permanent prosperity.

This is the true system. It may be accomplished in many ways. The working classes may do it for themselves, but they seldom can procure trustworthy and prudent agents. The agent of the operative class is apt to find the handling of large sums of money too much for his honesty; and the whole body is extremely gullible, or they would not think of settling with the Potters' Association in Wisconsin, in a Siberian climate, more than a thousand miles into the interior, when Canada West is nearer, and under every aspect infinitely preferable.

Associated parishes might in this manner send out to some prepared locality their redundant hands, under the guidance of a discreet bailiff. In this case the prospect is not so good, from the inferior capacities of the emigrants; but eventually, in one way or another, good would be done.

Capitalists who can wait for returns would find this kind of planned emigration a safe and sufficiently lucrative investment. I believe the two great companies now at work in this manner in the Canadas are satisfied with their prospects. There are few communities so prosperous as those of Guelph, Galt, and some other townships created under the auspices of the Canada Company.

The British Government can do all this with greatly increased facilities; but the precise manner, although sufficiently obvious, it does not enter into my plan to develope. I have said that they are bound to make a speedy commencement.

Allow me to make a comparison. If I give the form of an axe-head to a suitable piece of iron, sharpen the proper edge, and attach to it a stout handle, I am sure that with my new tool I can fell a tall oak, and perhaps a thousand. Now I am just as assured that if a skilled agent take twenty, or two hundred families, healthy, industrious, with some workers in wood and iron among them, and plant them in some select spot in fertile Canada West, they will in a few years be a prosperous community, not only above want for ever, but able to repay the expenses of migration.

The comparative cheapness of sending families to Canada must give it a permanent preference over Australia and the Cape.

The English man and woman leave their native village, hedge-rows, and old familiar faces, with reluctance. In the midland counties there is not so strong a temptation to go as in Wiltshire and Dorsetshire, where the labourers are in extreme poverty. An influential and active clergyman in

Wiltshire confessed to me, that how his poor got on at all on their wretched wages was to him the problem of problems, and far more difficult of solution than anything he had met with at Cambridge. The well-informed and ambitious Scotchman is quite ready to embark for a colony. Half Ireland would go at a word; and they are right. I once saw four thousand Irish at Lockport, in the state of New York, making a canal. They were delvers only, under American inspectors. Such specimens of bone and muscle; such activity and fun; good eating and hard drinking, alas! I never beheld. Some of the money thus earned would buy a share of the neighbouring forest. Ten or fifteen years from that time would find some of these people independent and rich; the others still poor, because wasteful.

For their own benefit, and that of others, distressed labouring men should emigrate with their families, if healthy, hopeful, and willing. Character must be touched on tenderly. If possible, they should go out young: it is then that they possess the ductility required in a new world. Farmers, tradesmen, and artisans with some capital, may reasonably expect to do well. Wages are high, considering the price of necessaries. It is in the upper or western country that these men are needed, not in the sea-board towns.

Thirty different artisans, who arrived at Guelph, in Canada West, in 1833, 1834, and 1835, were without money, furniture, and nearly without clothing. Six years afterwards, they would not take from 200*l.* to 500*l.* each for their property! Some who had a few pounds would not take double these sums for their gains, while there are a few tradesmen who, to judge by their buildings and farms, must have acquired large capitals.

The prices of British manufactures are moderate in the Canadas, from the low rate of custom-house duties, competition, and improved roads; but the poorer settler should, as much as possible, make his articles of consumption at home—spin, weave, dye, make soap, candles, &c. He can often sing—

> "I grow my own lamb,
> My own butter and ham;
> I shear my own sheep, and I wear it."

Gossip must not be thought necessary to a young emigrant's happiness. A life of retirement—save a holiday now and then—self-dependence, and the pleasurable feeling of advancement, must suffice for a time. He must beware of new friends. The highways and byways of America are full of active and plausible villains. The very woods have some caves of Adullam. He must beware of early becoming a politician—for politics are apt to lead into a whisky-shop—and perhaps his opinions are not worth propagating. Try to be content with the homely fashions of your neighbours. Depend upon it there is a fitness in them.

The agricultural inhabitants of the remoter districts are especially ready to assist one another, both on great and small occasions. The nature of their position leads to this, and each, in his turn, finds his account in it. Their solitariness, constant occupation, and palpably growing prosperity, have produced among the country people an unsuspecting friendly habit of mind, great openness with strangers, and, consequently, a large hospitality; so that manners and ways, which in England would be imprudencies, and even improprieties, cease to be so here.

To shew my meaning by an apparently trivial circumstance. I was one day refreshing, at a sort of half inn in the woods, on one of the branches of the beautiful river Trent, thirty or forty miles north of Lake Ontario, when the eldest daughter, a fine girl of sixteen, came and sat by my side on the bench before the house, which commanded a wide wilderness view. She readily, and with genuine modesty, told me the whole history of her family, of her own doings, and those of all her young acquaintance, ending by singing a song, sweetly and naturally.

She came from the Black River, in the state of New York, and had been in Rawdon four years. All this would have been impossible in England; but here it is an ordinary event; and this partly because, in this abundant country, hasty marriages are not fatalities, although probably unwise.

The settler should determine to make his new abode his resting-place for life, and he will be the happier. He must think little about England, except when a countryman asks his hospitality and his advice.

The emigrant should have solid reasons for leaving Britain:—for instance, because he and his cannot live in comfort, and because in Canada he can. He must not leave in a fit of ill-temper or idleness, but to labour for a high remuneration; for *that is the great and real advantage of emigration.*

His new residence will have its disagreeables in the odd, but, in the main, suitable ways of the new people — the vile roads — the distance from markets, shops, church, acquaintance — and, in the summer, the plague of mosquitoes. But what are these, in comparison with the ruinous disappointments and maddening struggles for existence, but too frequent in Europe?

As a rule, but not without exceptions, bulky articles should not be taken from England (not purchased there, at least),—such as agricultural implements, furniture, crockery, &c. They can be had cheap and good on the spot.

The best month to arrive in Canada is May; a productive summer is before the stranger.

All the principal towns have energetic public institutions, for the benefit of the sick and destitute; and public works are almost always going on, which afford regular and good pay.

Any money taken out will turn to most profit in good bills.

Hitherto, I have been speaking to the working man: now a few words to the capitalist.

There is not a more advantageous position on the face of the globe in point of climate, comforts, society, security, and general prospects, than a farm near one of the numerous centres of business in Canada West, for the family (once, perhaps, sorely pinched in England) of a half-pay officer, small annuitant, or somewhat reduced gentleman. Very few of the privileges of the old country are here sacrificed; for good society clusters round these places — such as Hamilton, Toronto, the Ottawa River, &c. All the members of the family meet, with their appropriate occupations and pleasures, out-door and in-door. Good markets are nigh at hand. London news is only a fortnight old, and local intelligence spreads rapidly; while the farm, with or without half-pay, should support all in light-hearted abundance. The half-pay is chiefly useful in maintaining gentility.

Canada ought to be the paradise of this large and worthy class; and is so, comparatively, to thousands.

Such farms, with their necessary buildings, are still to be had, at very moderate prices.

A raw country and their population will seldom suit the great capitalist. The delicate habits in which he has been educated will be subject to an endless succession of shocks and jars—intolerable, unless neutralised by the natural or morbid stimulus of a darling project. Here is one great defect in Wakefield's beautiful scheme of colonising with capital and labour combined. As a rule, capital refuses to go where the owner must accompany it—the scheme halts, and is, in fact, defeated. It is very unsafe to send out capital to take care of itself. "I will not go; for I can find in England tolerable employment for my capital, and can, at the same time, enjoy the thousand nameless *agrémens* and conveniencies of an old country."

As a specimen of the daily small annoyances that are here met with. A large capitalist invested in iron mines and forges in Canada West. He built and furnished a house in the English style. He had occasion to advertise for tenders to clear some land. A master woodcutter, an off-handed Yankee, thinking of nothing but timber and dollars, came with his offer. He was introduced into the parlour, bright with its newly-papered walls, and figured carpet. The American, as he struggled for his price, balancing his chair against the wall, rubbed his wet greasy hair against the paper, when Mr. Charles Hayes begged him to keep his head off the wall, which he instantly did; but soon afterwards, very unconsciously, rolled his quid, and spat on the new carpet. Mr. C. remonstrated, when the woodman waxed warm, and said, "Neighbour, I see we are not likely to do business. You are a hard man, and make bothers. You know I'll do cheap; and yet we don't progress." "Yes," said the Englishman, "we shall progress, if you will step out with me into the garden;" where, in fact, terms were agreed upon in a few minutes.

Some persons blindly rush beyond the limits of civilisation, and are surprised to find themselves neither happy nor useful. Many a town-bred lady has found herself thus.

For the sake of the female part of his family, no man should venture into the Canadian woods unless he can very materially better his condition. The ladies must milk their own cows, cook their own mutton, scald and cut up their pork, and so forth. But there are hundreds of cleared farms in the upper province, to be had on easy terms, where none of these things need be done.

No purely professional man, excepting, perhaps, the minister of religion, can expect an income in Canada. Law and physic are overstocked. The importing merchant treads on slippery ground; but the shopkeeper does better.

For a person in easy circumstances to retire to Canada might not be unwise; but for such a person to fix himself in the United States, would argue great ignorance or perversity. In fact, it is rarely or never done. If an Englishman present himself as a resident at Philadelphia, or New York, without an ostensible calling — being neither a merchant, diplomatist, soldier, nor naturalist, the people of the place patiently wait until the ugly secret of his being there explodes, which sooner or later takes place with great certainty, when he is cut by everybody worth knowing. The tone of society in the United States is disagreeably different from that of England — it is more angular and obtrusive. This remark extends to Canada West, but in a much less degree.

Society in the United States is constantly fluctuating: all is change and dizzy agitation. Local attachment scarcely exists. A man will, at a moment's notice, sell the farm on which he was born, and move westward a thousand miles. His neighbours justify him.*

I think life is shorter there. Perhaps the universal fever of accumulation tends to premature decay. As Mr. Sidney says, in one of his able little books, "The defects of the climate of the United States are notorious. The thin, sallow, wrinkled appearance of the men, and still more of the women, proves the fact at one glance." "In the Western States," a respectable American merchant observed to us the other day, "we take calomel and quinine by the pound, and expect fever and ague, as your lords do the gout, annually." A good set of teeth is a rarity in America past thirty years of age.

A rough animal happiness is diffused all over North America; and I rejoice to know it. But grumblers are everywhere — you cannot escape them;—some on speculation, others because they are injudicious, idle, intemperate, or sick.

* The philosopher justifies him thus:—"The American uses things without allowing himself to be taken captive by them. We behold everywhere the freewill of man overmastering nature, which has lost the power of stamping him with a local character, of separating the nation into distinct peoples. Local country, which had great sway in the Old World, no longer exists. The great social country wins all interest, and all affection: it over-matches entirely geographical country." —ARNOLD GUYOT, *Earth and Man. Lectures*, p. 301.

There is not much of the picturesque near the usual home of the working emigrant. A clearance in the woods is very offensive to the eye, being a dismal scene of uncouth log-huts, blackened stumps, leafless scorched trees and awkward zig-zag fences.

It is in Canada as in every other part of the globe. A producing country lies low, and is unattractive: fine scenery is usually sterile. The Indians, lingering among the whites, are not picturesque. Cotton Mather, the old Puritan of Massachussets, quaintly and truly calls them "doleful creatures, the ruins of man." The place where they become so is seldom an advisable residence for the emigrant.

I was sorry to observe, in the more retired parts of Canada, that when the difficulties are surmounted, and all is secure and comfortable, the settler is apt to fall into a dull and moping state. There is now little to interest; the farm and the boys work well by themselves; neighbours are distant. There is no stimulus at hand preservative of the domestic proprieties. All are necessarily careless of dress in summer; while in winter a whole wardrobe of old clothes is called for at once. In summer, while on travel in an open boat, I have not seen my coat for a month together.

The females, I am bound to say, bear a woodland life far better than the men; are cheerful, active, and tidy in their persons. I have been often very pleased with their healthy, satisfied, and smart appearance while mounting their Dearborn spring waggon on Sundays to go to church, driven by a brother.

I have repeatedly witnessed the whole progress of a new settlement from birth to maturity—from the first blow of the axe to the erection of churches, hotels, and mansions of cut stone.

While encamped on a woody island for three weeks in the River St. Clair (Michigan), I one evening saw a boat bring to, on the east or British shore, not far from me, and then a forest. I paddled over in my canoe to see what the arrival was.

It was a large boat laden almost to sinking with a hearty family of five persons (the parents and three children), with all sorts of lumbering chests and rude furnishings, a long gun, tools, axes, hoes, spades, a dog or two, a few poultry, and a barrel or two of flour and pork. This was the true pioneer family.

While I loitered about them, not unwelcome, for a couple of hours, they landed and arranged their goods, and went to sleep on matting, snug under the fragrant shelter of pine branches.

Two days afterwards I found my friends comfortably housed in an oblong log-hut well caulked with clay. For such expeditious building they must have had help from others.

I shall not ask you to accompany this settler through his cheerful winter work of felling and girdling trees, of burning and clearing away the underwood of his intended farm, and now and then bringing home a deer or wild turkey.

Many such scenes I have witnessed. I have returned to the spot two or three years afterwards, and found the family, if strong-handed, or if they have had a little capital, in possession of a comfortable log-house, out-buildings, oxen, a cow, and pigs and poultry innumerable. From five to thirty acres have been cleared and planted, while perhaps a hundred more remain, and as yet only yield pasture and fuel. In from six to ten years, additional comforts spring up with an enlarged clearance. The original hut may be a stable, and a two-storied frame-house may have been built, shining all over with white paint and bright green doors and window-shutters.

By this time neighbours have approached, roads have been struck into the more recent settlements, and the Englishman, at least, is pleased to find the human tide flowing towards him, bringing consumers for his produce and enhanced value to his land.

These people are plainly, but warmly clad; on Sunday with great propriety, even if thirty miles from a church; which seldom need be the case.

All this has been repeatedly accomplished by an Irish desperado, whose life at home was divided between the drunken party-fights and hopeless starvation.

I once spent four days in a town in the state of New York, with three fine churches, many inns, a public library, museum, and eight thousand inhabitants, standing upon ground which, five years before, was a beech forest, unconscious of stir or sound, save of the adjacent cascades. Some stubborn tree-stumps were still in the back streets (Rochester). To use the graphic language of Birkbeck, "If you look at such a place as this after the lapse of thirty years, or less (Sandusky, Cleaveland, &c.), what a mighty change has been effected! The village is a city, and contains its congregated tens of thousands, its streets, squares, halls, fanes, hospitals, and all the civic machinery of an Hanse town. There may be in the neighbourhood a black stump; but the raw desolation is gone: the rich corn-field waves in the breeze, and fruits and flowers surround the dwellings. The wild stream is tamed, and labours like a servant in the factory; the woods retreat, leaving a few trees for friendly shade; and the wolf and bear steal away from a place which is no longer for them."

By way of conclusion to these little jottings on a most important subject, I will repeat, that in Canada the labourer and artisan have two great advantages,—far better wages and better investments than in England. To the capitalist I may make the encouraging remark, that the more you invest prudently the greater your gains. Your first year or two, however, should be spent in observation, in learning rather than in acting. With good sense and industry the ordinary emigrant may, after a few years, rest assured, with the blessing of God, of ease and competence. Instead of want and hopelessness, he will see a yearly increase in the value of his possessions, partly from his own exertions, and partly from the generally increased value of land. His children's prospects are still higher. They may look forward to opulence. Many of the sons of poor settlers, Irish or British, are members of the colonial legislatures.

I advise for settlement, at the present time, the vicinity of the River Ottawa, the north and west shores of Lake Ontario, the shores of Lake Simcoe, the vast peninsula between the three Lakes Ontario, Erie, and Huron, and, finally, the eastern townships of Lower Canada which border on the states of Vermont and Maine.

I greatly prefer the Canadas, as an emigration-field, to the United States, and am deeply concerned to see so many of my fellow-countrymen burying themselves in the unhealthy and otherwise undesirable regions of Ohio, Illinois, Indiana, and Iowa. I wish they would remember, that even in the wilder parts of Canada life and property are safe, laws are respected, and religion held in its due reverence, which is not always the case in the above-mentioned parts of the United States.

In Canada the climate is healthy, in Upper Canada particularly so, except in the extreme south-west. The air is remarkable for its clearness, dryness, and exhilarating effects. It is quite common for an invalid from England to lose his complaints, gather great strength, and live to a good old age. The average number of rainy days at Toronto, for the nine years ending 1845, was only 87. It was 178 in London. The temperature of Upper Canada is much milder than is generally supposed. The vast bodies of water occupying the valley of the St. Lawrence must mitigate both the heat and the cold.

The markets are good and near, the population friendly and comfortable, ready to teach new comers the best methods of labour.

Land of the first quality is plentiful on moderate terms, either wild or cleared. European goods are much cheaper than in the United States. Taxation is almost unknown. Internal communication is easy and rapid, by canals, lakes, rivers, and highways. All Christian denominations receive public support. There are more ministers of religion, in proportion, than in England. The acts of Government are usually, and their intentions always, truly paternal. The United Province, *de facto*, governs itself. Newspapers abound, filled with British intelligence.

I could be well content to pass the remainder of my days within the sound of the Falls of the Chat, on the Ottawa River.

The fever at the Hawksbury settlement having been apparently extinct for ten days, I bade an unwilling adieu to my kind but unfortunate hosts at Hamilton Mills, on my return to Quebec.

I determined to walk the whole way to Montreal, sixty miles, and left, not overpressed with baggage, early in a dewy morning, "just as the sound of a going was heard in the sycamore trees."

The dense, dripping woods through which my path for the nine first miles lay, with now and then a bog-hole, soon soaked my smart boots through and through. My wet stockings so chafed my feet that I was fain to walk in boots only. In much pain I made twenty-five miles that day, through alternate clearances and forest; but towards night, when the stars broke forth above the tree-tops, I wished for a resting-place.

Walking on, however, through the woods until it was quite dark, and every bush was a bear, I thought good to get a thick stick instead of the slender one with which I slung my bundle over my shoulder. Scarcely had I done so when I heard the barking of dogs, and a turn in the dusky path shewed me the glimmer of a cottage window.

The dogs were soon upon me; but my stick kept them at bay until I got within shouting-distance, when, at my cries, the large door of the house opened, and poured out such a rejoicing flood of light as only an American wood-fire can produce.

It was a humble house of entertainment (Schneider's), to me most welcome. Excellent bread, milk, honey, and a little bacon, was all it could offer, and all I required; but the genuine kindness, the foot-bath, the snowy bed-sheets of that night, are still most pleasantly remembered.

The next morning I went on my way. While

creeping round the great bay at the mouth of the Ottawa (west shore), a miller, out of spontaneous compassion at my foot-sore state, took me into his cart for two miles. The same evening I arrived at La Chine, within nine miles of Montreal.

The next morning, lame and weary, I set forth as a humble pedestrian for Montreal.

I had been heavily dragging foot after foot for about five miles, but not without being pleased with the activity of the motley population of French, Irish, and Scotch on the road, and with the richly-verdured heights on the north, in all the gaudy tints of autumn, when, while skirting the ancient sea-banks of St. Henry, I saw a girlish figure creep from under the dry arch of a bridge which crossed the road, and begin to dance.

She was soon surrounded by a group of children from three or four cottages close by; but she kept up her dancing, and threw off, first, her bonnet, then her shawl, and then her under-neckerchief, singing and jumping wildly about, with her long hair all loose about her shoulders.

Not being very lively at the moment, I was paying little attention to this scene, although now very near, when on a sudden the poor woman rushed on me, and flinging her arms wildly round my neck, and so violently that I could hardly stand, exclaimed,—

"Doctor, I am Polly White! Polly! that came in the same ship with you! Save me, Doctor: I am dancing to keep these people from murdering me, as they did my William. I have given them all my clothes, and they are not satisfied," &c. &c. in an endless flow of piercing tones and sobbings, never heard but from maniacal lips.

Looking narrowly, and not a little frightened, at the flushed, demented face, I saw truly that it was Mrs. White, a fellow cabin-passenger from England, the young mother of three children, and going out to Canada with them to join her husband, who held some small government employ at Montreal.

Her gentle manners, obliging disposition, and well-behaved children, had made her quite a favourite among us.

How or why she was here, and in this poor plight, and what a weary stranger like me, accidentally all but penniless, was to do with her, was past my comprehension. I knew of no provision for such a calamity as this in Montreal or in Canada, for I had only been two hours in the former and two months in the latter.

However, I tried to soothe her, and gradually drew her into the nearest hut.

After listening for some time to her shrill torrent of incoherence, as she sat and stood by turns, I tried to put a few questions to her; but getting no answer, I sat ruminating what to do.

The door being open, and looking aslant up the road from Montreal, I saw a stout, elderly gentleman slowly approaching on a bay mare.

Several neighbours had come in—poor people, but women, and much distressed for this poor waif of their own sex; so, making a sign to them to take care of Mrs. White, I advanced to the gentleman, and told him what must be called *our* case.

He proved to be a magistrate, and kindly dismounted. After having looked at the poor lady, he requested the tenant of the cottage (to whom he was well known) to take care of her for an hour or two, by which time he would send a district officer to take her to Montreal.

I afterwards heard, that on her arrival at Montreal from England she found her husband dead, and herself and children all but friendless. This sudden and heavy blow bereft her of reason.

When I met her, she had escaped from some place of confinement.

As I mournfully left this poor thing, like a

crushed flower, I remembered, with Archbishop Sumner, that this world is initiatory, not final—that our peace here is not to flow as a river, and that " every sorrow cuts a string and teaches us to rise."

In a couple of days I left Montreal for Quebec per steamer.

Canadian Geology p 243
about 1819-1821

EXCURSION THE SECOND.

MONTREAL, THE OTTAWA, &c.

Montreal; Island, City, and Society—North-west Stores—Peter Pond—Boat Song—Dancing Pheasants, &c.—North-west Fur Traders—Lake St. Louis—Ottawa River—Light Canoe—M. de Rocheblave—Munitions de Bouche—Voyageurs—Indian Village—Flooded River—Gaelic Maid—American Farm—Hull—Philemon Wright—Lakes Chaudière, Chat—Falls of La Montagne and Grand Calumet—Rivière Creuse; Western Branch, Tesonac—Miss Ermatinger—Lake Nipissing—French River.

In the spring of the year following my mission to the sick settlers at Hawksbury, the Colonial Government was pleased to send me through Upper Canada to make a general report upon its geology, of which at that time nothing was known. Since then the province has appointed an official geologist. Logan, see note

I was very glad of the task, although the pecuniary aid with which I was to prosecute this journey of nearly 2000 miles was absurdly small,*

* Twenty-six pounds. I mention this in perfect good humour; but travelling in barbarous or semi-barbarous countries is very

something like Sir Francis Head's outfit for his vice-royalty.

Had it not been for the kindness of the North-west Company of Fur-traders, and my own limited resources, the objects in view would have been very imperfectly fulfilled.

This Company very handsomely granted me a free passage in a light canoe to the Falls of St. Mary, at the outlet of Lake Superior, by which means a large and interesting region, rarely visited by scientific persons, was laid open to cursory inspection.

As I shall, in the sequel, have better opportunities of sketching Lake Huron and the other parts of Upper Canada, I shall limit this excursion to the Rivers Ottawa and Des François, with Lake Nipissing, premising some remarks on Montreal and the fur-traders.

I arrived at Montreal early in May to join the light canoe; but as it did not set out for a few days, I wandered about the environs, and partook of the hospitalities of the town. The picturesque

expensive. On the north-east shore of Lake Erie I paid 3*l.* 10*s.* for being taken in a cart sixteen miles in five or six hours. In 1845 a bill was passed by the Canadian House of Assembly to appropriate 2000*l.* annually for five years, to make an accurate and complete geological survey of the Canadas. An experienced and energetic geologist, Mr. Logan, was appointed for this duty, with assistants. His services have already proved very valuable.

and fertile island of Montreal, upon the south side of which the metropolis of British North America is situated, is thirty-two miles long by ten in its greatest breadth, and with a somewhat triangular shape.

With the exception of Montreal Hill and its dependent alluvial ridge, the island is tolerably level, and it is watered by several rivulets.

Montreal Hill is almost wholly of basalt. This rock has risen obtrusively above the surrounding layers of limestone, without disturbing their horizontality, and has solidified in its present form. Not only so, but, as is very curious, it sends forth arms, rays, or dykes, from one to fourteen feet thick, which run at right angles with the mountain a mile or more into the plains around. Masses of shell limestone, and single shells, are seen imbedded, and unchanged, in the basalt, which is both of the hornblende and augite species.* I am not aware of anything similar elsewhere.

Montreal Hill almost immediately overlooks the city. It is three miles long, and comparatively narrow; its height is 650 feet, as measured by Lieutenant-colonel Robe, lately Governor of South Australia. It dips, on the east and south-

* *Vide* "Transactions of the Lyceum of Natural History, New York."

east, precipitously from a rounded summit of scantily wooded rock, and is elsewhere in hummocks, or steep declivities, clothed with beech, maple, and fir. The sides and base are occupied by orchards, farms, and gentlemen's seats. The view from the top is extensive and varied. To the south it is much the same as from Mr. M'Gillvray's drawing-room window; to the north it exhibits an undulating country, well cultivated but woody, with glimpses of the St. Lawrence and the Ottawa; the whole bounded by high lands trending north-east. This "Mountain," as it is here called, is a striking object from its massive solitariness.

Montreal is a stirring and opulent town, with a population exceeding 50,000, and therefore larger than Quebec. Its inhabitants have always, as the Americans say, been on the commercial "stampado." * They are enterprising and active, pushing their merchandise into the most remote wildernesses where there is the chance of a market.

Montreal does not wear the heavy, sleepy air of Quebec. The social, easy-going Canadian, is suffering from a great invasion of Americans and

* A phrase taken from the stampado of the bison in the plains. Vast herds meet on certain occasions, and shake the earth for miles round by their incessant and fierce stamping.

British, who, it is to be confessed, have possessed themselves of the bulk of the upper-country trade; but the French labouring class is still very numerous.

Its situation and its environs are very beautiful. Few places have so advanced in all the luxuries and comforts of high civilisation as Montreal, or is so well supplied with religious, philanthropic, and scientific institutions in full activity, including both a hospital and a college for Protestants, besides the rich educational establishment of St. Sulpice for the Roman Catholics.

This town, since I was first there, has been renovated—nay, newly-built and greatly extended. Some of the show-shops rival those of London in their plate-glass windows, and its inns are as remarkable for their palatial exterior as they are for their excellent accommodation within. Its magnificent quays of wrought stone which line the St. Lawrence are the admiration of strangers.

The main cause of this prosperity is the rapid peopling of the country westward and southward for 600 miles and more.

In 1842-43 the population of Upper Canada, the trading-ground of Montreal, was 401,000 souls; in 1848 it was nearly 700,000. To this we must add a large public expenditure, and, doubtless, a very extensive illicit trade with the United States along the frontiers.

It does not enter into my plan to describe the splendid Roman Catholic cathedral of this city, the more modest and yet large Episcopal church, the Nelson monument, and other public buildings. They have been well represented by Mr. Bartlett in his "Canadian Scenery."

I humbly confess my error. I found, but did not expect to find, at Montreal a pleasing transcript of the best form of London life — even in the circle beneath the very first class of official families. But I may be pardoned; for I had seen in the capital of another great colony considerable primitiveness of manners, not to mention the economical and satisfactory device of the lump of sugar candy tied to a string and swung from mouth to mouth at a tea-party in Cape Town, not very long fallen into disuse (1817).

At an evening party at Mr. R——'s the appointments and service were admirable; the dress, manners, and conversation of the guests, in excellent taste. Most of the persons there, though country-born, had been educated in England, and everything savoured of Kensington. There was much good music. I remember to this day the touching effect of a slow air on four notes, sung by a sweet voice, and supposed to be a hymn sung before a wayside oratory in Tuscany.

I had the pleasure of dining with the then great Amphytrion of Montreal at his seat, on a high terrace under the mountain, looking southwards, and laid out in pleasure-grounds in the English style.

The view from the drawing-room windows of this large and beautiful mansion is extremely fine, too rich and fair, I foolishly thought, to be out of my native England.

Close beneath you are scattered elegant country retreats embowered in plantations, succeeded by a crowd of orchards of delicious apples, spreading far to the right and left, and hedging in the glittering churches, hotels, and house-roofs of Montreal, whose principal streets run alongside the St. Lawrence.

To the left of the town nothing particular presents itself; but to the right, or south-west, you have the pretty village of St. Henry close under the steep ridge of St. Pierre, and then the railroad and canal leading to La Chine, passing through copses and farms, and from time to time betrayed by a glancing locomotive or the broad sail of a barge.

The wide, tumultuous river, and the island of

Probably M'Gilvray (p108) fur trader

St. Helen, come next into view beyond Montreal, with the opposite shore studded with white dwellings, among which the large village of La Prairie is conspicuous, with its shining church. Directing the eye still farther south, it ranges over a level and populous district of great breadth, till arrested in one direction by the fine hill of Belœil, and in another by the still more remote and lofty mountains of Vermont and New York.

Mr. M'Gillvray was accustomed to entertain the successive governors in their progresses, and was well entitled to such honour, not only from his princely fortune, but from his popularity, honesty of purpose, and intimate acquaintance with the true interests of the colony.

I hope to betray no family secrets in the following little sketch of the doings at the dinner-party.

My host was then a widower, with two agreeable and well-educated daughters. The company was various, and consisted of a judge or two, some members of the legislative council, and three or four retired partners of the North-west Company of Fur-traders. Our dinner and wines were perfect. The conversation was fluent and sensible, far above my sphere at first, about large estates, twenty to thirty miles long, and how to improve them by draining, damming, road-making, and so forth—operations only in the power of great capitalists who can wait for returns.

For myself, a young man, I listened meekly as "*de profundis;*" but at length the talk turned to a subject more attractive—the Indian fur countries, on whose frontiers I was about to wander.

I was well placed at table, between one of the Miss M——'s and a singular-looking person of about fifty. He was plainly dressed, quiet, and observant. His figure was short and compact, and his black hair was worn long all round, and cut square, as if by one stroke of the shears, just above the eyebrows. His complexion was of the gardener's ruddy brown, while the expression of his deeply-furrowed features was friendly and intelligent, but his cut-short nose gave him an odd look. His speech betrayed the Welshman, although he left his native hills when very young.

I might have been spared this description of Mr. David Thompson by saying he greatly resembled Curran the Irish orator. *

He was astronomer, first, to the Hudson's Bay Company, and then to the Boundary Commission. I afterwards travelled much with him, and have now only to speak of him with great respect, or, I ought to say, with admiration.

No living person possesses a tithe of his inform-

Thomson.—See Coues'

ation respecting the Hudson's Bay countries, which from 1793 to 1820 he was constantly traversing. Never mind his Bunyan-like face and cropped hair; he has a very powerful mind, and a singular faculty of picture-making. He can create a wilderness and people it with warring savages, or climb the Rocky Mountains with you in a snow-storm, so clearly and palpably, that only shut your eyes and you hear the crack of the rifle, or feel the snow-flakes melt on your cheeks as he talks.

The two other north-westers were elderly, business-like Scotchmen, strong-featured and resolute. One of them (of great frame and stature) was literally driven from the Indian territories.* These

* He was a leading partner of the North-west Company of Fur-traders, stationed near the head waters of the Saskatchawine. Unwittingly he offered what was considered a great insult to the child of a powerful Indian chief, who was expected home that night. A people which has its meat chewed beforehand by old women may have extraordinary notions of hônour. Mr. M—— was advised to take fleet horses, as soon as it was dark, and flee for his life; and so he did, although one of the bravest of men. He struck into the rocky wilderness towards the Arctic circle, and there hid himself for six months, living perhaps upon his horses. He let his beard grow, and finally crossed the American continent as a Canadian boatman, in white capote, green tasselled belt, and ostrich feathers in his hat. When the chief heard his child's story he pursued with all his tribe, but in wrong directions — towards Canada, the Rocky Mountains, and into the southern plains. Mr. M—— never returned into the fur countries. A few years ago he was deputy-lieutenant in a Highland county of Scotland.

countries are sometimes called Rupert's Land; their geography and productions, the romantic incidents of a fur-trader's life in hunting and in battle, being then quite pet subjects at Montreal. The rest of the evening was passed, to my great content, in listening to the tales about them by one or other of the company.

Mr. Thompson told us that in his youth he had served under Sir Alexander Mackenzie, one of the first to cross the American continent in these latitudes (now done every week in the year); and he spoke very highly of his endurance, skill, and bravery. He said that Mr. Roderic M'Kenzie, then a clerk in the North-west Company, an industrious, methodical man, wrote the history of the fur-trade in Mackenzie's volume of travels; and that he himself (Mr. T.) furnished the geographical sketch of the north-west territories, with alterations by Sir Alexander; some of which are inaccurate, as, for instance, the introduction into the map of imaginary hills between the Beaver and Saskatchawine Rivers.

Mr. Thompson gave some curious historic anecdotes, shewing how Dr. Franklin obtained the local information which enabled him to obtain so favourable a boundary line between the

Canadas and the United States from Mr. Oswald, the British commissioner.*

Dr. Franklin was indebted for this to Peter Pond, a native of Boston, United States, an observing, enterprising, unprincipled Indian trader in the regions beyond the great lakes. This person obtained great influence over his *voyageurs* by mingling in their carousals, by his ability and courage. With the quiet foresight of a New Englander, he noted down the topography of the countries he visited, and with the help of Mr. Cuthbert Grant, then a young clerk in the trade, made a tolerable map of them. But such was his violent and rapacious disposition, that he was taken out of the fur countries for at least one murder. The sufferer in the first case was a half-pay German officer named Wadanne, much liked by the Indians, and therefore in Pond's way. He was trading with a small outfit from Government and a permit, as was then the practice.

At a portage called Isle à la Crosse, Pond and a confederate agreed to get rid of him. It was effected thus. They invited Wadanne to sup

* The natural point of departure from Lake Superior for the boundary line is the River St. Louis at its upper end. This would have been advantageous to Great Britain, in securing to her the Upper Missouri, &c. &c.

with them alone in their tent. Over their cups the conspirators engaged in a fierce mock quarrel: both seized their guns. Wadanne tried to mediate, and was *accidentally* shot in the scuffle. His thigh-bone was broken, and he died a few days after. Mrs. Wadanne was close by; but the mischief was done before she could interfere. I saw her daughter afterwards at Fort La Pluie (J. J. B.).* Pond was brought down and lodged in Montreal gaol, but was acquitted for want of evidence.

The Montreal merchants furnished him with an outfit, and he returned to the north-west countries, wintering in Athabasca, near a fort belonging to a Mr. Ross. Peter pursued his usual roystering, plundering career. He persuaded his men to rob Mr. Ross of a load of furs in open day. In the course of the altercation Mr. Ross was shot, really by accident, from a gun in the hand of a *voyageur* named Péché. Pond was blamed, and again brought to Montreal.

While the lawyers were disputing for some months whether the Crown had jurisdiction in the Hudson's Bay territories, Pond broke out of

* It is to be confessed, that until the Hudson's Bay Company had uncontrolled sway over the Indian countries, rapine, drunkenness, and murder, greatly prevailed therein. Indians and Europeans suffered alike. It is not so now.

his wooden gaol, and escaped into the United States. There Franklin picked him up. It is understood that Pond was poorly rewarded. Franklin tried to employ him, but in vain; he was untrustworthy and intractable.

Mr. Oswald signed, it is said, the Boundary Treaty without the necessary information. A few hours afterwards some Montreal gentlemen arrived to supply his deficiencies. During his interview with them Mr. Oswald shed tears.

A couple of years after this an Indian trader of Montreal, arriving from England at Boston, accidentally heard of Pond being there. Calling at his lodgings, he found Pond at dinner, with two or three other people. As soon as Pond saw him, up he jumped, seized a carving-knife, and swore he would stab the first man that touched him. "Oh!" said the trader, "I do not come to arrest you, but only to have a little fur gossip." "I do not believe you," cried Peter; "the sooner you leave the room the better for you." The gentleman took the hint. Pond also left the town, and was next heard of at Philadelphia. He died in poverty. His son was lately a blacksmith in Lower Canada.*

* After this was copied from my notes, I found part in Mackenzie's "History of the Fur Trade;" but my information is derived as above, and is much fuller.

The guests at the wine table now joined the ladies for coffee, when one of the Miss M'Gillvray called to Mr. M——, and insisted upon his singing a wild *voyageur* song, "Le premier jour de Mai," playing the spirited tune on the piano at the same time with one hand.

Thus commanded, Mr. M—— sang it as only the true *voyageur* can do, imitating the action of the paddle, and in their high, resounding, and yet musical tones. His practised voice enabled him to give us the various swells and falls of sounds upon the waters, driven about by the winds, dispersed and softened in the wide expanses, or brought close again to the ear by neighbouring rocks. He finished, as is usual, with the piercing Indian shriek.*

When this was over, and the lady had obeyed a call to the piano frankly and well, a gentleman asked Mr. M'Gillvray what truth there was in the accounts of the dancing pheasants in the north-west, adding, that although he was at first incredulous, he could scarcely remain so after Mr. Gould's statements respecting the pastimes of the bower-bird of Australia.

Here our friend Mr. Thompson said he had repeatedly stumbled upon what might be called a "pheasant's ball," among the glades on the east-

* The words are in the Appendix. p 323

ern flanks of the Rocky Mountains. In those grassy countries the almost noiseless tread of the horses' feet (unshod) sometimes is not noticed by the busy birds; but the intruder must not be seen.

"The pheasants choose a beech," said Mr. T. "for the dance, a tree with boughs, several on the same level, and only full leafed at their ends. The feathered spectators group around. Six or seven pheasants step on the trembling stage, and begin to stamp, and prance, and twinkle their little feet like so many Bayadères, skipping with '*balancez et chassez*' from bough to bough; or they sit with curtsey and flutter, arching their glowing necks, and opening and closing their wings in concert; but, in truth, the dance is indescribable, most singular, and laughable. When it has lasted ten minutes, a new set of performers step forward, and the exhibition may last a couple of hours."*

* The following extract confirms in a remarkable manner this account of the pheasant dance. It is taken from Schomburgh's "Third Expedition into the Interior of Guiana," recently published in the "Journal of the Royal Geographical Society" (x. 235). "Not far," says Sir Robert, "from a high peak, called Arapami, near the River Kundanama, while traversing some mountains, we saw a number of that most beautiful bird, the cock of the rock, or rock manakin (*Rupicola elegans*), and I had an opportunity of witnessing some of its very singular antics, of which, though I had heard stories from the Indians, I had hitherto disbelieved them.

"Hearing the twittering noise so peculiar to the *rupicola*, I cautiously stole near, with two of my guides, towards a spot secluded from the path, from four to five feet in diameter, and

I confess to have been at the time greatly staggered by this story; but we see it has been verified, as well as another as incredible, from the same gentleman. He told us that in the far north-west, near the Arctic circle, the ice forms over a river, and the water sometimes deserts its bed. There is a dry channel, with a high arch of rough ice overhead, tinted white, green, and earth-coloured, if the banks are lofty. He said he had travelled for the best part of a mile in such a tunnel, simply because it was the best road.*

which appeared to have been cleared of every blade of grass, and smoothed as by human hands.

"There we saw a cock of the rock capering to the apparent delight of several others; now spreading its wings, throwing up its head, or opening its tail like a fan; now strutting about, and scratching the ground, all accompanied by a hopping gait until tired, when it gabbled some kind of note, and another relieved him. Thus three of them successively took the field, and then with self-approbation withdrew to rest on one of the low branches near the scene of action.

"We had counted ten cocks and two hens of the party, when the crackling of some wood on which I had unfortunately placed my foot alarmed and dispersed this dancing company."

My notes from Mr. Thompson were written some years before I met with Sir R. Schomburgh's narrative.

* "Journal of Royal Geographical Society of London," ix. 119. Baron Wrangel, while riding to the north of Yakutsk, in latitude 65°, over a large river; the ice suddenly giving way, he was thrown forwards and escaped, but his horse went under. He was lamenting the loss of his steed, when the Yakutskis, laughing, told him the horse was not only safe but dry; and eventually, when the ice was broken away, it was discovered that there was no water beneath,

It is hardly necessary to say that I passed a very agreeable evening. Our host was a large, handsome man, with the pleasant, successful look of the men of his habits and mode of life. I hope that what entertained me will entertain others.

The North-west Company of Fur-traders originated in the year 1783, from the united stimulus of gain and adventure. It was scarcely possible to abstain from endeavouring to share in the apparently enormous profits of the Hudson's Bay Company. Furs from the north-west were daily sold in Montreal, at a profit of from 1000 to 2000 per cent upon the prime cost among the Indians. It was eagerly believed that the Hudson's Bay charter did not include the vast extent of country then and now claimed by that Company, which, for all the grantors knew, might in truth have been salt water—a portion of the Pacific Ocean.

A number of young men, chiefly of good Scotch families, able, daring, and somewhat reckless perhaps, formed themselves into a company in order to traffic in the forbidden land in spite of the char-

and that the animal was standing upon the perfectly dry bed of the river.

Similar streams, some rather large, others fed only by superficial springs, are now not unknown to the Hudson's Bay Company; and one has been mentioned by Sir John Richardson.

ter. They neither wanted the necessary capital nor the requisite knowledge.

Among these were M'Kenzie, Mactavish, Frobisher, M'Leod, Rocheblave, and others—men who have become celebrated for their painful wanderings and perils extreme in search of furs. Their most prominent member, Mr. M'Kenzie, was knighted—an honour which seemed to legalise their proceedings.

They went boldly to work. Close to each Hudson's Bay Company's fort they planted one of their own, to undersell and beard the old people. When disputes arose, as was sure to do, the partner of the new concern was always prompt to appeal to the pistol, making it a personal affair. In fact, the quiet, inky-fingered clerk of the old Company, expecting only his poor salary, was no match for the fiery youth who worked on shares.

Not only did the North-west Company dispute successfully the known hunting-grounds, but they pushed strong parties far beyond, down the Fraser, Peace, Thompson, Columbia, and other rivers, even to the Arctic circle and the Russian dominions in America.

The adventure was successful. Every year brought with it enlarged operations and accession of capital. The early part of this century found the North-west Company almost irresistible in Canada—an extensive purchaser in her markets, employing thousands of her population, and enriching all connected with them.

During the last war with the United States they sent into the field three regiments of hardy *voyageurs*, of eight hundred or one thousand men each; and this at a time when the British Government required such countenance and succour.

Every device was used to stimulate their agents in the Indian countries to unusual exertions. A scale of ranks and emoluments was introduced,—occasional furloughs granted to enable the successful to enjoy themselves. The celebrated Beaver Club of Montreal was established as a point of recreation and of union, and where, I have been told, on certain great occasions the last plate put on the table before each member held a cheque for a sum of money.

I noticed that the members of the North-west Company were often relatives. This arose, I doubt not, from the enticing descriptions which were sent into the Scottish Highlands, from time to time, of the adventurous life of the wilderness, of hunting and war, of alternate indolence and desperate toil, and lastly and particularly, of the acquisition of splendid fortunes.

A first-rate Indian trader is no ordinary man. He is a soldier-merchant, and unites the gallantry of the one with the shrewdness of the other.

Montreal was then the best place for seeing this class of persons, as St. Louis at the mouth of the Missouri is at present. What sailors are at seaports they are at these places. They spend fast, play all the freaks, pranks, and street-fooleries, and originate all the current whimsicalities: but this is their brief holiday: when they turn their faces westward, up stream, their manners change.

The Indian trader is a bold, square-chested, gaunt man, sun-burnt, with extraordinary long hair as a defence against mosquitoes. He is equally at home on horseback or in the canoe—indefatigable when needful, careless of heat and cold, and brave as steel, as though he bore a charmed life, in countries where the Queen's writ scarcely runs, where the law only of personal authority takes effect. Often he has not only to contend with the Indians, and to right himself on the spot with other traders, but he has to fight his own men hand to hand. Kindness, vigour, and sagacity, usually render but one such affair necessary.

It had become evident in 1816, and before,

that the competition of the two companies was injurious to all concerned, that their strife was devastating the fur countries, and that their mutual attacks (on one occasion sixteen Scotchmen and Englishmen were massacred) would be tolerated no longer. They cannot have desired the continuation of such a state of things. An amalgamation therefore took place in 1821; and all has been peace since that period, greatly to the benefit of all parties, and most so to the Indians;—although it is true that these last are only the hunting-slaves of a company of whites in Leadenhall Street.

At length the day of departure, the 20th of May, arrived. Together with a pleasant young clerk of the North-west Company I left Montreal in a long-eared calash,* drawn by two stout black horses, for the mouth of the river Ottawa, at the upper end of the island of Montreal—there to embark in the light canoe.

The main business of the canoe in which I was granted a seat was to convey Mr. Rocheblave, a

* It is like an English gig, but much stouter, the horse farther from the body of the carriage; and this allows of room for the driver, whose seat rests on the footboard. Instead of doors, like our phaeton, it has high sides, for warmth and other reasons. The driver's seat and the board which supports it fall by means of hinges when the passengers get in, and the board and seat are then hooked up again to their place when the driver mounts.

partner in the North-west Company, and his clerk, to Fort William, in Lake Superior; and M. Tabeau, a Roman Catholic priest, and myself, to the Straits of St. Mary, the outlet of the above lake, and my furthest point on this occasion.

We were soon at La Chine, and were trotting along the good road which skirts the shores of Lake St. Louis, when, to my great gratification, we had not gone far before we found the shore lined with flat-bottomed boats filled with six companies of the 68th Light Infantry, on their way to Kingston in Canada West.

Most of the officers were walking leisurely on the road, some of the juniors, however, standing erect on the stern-thwarts, pole in hand, making respectable proof of their river-craft.

The officers' wives were in boats with awnings —sitting cool and happy, while the soldiers, their baggage and womankind, crowded the other barges.

Inexperience in a strong opposing current is as bad as in taking a cross-country ride. So our friends found it,—especially in rounding a point, when too often, in spite of clamorous warnings innumerable, the boat's head would be caught by the stream; and away she would dart Quebec-wards, to the great amusement of all but the principals concerned.

Passing along an endless string of white cottages, with dome-shaped ovens, and primitive wells by their sides, we arrived at the pretty village of St. Clair, when another spectacle awaited us. For some miles previously we had noticed that all the houses were shut up. This was now explained.

A sudden turn in the road shewed us on a long low point, advancing into the lake, with a grove and a church at the end, drawn up before a large wooden cross, a large procession in honour of Ascension Thursday. Foremost stood a body of stoled priests, with their acolytes dressed in white, with blue sashes, and behind them a prolonged file, four deep, of neatly-dressed females, having among them a tall red banner; while their male friends stood behind in less orderly array, and looking wistfully at sky and water, as if their minds were elsewhere—perhaps in the young wheat-fields. I was surprised to find among these good men the same rustic style of dress as in Normandy—the same short-waisted blue coat and brass buttons, the immense flapping shirt collars, and the same high and heavy broad-brimmed hat.

The scene was beautiful, and called out many thoughts, both as a Christian and a lover of the picturesque. It would have just suited Peter de Wint — full of quiet heavy masses of foliage, black in the outstretching shadows of a declining sun, but cheered by the pilgrim group, their banner, the church, and the wide waters sparkling from afar.

We jogged on nine more miles, past St. Anne's, celebrated by the poet, to Château-brillant, a small fort, venerable in ruins, overlooking from a mound the Narrows at the mouth of the Ottawa. It is overgrown with ivy and young trees, and was once meant to overawe the neighbouring Indians.

The only quickset-hedge I ever saw in Canada occurs on the little farm close to this ruin.

Our *voyageurs* were to have awaited us at Château-brillant; but, save for our own shouts, all was still among its shadows. Returning a couple of miles, we found them at Forbes' Tavern; and they said, forsooth, that as good Catholics they could not but stay to assist in the holy procession at St. Clair.

I was now introduced to our leader, M. Rocheblave, a senior partner of the North-west Company, a tall dark Frenchman, with a stoop, born at New Orleans. I found him well informed, obliging, and companionable. He would have been more so during the first few days of our voyage, but he had been only *very* recently married.

Let me not forget M. Tabeau, the curé of Boucherville, a stout, rosy, happy-looking priest of middle age, of unaffected and even polished manners, fond of music, and reasonably so of good living. He was (and I hope still lives) a good man, and had nothing of the livid complexion and gloomy pugnacity of many of the Roman Catholic clergy in England.

I have already mentioned Mr. Robinson, the clerk. At once I felt that I was fortunate in my companions, and took my seat in the canoe at Forbes' Tavern, not a little excited by my new position, and by the romance (to me at least) of ascending almost to the source of the lovely and beautiful Ottawa.

It may be well here to premise that the Ottawa is throughout, and in many points of view, an interesting river. It is always very broad—from half a mile to two miles—and five hundred or more miles long; for Lake Tematscaming is not its source, but only an expansion. It is not so much a river in the English sense of the word, as a chain of lakes, or long sheets of quiet water, twenty, thirty, and sixty miles in length each, connected by narrows and rapids, by which the river forces its way through high and rocky lands in a series of cascades and foaming currents.

The countries adjacent will soon be the seat of a thriving population, for they seem for the most part fertile—fit for either pasturage or arable. Clearances on the Ottawa are now found two hundred miles above Montreal, and they are multiplying. Mr. Sheriff reports that the region between Lake Nipissing and the upper part of the Ottawa is a well-timbered high table-land, inviting the labours of the poor but diligent settler. The Ottawa has long been the chief resort of the lumberer, who supplies England with great quantities of pine. Nowhere have I seen such lofty and large firs as on the Ottawa.

bleak: rocky

Our canoe was thirty-six feet long, sharp at each end, six feet wide in the middle, and made of birch bark, in sheets sewn together with vegetable fibre, and the seams gummed up close. The sides are strengthened and steadied by four or six cross-bars lashed to the rim of the canoe, and the inside is protected by slender ribs of a light wood, but the bottom only by a few loose poles. It is called a light canoe, or "canot lâche," because intended to go swiftly, and to carry only provisions and personal baggage. Its

* 36'x6' canoe

light canoe

* For "North canoe" manned by 6 voyageurs See Vol 2 p 236

usual complement is nineteen—that is, fifteen paddlemen and four gentlemen passengers; the latter sitting each on his rolled-up bed in the middle compartment.

The North-west Company provided *munitions de bouche* on the most liberal scale—port, madeira, shrub, brandy, rum, sausages, eggs, a huge pie of veal and pheasants, cold roast beef, salt beef, hams, tongues, loaves, tea, sugar, and, to crown all, some exquisite beaver tail. The men were provided well in a plainer way, and had their glass of rum in cold and rainy weather.

I was disappointed and not a little surprised at the appearance of the *voyageurs*. On Sundays, as they stand round the door of the village churches, they are proud dressy fellows in their parti-coloured sashes and ostrich-feathers; but here they were a motley set to the eye: but the truth was that all of them were picked men, with extra wages as serving in a light canoe.

Some were well made, but all looked weak in the legs, and were of light weight. A Falstaff would have put his foot through the canoe to the "yellow sands" beneath. The collection of faces among them chanced to be extraordinary, as they squatted, paddle in hand, in two rows, each on his slender bag of necessaries. By the bye, all their finery (and they love it) was left at home.

One man's face, with a large Jewish nose, seemed to have been squeezed in a vice, or to have passed through a flattening machine. It was like a cheese-cutter—all edge. Another had one nostril bitten off. He proved the buffoon of the party. He had the extraordinary faculty of untying the strings of his face, as it were, at pleasure, when his features fell into confusion—into a crazed chaos almost frightful; his eye, too, lost its usual significance: but no man's countenance (barring the bite) was fuller of fun and fancies than his, when he liked. A third man had his features wrenched to the right—exceedingly little, it is true; but the effect was remarkable. He had been slapped on the face by a grisly bear. Another was a short, paunchy old man, with vast features, but no forehead—the last man I should have selected; but he was a hard-working creature, usually called "Passe-partout," because he had been everywhere, and was famous for the weight of fish he could devour at a meal. He knew the flavour of the fish of each great lake, just as the man who had been ordered by Boerhaave to live on broth made of grass came to know the field from whence it was taken. Except the younger men, their faces were short, thin, quick in their expression, and mapped out in furrows, like those of the sunday-less Parisians.

Nothing could exceed their respectful and obliging behaviour. The same must be said of all of this class with whom I had anything to do. Their occupation is now gone—gone for them the hot chase of the buffalo, the fishing-spear, and echoing cliffs of Lake Huron. I look upon them with the same mysterious awe and regret as I should do on the last Dodo or Dinornis, the ultimate vestiges of a lost race. Our worthy priest, M. Tabeau, while on shore, shook every *voyageur* by the hand kindly, and had a pleasant word for each. We then embarked at thirty minutes past three P. M.

As soon as we were well settled down in our places, and the canoe began to feel the paddles, Mr. Tabeau, by way of asking a blessing on the voyage, pulled off his hat, and sounded forth a Latin invocation to the Deity, and to a long train of male and female saints, in a loud and full voice, while all the men, at the end of each versicle, made response, "*Qu'il me bénisse.*"

This done, he called for a song; and many were gleefully carolled—each verse in solo, and then repeated in chorus, north-west fashion. Of such use is singing, in enabling the men to work eighteen and nineteen hours a-day (at a pinch), through forests and across great bays, that a good singer has additional pay. The songs are sung with might and main, at the top of the voice, timed to the paddle, which makes about fifty strokes in a minute. While nearing habitations, crossing sheets of water, and during rain, the song is loud and long. The airs I suppose to be ancient French. They are often very beautiful. Now and then the words are evidently Canadian, like the one which commemorates the death of a *voyageur* at the Falls of La Montagne (where we shall soon be), or that in which the lover entreats the lady to fly with him and hide among the wild and verdant isles of the Ottawa.

The current, as we ascended the Ottawa (open, or spotted with islets, by turns), from Forbes' Tavern, was strong against us; but in an hour and a half we arrived at the pretty Indian village of the Lake of the Two Mountains, which straggles over and about a sort of green, with mounts of sand behind, overhung with woody hills. The Nipissing, or Witch Indians, inhabit the left half of the village, in neat, painted houses (so they looked at a distance); but the other half, belonging to the Iroquois, seemed desolate and neglected. I suppose they were still at their winter hunting-grounds. As we skirted close past the church, which is near the water-side and in the centre of the village, we saw sitting on a gravestone, under a lofty elm, the old priest Humbert,* with his large serious features, in cassock and sombrero. Singular to say, Mr. Bartlett, in his "Canadian Scenery," has given us the self-same picture, taken some years after my visit.

At the further end of the village we delivered a bag of silver money to a trader of the place. There gathered near us a group of dark, handsome, gipsy-like men, wrapped in blankets with scarlet borders; filthy, ugly women; and frolicsome children, all peaceable, and pleased to gaze upon us. The strange, uncouth spot, the bandit faces and dresses, made me think I was at the world's end.

Half a mile above this village, we encamped for the night in a wood of tall beeches and elms. The gentlemen occupied one small square tent of thin canvass, pitched by their own hands, as the custom is. We soon had a roaring fire, took tea, and lay down to sleep,

> "Lulled by the sound of far-off torrents,
> Charming the still night."

My bed, a blanket folded four times, was near the entrance of the tent. As I lay, I could see the gleam of the rippling waters hard by; and

* His brother, General Humbert, commanded the French in their invasion of Ireland, in 1798.

the stars of a lovely summer's night were among the tree-tops. The *voyageurs* were asleep in their blankets around the fire; one alone was up and about, on watch, and cooking their next day's soup. Baggage lay strewn in all directions.

We heard at a little after two in the morning, while yet dark, the loud and startling shout of "Alerte!" and in a few minutes we were afloat on the broad bosom of the river, here called the Lake of the Two Mountains, twenty miles long, and reaching to Point Fortune, at the foot of the Long Sault Rapids, of which we spoke in our last Excursion.

We breakfasted some distance higher than Point Fortune. While thus comfortably engaged, some men in great haste came and inquired if we had seen some timber rafts driving down the stream. Truly had we — in the boiling rapids, both above and below us, dashing along at a prodigious rate, and sure to be broken to pieces on the rocks. They had escaped from their fastenings, while the men were at a tavern three miles higher up.

Our canoe now crossed to the east side of the river and landed her gentlemen, in order the better "to force" the rapids, which are long and strong, and particularly violent at a bend where six Iroquois had been drowned a few days before, by the breaking of their tow-rope. The river being this season eight feet above its usual level, the rapids were unusually vehement, and, in places, the woods around were flooded.

We walked the nine miles to the head of the Long Sault Rapids, through swamps and woods. To avoid wading, Mr. Robinson and myself struck deep into the forest, lost ourselves, and wandered about uneasily, until we came upon a decent log-house in a small clearance (township of Grenville). After some rapping, the door was opened by a very handsome tall young woman, with auburn hair, tidily dressed. I inquired our way. She shook her head without a smile. In great surprise—for she looked British all over—I addressed her in French; but I only got another shake of the head, when her brother appeared, and told us that they were Highlanders, and that his sister could only speak Gaelic. He put us in the right way for the head of the rapids. These people were dissatisfied, and longed for the hills of Blair Athol—almost the only instance I ever met with.

We regained the river Ottawa opposite the Hamilton Mills, and found our friends at Major M'Millan's, a considerable landowner, waiting for the canoe.* One of the Major's children had

* A summer or two after this I spent a fortnight at a charming encampment, a few hundred yards below Major M'Millan's, of two

swallowed a halfpenny: I sent down after it some rhubarb and dry bread, but I could not wait the effect. We soon afterwards embarked, and made a quick and merry dinner on the grass, half a mile above the Major's, and paddled up the splendid sheet of water, sixty miles long, which leads to the falls of the Rideau and Chaudière, to the village of Hull, and now to the far more important place, Bytown. ×

Since I made this canoe voyage, the country has been much settled, and one or two steamboats 1819 see p 126

companies of the Staff Corps, then constructing the Grenville Canal, to avoid the Long Sault Rapids. I passed the day in geologising, and the evening in listening to the guitars of two accomplished sisters, Sicilians, who had married officers of this corps.

I was the happy guest of Col. Robe, then a studious and zealous lieutenant in this useful regiment. I wish I had time to describe the primitive kraal-like huts of the officers, and other droll makeshifts of the wilderness.

Col. Robe was so enthusiastic a geologist, that in mid-winter he went from Montreal to Lanark on the Ottawa (100 to 120 miles), on my information, to secure some bones found there in a limestone cave in the woods. But they proved to belong to an unfortunate deer who had slipped in by accident; and we lost a Canadian gaylenreuth.

The Staff Corps was here, I think, two summers. One day Major Rochfort Scott (author of "Travels in Candia and Spain"), then a gallant young sub, made a dash into the melancholy woods, which began at the back of his tent and extended to the Arctic circle. Taking with him a soldier, he went almost due north for eighty miles, across rivers, morasses, woods, rocks, and hills, and skirting the lakes. He was many days out, and returned when his provisions failed. He found a large deposit of plumbago. plumbago

× Bytown, for Col. By, Engr. of Rideau Canal, now called Ottawa

navigate this lake, as we may call it, daily; but at the time I am speaking of, it was chiefly in a state of nature. The gentle acclivities on all sides were covered with forests of hard wood—thus indicating a fertile soil; but the signs of man were rare. They were, a little pirogue, with a man and a girl in it, creeping close in shore; or the hut of a family arrived last autumn. A punt stands before the door, a plank is pushed a little way into the river, and there fastened, to draw water from; and perhaps you may see a thin, scantily-clad female, dipping a vessel into the stream. Pig, ox, or cow, they have not yet acquired. They subsist on the potatoes, pumpkins, and maize, which have been planted among the stumps, with a little salt pork. About twenty-five miles from Hamilton Mills, at nine P. M., we arrived at La Petite Nation, (a seigniory of eight hundred and twenty-six settlers in 1842, belonging to Mr. Speaker Papineau, the celebrated agitator.) We found his brother there, in a goodly house, on an island surrounded by a wide-spread inundation. Here we pitched our tent for the night, and invited Mr. C. Papineau to sup with us. He was a dark quick-eyed man, with a small hooked nose. As he was not ignorant of the good purveying of a light canoe, our society, perhaps, was not his only inducement to join us.

The next day we were off by three A.M. (May 22), and in the course of the day passed over thirty miles of broad waters buried in dense forests. Just before we landed to dine, near the house of an American farmer, we overtook five loaded canoes of the North-west Company, with sixty men. As soon as they were in sight we began to sing, and when abreast there was a lively exchange of travellers' wit between the parties. While we were at dinner our friends passed us, and sang most sweetly, with a full chorus of all the crews — distance softening down any occasional harsh note from a novice.

The American had been at this large clearance some years. He had cows and horses, and no small substance. I saw five or six stout fellows about the premises, and some hearty girls — "Madges of the milking-pail." The mother chattered fast to us during our meal, and wished to buy our broken victuals, although they seemed in good case. Mr. Rocheblave gave them some.

I was sorry to see an idiot boy, fifteen years old, going about with literally nothing on him but a very dirty calico shirt.

The land around had been slowly rising from our dining-place; and at six or eight miles from thence we came to a bend of the river to the right (east). This, of course, we followed, and soon beheld an uncommon landscape.

We were at the lower end of a reach two miles long. At the western angle of its upper end the Rideau Fall leaps into the Ottawa in two massy sheets of water, from a height of sixty feet, and about a hundred yards apart. They are of unequal size: the larger perhaps three hundred feet broad, the smaller one hundred feet—the larger also being guarded by a high precipice crowned with pines. An island divides them. The environs in almost every direction are covered with great pines, stripped, blackened with fire, and pointing, needle-like, far into the sky. The extreme distance behind the Falls, and to the north, visible to us on the river, rose into uplands and hills, also covered with fired pines.

Such was this scene in 1821, when man had only begun his changes. Bytown has been built since near these falls; gigantic locks and a very large canal are close to it. A great part of the traffic between Montreal and the upper country was expected to pass through these works; but this route has been neglected since the St. Lawrence Canal has been finished; the latter being the shorter and more economical line of transport. The Rideau Canal will be of little use, except during war. This interesting landscape now wears another kind of beauty, which has been exquisitely well transferred to paper by Mr. Bartlett.

Continuing our course up the reach, delighted with the high and often rocky scenery, a strong back-water eddy drove us up a narrow pass among cliffs, bare but for young firs in the clefts. Three openings now presented themselves; the most distant one, to our left, displayed a broad half-rapid, half-cascade, sweeping down among islets of pines. The middle passage seemed very narrow, and conveyed away in a state of commotion the waters of the Kettle Fall (the Chau[illegible] proper), while the near or right passage, in that our canoe was dancing, led by a winding [illegible] into a rocky cove, where we landed for the portage, usually two hundred yards long.

[illegible] these turbulent waters, we were [illegible] ourselves amid a complete encampment [illegible] lodges (twenty-two), belonging to the [illegible] Company; and ten or twelve [illegible] belonging to the Iroquois [illegible] of the Two Mountains, [illegible] winter hunt, with their families [illegible] being very fond [illegible] dressed [illegible] and fringed [illegible] greater number were tipsy, especially one, who rolled rather than walked down a steep footpath, very drunk, loaded with furs, and nearly threw me into the river. The clamour, jargonings, and confusion, rising up on all sides in this mixed and impetuous multitude, cannot be described.

When we had mounted the landing-place, we stood on a platform of naked rock. On our right, on slightly rising ground, and backed by woods, was the village of Hull—half-a-dozen good houses and stores, a handsome Episcopal church,* and many inferior buildings. Before us was the river, nearly a mile broad, and sweeping through the forests in strong rapids towards the Falls. One hundred yards on our left was the Kettle Fall, with the disappointing look of a mill-dam, and a fall of thirty feet. A long and severe thunder-

* From the church-tower I looked over the whole region around; then to the west and north-west, a waste of waters and woods. Northwards and eastwards Mr. Wright's farms are close about us, and then the forests. Mr. Willis (Bartlett's "Canadian Scenery") says the hills behind Hull are 900 feet high. I doubt this. In the direction of Bytown there are extensive clearances, from the great population assembled there for commercial purposes.

Lieut.-col. Robe made a charming sketch from this tower during a visit I afterwards made with him to the deposit of iron ore in this neighbourhood. The sketch I gave to the present excellent British Consul of New York. This iron deposit is five miles north of Hull. It was brought into view by the falling down of a part of the mound on which it occurs. We were guided to it by a blaze in the woods.

storm prevented me from examining it properly. I saw the forked lightning strike a pine-stump fifty yards off. So greatly increased was the flood on the river since the day before, that we were delayed here three or four hours, and had to make two portages.

One description of the *voyageur's* method of passing a portage will suffice. The whole cargo is distributed into loads of 95lbs. weight each. No single article is allowed to weigh more. Of these each *voyageur* takes one, two, or three at once to the further end of the portage, if it be not too long, and at a slow trot, with the knees much bent, stopping for a few minutes every half hour, this rest being technically called a pipe. The load is made to rest upon the head and shoulders by means of a broad strap, which passes over the forehead. The canoe is carried most tenderly on the naked shoulders of six men, and is pushed, cushioned on beds, up ledges and precipices. The gentlemen carry their own small articles, and any others which may come to hand, such as poles, paddles, or kettle, &c. One of us lost the lid of our kettle, whereby we suffered more inconvenience than can be readily conceived. The road is usually as bad as possible, over fallen trees, slippery rocks and rivulets, through marshes and dense woods.

At seven P. M. we made our final start from Hull,* and were towed up some temporary rapids for a couple of hours, so close to the bank as to be brushed by the foliage, when we encamped for the night in a little glade.

Here we found waiting for the morn seven

* Mr. Philemon Wright came here in 1806. He is a Loyalist from the United States, and brought with him capital, talent, and many hard-working settlers. He is (or was) a plain little man, in constant motion, teaching and being taught—a true pioneer, an enthusiast in reclaiming and cultivating wild land. He has personally brought over from England the finest rams, bulls, oxen, cows, and horses money could procure. He has three or four extensive farms in his own hands in the rear on the river Gatineau, and has a rather numerous and I believe thriving tenantry. He has built the greater part of Hull. He was so good as to shew me the tree under which he slept on the night of his arrival. I felt that the tree was memorable, in a manner sacred, and that I was in the presence of a considerable mind; not perhaps able to figure in a ball-room, but able to gather and nourish a happy population. The schoolmaster of the place was his factotum, a quiet shrewd person, of like eager agricultural impulses with Mr. Wright. They passed one winter at Quebec in a small lodging, probably to obtain some facility or other from Government. Both master and man lived in a world of their own—not in the present, but in a great future. Many a time at midnight have I passed their little window (without a blind) and saw them with one poor candle, compass and pencil at hand, poring abstractedly over a MS. map, elbows on table, and their heads firmly clasped in their palms; the fire extinct in the stove, most probably, in that intensely cold climate.

Mr. Wright has an excellent house at Hull, where he and his large household live plainly and plentifully. There I drank tea with him. We had also beefsteaks and cold boiled peas: but I have partaken of things as incongruous in one of the best Quaker families of Philadelphia.

loaded canoes and eighty *voyageurs* belonging to the Hudson's Bay Company. Our leader warned his men against quarrelling with their neighbours.

It was an uncouth scene. There was a semicircle of canoes turned over on the grass to sleep under, with blazing fires near them, surrounded by sinister-looking, long-haired men, in blanket coats, and ostrich feathers in their hats, smoking and cooking, and feeding the fires. I particularly noticed one large square man, squat on the wet ground, with a bit of looking-glass in his hand, intently watching his wife, as she carefully combed out his long jetty hair, undisturbed by a sharp rain, which the powerful fire did not permit to penetrate.

May 23d. The weather has changed: it is very cold, and will snow.

We set off in the dark at three A.M. I had the agreeable addition, to the usual comforts of these expeditions, of stepping nearly knee-deep into the water (iced in the north), a stone from which I was stepping into the canoe having unkindly rolled over. My hat was also soon afterwards knocked overboard by a paddle, and restored to me full of water.

Daylight found us on the Chaudière Lake, thirty miles long, and varying in breadth from one to two miles, turning westwards at its upper

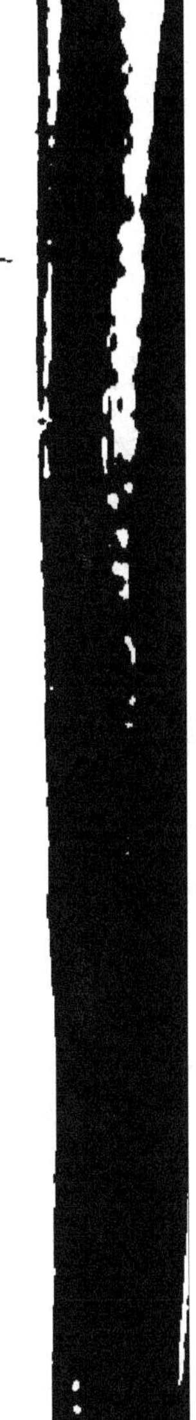

end, and filling with population. The banks, richly wooded, were often high, and faced with little beaches of yellow sand. A mile from the north shore a range of hills presented themselves.

At nine A.M. we breakfasted among the rank grass of a deserted clearance. It being Sunday, Mr. Tabeau had the tent set up; and he dressed an altar within it with crucifix and candles, little pictures, and clean linen cloth. With his singing-boy and bell he performed a religious service, all the *voyageurs* kneeling round the tent door with great seriousness. I was glad to see this. Roman Catholic light is infinitely better than unbelieving darkness. One thing struck me at the time; that while the common run of Protestants seem ashamed of the simple but sublime and comfortable truths found in the Bible only, the various superstitions are openly and proudly confessed, beginning with Mariology, and ending with African Fetishism.

Leaving this, and paddling along on the south side of the lake, we not long afterwards arrived within two miles of the splendid Falls of the Chat. Saving always the Falls of Niagara, we had before us, in the exaggerated state of the river, the finest burst of waters I have seen in America.

We were at the apex of a triangular sheet of

water. Before us, a couple of miles off, was a base-line half a league long, and for the most part occupied by a massy, voluminous cataract, forty and sixty feet high in portions, rushing down into a lower country through the intervals of piny islets; the remainder of this base-line on the east being a barrier of rocks and trees, with two small impetuous falls at the very end, forcing a devious passage through thick foliage.

Mr. Bartlett has not done justice to the main cataract; but I doubt not the spring-floods added greatly at this time to the magnificence of the spectacle. The River Ottawa, like all streams from the north, is liable to freshets from the rapid melting of snow.

The billowy tumult of the widened stream continues for some distance below the principal cataract; but our skilful steersman conducted us (dangerous as it appeared) delightfully across it, his men answering his signals of hand and eye as prompt as thought. We soon landed at the portage, at the foot of the smaller falls, so well delineated by Bartlett.

Here, screened by huge masses of rock and by coppice, we found an Indian hut filled with men, squaws, and children, all astonishingly dirty,—and with such long, filthy finger-nails! It was a scene of noise and confusion seldom equalled; cascades thundering, *voyageurs* toiling, children screaming, ladies (!) begging, and dogs barking.

We soon clambered up the rugged height before us, the men pushing up the canoe, stage by stage, supported on our beds.

But now began some very nervous work for two hours. The river was so swollen and furious, overleaping its banks into the adjacent woods, that previous experience was at fault. We placed the loaded canoe in the water some yards above one of the two narrow falls, and had pushed off, when, to our dismay, in spite of every effort, we found that we were being sucked into the cataract. I shall never forget the fright, nor the eagerness with which we soon clutched at some willow boughs, and were saved. Two Indians had been drowned that week near the same spot.

We could not venture on the river itself, full of islets there; its current was above our strength. We therefore crept with exceeding slowness through the woods by temporary channels, and crossing basins when favoured by eddies. Great was the skill and coolness of our men, ill-favoured little folk as some of them were. In a moment we shot across one very dangerous pass, all hands clinging to the trees for safety.

At length we reached something like still water, to the great content of all; not excepting our worthy priest, who had been perpetually catching at trees, and vociferating, "Hauw! hauw!" an Indian equivalent to our own energetic "Go it! go it!"

Reaching an inundated island, composed of fine white marble, we dined. The men dried themselves, had their glass of rum, myself one of port, and all was cheery again. At this place we found two Hudson's Bay canoes repairing damages. This is chiefly done by patching with birch bark, and caulking with gum from a certain kind of fir found throughout North America, which softens under heat, hardens in contact with water, and adheres with great force to birch bark.

The Hudson's Bay people went off first; but we soon overtook them, singing as we drew near, when a race began, which after a short contest we won, as we were light. M. Rocheblave, waking up out of an after-dinner dream at the shout of victory, was not pleased.

We had now entered Lake Chat, sixteen miles long by one or two broad (Mr. Sheriff), and coasted its southern shore crowded with trees. We saw some scanty openings in the woods. Not long after, the Chief Macnab with some of his clan established themselves here.

Here and there, especially on the north side of the lake, small fertile islands are scattered.

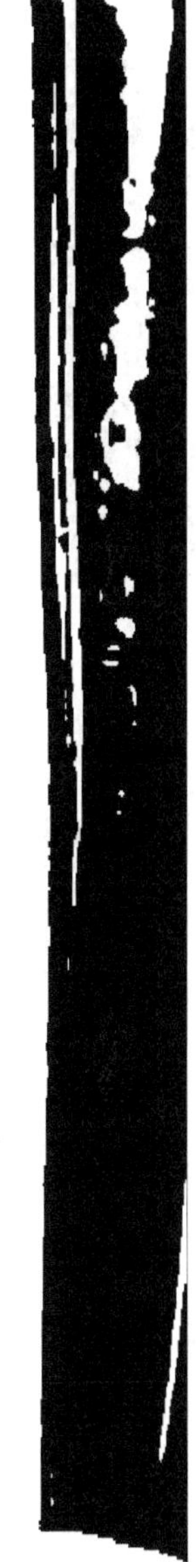

My information respecting this lake and that of the Chaudière is but scanty.* It rained incessantly; our heads were under a large tarpaulin. To prevent being stifled every now and then, I peeped out and scanned the neighbourhood. The youngest man of the crew, a handsome, gallant fellow, sat behind and next to me. I was surprised to find him naked, save a pair of linen trousers, in the cold rain. I told him I wondered at his rashness; but, shaking the wet out of his long locks, he laughed and said he was warm, and that he should have his clothes dry to wear at night. Looking about, I saw others had done the same.

Towards evening we began to encounter the rapids of the Richelieu (or "the Cheneaux"), four miles long. They are caused by the river becoming at times narrow, shallow, and full of islands. At their foot there is a great boom thrown far into the water, to stop the stray logs of timber which the lumberers send down marked.

We avoided the greatest violence of these rapids by creeping close to the sedgy bank, among fallen pines, overhanging oaks, and beeches. Sometimes, however, we were obliged to use the tow-rope.

* The map of the St. Lawrence valley attached to this work gives a fair general idea of the upper parts of the Ottawa River.

Our course, however, was not always so harassing, for sometimes the flood overspread low lands, and the current moderated. It was very new to me to float in the twilight of thick woods, among their gnarled and huge trunks, their foliage drooping and drenched, with these half-naked men of shaggy locks, carolling with boundless gaiety. It is not often that we see in Canada such large bowls and grotesquely twisted boughs as are found here.

I could not but admire the great diversity in colour and form of the trees of these romantic spots. There were cedar, oak, birch, and beech, with pines on the higher grounds;—the last often blasted by lightning in single trees, or fired by Indians in large tracts: more usually, however, the pine stood erect, flinging its rough limbs deep into the sombre forest. The birch and trembling poplar commonly adorned the foot of a precipice, with pale grey or light green leaves, of a delicacy of tint contrasting finely with the dark masses around.

The interior of the country seemed to consist of short hills almost bare, from 400 to 500 feet high, standing in morasses, meadows, or lakes. White marble and sienite are the prevailing rocks for miles.

Five miles above these rude scenes brought us

to the Falls of La Montagne. A hilly ridge had followed the course of the river a little way off for a few miles, but it now (near the Falls) forms the immediate shore for some distance, and crosses the river to form the barrier forced by the cataract. All this neighbourhood is most picturesque, and promises peculiar geological interest, but heavy rain and snow prevented my either sketching or taking notes at the moment.

A curious disposition of strata is seen where the hill first strikes the river, which would make a good drawing.

The high, smooth, mural precipice of white marble, which forms the north-east side of the river, is traversed vertically by several (or many) broad black stripes of an hornblende rock (?), and looks like a vast hanging sheet of striped calico. As it nears the Falls the precipice becoms a slope clothed with pines.

The Falls are not more than fifteen feet high, but the water being pent up by high cliffs, they are loud and tumultuous.

We reached the foot of the carrying-place by dashing athwart some dangerous-looking rapids, and again found ourselves among numerous friends;—a brigade of loaded canoes being then engaged in passing over the rough little hill forming the portage, and 385 paces across.

Although at that moment the rain had changed into a heavy snow (May 23), and the whole landscape was fast turning white, there stood watching his men on a jutting rock a handsome young Scotchman, evidently fresh from the Highlands, his face glowing with the animation, novelty, and wildness of the scene. He was quite a picture, as he leaned on his fowling-piece, in a strong shooting-dress and Caledonian "maud," his broad bonnet hanging jauntily over his left ear.

This is the scene of one of the most beautiful of the Canadian boat-songs. I have heard it repeatedly, but did not take it down. It is supposed to have been found inscribed on the bark of a birch-tree a little above the Falls. This is its argument, as the poets would say. A canoe laden with furs is waylaid by hostile Indians, who are discovered crowding both banks of the river, at a bend where both falls and portage come in sight together. In their consternation the *voyageurs* appeal to the mild Mary, the Virgin Mother, who immediately appears to them in a rainbow amid the spray of the cataract, and beckons them onwards—to leap the fall. They obey, rush into the gulf, and are saved from torture and death. One unhappy man had just left the canoe: he saw the whole, but dared not shew himself.

Sometime afterwards he was found dead at the foot of the inscription.

The interval of eighteen miles between this portage and the next, the Grand Calumet, is very intricate. It is full of islands and rapids, threading an assemblage of hills. All the rock I saw is white marble, and so is the hilly portage of the Grand Calumet, one mile and a quarter across. There is a formidable rapid at the foot of this carrying place, and one or more booms to catch stray timber.

The cold rain and snow were so heavy that I took but little notice of anything from hence to Fort Coulanges. Hills and ruined precipices accompanied us for a few miles above the Grand Calumet, when the country suddenly lowered and became flat. The river has spread out, the banks are woody, marshy, or faced with sand-beaches and slight traces of fossil limestone.

Such without change, for twenty miles or more up the river, is the neighbourhood of Fort Coulanges, a small station belonging to the North-west Company, and used as a depôt or refuge in case of accident. The clerks in charge have cleared to profit about seventy acres of land.

We now forced the Allumettes Rapids, partly formed by a very large island, now partly cultivated, and adorned with a pretty church. They are the outlet of that portion of the Ottawa which is called the Lake des Allumettes. These rapids are distributed into a number of rocky narrows, one of which we ascended, taking us to a fall over a low shelf of gneis, where the canoe was carried a few yards and then pushed up another passage like a sewer or tunnel.

Lake des Allumettes (sometimes considered as two) now opens to us, twenty-one miles long (including the island) by the usual breadth of one or two miles. The current is just perceptible. It contains some low islands, and has flat banks, either sandy or wooded to the water's edge.

The landscape undergoes a sudden and extremely picturesque change as we enter upon the next portion of the Ottawa, " the Deep River," or Rivière Creuse, of the French. The stream is at once narrowed by steep hills, which are either totally barren or are merely dotted with dark patches of fir.

A few miles from the lower entrance brings us to Cape Baptême, when for a great distance the Ottawa washes the base of very high brown cliffs of gneis, either in great solid sheets, or split, torn, and dismantled, the surfaces often covered with the edible but indigestible tripe des roches, and the fissures harbouring solitary pines and numerous pendant scarlet flowers, bell-shaped. From one of these cliffs two contiguous streams leap boldly in slender jets, which dissolve in spray in mid-air.

Mr. Sheriff (to whom as an old acquaintance my kind regards) says "that from a hill at the foot of Deep River, from 500 to 600 feet high, there is a prospect which I have not seen surpassed. The portion of the Ottawa within view is perhaps the most remarkable and beautiful of its whole course. To the right is the Deep River, extending twenty miles along the base of the heights, perfectly straight, and yet lined with an uneven succession of rugged points (headlands). To the left is the whole of the spacious winding of the upper Lake des Allumettes, with its numerous islands; and a part also of the lower lake is visible beyond the great island. Several smaller lakes are seen on both sides of the river, and among the rest are two, singularly situated half-way up the hill from which the prospect is obtained. The land about here, except a rough ridge about the Ottawa, appears to be fertile." *

One of our *voyageurs* was once in the Deep River, when he and his mates espied a bear swimming across. As bear's meat is juicy and

* Transact. Lit. Hist. Soc. of Quebec, vol. ii.

good, the canoe gave chase and soon came up with the swimmer. A blow was made at him which missed, when the bear placed one paw on the edge of the canoe and fixed the other in the worsted belt of the man who struck at him. He was only prevented from swamping the canoe by a better aimed blow from the axe of a comrade, when the bear fell away, and was finally killed with long poles. These people had a narrow escape.

This defile of steep hills and precipices alternating for thirty-six miles is equal to the best part of the Rhine, apart from its ruins; a thousand pounds spent in erecting on a few commanding points some fragmentary castles would produce a splendid scene. It ends at the troublesome rapids of the Les Deux Joachims, when the country becomes depressed, but is still rocky and uneven. They are said to be three-fourths of a mile long, and are grand, being rather low cascades than rapids.

Nine miles further up, along a steady current, brings us to the River du Moine, near whose mouth the father of our priest, Mr. Tabeau, was drowned. Here the Ottawa drives for two miles violently down both sides of a steep island loaded with boulders, and having no vegetation but a few berries.

The River du Moine enters the Ottawa on its north-east side, and is of considerable size and length.

One mile above this again we have the rapid Du Roche Capitaine, where, singular enough, Mr. Rocheblave lost his father. It is also caused by an island four miles long. The pass being very narrow, the water rushes with great vehemence into a large circular basin below. We had to leave the canoe and scramble along shore as we could. The crossing here of a small river on a slippery chance-fallen tree I did not much like.

In our course up the Ottawa we passed many rivers, such as the Mississippi, Missisauga, Madawaska, River du Nord, without seeing them, as their mouths are so hid in trees, or otherwise concealed, that they are commonly undistinguishable at the distance of a few hundred yards. From hence to the western branch of the Ottawa, often called the Little Ottawa, about twenty-five miles, there is little obstruction. The north shore is high and the river wide. The quantity of *débris* in square masses is very great everywhere.

At the distance of 330 miles from the St. Lawrence, according to my rough calculations, the canoe route to the Falls of St. Mary leaves the main river for the western branch, which takes its rise north of, and near to, Lake Nipissing.

Where I reluctantly left the noble Ottawa, it was seen for a great distance, a mile broad and shallow, streaming down with great rapidity through a level woody country.

The entrance into the western branch,* called the River Tesouac by the Indians, is as broad as the Thames at Windsor; it creeps sluggishly through swampy grounds for awhile, but soon widens, and the vicinity rises into well-wooded uplands. A few miles, however, brings us to the narrows, which are even more contracted than at the mouth; and the river becomes deep sunk in mural precipices crested with half-burnt pines.

On the side of a lofty scarped rock, fifteen miles up the stream, is a triangular cave, called Hell Gate. It is shallow, and used as a land-mark. We were nearly lost here. The current at this spot was extremely swift and rough. Rounding a little point we were caught by a cross eddy and flung violently on a pine-tree which had fallen into and across the river. Providentially it still had all its leaves on, and so did not thrust us through and sink us. There would have been no escape; landing-place there was none for a mile or more.

The ravine or chasm in which the river here

* 578 feet above the level of the sea, according to the officers of the Magnetic Survey.—*Geogr. Soc. Journal*, vol. xvi. p. 263.

runs is so narrow and deep that the sun rises very high before it shines on the water, and hardly at all in winter. The gloom, therefore, is great, reminding one of the mouth of the classical Avernus; and it is heightened by the black colour of the rocks and the restless agitation of the waters. The woods around, when they are visible, through a momentary depression of the banks, are rather peculiar. Large tracts consist of fine healthy fir; then comes a district of fired trees, blackening all within the horizon, mingled with patches of the lively green of the wild cherry and young poplar, and here and there a single huge pine. The current seldom maintains an equable and moderate rate for a mile together: some descent or obstruction is continually occurring.

Two beautiful waterfalls are met with about thirty-five miles from the great Ottawa. One is at the Portage Paresseux, and resembles that of La Puce, near Quebec, in escaping from a dark channel of rocks and woods into a narrow dell. Its height is forty or fifty feet. The other fall, that of La Talon,* is remarkable for its nakedness and the fantastic shapes of the surrounding gneis rock. Marble appears here again. The

* The Portage Talon, according to the officers of the Magnetic Survey, is 689 feet above the sea.—*Geographical Society Journal*, vol. xvi. p. 263.

numerous portages on this sullen river are much alike, flat, swampy, or woody.

I had a great surprise at the Portage Talon. Picking my steps carefully as I passed over the rugged ground, laden with things personal and culinary, I suddenly stumbled upon a pleasing young lady, sitting alone under a bush, in a green riding habit, and white beaver bonnet. Transfixed with a sight so out of place in the land of the eagle and the cataract, I seriously thought it was a vision of—

> "One of those fairy shepherds and shepherdesses
> Who hereabouts live on simplicity and watercresses."

But having paid my respects, with some confusion (very much amused she seemed), I learnt from her that she was the daughter of an esteemed Indian trader, Mr. Ermatinger, on her way to the falls of St. Mary with her father, and who was then, with his people, at the other end of the portage; and so it turned out. A fortnight afterwards I partook of the cordialities of her Indian home, and bear willing witness to the excellence of her tea and the pleasantness of the evening.

Forty-five miles from the great Ottawa we left this branch, now rounding towards the north of Lake Nipissing, to cross three small but interesting lakes. These lakes are charming bits of scenery, oval in shape, three or four miles long each, and sprinkled with islets. Bluffs and cliffs form their lofty and irregular shores, moderately clothed with that mingling of flourishing and fallen trees so suited to a landscape so wild.

I shall only say of the intervening carrying places, that they are rocky and swampy by turns, especially the last, an abominable marsh, which we traversed in the dark, knee-deep in mud and tree-roots. We only found a sleeping-place at its west end by first laying poles down on some very tall grass (growing in six or eight inches of water), and then spreading out over them a large tarpaulin.* The men did the same, and contrived a fire-place. These ditches or swamps are the sources of the Vaz River, which is here ninety feet broad, and makes a leap of twenty feet into a lower region. The portages are well named the Vaz, or Mud Portages.

We embarked on the Vaz River, circulating slowly among rushes, reeds, cedars, and hemlocks. After a six miles' pull we entered Lake Nipissing at La Ronde, a post of the North-west Company,† a decent, ordinary-looking house,

* I only mark our eating or sleeping places when they present something worthy of remark.

† Now removed to an island on the north shore, half-way between the Vaz River and the River des François. It is considered to be eight or ten miles out of the canoe route to St. Mary's from Montreal.

not stockaded, with a potato-ground close to it, among marshes and gneis mounds.

The old name of this fine lake is Bis-serenis. Its waves ran high, and the wind was fresh and chill, after the smothering air and dreary twilight of the thickets we had just quitted. There are a few islets on its ample bosom. I saw neither island nor main on the north shore, although the day was clear. Certain flitting islands, however, geographers put in and out of their maps there at pleasure; which reminds me of a quaint and picturesque passage in old Hackluyt—"The like has been of those islands now known by the report of the inhabitants, which were not found of long time one after another, and therefore it should seem he is not yet born to whom God hath appointed the finding of them."—P. 502.

The first part of the south shore is a bay twelve miles across. Its banks are low, but the land behind them rises moderately in shelves, and from the canoe appears to be bare, bleached rock, with patches of dwarf pine. The south shore is forty-six miles long. We coasted it. Everywhere it wears the same aspect, except in the unfrequent occurrence of islets far out in the lake.

Twenty miles from La Ronde, and half a mile from the south shore, there is a large jumbled heap of slabs of rock, with edges as sharp, and surfaces as clean, as if they had been quarried for gravestones, and then flung down here yesterday as a breakwater. I do not understand this heap of rocks. There is no island near them.

The size and shape of Lake Nipissing, as expressed on maps, is only a rough guess. It seems to have two deep bays on its north side. The officers of the Magnetic Survey found it to be 695 feet above the sea.

When Mr. Sheriff ("Quebec Historical Society's Transactions," vol. ii. 286), says that the south shore of this lake is a level tract, with a rich, heavy soil, and extending many miles southwards, with little rise, he cannot mean the country within sight from the water. Good land in Canada is frequently at some distance from large rivers.

He goes on to state that about the sources of the Madawaska, near lat. 45° 15′, the interior of the country forms a great table-land, growing hard wood, and gradually sloping towards Lake Nipissing. Along the south-west route of the rivers Neswarbic and Muskoka this kind of country extends from within thirty miles of the Ottawa to the immediate vicinity of Lake Huron, 140 miles.

On the whole, Mr. Sheriff says (vol. ii. p. 239), "from personal inspection, that in this unnoticed part of Canada a fine habitable country will be found, millions of acres in extent. I hope it will, ere long, be rendered accessible to population." In the face of the prolonged and severe winter here prevailing, I fear that until the rich soils of Lakes Ontario, Erie, and St. Clair, are taken in possession, there is little chance for these wildernesses. They may be worked for marble, iron, or copper.

We leave Lake Nipissing by the Portage Chaudière des François. It is near the falls of the same name, and leads over low ridges of naked gneis, and here and there a cliff, to a backwater of the interesting River des François, by which this lake discharges into Lake Huron.

The falls are principally to be noticed for several smooth, funnel-shaped holes in the solid rock, near the lake, but twenty feet above its present level. One is from three to four feet deep, and as many across at the top, but only eighteen inches at the bottom.

They are supposed to be caused by the friction of stones whirled round by an eddy, as they have actually been seen where eddies have been known to exist. The other holes (or kettles) are smaller, as far as I recollect.

These appearances are common in Canada. I have even seen one on the Long Sault Rapid of the Ottawa on a large loose stone. In the granite of Cape Tourment, forty miles below Quebec, there is the commencement, the rudiments as it were, of a kettle—concentric excavated rings, each an inch in diameter, and the whole about nine inches across.

I shall not dwell long on the River des François, which we descended fast and gaily, lest I become tedious, although it is a very peculiar river. It less resembles a single stream than a bundle of watercourses flowing, with frequent inosculations, among lengthened ridges of rocks. The utterly barren and naked shores seldom present continuous lines bounding a compact body of water, but are commonly excavated into deepened narrow bays, obscured by high walls of rock and stunted pines. It is seventy-five miles long. Its breadth is exceedingly various, sometimes swelling into a broad lake for miles, and crowded with islands.

Few prospects exceed, in the grand and singular, those which are often here created by the groups of long and lofty islets, extending from a circle, in giant rays, far into some dark gulf-like bay; their rugged outlines and wild foliage reflected in the clear waters, and solemnised by the profound silence of these solitudes. In certain parts of the river, where the rocks are more distinctly stratified than usual, the freezing of crevice water has made great devastations, loading the land with shale, as in Lower Canada, and sometimes splitting off, and piling masses of vast size and weight upon one another. At one place, not far from half-way down (I think), the passage is nearly closed by a large heap of bare cyclopean blocks. Noah, as he stepped from the ark, must have cast his eye over a scene like this—not a pound of soil in fifty square miles — a region bruised, crushed, half-drowned, deserted by all living.

It was near this spot that a memorable massacre of missionary monks took place, but I have unfortunately lost the details.

Beside the Chaudière Cascade there is another called Des Recollets, twenty miles down the river. It is from fifteen to twenty feet high, but narrow, and divided into three portions by two fragments of rock. It is very beautiful in its white waters and dark walls, bristling with dead and living pine, almost naked heights being close at hand.

I was much interested by the ruins of an Indian fort, or look-out, which still remains on a point of land commanding a good view downwards, and, I think, upwards. It was a circular building, about five feet in diameter. When I saw it it was only four and a half feet high. It was

carefully constructed of the stones at hand, and would contain a couple of Indian watchers in the days when war seldom ceased.* Cooper's splendid powers of description and amplification would have ennobled this spot with thrilling adventure.

Indian drawings occur on the smooth face of a gneis mound not far from hence. They are rude sketches of animals and men in various attitudes.

Many rapids occur, but the most serious is that of Brisson. It is very swift and turbulent. As our canoe turned round and round in it, in spite of all our men could do, the sight of thirteen wooden crosses lining the shore, in memory of as many watery deaths, conveyed no more comfort to my mind than do the impaled bodies on the highways of Turkey to the feelings of their surviving robber-friends. The current is always strong, so that we swept down the river in one day.

In descending there is but one portage, that of the Recollet, and it is said, though I cannot believe it, that Indians have dashed over that fall. In ascending there are many portages.

At the upper part of the River des François the neighbouring country attains a moderate height, either in great piles of dislocated rocks or in stair-like ridges. Nearer Lake Huron its envi-

* There is one in La Cloche, Lake Huron, and several on the old route to the Lake of the Woods from Lake Superior.

rons are lower; and as far as is visible from the canoe, they are destitute of vegetation.

This river discharges itself into Lake Huron in narrow channels formed by parallel, smooth, naked mounds of gneis, a few yards broad, a few feet high, and broken into lengths of twenty to two hundred yards. La Dalle, from three to five miles from Lake Huron, a rapid of uncommon swiftness, is a gut of this kind. It is not more than ten or twelve feet wide, and an hundred yards long. Our canoe flashed through it almost in a moment. Either of its sides I could have touched with a walking-stick.

We now enter Lake Huron (a stormy water, a thousand miles round), among shallows, reefs, and tortoise-backed mounds. Its shores here are low and barren, but the back-ground rises higher. The blue line in the south, resembling a long low cloud, is the Great Manitouline Island. But it will be better here to leave my kind friends of the North-west Company and their untiring canoemen, as I shall be enabled to describe Lake Huron more fully and better in a future excursion.

I afterwards learnt that my companions returned in the autumn to Montreal in health and safety. My best wishes and grateful acknowledgments abide with them.

EXCURSION THE THIRD.

THE ST. LAWRENCE.

Calash Journey by Montmorenci and Château Riche to St. Anne, Ferry-house—Cottage life—Falls of St. Anne—Indian Family in the Woods—Feriole: Double Sunset—Cape Tourment—Walk round its Base to La Petite Rivière—Grand Scenery—Dangerous Precipices—Slippery Rocks—Mud up to the Knees—Dinner at a Cascade—Almost impassable Buttress—Mosquitoes—La Petite Rivière: Arrived disconsolate—Boat Voyage to St. Paul's Bay—Kindness of M. Rousseau and Family—The Peasantry—Earthquakes—A Tea-Party—Discussion with an M.P.P.—Cross the St. Lawrence to L'Islet—Sleep in a Hay Chamber—Walk along south Shore to Quebec.

The few of my acquaintances who had visited the St. Lawrence for any distance below Quebec were loud in their praises of its scenery and inhabitants. I was therefore determined to embrace the first opportunity of judging for myself.

Early in the month of September, on my return from the geological tour round Upper Canada, the head of the medical department for

Canada, Dr. Wright, invited me to accompany him and a young friend* to the Bay of St. Paul by land, a distance of sixty miles. If our excellent old friend had been better informed, I think he would not have made the attempt; the main and most novel part of the affair being to walk round the foot of the Tourment mountain, where it is for many miles bathed by the St. Lawrence.

We hired over night two of the high, creaking, shaking calashes of Lower Canada, invented in the sixteenth century, to take us—not forgetting a good store of provisions—to St. Anne the Great, a parish and river, twenty-eight miles below Quebec, and close to the great bluff just mentioned, called Cape Tourment.

In the mists of early morning we issued from the sombre Temple gate of the city into a dirty suburb, among river craft, timber-yards, docks, and the narrow Norman carts of the "marchedoncs," as their drivers are nicknamed, from their perpetual use of that "cry" to their cattle.

We were soon at the stout wooden bridge over the St. Charles, and on the highroad to (and through) Beauport, with its handsome church and long line of houses.

We successively trotted past the comfortable

* A promising young medical officer, who soon afterwards was sent to Cape-Coast Castle. Of course he died there.

inn at Montmorenci (nine miles), the pretty terraces, church, and presbytery of Ange Gardien (eleven or twelve miles), and then dipped at once into the marshes, famous for snipe, which border the St. Lawrence.

Although the herbs and foliage were no longer gushing and throbbing, and swelling with the hasty impulses of the early Canadian spring, still all was fresh and verdant. An almost tropical sun was glowing in the clear sky, and the cicada* was ringing its trilling note, loud, metallic, and ceaseless, from every bush.

We reascended these terraces at Château Riche (sixteen miles), at certain seasons a favourite resort for sportsmen. The old castle is there yet—four bare walls—scarcely worth a visit.

After having refreshed ourselves here, and taken a glimpse of the Falls of La Puce, not far from hence, we rode along a similar river-side for twelve more miles, when we gladly rested at St. Anne's, and took up our abode at a peasant's cottage, near a ferry, on the picturesque river St. Anne, not many hundred yards from the St. Lawrence.

Our harbour for the night was a Canadian

* A curious dumpy insect (the cicindela), rather less than one's thumb-end, and like it in shape, common in warm climates. The noise is made by rubbing the thighs against its sides.

house of the ordinary sort, accustomed to take in occasional guests like ourselves. It contained one large, low, common room or kitchen, with two ample windows in it, a cast-iron stove in the middle, and a large fire-place at one side. Then came, also on the ground-floor, a bed-chamber for the family, and another for visitors, with a cock-loft above all, entered by a ladder, for the grown-up boys to sleep in, among all sorts of provender and farming-tools.

The walls of all the rooms were adorned with rude religious pictures, and in each was an earthenware crucifix, with a receptacle for holy water attached.

I need scarcely say that the house was full of hardy boys and girls—the father more stupid-looking than usual; a kind of good-humoured bear. The mother was the ruling spirit, short, black-eyed, bustling, and flushed.

She received us gaily, and bade us go play at ducks and drakes with the flat pebbles* in the river, until she had prepared a good supper of fowl, potatoes, and soup.

She kept her word; and we husbanded our own providings for worse times. After supper,

* We did not play long with the pebbles, for we found the river loaded with erratic blocks, among which we met with coccolite, satin-spar, garnet, graphic granite, &c. &c.

some excellent rum-toddy disposed us for bed; and thither we went.

During the evening we had an opportunity of observing the domestic life of the Canadian peasant. Neither parents nor children made the slightest account of our presence. Gentle cuffs and "orders perempt" went on as usual. The whole family took supper together out of one large bowl of thin bouilli, into which were thrown large pieces of brown bread, cabbage,* and some herbs unknown to me, with a few small masses of fat. Each took care of himself in an orderly manner, with a short-handled broad wooden spoon.

Soon after supper, the whole family knelt round the largest of the windows for several minutes, the bright stars of evening shining in upon them, uttering in low tones their well-meant prayers.

The French Canadians are a devout people. Four out of five houses have domestic prayer regularly. Their worship, such as it is, carries with it an observable blessing in family unity and affection. Would it were better applied, and that their King and Redeemer had his full rights!

* Hence another Canadian by-name, "coup-choux," or chop-cabbage, applied to the peasantry.

This scene made me draw comparisons, and gave me a disagreeable twinge. Family prayer, morning and evening, does not exist in one Protestant house in ten, I fear, in Britain and elsewhere.

The next day we resolved to go up the river St. Anne a few miles, as far as the nearest falls. If we had taken with us one of the brave boys of the cottage, we should have fared better; but having a thread-like track of trodden leaves in the woods pointed out to us as the unmistakeable path, forwards we set alone; but in about a mile (and it seemed two), near a sudden rise of land, our single trace separated into several. Taking the likeliest, the river being out of sight and hearing, we trudged on for a mile or so, and were stopped by impenetrable underwood. Retracing our steps, we tried a second and a third foot-way with like result. But during the third attempt, as we were thinking of returning home wearied and disconsolate, we alighted upon an Indian family at a bark wigwam, weaving dyed baskets for sale in the neighbourhood. They were a well-favoured group, in decent attire, only Indian in part,—just such as a half-crazy person in an English village, fond of finery, and at the same time poor, might put on. I thought their life not so bad for summer-time. Our new friends soon put us in the way to the falls. They spoke French, and were Roman Catholics.

The falls are well worth a visit. I regret not to have a sketch of them; but there are very many as fine in Canada, which, like Sweden, is *par excellence* the land of cataracts.

The waters, embowered in fine trees, leap spiritedly into a deep chasm of primitive rocks, down whose sides a treacherous path takes us to the bottom of the falls, if we are very venturous and determined.

We were glad to find ourselves once more at the ferry-house of St. Anne.

The next day we set out in a calash for the romantic parish of St. Feriole, among the mountains, from five to ten miles back from the St. Lawrence.

At first we ascended a sandy terrace (whilome the river shore), across a stripe of cultivation among low clumsy houses without gardens; and then soon afterwards another—a broad one—also ranging parallel to the St. Lawrence for many miles up-stream. The soil of this upper flat being sandy, we drove through fragrant groves of pine over a road as good as in an English park, until we neared the rude and straggling village, when the occurrence of granite rocks made the ascent rough and sharp.

After having quietly surveyed the stern and singular scenery about the village, we struck a few hundred yards northwards upon the "Rose," a mountain torrent, ten yards across, always a violent rapid, and sometimes dropping suddenly into wooded abysses. Near one of these cascades a tall pine-tree had fallen across the stream. Nothing could prevent our younger comrade from tottering across it. Twenty fatal possibilities might have happened to him, but he went and returned in safety, and greatly self-exalted, I suppose.

The mountain village of St. Feriole is chiefly remarkable for a leaning sugar-loaf hill to the west, which gives rise to a phenomenon often spoken of in Canada—a double sunset. The sun sets to the inhabitants of the village as it passes behind this hill, reappears for a short time, and sets again behind the succeeding height. At certain seasons the effect is striking.

The late Colonel Forrest, an admirable artist, took several views in this vicinity, induced by me to visit it. The prevailing tint in the hill-forests of Canada, rifle green, is well seen here.

We now drove merrily back to our pleasant

ferry-house, and prepared for the greater feat of the following day—the walk round the base of Cape Tourment.

There are few objects in Lower Canada better known, and perhaps more carefully avoided, than the great headland of Cape Tourment, nineteen hundred feet high. It is the advanced portion of a great group of mountains, occupying a lofty inner country, untravelled, save by a few Indians. Near to, and behind it, is a massy summit somewhat higher than itself.

Government has cut a narrow road over this hill country, side by side with the St. Lawrence, to connect Quebec with St. Paul's Bay by land, and in the boggy parts has laid down a little corduroy.

When I passed over it (not in this excursion) there was not a habitation throughout the twenty-seven miles of woods: now, there is a log-hut and a little clearance every league.

The road is usually in steep ascents and descents, with swift brooks flowing in the bottoms, among large fragments of rock. Seven miles from St. Anne is the River Nombrette, or La Grande Rivière, which traverses a rich but neglected country in three branches, all crossed by the road near a wood of remarkably tall pines.

The traveller is so buried in trees, that rarely

along this dreary route is the fatigue of an ascent repaid to him by a prospect; but now and then scenes of grandeur and savage beauty never to be forgotten reveal themselves. The eye ranges over undulating surfaces, where only the tree-tops are seen, blending in patches all imaginable hues of green, from the fairest to the darkest.

Sometimes we see a forest-valley encircling a lake or morass, and swelling on all sides into hills; at others the landscape rises higher, becomes more abrupt, and presents a number of black, broad, steep, almost alpine mountain flanks, intersecting each other, as we see in the Swiss canton of Uri, with rapid streams winding through their narrow and rocky intervals.

From the near or west end of this gloomy and high track, just before descending into the low grounds of St. Anne, looking over the tops of the lower trees, we suddenly behold the wide St. Lawrence, the corn-fields and dwellings of St. Joachim and St. Anne in the bright vale below, with the Isle of Orleans farther off, and a dim vision of Quebec shining aloft.

The view from the other end of this woodland road, peeping down into St. Paul's Bay, is equally but differently beautiful.

Such is the immediate vicinity of Cape Tourment.

The day after the trip to St. Feriole, having breakfasted, we started with a guide secured at no ordinary wage. He carried our provisions and a coil of rope.

We purposed walking to the hamlet of La Petite Rivière, eighteen miles distant, without a habitation in the interval, and almost wholly an iron-bound coast, at the foot of Cape Tourment, and two-thirds washed directly by the waves of the St. Lawrence, save occasional beaches of mud or shingle.

Crossing the shallow and noisy St. Anne, and some fields beyond, we came to the foot of the huge bluff — Cape Tourment — up above, a pile of toppling crags — down below, a cliff with little ledges.

Up this cliff the waves swept, ever and anon, dashing sheets of water many feet higher than the usual common sea-level.

I was dismayed. My companions behaved better than I did. As we faced a precipice thirty or forty feet high, to be clambered up by us, "This cannot be the way," shouted I; "do you take us for Barbary apes?"

The good guide spake not, but shewed us one

or two footings, and then a broader ledge on which to take breath and fresh courage. Getting up himself first, he gave a hand to each in turn; and at length, with trembling knees and anxious eyes, we were planted on the summit, no little pleased with our success.

After walking safely enough over high masses of fractured rocks, we now followed our guide's example, and pulled off our shoes and stockings to pass over a series of slippery granite-mounds sloping into deep water, as smooth and shining as if they had been coated with French polish. We meet with precisely the same on the Hasli side of the Grimsel Pass. I was surprised how securely the naked foot clung to the glass-like rock.

This having continued about half a mile, a good deal of rough but safe walking succeeded, in the midst of which we came upon a splendid fissure, or cleft, in the mountain — another "Brèche de Roland," deep and narrow, and reaching far up the acclivity, composed of grand rock masses piled high in the air, with a few scattered pines here and there. It may be a water-course in winter, but there is none in September. It was beyond my pencil, and laughed audibly at my drawing-paper, eight inches by five.

Now the fall of the tide permitted our access to the beach, where for four or five heavy miles did we solemnly trudge barefoot, always over ankles, sometimes up to the knees, in smooth brown mud. Once or twice, in rounding a point, we waded nearly up to the middle. We loudly expressed our disrelish of this mode of progression; but there was no retreat.

About half-way to La Petite Rivière, we met with a charming little cascade dancing down from a mountain summit. Its sweet water and our need tempted us to dine by its side. Dining was pleasant; but mosquitoes soon found us out, and punished us severely. I suffered less than my friends, because instead of taking a nap I ran about examining the rocks. The little plagues bit poor Ritchie blind; at least he became so in an hour or two from the swelling of the eyelids and face.

After lingering about our cascade for four hours, on account of the tide, we set out again, and alternately climbed over piles of large *débris*, or crept round their bases. At length we were, to all appearance, stopped by a smooth round buttress, thirty feet across, the deep waters below lashing and washing high up the rock, while all above looked most forbidding. But straight across this buttress ran a horizontal ledge, a couple of inches broad. Upon this my two friends and the guide shuffled with vast tremor and hesitation, with

R. Young sc.

Les Eboulements — from below Cape Tourment.

many a stop and wistful look, declaring they could neither go on nor return. I did not like the thick tongues of water the tide every now and then spit upwards near the ledge.

I cried out energetically, and truly, that my dizzy head would not even allow of my trying to pass. So I hopelessly mounted the entangled steep several hundred feet above the buttress, and at last found a jumble of huge blocks, forming a kind of bore, tunnel, or passage. As it seemed to slope downwards and crosswise promisingly, I crawled into it, and, with sundry abrasions, scratches, and rendings of skin and clothes, on arriving at the other end, I saw myself on the wished-for side of the awkward "pas," my friends standing a good way below me, and gazing about uncomfortably.

The love of geology had enticed us into these perils. I bethought me of the old sarcasm uttered against all such crazy folk as we — "*I, demens, et curre per Alpes.*"

Vast dimensions, like those we see in Switzerland and the Himalayas, are not required to produce feelings of pleasurable awe. A walk under the heights of Dover will prove this. So we were well justified in being delighted with the scenery of Cape Tourment.

The mountain was steep—here in perpendicular

sheets of naked rock, there in heaped-up cyclopean ruins, overspread in parts with delicate foliage. Lofty headlands along shore shewed us labour to come; and a brisk wind which had sprung up, while it cooled the hot air, was whitening the waves with little breakers over the broad surface of the St. Lawrence.

Toward the latter third of our day's work the coast lowered. We fell in, fortunately, with a level beach of yellow sand for five weary miles towards La Petite Rivière. The finely-shaped hills of the Eboulements and Malbay seigniories now came into view. The last six miles I led my poor friend R., for he was stone blind. Of him it might be said, "He saw no man, but they led him by the hand." Our chief was also disabled. The insects and the mud-wading had greatly swollen his legs, and made them look like raw beef. Right glad were we to find ourselves, at about nine in the evening, in the first poor hut we met with—that of an aged couple, who kindly gave us shelter. The little collection of dwellings near the St. Lawrence offered nothing better. We supped upon our own provisions; after which, a blanket or two being spread on the floor, we were all speedily at rest.

Next morning my friends were not much better, and all were tired and suffering; but myself the

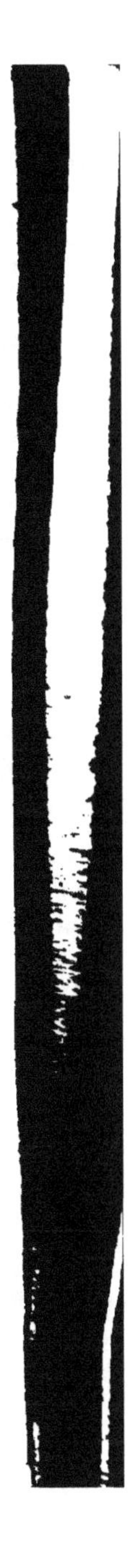

least. Walking any further was out of the question.

I should here mention that the seigniory of La Petite Rivière is a group of small farms in a break in the mountains, through which runs a gentle stream. The scene, overhung by Cape Maillard, 2200 feet high, is rural and more than pretty. The level ground consisted principally of hay-fields, and the people were busy gathering in their crop. White houses are dotted about; and far up the valley I espied a church-steeple. An Englishman is as seldom seen at this place almost as in Timbuctoo (in my time).

In the afternoon we hired a stout fishing-boat, and started with four civil Canadians for the Bay of St. Paul, twelve miles lower down the St. Lawrence, and on the same (the north) side.

We coasted the flats of La Rivière, animated by an active population; then by the side of a dark mountain curving round a deep bay, and bathed by the tide. We soon turned Cape de la Baie, the west angle of St. Paul's Bay, and came in sight of the seigniory and church of that name, placed at the base of a deep semicircle of undulating mountains, most of the houses hidden by a line of firs crossing part of the valley.

As we were approaching the mouth of the Gouffre, the river which drains the valley, we inquired of our boatmen for accommodation during our short stay. As in all the more remote seigniories, there is no inn, for the same reason that there is no doctor — the trade will not pay, our friends recommended us to try M. Rousseau, a very respectable farmer residing close by.

The wind drove us up the Gouffre rapidly for about a mile, when we brought to opposite a low, roomy, clap-boarded house a few yards from the river, with true signs of the comfortable about it —a good garden, outhouses, and several chimneys. An old soldier in a campaign always billets himself, if possible, upon a house with two chimneys at the least—never where there is only one; and for very obvious reasons.

We announced ourselves. M. Rousseau was at home, and, although perfect strangers, without introductions, received us with the greatest kindness—a kindness manifested with equal earnestness by his wife and family. A room was given to us containing two snow-white beds, and refreshments were soon on table.

Nature had been at best but niggardly to us in personal attractions; and we were then even less so than usual, being purblind, lame, and "used up," as well as roughly clad for a rough service. Poor Ritchie's face was as marred and speckled as if he had had the smallpox. Nevertheless, during our three days' stay, the attentions of this good family were unremitting. The invalids were carefully and successfully nursed. We fared well; the port was good, though but little drunk, and the beds were soft. When we left, in spite of our sincere endeavours, we were not allowed to make any remuneration for the trouble we had given.

After refreshment, leaving my friends in-doors, I stepped forth to examine our whereabouts. I stood in the middle of a semi-oval valley, four miles deep by two broad, screened all around by a high country of mountains and their peaks, save towards the St. Lawrence. These mountains again, are flanked in the valley at irregular distances by alluvial terraces, in descending series towards the River Gouffre, two or three in number, and not always perfect.* These terraces and knolls are studded with dwellings by twos and threes, and by clumps of beeches. Through this sweet scenery the River Gouffre pursues a winding and often destructive course from the interior, and has one or more noble belts of firs near its marshy embouchure.

The whole has a very Swiss look — a sea of mountains in the rear — the hamlets sprinkled

* On the east side of the outer valley of which I am now speaking is a great talus of large and small boulders and earth massed high up the hill-sides.

on the steeps — the corn in little patches among precipices—tiny cascades, the pretty church, and the roomy old houses half hidden by pine-groves.

As well as this outer valley, there is another within, which seemed little more than an umbrageous dell continued into the interior for several miles among primitive mountains abounding in iron ore, and giving passage to the Gouffre. I shall not sketch in further detail this colony of Normans, as two illustrations of it are given.

We had several pleasant rambles. The people were as comfortable and contented as well as may be in a world of trial. We seldom or never see in Lower Canada any of those slow, thick-skinned, unimpressionable rustics—barn-door savages, as I have heard them unfeelingly called—that fill our villages in England. In St. Paul's Bay they are rather a good-looking race—spare, active, with a quick eye, both men and women. The French Canadian has lively affections, great excitability; his feelings play freely, and are almost explosive. He is fond of money, shrewd in its acquirement, and retentive when he has it.

Although it is true that Lower Canada is a hard country — hard in its sky, hard in the earth and in wrinkle-begetting labour — yet, on the whole, the condition of its agricultural population is far preferable to that of the English labourer. The

He did not say "bosky dell"

chief drawback is the great expense of keeping cattle through the long winter, and the forced idleness of so extended a period of time.

The Lower Canadian acquires land easily; and there is plenty of room for his children after him. The frugal and industrious man, who lives within ten or fifteen miles of a town, is rich in coin also, as a rule. His market is remunerative. He has numerous religious holidays, which usually lead to gossip and merry-making. His spiritual director is commonly his adviser-general, and is taken from his own rank of life.

St. Paul's Bay is so healthy as not to require a medical man. There is nothing for him to do, although there are more than 3000 inhabitants in the vicinity. Several have been starved out.

Something either political or connected with the climate has of late disturbed the serenity of the Lower Canadians. Although they have an extreme distaste for the manners and habits of the Americans, they have been emigrating in considerable numbers to the State of Illinois within the last two years; a thousand in 1848 to Chicago.

Out-door work in so severe a climate injures the appearance and gait of females. We saw at a little dance, however, in a barn belonging to our hosts, some pleasing faces. I have observed that the hardships undergone by European as well as American mothers do not deprive their infants and young people of the round, blooming, hopeful features, the grace and general loveliness, we expect at their time of life. The almost supernatural ugliness and atrocious aspect of a full-blood Indian grandmother is beyond conception; the revolting idea has yet to be transmitted to Europe.

From time to time earthquakes and other singular appearances take place in this and the neighbouring seigniories. As far as I am aware, the last well-authenticated instance at St. Paul's took place in 1792. This has been described by Mr. Gagnon, in a letter to Capt. Baddeley, R.E., and by him quoted in "Transactions of the Historical Society of Quebec," vol. i. p. 145. As it is worth reading, I have made some extracts from it in a note.*

I believe that Lieut. Hall's sketch of this part of Lower Canada, made in 1814, is the last public notice of it.

* "At 7^h 15^m, Oct. 6, 1792, commenced at St. Paul's, a series of earthquakes for six weeks, from two to five daily, but much more frequent during the first night, though small. One shock had an eastern direction. Weather thick.

"On the evening of the 26th instant (Therm. Fahr. 57°), and on the 27th, (6^h 30^m, Therm. 79°), in the interval between two mountains, which afforded a long range to the eye, I saw a continual eruption of thick smoke, mixed with flame, sometimes shooting high in the air, and at others ascending in large round volumes,

Strangers being rarely seen here, our little rambles had not been unnoticed.* On our third morning, therefore, the member for the Bay and its vicinity in the Provincial Parliament, a little quick-witted, elderly person, called upon us, and with great politeness invited us to tea for the same evening. Our being without visiting costume was not held to be an obstacle; so we willingly surrendered, partly to shew a friendly feeling, and partly from a fancy to see the *ménage* of the leading individual (the priest excepted) of the locality.

Of the outside of Mr. Pothier's house I shall not say a word, because it is faithfully delineated from behind, in Irish fashion, in the accompany-

twisting and whirling about. During the whole night the spectacle was admirable. The sky was all on fire and agitated. There was a feeling of heat on the face, but no wind."

No one has seen the spot. In 1828, when Capt. Baddeley received Mr. Gagnon's letter, he thought it useless to try to find it, as every trace of the eruption would be obliterated by a luxuriant vegetation. Besides, Capt. Baddeley had not the necessary time at his command.

* My companions having been disabled by the walk round Cape Tourment, our geological and botanical excursions were very limited. We found some curious inter-stratifications of gneis and marble, with a small vein of sulphuret of lead and fluor spar, at a cascade on the west side of the valley; and I made a hasty rush into the picturesque upper valley for two or three miles, but I saw nothing worth noting, for want of time. I am persuaded that this vicinity would well reward the visit of a geologist.

ing drawing. This drawing gives us a pleasing idea of the secluded valley, its pretty church, venerable presbytery, full-foliaged trees, and warm dwellings scattered along the river-side. In the corner of the picture is a high pole; this marks the residence of a militia officer, where his men rendezvous when required.

We found that our new friend, besides being a proprietor and occupier of land, kept a store, to the great convenience of the public, at which might be purchased every nameable article suited to the place—rice and ribbons, tape and tobacco, bonnets and butter, &c. &c.

I was somewhat displeased that he did not ask our host and his amiable family—a neglect, I suppose, arising from some local mystery.

We found nothing new or shocking in our entertainment: it was English,—only better, in the opinion of those who are fond of liqueurs and confectionary. Unfortunately for my wish to meet a pure native, both Madame and her only daughter had more than once accompanied the M.P.P. to Quebec, where they would of necessity see much good society, and assist at the Governor-General's annual ball. For party reasons, as well as for better, the members of the Provincial Parliament were much courted at that time.

The ladies were quiet and simple in their manners, neat in their dress—some three years, perhaps, behind Bond Street; but that was no great matter.

Our chief suggested to me, by a little by-play, that I ought to be attentive to the young lady, as she was evidently an heiress; but I at once begged off, although she was both pleasing and intelligent. Taking my friend to a window, I explained to him that I was of too tender years to take upon me as yet the responsibilities of "*un homme fait.*" Neither was I inclined to spend the rest of my days in the hollow of a tree, and as such should I have felt even the sweet vale of St. Paul.

None are so home-sick as the damsels of the free and easy Canadas; very few of them bear transplanting, as hundreds of English officers know right well.

Our kind entertainer had designed that evening to fructify; for the tea-things having been removed, and the ladies settled to their tambours, he proceeded to play the member of assembly—that is, to indoctrinate our elder companion at much length into the griefs, as he called them, of his country. The French Canadians of the better class, who have been more or less educated, are often thoughtful, and fond of political discussion. Although they have few books, and those of a very old school, they have nimble minds, and spend much of the winter together—the young in frolic, and the older in grave debate.

It was only natural that we conversed on public topics. Mr. Pothier spoke on what deeply interested himself, and upon what he thought he understood. He really made quite a speech at one effort, and several smaller ones.

I shall write down this conversation fully, and, in its substance, with tolerable accuracy, as representing faithfully the state of French feelings at the time, and as shewing how deeply and universally the Canadians had at heart the great privilege of self-government.* Most, if not all the great public grievances then existing, have since been removed. They have self-government enough.

"Gentlemen," said he, the play of his features shewing a marked wish not to offend his guests, and yet a settled determination to open his mind to a party of officials, however humble and powerless in reality,—"I hope I do not presume too "far upon your forbearance, in laying before you "a few of my provincial notions this evening; "and before I say another word" (whereupon our good chief, who had been looking at his still swollen legs, pricked up his ears a little alarmed),

* It has been transcribed a year; and therefore before the present agitation.

"permit me to declare to you that the inhabit-"ants of my country are not insensible to the "many blessings they enjoy under the mild sway "of Britain.

"I am about to set things in a light new to "you—perhaps unpleasantly new, but still in "the true light. Public opinion in England is "strongly against our wishes; but this is simply "for want of consideration. On some subjects, "light reaches us all at one time, only through "a crevice, as it were, and is little better than "darkness; but after a while the crevice becomes "a window, and the window a bright oriel. May "it be so now! I hope to obtain our demands "by amicable means—a bloody struggle would "be too costly, as well as uncertain. It may "come to this; but I will not share in it.

"We ask not to intermeddle in the imperial "questions of peace and war, or of treaty-making; "but for an executive government, responsible "for all their acts to the people of the Canadas, "as represented in their Senate and House of "Assembly. We ask for the precious faculty of "self-management—for the power of transacting "all our business purely local and Canadian, "without reference to Downing Street. We wish "for the control of all monies levied in the "colony; the appointment and dismissal of all

" executive and judicial officials, who must be, " as far as possible, Canadian-born. In granting " this, it does appear to me that humanity would " receive a magnanimous lesson, and that all " parties would be great gainers.

" I am free to confess to you that my country-" men hourly sigh for their political rights" (I am translating from the French). "We feel it " to be quite as indispensable to communities to " manage their own affairs, and be responsible " for their own happiness, as it is to individuals; " and that no abundance of meat and clothing, " no security of person, can compensate for the " want of that moral schooling which is involved " in self-guidance, or for the loss of the whole-" some and joyous sense which fills the breast of " the citizen of a self-ruling state.

" It would be well to give the Canadians a re-" sponsible government. Who is so interested in " their welfare? who so minutely and accurately " informed about them? We are a colony num-" bering 1,500,000 souls, fifty-seven years in the " possession of a representative government—im-" perfect, to be sure. We feel equal to the task, " and see, with the blessing of Almighty God, a " great and prosperous future before us. Neither " are we left without the human instruments to " carry out the local administration of our affairs.

"We have men of ability sufficient and to spare, in all the public walks of life, to conduct with credit and ability the various departments of government, from the highest office to the lowest."

"Permit me to interrupt you, my dear sir, for a moment," hastily interrupted Dr. W., who by this time had brought his scattered thoughts to bear upon this sudden political onslaught; being now compelled to forget the flowers and fountains of St. Paul's Bay, in which he came to delight. "I think that, like certain ladies, you are speaking of one thing and meaning another. I fear that, while you talk of responsible government, you mean independence; and that is a very indiscreet topic with a servant of the English crown. I am aware that it is a widely prevailing opinion, that a total severance between the mother country and her Canadian provinces is not very remote; but this is only the mistake of a few short-sighted and dissatisfied men. No prime minister, however powerful, dares to ask the sovereign and his people to set you free, and part with one of the brightest and most glorious jewels of the British crown. Are you able to contend with the parent state? Are you capable of prosperous self-existence? I greatly doubt both. It was only through a remarkable concurrence of favourable circumstances, by the "uprising of many Americans of supreme talent "in the various departments of public service, "aided by a powerful European nation, and still "more by the justice of their cause, that the "United States were enabled to win their freedom. "A short and true story comes into my mind on "this subject. Some Loyalists waited upon Lord "North, the minister of the day, to explain to "him the various agencies at work in the Ame-"rican Revolution, its causes and motives. Their "story was long—seemingly endless, and not a "little confused. But Lord North interrupted "them, and said, 'Ah! I see how it is; the child "has burst his breeches.' You think you are "old enough and strong enough to do the same; "but you will find your pantaloons made of "tougher materials. You are not ripe yet for "self-government; when you are, I trust Eng-"land will understand her duty, and part with "you in an amicable spirit."

"No," said M. de Rouville Pothier; "you "never did emancipate a colony, and I fear never "mean to do so. Look at the millions you are "expending on Fort Diamond, which commands "the gate of the St. Lawrence, and can lay "Quebec in ashes in two hours. Look at your "vast defences and naval yard at Montreal and "Kingston; your ship-canals, &c. &c. These

" seem intended to overawe the people of Canada " for their own good, and to perpetuate the con- " nexion,—a connexion, let it be distinctly un- " derstood, I am as far as you, dear sir, from " wishing destroyed, and of whose benefits to us " I am fully convinced."

"I am glad to find I have mistaken you," replied the Doctor, who now warmed in the dispute, and hastened to say, " You must see that it " is a connexion not only of mere interest, but " also of the higher feelings of duty, gratitude, " and honour, the breaking up of which, except " upon extraordinary grounds, would be a calamity " to both parties. In case of separation, or if you " remain independent, but weak, and in constant " fear of your powerful neighbours, you must be " immediately and heavily taxed. Instead of the " present low custom-house duties, you must pay " forty per cent to meet your new expenses of " administration, of defence, and the local bur- " thens." (At present, 1849, they are twenty per cent below those of the United States.)

"If you annex to the United States, the entire " customs and land revenues would be placed at " the disposal of the Federal Government for " general purposes, while the Canadian people " would be taxed directly for all local objects. " The control of your own revenue would be gone.

" The Roman Catholic bishops and clergy would

" immediately lose the public salaries which for " fifty years they have received from the British " Government. Neither have I the least doubt " but that the proprietors of land under the French " tenures would eventually be beggared by a con- " fiscation, in spite of any proviso to the contrary. " In the councils of Washington it is well known " that the sacred cry of justice and of right is " stifled in the presence of personal or national " interest, just as much as in those of St. Peters- " burgh.—(*The Seminoles, Mexico, &c.*)

" If you were to separate to-morrow, a few " lawyers would be the chief gainers. They, with " their connexions, would fill all the public offices.

" The great body, I think I have shewn, would " suffer, and would not be slow in telling you so; " for few love money with the intense affection " of a Canadian peasant."—(Spoken plainly, I thought.)

" I made use of the word 'gratitude' just now. " How beautifully was the kindness of the home " Government shewn a few years ago in this re- " mote spot! Your crops barely suffice for your " population; you have scarcely any other re- " sources. At the time to which I allude, a deficient " harvest brought you to the brink of a famine."

" Your sovereign supplied all your wants, and " asked for no return. Perhaps your own hand " drew up the petition for this aid. I doubt "whether the Canadas in a state of independence "would have done so much, for the western people "are not overfond of their French compatriots. "The authorities of Washington, 900 miles from "you, would not have sent you a dollar."

"But to descend now to a more possible and "less violent political change, your having re-"sponsible government, the management of your "own affairs all but uncontrolled by the Colonial "Office, I am sorry to say that I have misgivings, "sound and deep, about that measure. When I "think of the few permanent residents in this "country, adapted by education, abilities, and "habits of labour, for the conscientiously dis-"charged burdens of office,—when I think of the "number of office-seekers, their poverty, love of "display and official distinction, I cannot but "foresee a vast increase of what I already observe "too much—of heartburnings, animosities, cabal, "and the sacrifice of public to private interests: "I am not prepared to grant even this smaller "measure of emancipation. And I am sure you "will allow that the intentions of the Imperial "Government are kind and paternal. It has no "other object than your well-being, knowing "that it operates directly upon that of Britain. "And see how you have prospered!"

"Well, my dear sir," retorted the eager but still friendly Pothier, whose flushed countenance had also tinted with carmine the sympathising cheeks of his wife and daughter. "But, pardon "me, I do insist, but with perfect respect, that "we have in Canada the requisite materials for "self-government, and that there is a sufficiency "among us of stability, honesty, common sense, "and knowledge. You are too hard upon us; I "can point out the men."

"I concede that the Colonial Office means well, "but its good intentions are marred by ignorance. "Your office people know nothing about us, and "mismanage us, as they do all the other colonies. "They seem to have neither sunlight nor star-"light to guide them. We have had a hundred "incontestable proofs of this. What good can "an over-tasked man, 3000 miles off, in a back "attic in London, do my country? What does "he know of its wants, modified by climate, cus-"toms, and prejudices, as well as by a thousand "points in statistics and topography—distracted "as he is with the cries of forty-two other colonies? "These things are only known to him in the "rough. He can direct and advise on general "grounds alone, and, therefore, too often erro-"neously. Besides, he is like one of your church-"wardens, only a temporary officer. He fears to "meddle, and leaves the grief to grow. If we "have a sensible, useful colonial minister to-day, "he is lost to-morrow; and we have in his place

" an idle and ill-informed, or a speculative, hair-" splitting, specious man to deal with — never " feeling safe, and sometimes driven half-mad by " his fatal crotchets."

Here Dr. Wright looked very uneasy, but held his peace.

"The blunders committed at home pervade all " departments. The Lords of the Admiralty send " water-tanks for ships sailing on a lake of the " purest water in the world. The Ordnance " Office (or some such place) send cannon to be " transported from Quebec into the upper country " in winter; one gun costing 1700*l.* to take it to " Kingston, where, by the bye, it never arrived, " for it lies to this day in the woods, ten miles " short of its destination."

"A man becomes a public defaulter to the " amount of 100,000*l.* and he is rewarded with a " baronetcy. A seigniory worth 1500*l.* per an-" num, belonging to him, is not attached, it being " supposed to have been given to the son; but " twenty years afterwards, a new governor, of a " bolder temper, seized it at once on behalf of " the public.

"Administrative difficulties at present weigh " upon us for six months, to which a week or a " day here would put a period, or which never " would have been a difficulty at all."

"My wonder, too, is," he continued, "how our "excellent governor in his castle of St. Louis gets "to know anything about us. The officials at "home are in a worse case still. I pity the per- "plexed governor walking amid the corruption "of clever and interested persons, who colour "everything to suit their own views. I have "heard it said that there is a gentleman at Quebec "who has a petition ready to be laid at his Ex- "cellency's feet for every and each well-paid "office as it falls vacant."

"There is a grievance which we feel most "acutely, that I may be allowed to state: it is, "that the greatest number, and the most lucra- "tive, of our public offices are given to strangers. "Every vacant place almost is filled up by the "second cousin of a member of the Imperial "Parliament, or by some one who has been useful "to the ministry in some obscure county election. "Our peasantry have a notion that soldiers are "stored up in barrels at Chatham, fully accoutred "for use in Canada, so soon and surely are they "sent out when wanted. And verily, I believe "there is something of the kind among the men "of the law, the custom-house, and other branches "of the civil service. At present, therefore, our "own young ambitions are in despair. I can "shew you a hundred young men of family, with

" cultivated and honourable minds, absolutely
" running to seed for want of occupation, and
" exasperated at finding themselves neglected.
" These, under a better order of things, will find
" new duties, new subsistence, and be made de-
" voted servants of a just government.

" It is only prudent to do what is right by the
" Canadians, for their country is in the grasp of
" the United States at any moment; contingents
" from the four nearest states would take it irre-
" vocably in one campaign. You will remember
" that it has become a fashion among American
" Presidents to signalise their four years' reign by
" some distinguished acquisition. Neither prin-
" ciple nor their true interests will stop an excit-
" able people like the Americans, with an ambitious
" politician at their head." *

Here our worthy chief's face began to gather blackness. He was tired of the discussion, and walked to the window to gaze upon the placid scene close to his eye — the well-kept church, the presbytery, nearly smothered under one huge tree; the burial-ground, full of black wooden crosses, hung with wreaths of amaranth and the tinsel gauds of humble affection.

* General Winfield Scott, an able and very popular officer, has recently bid for the Presidency of the United States by making proposals tantamount to the annexation of the Canadas (1849).

After a little time he returned to his seat with recovered features, and said, "I think we have "talked enough to-night. Although no revolu-"tion is meant, still it is well to remark, that "great political changes are too often fruitless ca-"lamities, devouring their own children. Might "we persuade Mademoiselle to favour us with a "little music?—I see a new piano."

The rest of the evening passed off well. We had some old French airs, sung not amiss; some delicate preserved fruits and cream, with Martinique liqueurs; and parted.

In the passage near the door, while M. Pothier was finding Dr. Wright's hat and stout stick, he could not help quoting the old Frenchman who said, that "He who lives in the mist of the valley "is too apt to laugh at the cries of the sentinel "on the clear hill-top."

"Excuse me, my good sir," replied the Doctor, "if I say, very seriously, that Papineau and his "fellows are using your honesty and your in-"fluence to prepare for the Canadas 'the day of "slaughter when the towers fall.'"

This conversation actually took place many years ago, but not so methodically as reported.

M. de Rouville Pothier is one of the moderate opposition.

While walking home, Dr. Wright, a mettlesome

old man, shewed many signs of disturbance. He declared he was not prepared for such an attack from a man never heard of in the House of Assembly.

"It shews that there is not only discontent, but power, out of sight. The worst of it is, that there is much truth in what he says. Do you think they will ever try an open insurrection?"

"Yes, sir," I said; "the men who are planning "it are known even now. Politicians and sol-"diers spring up in a new country before philo-"sophers and poets. They have seventy thousand "tainted militiamen, and a hardy peasantry. "There will be no want of generals. Permit me, "dear sir, to say that you manifested great tact "and prowess in this very unexpected skirmish."

If I am to be allowed to express my own humble opinion, I should say that at the present hour the Canadians have obtained in responsible government all that a sensible people can require for their real good; but that as soon as they are able to stand comfortably alone, and can shew that three-fourths of the population desire it, we should amicably set them free, with certain payments for fortifications, and not without a treaty of alliance.

This should be done because it is right, in defiance of an apparent expediency. Nations are as much bound to act on the Christian principle of doing to others as they would be done by, as individuals.

Plausible reasons against such a policy are not wanting, such as that it would be a national dishonour, that Canada is an outlet for our surplus people and our manufactures, a nursery for our sailors, &c.; but, of necessity, so it would remain. We should be no losers. What have we lost by the emancipation of the United States? They are our outlet, market, and naval nursery twenty-fold. Two shillings a-month of additional pay would fill our navy with the finest seamen in the world; and the Canadians are far too shrewd not to buy in the cheapest market and sell in the dearest. As to the dishonour, I see none, having for some time a strong feeling upon the sin of dominating over more tribes and wider regions than can be superintended beneficially. For this, I fear, more empires than one will on a certain day be awfully rebuked.

I am much inclined to agree with Sir Henry Parnell when he says, that "the possession of colonies affords no advantages which could not be obtained by commercial intercourse with independent states."

Mr. William Gladstone, speaking in the House of Commons (April 1849) of a wise system of colonisation, says, "Then the connexion between "the dependency and the mother country will "subsist as long as it is good for either; and "when it ceases, I hope the time will come when "the separation shall take place, not violently, "but by the natural operation and vigour of its "energies, to suit it for a state of self-government "and of independence; and then there may still "subsist that similarity of laws, feelings, and "institutions, which are infinitely more valuable "than any political connexion whatever. (Hear, "hear!)"

Foreigners (Castelnau, "Vues et Souvenirs de l'Amérique du Nord") already perceive that the separation we are speaking of is certain, and a mere matter of time.

If a general and well-planned attempt to shake off the allegiance to Great Britain were to occur, I have great fear for the issue.

The population of the Canadas is numerous, rich, intelligent, and warlike. Then, again, nothing could prevent the idle young men of the United States (full of meat and of pothouse glory, shabby and false, acquired among the Indian levies and distractions of Mexico) from helping, and eventually dragging the great Confederacy itself into the contest, to the sincere grief of all considerate persons. I regret to say that the

Point of view in 1849

peaceful and high-minded blacksmith, Elihu Burritt, is but a sorry representative of the American public (1849).

Early in the evening of the next day we left this sweet valley, of which the best drawings give a very inadequate notion.

We again and again thanked our kind hosts, the Rousseaus, who, I repeat, would hear of no remuneration. The only return ever made to them was in the form of a champagne dinner to the eldest son during one of his rare visits to Quebec.

An excellent boat, with civil boatmen, conveyed us swiftly across the St. Lawrence to its opposite or southern shore, a traverse (12–16 miles) of rough waters, as they proved to us, studded with pilot and fishing-boats, with now and then a large European vessel, under whose bows we shot, while their passengers leaned curiously over the bulwarks, and up among the rigging, to examine us.

After having got a-ground, near the shore, in the mud, and there remained in the dark for an hour and a half, we landed in the parish of St. Anne, and found shelter in a cottage hard by. It afforded us only one small, sweltering bed-room; we (the two young folk), therefore, after a supper of black bread, bacon, and a

L'Islet on the St. Lawrence

decoction of burnt beans (called coffee), retired to a barn full of fragrant hay, where we slept very comfortably in our clothes. But the next morning we were much grieved to find that our chief had suffered a small martyrdom under the combined assaults of insects, heavy bed-clothes, and bad diet. So disconcerted was he that, having procured with some difficulty a calash, he started forthwith for Quebec, taking with him my friend Ritchie.

He did well. It is only for the young to go on tramp in a country without inns. Water from a dirty lake is neither wholesome nor palateable after iced champagne every day. I was now alone, with a few necessaries in a little bag, trudging on foot towards the small town of St. Thomas, distant twenty-one miles.

I found this part of the south shore of the St. Lawrence broken up into low, rocky ridges (of inclined clay-slate and conglomerate), with smiling corn-fields in the intervals, the crops of wheat astonishingly fine. Here and there along the road, and near the houses, the dropping wyche-elms were large, and almost artistically planted. —Plate represents a scene in the parish of L'Islet.

After three hours' brisk walking I was cheered by being told I was within six miles of St. Thomas, and as much mortified when, after an hour's further march, I found I had yet eight miles to go.

In due season I arrived, and at the entrance of the town crossed two bridges over the River du Sud, evidently a large body of water in winter from the breadth of its bed.

I had scarcely heard of this little place. It has a thousand inhabitants, among whom I saw many cheerful faces in its four or five short streets. The houses were in the roomy, heavy French style, in good repair, and white-washed. The environs are woody. It is the market-town for a considerable interior, and has mills.

The next day I plodded on to Beaumont. It was a Roman Catholic fête-day. I must have met the entire population of the neighbourhood on their way to church, some on foot, some in calashes, all looking happy and well-attired. I wish that we Protestants would mix a more social spirit with the practical part of our religion. We might, on the anniversaries of missionary and benevolent institutions, for instance.

The whole country, from St. Thomas to Beaumont, perhaps eighteen miles, is very pleasing, and is spread out in grass and corn-fields, with young woods of pine and birch on terraces, just high enough to shelter the cultivated land. The road usually skirts the St. Lawrence, and is a series of long ascents and descents.

The seigniory of St. Michael is soon attained, and looks beautifully as we approach from the east. Stretching far into the interior we see a broad valley, alive with an industrious population, through which, during summer, a scanty river wanders, but which, in spring, is an abounding torrent.

On the west side of the village of St. Michael the road rises, and we see in front of us the strongholds of Quebec, faint and blue in the distance. Southerly (to the left) we have the dark pine-ridges of Lauzon, skirted by fine meadows. On the north-west is the large isle of Orleans, and the broad St. Lawrence, with a solitary ship, perhaps, labouring on its bosom.

I happily arrived at Beaumont just as a very severe and protracted thunder-storm broke over our heads.

Near this village, on a woody cliff, overhanging the St. Lawrence, is an incomparable little inn, something like the best on the lakes of Cumberland, redolent of roses and honeysuckles, picturesque, wholesome—neatness itself—larder excellent. I recommend it, and its pleasant walks, to those who wish to spend a convalescence, or a still more pleasing period, in the country. It is (or was) kept by a worthy Scotch family of the name of Fraser.

I took a carriage from Beaumont to Quebec, fourteen miles, the last half-dozen of which are varied, rocky, and high, or running into dells. Habitations, farms, and gardens, covered the country, which was full of the agreeable cries of pigs and poultry, and cattle of all sorts, growing up for the market of Quebec nigh at hand.

I have passed Point Levi, with its pretty Roman Catholic church in a nook, have left the uplands, and am at the Quebec Ferry, at the foot of a crumbling precipice, crowned with pines and a Protestant church with a handsome tower. The river is crossed and Quebec is entered.

I need not say that, travel-stained and rather weary, the city, with its tumultuous summer commerce, was very welcome, and so was the easy chair in mine inn; and no less so the cordial greetings of the presiding lady, Mrs. Wilson, whose good deeds in my behalf may I never forget!

EXCURSION THE FOURTH.

KAMOURASKA AND MALBAY.

Steam Voyage to Kamouraska—Company on board—Anecdotes—Migrating Spiders—Kamouraska—Cross to Malbay in an open Boat—The Brassard Family—Malbay—Curious Mounds—Valley of St. Etienne, a deserted Lake—Singular Fog—Earthquakes—the Musician—Anecdotes—Peasantry—Aimée's Toilet—Salmon River—Lake St. John—Homeward on foot by North Shore of St. Lawrence—Eboulements—Hospitality.

After due refreshment, a fortnight after the last excursion, I started in a steamer for Kamouraska and Malbay, situated on the St. Lawrence, opposite to each other, thirty miles below St. Paul's Bay, and therefore ninety miles below Quebec, Kamouraska being a little sea-bathing place, while Malbay is a secluded seigniory of great interest, occupying a valley among the hills of the north shore.

My intention was to go first to the bathing-place, then cross over to the opposite shore, and work my way on foot to Quebec among the mountains and partially-cultivated districts bordering the river.

European steam-boats are unclean tubs in comparison with those we meet with in America. It was early in October that I stepped on board a splendid vessel, bound to Kamouraska on a pleasure excursion, with a gentlemanly captain and an obliging steward.

The morning mist promised a warm day: the air was fresh and elastic, such as can only be felt in a region where man cannot infect—where he is to surrounding nature as the bee to the wide heáth.

A steam-boat is everywhere a Noah's ark, to which the neighbourhood sends representatives of each of its classes, with a few stragglers from afar.

So we had a few officers of the garrison of Quebec, with their wives; Mrs. Thomas Scott, of the 70th regiment, and her fine family; she was sister-in-law to Sir Walter Scott, the poet and novelist. There were some merchant families with well-stored baskets, the English from Montreal, the French from Quebec. We had likewise some stray American tourists, who, I am glad to say, every summer flock in great numbers to the Canadas.

The American, while young, stands out here in strong relief. He is instantly recognised by his abrupt address, wiry, nasal tones, his long, pale face, straight hair, loose gait, and unbrushed hat.* The French Canadians of the middle or upper classes have short lively faces, with dark complexions, and they are apt to be rather negligent of their attire. The British officers on board, in their belted blue surtouts and foraging caps, were, as all the world over, gentlemen; a thought too reserved perhaps, being usually too

* This crusty exterior very often conceals a well-trained intellect, a gallant and susceptible heart. Many such have I met with, especially at Philadelphia.

Some parts of the United States have a bad character.

I went one spring to Yale College, Newhaven, to read there for a few weeks. In searching for lodgings, I found a quiet street behind the College.

Entering by an open door one of the houses, which had "Lodgings to let," in the windows, I was immediately met by an active, middle-aged woman.

"Have the goodness, madam," I said, "to shew me the rooms which are to be let."

"I won't," she replied, with a face on fire: "I know who you are!"

"I think you do not," was my answer, and was about to explain further, when she rushed in upon me with,—

"I do know you. You are an impudent Virginian, with your tobacco, your brandy, and dirty nigger servants. If I were to let you my rooms, you and your fellows would give us Satan's delights every hour of the twenty-four."

I had opened my mouth to tell her I was an Englishman, &c., but she shouted, "Get out of this!" so vehemently that I was glad to run away.

This good woman must have had very bad luck in her inmates, for which all Virginia is not to be blamed. When far from home, with a well-lined purse, bachelors' revelries are apt to be inexcusably "funny and free."

sublime to begin a conversation with a stranger. We except the happy and thoughtless subs.

Among our American companions were two charming sisters from Boston, United States, who shone out like stars from among the general company.

> " So shews a snowy dove trooping with crows,
> As yonder lady o'er her fellows."

They were truly lady-like and beautiful, each in her own way: the elder was calm and queenly, while the younger, scarcely seventeen, of a more slender form, was all movement and grace. Their father accompanied them. I had the pleasure of their previous acquaintance in descending the rapids of the St. Lawrence with them.

We stopped at the lower end of the island of Orleans to allow us to wander among the pretty thickets of nut-trees and beech, for which the place is noted. In an hour the signal-gun called in the wanderers, and all came but one couple—the younger American fair and a handsome young officer—and they made their appearance in a few minutes, flushed with running. The flush was not a little heightened when the excellent band on board struck up a then popular air, " Will you come to the *Bower* I've shaded for you?" in allusion to the gentleman's name.

We were soon off. With a tide of six miles an

hour in our favour we swiftly passed the successive islets below that of Orleans, amid the mixed scenery of rock, water, and shipping, which had so much delighted me on my first entrance into Canada.

So numerous a company must be expected to contain some very volatile young men. One of these pointed out to me a female figure in the deepest widow's weeds, sitting with her back to us near the stern. "Take an opportunity," said he, "of looking into that lady's face. You will be repaid." I did so; but instead of a bowed lily, all beauty and resignation, I was shocked to see under the pretty mourning-gear a square sallow face, pock-marked, with a slight hare-lip, and a red, sullen eye, like that of a baffled tiger-cat. "A widow, you see," said the lieutenant. "What could the poor man do but die? It was the only move." I turned away from him, thinking his wit vastly out of place. But it was a fearful physiognomy.

When half-way on our voyage we were much surprised by seeing, high in the air, streaming across the St. Lawrence, a number of grey, fleecy, island-like masses, each an acre or more in extent, in oblong sheets, torn as it were, and too thin and filmy for clouds. As portions now and then dropped on our deck, we found that it was a migrating party of small black spiders, every one upon his own long grey string or web. In a quarter of an hour they passed out of sight. I had seen the same before, but not in such numbers.*

Where was this army going? Was it pursued or pursuing? By what imperious instinct were its members impelled to start on a given day? Who are their leaders? Are they elders who have made the journey before?

They seemed bound to the great lake of St. John in the north, perhaps to make war upon the little black fly, whose sting is red-hot torture, and which loves the warm sands of a lake shore; or were they only going to burrow and breed there in peace? He that prepared a path for this mighty river, and gave wings to His angels, had prepared theirs.

The land crab of Jamaica has a curious provision for his journey to and from the sea to his mountains. His branchiæ (which serve as lungs) are of use only in water. They therefore float in water-bags provided for that occasion only, and so operate the necessary change upon the blood.

To within a minute of the appointed time we

* Probably *Aranea Obtextrix* of Beckstein and Strack, referred to in Kirby and Spence's Introduction to Entomology, sixth edition, vol. ii. p. 277.

came to anchor at Kamouraska, before a row of fifty neat-looking houses on a bank a mile long. This little port is formed by a shallow bay, defended from without by several rocky islets.

Our party rapidly dispersed, some to cross to the opposite shore, some merely to run about until the steamer returned, and others, with myself among the number, to obtain shelter in some boarding-house.

I was fortunate in my selection. I found some agreeable French society with whom to pass the evenings. The first thing I caught sight of in the "Salon" was a good guitar, which was often and agreeably played by a lady from Montreal, or it might have been from the Faubourg St. Honoré, so well did she preserve the traditionary manner and costume of France.

I have little to say of Kamouraska. It answers its purpose to the Canadian gentry. The waters of the St. Lawrence are salt; but dipping, as the bank does at each end, in extensive cranberry marshes, with here and there groups of bare, low rocks, I should fear malaria. In the back country are ranges of high, naked hills.

The view from our windows was very cheerful. The St. Lawrence, eighteen miles broad, is always, in summer, alive with shipping and pilot-boats. The opposite shore is very steep and high, and casts a deep shadow far into the waters. It is a sort of cloud-land, and seldom wears the same face for a couple of hours together.

I left Kamouraska, with its grand Indian name, on the third day for Malbay. Some peasant fishermen engaged to take me there in an open boat. We left at noon, with a gentle and favouring breeze, which in an hour veered round in our teeth. We now made long tacks for several hours, and at the wrong end of a long stretch we lost the little wind we had. All that autumn night we toiled at the oar, not perhaps with the vigour of a post-captain's boat's crew, but we toiled, and fetched bay and river at three next morning.

I was left in the dark of a raw foggy morning, with my small baggage, on the muddy beach, cramped, cold, and hungry. I was told truly, that save at Kamouraska there was no inn within sixty miles; but that about six o'clock I would be kindly received at Antoine Brassard's, a peasant, whose one-chimneyed house, on the bank above me, was just discernible as a dim black mass.

While waiting, like a forgotten ghost, shivering on that bleak shore, I cannot say that I took much delight in the concert around me of lowings, and bleatings, and barkings, by which animals express their wish for the sun, and which poets say are so delicious in early morn.

While sitting on my bag, chin on breast, I had one or two ugly frights from the swoop of a sea bird, who at that indistinct hour fancied I might be eatable. But day-light and six o'clock came punctually, and I was readily and politely received by Monsieur and Madame Brassard. They were obliging people: great was the stir they made for me. I was allowed to warm myself for a few minutes, and then requested to go to bed while breakfast was preparing.

Following my stout hostess and one or two stumpy laughing daughters, I ascended into the cock-loft, where was my bed for that nonce.

"Get out of that, Granny," cried my conductress. "What's to get out?" said I; "and from where?" "From Granny's bed, sir, and she's in it." I intreated that she should not be disturbed, and the more vehemently as the dim light showed that the chocolate-coloured sheets had never been washed since the days of Montcalm; and that Granny, on rising promptly to the call, was a most mummified creature, whose parchment skin reminded me of Ziska's when it headed a drum. Yet I afterwards found that this extremely aged and decrepit woman, weary of life perhaps, had no small share of feeling and intelligence; and as is usual, vastly to the credit of all semi-civilized or barbarous people, was kindly and respectfully treated. So I descended to breakfast, and then walked out.

I found Malbay, or Murray-bay, as the Seignior likes to have it called, a round indenture in the north shore of the St. Lawrence, about two miles in outer diameter, overhung by steep, pine-clad hills, at whose feet (in the bay) are grassy diluvial terraces, on which stand some houses and a neat church.

Near a principal house on the west side of the bay is a remarkable assemblage of detached barrow-like mounds, from ten to twenty feet high, covered with shrubbery. They are on a level with tide-water, and seem to have been deposited at the neutral points of conflicting currents in another state of things.*

A considerable breach about the centre of the rampart of hills permits the noisy River Malbay to join the St. Lawrence, and discloses in the rear a low country called the Valley of St. Etienne, sheltered on all sides by mountains.

This valley is not only picturesque, but highly interesting to the geologist. It has, in fact, been the bed of a lake which has undergone more than

* It is worth noticing, that a little beyond the east corner of the bay there is a primitive rock so full of garnet crystals, of the unusual size of an infant's head, that the original rock is almost obliterated. Fine specimens could only be obtained by blasting.

one depression in level, possibly by successive lowerings in its side or rim at the present outlet. The vestiges of this are yet very evident.

Having given a sketch of this valley, I hardly need be more particular than to say that it runs north and south for six miles, with a breadth exceeding a mile (at a guess), and is a straight, uneven, strip of land, with the shifting bed of the Malbay in the centre, and certain horizontal terraces on the flanks around.

These terraces may be described thus. On the eastern uplands, about 500 feet above the river, a flat and uniform embankment, like a regularly-made carriage-road, a few yards broad, runs along the whole length of the valley, cut through at intervals by winter torrents. At a given and uniform distance below this comes another terrace and bank correspondingly breached, and descending swiftly down to the broken ground and tumuli of gravel and clay near the river. These ancient shores pass all round the valley, but perhaps not quite so perfect and striking on its west side.*

* These beaches must have been deposited slowly, tranquilly, under water, and when the district was at a different level from the present; for water at the level of this day would drown four-fifths of America.

The lofty beaches of St. Etienne I could not examine with care, but the materials composing those of the river Notawasaga in Lake Huron are laid down horizontally, and often in thin strata, the

At the upper and north-east end of the valley there is a very large breach in these terraces (with perpendicular sides), which is lost sight of in the woods of the interior. It is evidently the bed of a great stream (the ancient river, probably) feeding the lost lake. (*Vide* Plan in Append. vol. ii.)

I cannot but think that its powerful current has scooped out a noticeable feature in the valley yet to be mentioned. It is the great bowl-shaped hollow, evidently a deserted bay, which we find at the north-west corner of the valley, opposite the bed of the ancient river just referred to. It is half a league in diameter, with very steep sides, terraced like the rest of the valley.

I never read of (except the Coquimbo and Glenroy Roads), or saw, any spot exhibiting so beautiful and compact a record of those times when not only this little valley, but all North America, was comparatively a drowned land, tenanted chiefly by aquatic and amphibious animals. Whether this

shells being identical with those now existing in the lake in perfect preservation, the bivalves being either empty or filled with smaller shells and sand.

The large terraces of the north shore of Lake Superior are composed of small fragments of the *rocks of the vicinity*, in the state of rough grit (or bowlders) sometimes confused, at others in horizontal sheets. The number of terraces varies in the space of a mile, sometimes from one to six: why, I could not discover. I suppose that slow elevation and the desiccation consequent on the loss of feeders have produced the present levels of the great lakes, &c.

The Valley of [illegible]

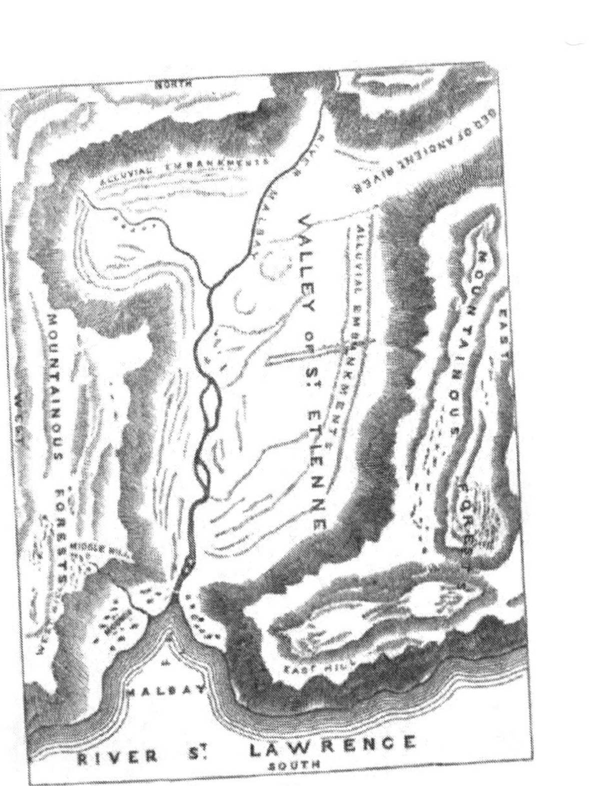
NORTH
ALLUVIAL EMBANKMENTS
RIVER MALBAY
BED OF ANCIENT RIVER
VALLEY OF ST. ETIENNE
ALLUVIAL EMBANKMENTS
MOUNTAINOUS FORESTS
WEST
MIDDLE HILL
EAST
MOUNTAINOUS FORESTS
EAST HILL
MALBAY
RIVER ST. LAWRENCE
SOUTH

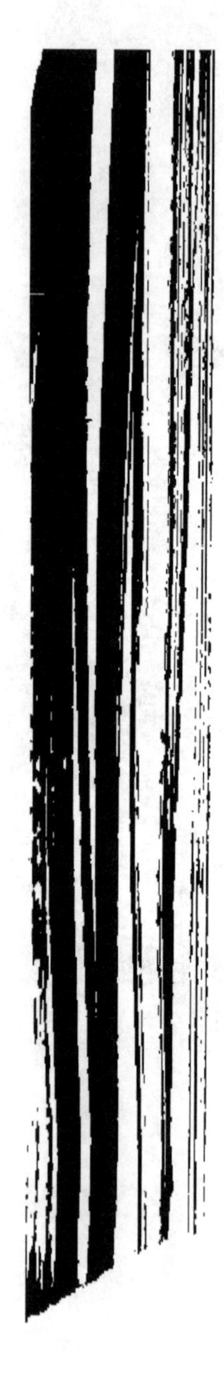

continent has been drained by breaching, or by a general change of level, we must not here discuss. I cannot help thinking how delighted the amiable and gifted Dean Buckland would be to look over this clear page of nature, followed by his galloping squadron of eager pupils.

The river of the present day enters the valley by a waterfall at its upper end, at some distance from the ancient river bed, and at the head of a woody ravine, whither I followed up the river at the expense of many a fall and many a rent.

About a couple of miles beyond Etienne, and separated from it by high grounds partly cultivated, is a small lake, one of many hereabouts, full of delicate trout. This lake is bounded on one side by precipices, and elsewhere by woods and clearances, backed by sugar-loaf mountains.

The materials for these sketches and descriptions I obtained in the course of five days, and chiefly on foot. I was prevented from doing any thing on the second day by an extraordinary fog of a deep coffee colour, lasting the whole day, and requiring in-doors strong artificial light. On walking out I could not see objects three yards off. I descended to the beach and saw nothing. I only heard the ripple and lazy plash of the wave. I have not seen any London fog at all equal to this in density. It left no deposit, and had no smell.

The celebrated dark days of Canada, in 1785 and 1814, were almost certainly caused by the eruptions of distant volcanoes, coinciding in time with local thunderstorms.*

* "On the Dark Days of Canada." By the Hon. Chief-Justice Sewell, President Literary Historical Society of Quebec, vol. ii. p. 231.

"On the 16th of October, 1785 (Sunday), after a foggy morning, but which had dispersed by ten A.M., black clouds rapidly advanced on Quebec from the north-east, and by 10° 30′ it was so dark that ordinary print could not be read. This lasted for upwards of ten minutes, and was succeeded by a violent gust of wind, with rain, thunder, and lightning; after which the weather became brighter, until twelve o'clock, when a second period of so much obscurity took place that lights were used in all the churches. Other periods of obscurity came on at two, three, and half-past four P.M., during which times the darkness was perfect—that of midnight.

"During all these hours vast masses of clouds, of a yellow colour, drove from north-east to south-west, with much thunder, lightning, and rain. The periods of total darkness were ten minutes, the intervals affording but little light.—(Barometer 29° 5′, thermometer 52° 50′.—Dr. Sparke.)

"The rain-water was very black, and upon its surface a yellow powder, sulphur, was found.

"These appearances occurred also at Montreal, but did not begin till two P.M. They extended from Fredericton, North Britain, to Montreal.

"The dark day of July 3, 1814, was much the same as that of 1785. There was darkness, continuous, with fall of sand and ashes. Chief-Justice Sewell was eye-witness to this off the banks of Newfoundland.

"Charlevoix says that it rained cinders for six hours, in 1663, at Tadoussac, on the River Saguenay, thirty miles below Malbay.

"Upon the 23d of November, 1819, a very remarkable black rain fell at Montreal, accompanied by appalling thunder. It was preceded by dark and gloomy weather, experienced all over the

Malbay is often overcast in this manner; why I cannot say. It is also remarkable for frequent earthquakes according to numerous testimonies, of which that of Captain Baddeley, R.E. (at second-hand), is the most recent.

While at Malbay, on a tour made by order of Government, he was informed by Mr. and Mrs.

United States. At times the aspect of the sky was grand and terrific.

"In Montreal the darkness was very great, particularly on a Sunday morning. The whole atmosphere appeared as if covered with a thick haze of a dingy orange colour, during which rain fell of a thick and dark inky appearance, and apparently impregnated with some black substance resembling soot.

"At this period many conjectures were afloat, among which that of a volcano having broken out in some distant quarter. The weather after this became pleasant until the Tuesday following, when, at twelve o'clock, a heavy damp vapour enveloped the whole city; it then became necessary to light candles in all the houses and butchers' stalls.

"The appearance was awful and grand in the extreme. A little before three o'clock a slight shock of an earthquake was felt, accompanied by a noise resembling the distant discharge of artillery. It was now that the increasing gloom engrossed universal attention.

"At 3° 20′, when the darkness seemed to have reached its greatest depth, the whole city was instantaneously illuminated by the most vivid flash of lightning ever witnessed in Montreal, immediately followed by a peal of thunder so loud and near as to shake the strongest buildings to their foundations, which was followed by other peals, and accompanied by a heavy shower of rain of the colour above described.

"After four P.M. the heavens began to assume a brighter appearance, and fear gradually subsided."—THOMPSON'S *Meteorology*.

M'Nicol, who reside there, that shocks are most frequent in January and February, and occur nine or ten times a-year, most generally in the night, being accompanied by changeable weather. Their direction seems north-west, the shock lasting one minute.

Notice is generally given by a noise like that of a chimney on fire, followed by two distinct blows.*

During the day of coffee-coloured fog, of which I have been speaking, and which was local, I was reading in a little bed-closet, more like a bulge in a crazy-wall than a room, when I suddenly heard, within the house, two or three short, delicious strokes of a fiddle-bow, succeeded immediately by a masterly execution, on one of Amati's best violins, of "Nel Silenzio," that mysterious and mournful air in "Il Crociato," which again instantly ran off into one of the gay galloping melodies of Rossini.

Such music in a hut!—such wild capriccios, and passionate complainings, in the murky air of an American wilderness, astounded me. Rushing to see whence it came, I found in the living-room (kitchen, &c.) of the house, playing to the family and some gossips, a slender, pale young

* Transactions of Historical and Literary Society of Quebec, vol. i. p. 142.

man, in corduroy and fustian. I need not say that the violin did not cease; but that the musician received a reward, humble indeed, but in proportion to the means of his Mecænas.

He was a thoughtless, and possibly a dissipated, London artist, named Nokes, on a free ramble through the Western world, and subsisting on his violin.

He had been to Kamouraska, which, having proved neither Brighton nor Ramsgate, he was working back to Quebec, not knowing whether the next stage would bring him to a city or a desert.

I afterwards formed a part of a delighted audience at Quebec, at a concert given by him and a M. Barraud, who, on a similar occasion, soon afterwards, at New York, acted as money-taker at the door, and left the city abruptly with all the proceeds.*

* Most musical people seem bit with the gad-fly. They embark for distant lands at an hour's notice. Huerta, the splendid guitarist, of St. Sebastian, met at Havre some Americans who were to embark the very same day for New York. They asked him to accompany them. He agreed, bought a few shirts, and the next day found him sea-sick in a packet-ship, his guitar hanging on a peg.

I was present at the crowded concert he gave on his arrival at New York. He made the large hall ring and echo with his Riego's March and Spanish Boleros.

In the fifth row from the front there sat a very young Italian

I go on to say that the soil of Malbay is indifferent, frequently all sand or all clay, and seldom level. All kinds of grain ripen late. Indian corn is hardly worth sowing, and tobacco often small and stunted.

The inhabitants are wholly without school-education. There is no medical man, lawyer, or tavern-keeper, but two or three shoemakers, and five shopkeepers (1823).

The priest has the love and respect of his flock, although he does not permit dancing.

The peasantry live hard, but are active, cheerful, and obliging. Marriages are early and prolific. There were but two childless couples out of 450, at my visit, and they were wondered at.

It is not uncommon for aged people to give up their little property to their children, reserving a rent. I saw an example of this near the village-bridge. The house was the neatest in the place, small, but conspicuous in red, black, and white paint, with a garden of roses and balsams on one

girl, the daughter of a miniature painter, joyous, fair, and musical. She was delighted with Huerta and his guitar. Three days afterwards she was a married dame, and the guitar had to carry double—all very imprudent and naughty; but I sometimes think that tipsy sailors and young couples have a kind Providence of their own.

We frequently meet with great musical talent in the most unlikely places.

side, and a considerable patch of ground planted with onions and cabbages on the other. My guide did not approve of this custom.

I saw a good deal of itch in the place; and now and then the sivvens, a very disgusting disease, makes its appearance. They are a dirty race.

Milk, black or brown bread, and soups, form the staple diet of the people all the year round; but in the months of August and September they live much upon bilberries, raspberries, and thin milk—and so did I while among them—a very cooling diet; and not likely to give any one "the burning palm, the head which beats at night upon its pillow with dreams adventurous," as Wordsworth speaks.

With the exception of a few near the church, the houses in the valley of St. Etienne were the best; but to my English eye many appeared small and neglected, with little or no garden.

I visited a small farmer's establishment, five miles up the valley, relations of my host, and was pleased with its tidiness and family harmony. They had collected from the rocky wilds around immense pans full of bilberries for food.

The young people, men and women, showed no shyness, although their threshold cannot be crossed by a stranger once in twenty years; and they entered into conversation with me agreeably and sensibly.

Upon the whole, and saving the dirt, I liked the Malbay peasantry. Nothing could be more obliging than the Brassard family from first to last. Of the two or three upper-class families I saw nothing, my business lying with hills and valleys more than with my fellow-men.

The charges of Madame Brassard for lodging and board — poor, simple woman! — were very moderate. I might have staid longer, but at six o'clock in the morning of my sixth day, I saw Mademoiselle Aimée at her ablutions before the house-door. She might have half-a-pint of water in a little bowl. With this she washed her hands, filled her mouth with the same, and, spirting it into her hands, most economically washed also her face. I shuddered as I thought of her milk and cookery, and resolved on instant flight to a land where water was less precious.

I ought here to say, that on my fourth day in these districts I went in a boat nine miles further down the St. Lawrence, to the River "des Trois Saumons," along an iron-bound coast.

This is a savage river, abounding in salmon, and escapes from the rugged interior through a deep ravine. The scene was quite melo-dramatic. On a naked rock in the troubled waters was a hut, hung round with dusky nets. At the door stood an unshaven, bronzed fisherman. Close upon us were white marble rocks, high and interleaved with more common primitive strata, with a screen of woods over all.

I spent a long hot night here for the benefit of hosts of mosquitoes, and began to feel geology a rude trade, saying, with St. Bernard, "Je me vois un petit oiseau, sans plumes, presque toujours hors de son nid, exposé aux orages."

I am sorry I have no sketch of this wild spot; and at the time greatly desired, in spite of mosquitoes and rude waters, to have gone some thirty miles further down, to the magnificent River Saguenay, but it was impossible.

West and south-west from the Lake of St. John, sixty leagues up the Saguenay from the St. Lawrence, there are several millions of acres of valuable land, fit for immediate settlement, with a remarkably healthy climate, resembling that of Montreal, according to Government-surveyors.

At the old Jesuit establishment on this lake, three hundred acres have formerly been in cultivation; but at present it is running wild. (Captain Baddeley, R.E.) In attempting a mission in a scarcely-inhabited country, dreary, distant, and Siberian in climate (whatever may be said to the contrary), the inexorable fathers must have had strongly on their minds the axiom of their founder, "He who desires to do great things for God must not be too prudent" (nor self-sparing). So I departed from Malbay, and not without regret.

I took my way on foot up the north shore of the St. Lawrence towards Quebec, and after many a painful step for eighteen miles I reached towards evening the little village of the Eboulements, so called from the prevalence there of earthquakes. The road from Malbay, such as it is, leads chiefly over mountain slopes and into deep gullies; but sometimes likewise along the river beach. Five miles from Malbay there is a sawmill in a picturesque gully, whose stream is choked with large erratic blocks. The slopes are more or less under cultivation. The white dwellings seemed numerous, being 250 at the time of my visit, but not going far back into the interior. These heights afford magnificent and ever-changing landscapes. On my right the inland country rose into mountain peaks, naked or scantily covered, except on their flanks and in the ravines, where the trees are fine and plentiful. On my left the St. Lawrence rolled at my feet. On its surface a ship was a speck. Its near or north shore is always bluff or precipitous, while the south shore is low and populous, swelling slowly into faintly-discerned

Cape Tourment and the N. Shore of the St. Lawrence

hills. If the spectator be near the village of the Eboulements, the eye is conducted for forty miles up the river along the successive promontories of Cape Corbeau, de la Baie, Petite Rivière, and Tourment, which last dips at once from a height of 1900 feet into the water, to where the rich island of Orleans and its attendant islets terminate the view. (See Plate.)

The highland districts, in which I now am, are remarkable for one feature which must not be left unnoticed. They are everywhere more or less buried in fragments of the underlying rock, with very few travelled rocks among them. There is good reason to believe that it is the freezing of the crevice-water which has thus deeply split up this rather slaty quartzose rock.

In many places this *débris* covers not only rock, but soil several feet deep. With immense labour, therefore, the peasant collects the stones into mounds of almost incredible number and size before he can have a blade of corn or of grass. I saw on my road two narrow gullies, 300 feet deep, entirely faced with them, and the rivulets buried out of sight. These splinters of rock are not so numerous in other parts of Canada, but are conspicuous in the narrows of Pelletau in Lake Huron.

The effect of extreme cold in shivering rocks is

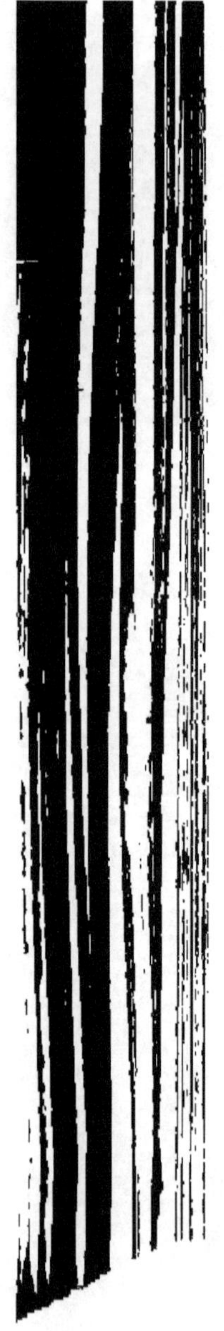

very well seen in Hudson's Bay, where the act is frequently accompanied by considerable noise. A conflagration in the woods always comminutes the rocks to a considerable extent.

The grass fields of the Hawksbury Settlement on the Ottawa are often strewn with loose rocks, not rarely from ten to twenty feet long by five to ten feet broad. They are broken up into large flakes like palm-leaves by keeping a wood fire in full play upon them for twenty-four hours, and then suddenly drenching them with water.

I soon obtained most comfortable quarters at a private house, among kind people, who thought themselves well paid by the latest French Canadian news from Quebec; a mode of remuneration very onerous to a weary man. On leaving this hospitable house I confess having put a dollar under a candlestick.

The village of the Eboulements is on the flank of a cultivated mountain, which slopes swiftly on the left into the St. Lawrence, and in front into a broad marshy meadow, through which wanders a little stream hid in alders.

From this meadow, perhaps seven miles from the valley of St. Paul, the road winds about the rough hilly region called La Misère, from the poverty and wetness of the land, to the summit of the lofty barrier overlooking St. Paul's, into which we descend almost perpendicularly.

Like many mountainous countries, such as the Sardinian Alps, the Scottish Highlands, &c., the seigniory of Les Eboulements and its vicinity is liable to frequent but slight earthquakes.

There is no reason to believe that there is any volcano north of 45° north latitude in America. Mr. Thompson, of whom I have already spoken, one of our greatest travellers among the Rocky Mountains and the Indian territories bordering the Arctic Seas, never saw or heard of one.

Having gratefully visited the excellent Rousseau family of St. Paul's, I left direct for Quebec on foot over the summits of Cape Tourment and its neighbouring heights; but as I have nothing particular to tell I shall now close this excursion.

EXCURSION THE FIFTH.

PART I.

LAKE ERIE AND THE RIVER DÉTROIT.

The Boundary Commission, its officers, objects, labours, &c.—Lake Erie—Mr. Beaumont—Rev. Mr. Morse—Amherstburgh—Captain Stewart and his negroes—Chevalier and Madame de Brosse—Rattle-snake hunt—Indian cure—The Prophet—The Kickapoo Indians—Détroit—My Inn and its guests—The Professor, the Judge, and the Barber—Moy—The Mennonites.

I BELIEVE that the report of my geological tour (the northern part of which up the Ottawa River, &c., forms the second Excursion), gave satisfaction. True it is that my masters did not know much about the matter, scarcely "quartz from pints," as a witty Irish lady once said of herself, but they had the wisdom to see how little could be expected from a solitary individual flung helpless into a tangled forest, or on the rugged shore of an oceanlike lake.

My tour of nearly two thousand miles showed,

as far as could be discerned from shores, and banks, and broken hill-sides open to examination, that some of the rock formations had not found a place in geological classification,* and that all were too old to contain bituminous coal. Canada West was found to be abundant in iron ore, limestone, fine marble, serpentine, gneis, and granite. I sailed within a mile of the copper mines of Lake Huron, but saw no traces of that ore, because I did not land. In the discovery of new fossils I was fortunate.

During the following winter I received the appointment of British secretary and medical officer to the Boundary Commission, under the sixth and seventh articles of the Treaty of Ghent.

This Commission consisted of two portions, British and American; each with a commissioner, an agent,† secretary,‡ astronomer, two or more surveyors, steward, and a number of *voyageurs* and boatmen, varying according to circumstances from ten to fifteen.

* I had neither the practical experience, the science, nor the ability of Sir Roderic Murchison. He saw the same order of rocks in other parts of the world, and had the honour of working out and proclaiming a grand discovery, the Silurian system.

† The agent was an assessor and adviser to the Commissioner. He corresponded directly with his own Government, addressed state papers to the Commission, and managed the accounts.

‡ I succeeded Mr. Stephen Sewell, brother to the Chief-Justice of Lower Canada, who resigned, and soon after died.

During two summers the Commission had the assistance of two schooners, the Confiance and the Red Jacket, on Lakes Erie and Huron; one belonging to each Government.

Of the Red Jacket I know nothing, having never seen her. The Confiance had a crew of twelve seamen, and was commanded by Lieutenant John Grant, R.N., an excellent officer and truly amiable man.

The Commission had been in existence three or four years when I joined it, and had worked from the starting-point up to the head of Lake Erie, 550 miles, through districts in parts exceedingly intricate.

It was the duty of the Commission to examine, designate, and trace upon correct charts of their own construction, a boundary line between Upper or Western Canada and the United States, along the middle of certain water communications, commencing at the Indian village of St. Regis on Lake St. Francis, where the 45th degree of north latitude strikes the St. Lawrence, and passing up this river, through the middle of Lake Ontario, of the river Niagara, of Lake Erie, of the river Détroit, the Lake and river St. Clair, of Lake Huron, the Straits of St. Mary, and of Lake Superior, as far as the Grand Portage.

They were to decide to which of the two contracting parties the several islands, more or less struck or approached by the boundary line, respectively belong, in conformity with the Treaty of 1783.

From the Grand Portage on Lake Superior the Treaty of Ghent directed the boundary to pass up Pigeon River and along the water-communications, a chain of lakes, rivers, and swamps, which lead to the north-west corner of the Lake of the Woods; from which point or corner a line was to be struck due south to north latitude 49°, and from thence along that parallel across the American continent to the Rocky Mountains.

The country to be examined and apportioned was, for convenience sake, designated in two articles, the sixth and seventh, of the Treaty of Ghent; the former ending at the Straits of St. Mary, and the latter continuing the line to the Lake of the Woods.

An accurately-described co-terminous line between countries so extensively and closely contiguous as the Canadas (with Prince Rupert's Land) and the United States is of the first importance, both in a civil and military respect; chiefly, however, in the former.

Positions of military offence and defence on the Canadian frontier are innumerable on both sides, so that the national interests are on that point but little affected as far as the 6th and 7th articles of the Treaty of Ghent are concerned. But a clear and acknowledged boundary is indispensable in questions of allegiance, of fiscal and legal jurisdiction, of general and local taxation, and among other particulars, in the pursuit of criminals, debtors, and deserters from military service. It also apportions territory, often of great value, and is advantageous in other ways which need not now be enumerated.

The details of the work evolved from time to time many difficulties, arising from a variety of circumstances, of which I can here mention only a few.

The want of any established precedents in international law was a good deal felt. They would have greatly facilitated discussion. The words used by the treaty-makers, whose topographical knowledge was limited, were sometimes vague. For example, it was uncertain whether the term "water communication," employed in the treaty, had a commercial or geographical signification. The Commissioners decided on the latter, as being the most useful.

The "north-west corner" of a lake was another debateable expression, which occasioned great difficulties.

Commercial routes were sometimes double.

They might be used or disused (who was to say?). Portions lay between main and island, both occupied by the same nation, and so necessarily falling to that nation, to the great discontent of the neighbouring inhabitants, who forgot that their right of passage and other uses would be secured afterwards by treaty.

The distribution of the very numerous and often fertile islands caused great labour in soundings, measurements, and valuations. The islands which were unequally divided by the boundary-line were usually given to that party which became entitled to the largest share, compensation being made in some other part of the frontier, as contiguous as possible. The inconvenience of two nationalities on one small island was not to be endured.

Good-feeling, caution, ingenuity, knowledge of various kinds, were required from time to time in both parts of the Commission, to avoid apparently insurmountable obstructions—dead-locks, as they are called—and to decide wisely in doubtful cases.

The Commissioners acted very much upon a set of principles tacitly or openly laid down from the first as general rules.

I feel assured that the work was faithfully and well performed, both from my own near observation,* and from the telling fact that the award neither a take-in nor a triumph to either natic

The quantity of fertile and commodious l which was set at liberty for public sale and enjoyment on both sides of the boundary was large, being equal on the British side to a cou ninety-five miles long by four broad; for this designation had taken place no titles c be given. By far the greater portion of the is of excellent quality, with a tolerably d population either surrounding it or creeping towards it, and worth all the expense incu twenty-fold and more. The British came secure possession of Wolfe, or Grand Is (31,283 acres), close to Kingston on Lake tario, of Wells, Howe, and other valuable isl in this vicinity. The island of St. Mary, in I St. Clair, and the rich and beautiful St. Jos in Lake Huron, seventeen miles by twelve, fell to the share of Upper Canada.

Although I speak without having the acco before me, I believe that the whole expens the Commission during nine years, the ter its existence, was under £110,000. It was in equal shares by the two Governments cerned. As an elaborate topographic and d

* I was five years in the Commission, and left it on acco my health.

Sec. for 5 years 1819-20 to

matic labour, undertaken by two great nations, and carried on for a series of years, the expense incurred cannot be considered great. The space under survey and decision was about 1700 miles long by a variable breadth, for the most part wilderness, very distant, often most intricate, and only accessible in the summer.*

All this stretch of country had to be mapped accurately, as a standing official document in evidence—a work which includes minute surveys by astronomical observation, and by triangulation, various measurements, &c., and the construction of numerous maps on a large scale in quadruplicate,—a copy for each Government and each Commissioner.

I need not say that the field service of this Commission was rendered arduous by the heats, severe labour, by the provisions being salt, by annoying insects, heavy rains, and by the unhealthiness of some of the districts under examination.

Several of the surveyors, although in high spirits at first with their good salaries and new mode of life, soon left us, subdued by toil and exposure.

I have in my eye now one gentleman of con-

* The topographical survey of Great Britain has already cost 1,500,000*l.*, although its officers and men are mostly taken from the military service, and therefore work very cheaply.

siderable energy, sitting by the half hour on a h
rock in the sun, wiping his perspiring face,
in angry contention with a cloud of mosquit
He soon went away. Another resigned beca
work was begun at four o'clock in the morni
or, as he called it, in the middle of the night.

It was, however, at the upper end of L
Erie that sickness effectually disabled the un
Commission. Scarcely a man escaped either a
or bilious remittent fever under severe forms.

The whole American party, General Po
(the Commissioner), included, caught one or ot
of these diseases among the marshes of the Mi
River, or at Point Pelé in Lake Erie. Not
of them died; but many had narrow escap
and few recovered until the succeeding spring

Mr. Ogilvy, the British Commissioner,
taken ill on the 12th of September, 1819,
Boisblanc Island, in the river Détroit, and
days after died in the contiguous village
Amherstburgh. He did not complain much,
suffered chiefly from utter prostration. For s
ral days he lay in a lethargic state;—in f
until a few hours before death.

Mr. Ogilvy died at the age of fifty, much
gretted. He was on the whole fitted for his t
being familiar with the country with which
had to deal, both in Canada and in the Ind

territories, and he understood the views and interests of the respective nations. There was about him, I am informed, an unusual amount of public spirit and talent; but he was variable, apt to be obstinate in trifles, and immediately afterwards too pliant in matters of more importance.

He was in good circumstances, and during the last American war lent Government three or four thousand pounds; for which seasonable aid he was offered (but declined) a lucrative public appointment.

During the last five or six years of his life he spent seven or eight thousand pounds in improving his estate of Airlie, near Montreal, and in land speculations which his unexpected death prevented from ripening.

Mr. David Thompson, the British astronomer (already introduced to the reader), fell sick early in the same September, at first with extreme weakness, and then with high fever and delirium. He was ill twenty-one days, and as soon as he was able, left for his own home on the St. Lawrence, near the Glengarry settlement. There he remained, feeble and out of health, all the winter.

Two of the British boatmen died of remittent fever; one at Amherstburgh, and the other at Montreal.

The whole country about Lake Erie (always

unhealthy in the warm months) was visited
year (1819) with unusual sickness. I was
on my geological tour; and in due course arr
in Sandusky Bay, at the south-west end of I
Erie, usually a gay and interesting scene,
then most pestilential, and therefore dese
The greater part of the inhabitants of
dusky city had fled, while the adjacent s
town of Venice was left by all its popul
(1500), excepting one man aged seventy y
It was most melancholy to walk among the
trodden streets, the empty houses, wharfs,
warehouses. Venice stands in a swamp, the w
of which is more than milk-warm in summer

As the Commission had again to work in I
Erie, and in the sickly regions on the wa
Lake Huron, it was resolved to place a me
man in the office of secretary, then vacant b
resignation of Mr. Stephen Sewell; and I
appointed.

Lord Castlereagh, then holding the fo
portfolio, conferred the vacant commissione
on Anthony Barclay, Esq., of the London
brother to Col. Delancey Barclay, of the Gu
aid-de-camp to the late Duke of York, and s
the late Col. Barclay, who for many years
various important employments in the U
States, on behalf of the British Government.

Mr. Barclay was selected with peculiar felicity, if fitness for office be determined by personal character, by great diligence, ability, and firmness of purpose, and by a large acquaintance with its duties, acquired as secretary to a similar Commission under the 4th and 5th Articles of the Treaty of Ghent; while he of all men was enabled, by previous education and quiet amenity of manner, to cope with the eager and exacting temper of American diplomatists, and to make good the right thing.

I am at the same time far from saying or hinting a single word to the moral prejudice of the United States' portion of our Commission. They were men of strict honour, and frank and friendly to all—to myself personally most kind. But it is well known that American civil servants are under strong pressure, and ever anxious to establish new claims upon the gratitude of the republic. The length of their state-papers, notes, replies, rejoinders, &c. &c., was wonderful to me, unacquainted as I was with the style and method of official correspondence.

It had been arranged in the winter of 1820–21 that the United Boundary Commission should meet at Amherstburgh, as early in the ensuing spring as it was possible for the surveys to be prosecuted.

On the 7th of May, 1821, therefore, the

1821 May 7 British Commission, including my humble arrived at Waterloo, a sleepy little cluste houses at the head of the river Niagara, an the Canadian side of Lake Erie.

It was impossible to proceed further. Lake was blocked up by a fixed mass of rough ice, miles long. From a neighbouring height, we glad to think we saw a narrow lead-coloured the open lake, beyond the great white expans

We were told that, by the help of a st south-west wind, all that immense body o would crack and rend, and come tumbling d the river Niagara in ragged fragments. An it fell out; but we waited in a wretched house for six days.

The passage of the ice down the Black-R rapids was an interesting sight. We watched the jammed masses, blocks and sh of all shapes and sizes, hurrying down the r at peace, however, among themselves, ex near the banks, where there was an abund of quarrel and mutual damage. But wi cautious start from either bank, crossing see quite safe. The boat and the ice were passive as regards each other, because drive the same current.

We crossed several times. Of course it tedious affair, as the boat is taken the best of a mile too far down. On one occasion we went to a pleasant dinner at Black-Rock, at the large and commodious house of the American Commissioner (General Porter), the very house which was sacked a few years before by the 41st British Infantry. The soldiers fell principally on the larder and cellar, and were not disappointed, as an eye-witness informed me. Although a grievous act of barbarity, the affluent American general could speak on the subject with the greatest good-humour. The whole frontier was ravaged by the British by way of reprisal. Gen. Porter

On the 13th instant the ice had almost all disappeared;* and we embarked in the Buffalo steamer for Amherstburgh, a distance of 224 miles, where we arrived on the 16th instant. There are now (1848) the surprising number of one hundred steamers on this lake alone.

We rarely saw the Canadian shore, as we kept close to the American the whole way, calling at Dunkirk, Erie, Cleveland, and other places, to land and receive passengers and cargo.

This shore is a remarkably straight and mono-

* Does not this show that forty miles of water left the lake in less than six days,—*i. e.* from the moment the ice broke,—each mass descending with the water it floated in? Mr. Allen has calculated that 701,250 tons of water flow out of Lake Erie at Black-Rock every minute. — "American Journal of Science," vol. xliv. p. 71. *

Probably a W. or a S W wind moved the ice

* 119000 second feet — not an improbable value for the "low water of 1819-20"

tonous line of rich sloping woods, with a clearance here and there. There are no materials for description of scenery.

We were favoured by no incidents, except that the servant of the British agent was robbed of a shoe, taken from off his foot while asleep on the deck at night. His great lamentation was the uselessness of the parted shoes to anybody.

If, during our three days' voyage, we escaped dulness, the merit lies with the passengers. I was much pleased with the agreeable manners and extensive information of Mr. Beaumont, a surgeon in the American army, on his way to Michilimackinac. He there had soon afterwards the good fortune to meet with Martin the Canadian, whose process of digestion could be seen through an aperture in the abdomen; and the world had the good fortune to have so important a phenomenon fall in the way of an observer as able as Mr. Beaumont.

* Dr. Beaumont

It will be recollected that Mr. Beaumont witnessed in this man's stomach (laid partly open by a gun-shot wound) all the successive steps in digestion—the accumulation of blood in the stomach, the effusion of the pale gastric juice, the curious muscular, movements of the organ, and finally, the disappearance of the changed food,

* At one time much quoted experiments on the human digestion

He made also very curious observations on the comparative digestibility of most of our ordinary articles of diet.

I was very much attracted towards a young cabin-passenger, named Hunter, from Maryland, a most prepossessing fellow, full of ability and spirit. He said he was a descendant of Pocohontas, the Virginian princess, who saved the life of Captain Smith, and afterwards married him. He had still very evidently the clear bronze of the Indian, and his never-to-be-forgotten eye. He was on one of those exploratory tours so frequently made by American youth, and bound for Lake Michigan; from thence to make his way by Greenbay and the Fox River to the Mississippi, and so round home. I longed to be his companion. The ivory haft of a dagger occasionally peeped from within his waistcoat. I asked him the use of it. He answered, that he hoped it would be of no use, but that it was best to be prepared for the lawless borderers of the west.

The young men of the Atlantic shores of the United States may often feel competition at home too strong for them, or may wish to know personally the capabilities of other regions, in fertility, water power, or commercial openings.

Again, we had an American clergyman on board, the Rev. Mr. Morse, very distinguished at that time for his exertions in the cause of missions. He was dressed with a preciseness very unusual in the United States—wholly in black, with small-clothes and silk stockings. His coat was single-breasted, descending to his heels, and was adorned with large cloth buttons. A white neckcloth and broad-brimmed hat I must mention, and then go on to say, that his physiognomy was mild, pleasingly devout; his nose aquiline, giving his face the convex profile we see on the coins of Louis XVI. of France. He was fit for his work, and while not without the wisdom which is from above, possessed the activity, frankness, and tact of the man of the world,—and the decision, let me add, of which his dress was the symbol. He was always amiable and accessible, but always the minister. He did not act upon the Jesuit maxim of entering a man's heart by *his* door and coming out at your own. The use of his pen was incessant; his note-book was flooded with remarks, but upon what, was past my comprehension.

I have said that Mr. Morse was a good man; and therefore could not help sighing when I saw the triumphant eagerness, the large flashing eye, with which he mounted a high railing, to mark and talk over, in the presence of Englishmen, the exact locality where, a very few years before, the

British and American squadrons had met in battle,—an open sheet of water, as smooth as glass when Mr. Morse was gazing upon it, with the Put-in Bay group of islets close at hand, other islands farther off on the north, and the low, woody, south main almost disappearing in the distance. I perceived that in the mistaken patriot we had lost, for the moment, the Christian. Did he not know that his country was fighting the battles of Napoleon the oppressor, and against her agonising parent? and that a war against Great Britain at that juncture was base, matricidal, and a political mistake? Hundreds of thousands of American citizens held up holy hands against that war. We can now rejoice that public opinion is vastly purified, and that thoughtful men seldom find pleasure even in victory.

The American papers soon afterwards told us that the Rev. Mr. Morse did not go beyond Green Bay, in Lake Michigan. He was laid up there by sickness.

The Boundary Commission left the steamer at Amherstburgh, at that time a village of about five hundred inhabitants; but now having, with double that number of people, a new court-house, market-place, five churches and chapels, and other remarkable improvements. In 1821 there were two companies of infantry at Amherstburgh, under a lieutenant-colonel, a man of talent and refinement, an excellent officer, but an invalid in an unhealthy station, and obliged by his duty to live here in a crazy cottage, with little or no society. Such is life in the army.

We met with every civility from the slender garrison. I here first tasted the grey squirrel. Although I am not fond of new flavours at the dinner-table, I thought this an excellent dish.

Our business here was confined to the settlement of accounts, and to framing directions to the surveying parties as to the summer's work. They were ordered to make a map of River and Lake St. Clair, with the upper part of the River Détroit, and the head of Lake Erie — a very unhealthy district.

The two commissioners, the English agent and the American secretary, returned home; the American agent and myself remained, to accompany the working parties.

As the British schooner Confiance, on board which we were frequently to reside, and which was to convey us to the seat of work, did not arrive for a week afterwards, I passed this time very pleasantly at Amherstburgh and at the American town of Détroit, eighteen miles above Lake Erie.

The river and lake of St. Clair, with the River

Détroit, form the water communication between Lakes Huron and Erie, taking from the former to feed the latter. They are noble bodies of pure, transparent water (except certain parts of Lake St. Clair), flowing through an immense plain, through millions of acres of forest, full of smaller rivers, sometimes consisting of dry, useful land, at others sinking into swamps or even extensive lakes. The hand of man is only felt on the principal streams; all else is in a state of nature. It is now, however, fast replenishing with an industrious population.

The Rivers Détroit and St. Clair have a lively fringe of comfortable and even pretty dwellings, embowered in pear, apple, and peach orchards, with here and there a church-tower or a clump of wych-elms shadowing an advanced bank of the river. Productive farms stretch out of sight into the woods behind. When first I saw this region of plenty and beauty, I was enchanted with it; but nearer acquaintance moderated my admiration.

Even at and about Amherstburgh there was much to interest,—not the moist, flat, half-cultivated environs, nor its couple of streets, humble and narrow, but some of the temporary residents.

The climate, aguish and worse, and the great heats of summer, may account for the drooping, aimless look of the people of this village, as well as its stagnant appearance generally.

The shopkeepers and small exporters complained of the times; but their stores were well filled; they were bartering freely with the back settlements in tobacco, wheat, Indian corn, &c.; steamers and sloops were constantly bringing and taking away. The shopkeepers had a news-room and library—a sure indication of life and spirit. So I concluded that, upon the whole, things were not very bad.

The farmers complained to me that the shopkeepers ruled them with a rod of iron, because they were mostly their debtors, and had to sell to them, their creditors, produce at a very low rate, or receive a visit from the sheriff's officer. This says very little for the prudence or energy of the farmer.

I remarked that, except when the climate had touched them, the general appearance of the country people was tolerably good, and indicated easy circumstances. I never saw in England better crops of wheat; and their tobacco brings a high price.

Strong drink is the bane of Canada West, especially on outlying farms, and still more especially, I fear, among half-pay officers. All goes on soberly and pleasantly while the buildings and land are getting up and into order; but as soon as this is done time hangs heavily, annoyances arise, vain regrets are felt, infirm health is apt to follow; when the only resource seems to be the whisky-bottle. The man begins to remember only the pleasant part of English and military life, and laments his chair and plate at the regimental mess. He is very glad of an invitation to dine with the little garrison twenty miles off; and in the end sinks into the sot, and drags his sons, if he have any, down with him.

The gentleman settler is unfit for the gloom of the woods, and should select a ready-made farm, not more than ten miles from a town. This can be done any day on reasonable terms.

There were in 1821 some remarkable persons in and near Amherstburgh, to whom I had the good fortune to be introduced. I am sure I shall be satisfying my own feelings, and doing honour to a man of high merit, in giving a brief account of Captain Stewart, late of the Honourable East India service.

Although Captain Stewart resided at Amherstburgh, and was still not thirty-five years of age, he had passed many years in India, and had had some concern with the mutiny at Vellore; but his part in the affair must have been small; for his jealous masters dismissed him with full pay for life. He was handsome, frank, and energetic. His iron frame was indifferent to luxuries or even comforts; any hut was a home, and any food was nourishment, provided he could be doing good to others; for he was, and is, a working Christian.

At this time he was waging successful war with the negro slavery of the United States. As a branch of this holy enterprise within the grasp of an individual of small means, and totally unaided, he devoted himself to providing a home for runaways from the slave states.*

Being at least twenty years before his generation, and having views as much above those of the careful traffickers of Amherstburgh, as the heaven is above the earth, the excellent captain was totally misunderstood, and well abused, for bringing them customers, forsooth.

His design was to establish in the neighbourhood a negro colony. For this purpose he bought a small tract of land in the rear of the village. As the poor fugitives came in, friendless and breathless, though exulting, Captain Stewart offered them protection and subsistence; the first being still necessary against the stratagems,

* In 1847 I had the pleasure of meeting Capt. S. at Bristol. I knew him instantly; there was the same carelessness about the outer man, and the same restless zeal for the old object.

and even violence, of their pursuers; the latter his land supplied.

The greater portion of these negro refugees became his tenants, and to this day form an orderly body of British subjects, numbering 174 in 1842. So well known throughout the United States is the fact that there is such an asylum for the wretched slaves, that from 1820 to the present day, at least 15,000 persons of colour have come and settled in Canada West. That number is supposed to be there now, with churches and schools in different parts of the province. During the late rebellion, when the American sympathisers invaded the British possessions, the blacks eagerly offered their services to Government, well knowing their fate if Canada should glitter as an additional star in the spangled banner of the American Confederation. Their offer was accepted. There is (or was) a coloured company of soldiers at Stone Bridge, Lake Erie.

I spent a very pleasant evening at the cottage of Captain Stewart, a plain but comfortable abode on the edge of his purchase, in which he lived with his widowed sister, and her numerous and fine family.

The negro village and the clearances were then but just begun. As it was a very rainy season, the land seemed to be a swamp, and the huts very indifferent affairs, but were thought to be palaces by the freemen who inhabited them. Subsequently heavy crops were obtained from their farms. Captain Stewart had the goodness to walk over some of them with me; and I am glad that I had the discernment to cheer him on in his difficult undertaking. Happy is the man who, with wisdom, selects and pursues some great, unselfish object. Its influence upon himself is most beneficial, as well as upon others, and will not cease with this life.

"A good man *seen*, though silent, counsel gives."

If this had been Captain Stewart's only work it would have been a noble benefaction to his fellow-men—well worth a life.

There was near Amherstburgh, at this time, a family in which all must have been greatly interested, a lingering relic, in the distant western world, of the old court of France.

Medical men have a very general *entrée* into the domestic circle. Sooner or later their services are indispensable, and they often become almost integral parts of the family. So it was here. The medical officer of the garrison was on these intimate terms with Chevalier and Madame de Brosse.

Dr. N. thought fit to take me with him to spend an evening with his French friends.

They resided a couple of miles from Amherstburgh, at the extreme point of the river, just where the fine woodland expanse of Lake Erie comes into view. In walking there we passed much pretty scenery, cottages with verandahs, clumps of drooping willows, park-like openings, and sand-banks overrun with sweet-briar, vines, and briony.

The cottage of the Chevalier stands between the lake and the highroad, and is a convenient jumble of added parts, each under its own little roof. The apartment with which I was best acquainted (the family sitting-room) looked with a wide bay-window upon the water. The large garden and the offices were on the opposite side of the road, upon rising ground, and sheltered the cottage from the cold north winds. They had a handy black galloway, and a Dearborn waggon on easy springs, to carry them about to the Canadian French families in the vicinity.

The moment I entered this sitting-room I felt myself in France. I was among the fanciful articles of *virtù*, the *bijouterie*, and feminine knick-knackery with which Madame de Genlis has made the untravelled English familiar. There was no carpet, but little rugs instead, in favourite spots, before two short hair-seated sofas covered with yellow plush, with four arm-chairs to match close by (*à la* Louis XIV.), and none of the newest. The tables were of the native walnut, and very beautiful. They were more or less covered with books and culled flowers, and the one in the middle of the room had a large Limousin plate, painted over with blue and white saints, and holding fans, seals, and medallions. For dear Versailles' sake, well remembered through a vista of chequered years, Madame had preserved, or somewhere picked up, a somewhat shattered cabinet of marqueterie.

Portraits adorned the walls of the room; an excellent likeness of Marie Antoinette, in the gloomy mezzotint of fifty years ago; a dashing powdered likeness of Madame de Brosse when very young; and another, much more humble and more modern, of her only daughter, a pretty little brunette, recently married to a worthy Frenchman, living on his property, twelve or fifteen miles off.

I must not forget two Watteaus, pictures of shepherds and shepherdesses, risking good looks and gay clothes on wet grass, with open mouths and music-books.

If there were a transcript of the ample and genial face of the Chevalier, I did not see it. I hope there was, for there are few so worthy of the painter's pains.

A tolerable piano was not wanting, and two or three capital guitars stood in corners upon piles of music.

I had been long familiar with Grimm, Marmontel, and other describers of French life in 1770–1790. It was, therefore, most agreeable, as well as unexpected, to find before me a very pleasing representation of the *vieille cour en action* in the heart of North America—not for a moment wishing the *vieille cour* back again.

I was received at the door by the Chevalier, with the warm but refined welcome which high-breeding alone can give. He was a magnificent person, six feet five inches high, under sixty years of age, with an open, gentlemanly physiognomy, and a free, springy carriage even now. There had been a time when he was finely proportioned, but an indolent life of twenty years had added more to his bulk than to his beauty.

He led us very pleasantly into the sitting-room. There, ensconced in an easy chair, close to the bay-window, and its quiet scenery of cypress, and willow, and shining lake, we found Madame de Brosse, a portly old lady, once fair, and certainly handsome, now lively and gracious, with a certain high manner blending in, but anything rather than offensive. She received us most cordially.

The new-married daughter, in a simple dress, sat by her side, evidently ready to contribute to a pleasant evening. How she came to be a brunette I do not know.

In a few minutes their only son, a lieutenant on the half-pay of a Canadian regiment, walked in. He strongly resembled his father in everything but his hilarious features, for those of the son, with a woodland negligence of dress, were decidedly pensive, and that perhaps from vain regrets for the lost distinctions and pleasures of his ancestors.

We had of conversation great plenty. The Chevalier and his lady were full of anecdote about courts, and camps, and lengthened wanderings. They found in me, at least, a new and respectful listener.

After coffee Madame called upon her daughter for a romance to the guitar, which she gave at once, very unaffectedly and well. Then M. de Brosse himself thundered out a "*Chanson à la chasse.*" It was too loud to be musical. I feared for the windows. In the duet that followed between himself and Madame de Brosse he sang the old French air upon which it was based as gently and sweetly as he had been boisterous before. Madame's organ might be thin, but her singing was correct and tasteful. Throughout the evening the amiability of this family, and their determination to look brightly on the present, and confidingly on the future, was delightful.

Having been a very humble cultivator of the gay science, I tuned up my small pipe in two or three French airs which had not as yet been wafted so far west. Having the great advantage of being "a new man," I was approved, and more than once repeated my visit. Gâteaux, creams, and fruits, I ought to add, ended the evening very agreeably. This interesting family were then in their best spirits on account of the marriage of their daughter.

The Chevalier had fallen in love with his lady at the court of Versailles, where they held some (perhaps) subordinate situations about the person of Marie Antoinette in the beginning of the first French revolution. That great political tempest drove the aristocracy of France, and these two young people with them, to the four winds.

After a variety of painful adventures M. de Brosse found himself an officer in the De Watteville regiment, in the pay of Great Britain, and having always corresponded with his Léoline, soon afterwards married her. They were in Spain, Sicily, England, and latterly in the Canadas, where he took leave of active service upon the half-pay of a major. He purchased a farm, and settled on the Détroit, where the comforts of life are readily procured, and where there are several French families of property and consequence.

Do they regret the elegant frivolities of the Trianon, and do they esteem themselves driven from Paradise?—Yes! certainly. Youth and distance have given lustre to the gay, and softness to the darker parts of their early life. The brightness of the scene immediately around them, and the amiability of their master and mistress, had shut their eyes to the miseries of universal France, which it was the design of Providence, by the revolution, to lessen.

My medical friend one day made a party to hunt rattlesnakes in the marshy islands, a little below Amherstburgh, as I had never seen one. We put on strong boots, reaching nearly to the knees, and thick pantaloons. We therefore did not fear a bite. As to our weapon of offence, we had a long elastic switch.

We landed on a field of long grass, twenty or thirty acres in extent, and found mowers at work, defended by pieces of blanket tied round their legs. They said they had seen several rattlesnakes in the course of the morning, and we were not long in finding six—three among the long grass, and three among some fallen timber. We had the pleasure (such as it was) of several runs, and of hearing the dread rattle in full force. We killed two, each more than a yard long.

Amherstburgh is famous for rattlesnakes. Dr. N. told me that a few months before, one of the children (aged six years) of an officer was bitten. The usual symptoms set in with severity. He used all the known remedies assiduously, external and internal, but the child only grew worse. As its life was now despaired of, the parents sent for an old Indian woman with the medical man's full concurrence. After having looked upon the child she hastened into the woods, and returned with some rattlesnake root (*Goodyera pubescens*). Of part of the leaves she made an infusion, of which she caused the child to swallow doses at certain intervals, and of part she made a poultice, which she applied to the wound. The child soon began to improve; one by one the symptoms disappeared, and in forty-eight hours the little sufferer was out of danger. This is a well-authenticated case, and very remarkable.

The only other circumstance worthy of note, which occurred during my stay, was the gathering of the Indians of Wisconsin, Iowa, and other parts of the United States, for the purpose of receiving their annual presents from the British Government. Some of them were brawny, well-fed, but sullen men, of middle-age, with little covering but a blanket, blue middle-cloth, and necklace of large bear's claws. Among them I saw the most interesting Indian of these regions, as much on account of his own great capacity and influence as because he was the brother of the renowned Chief Tecumseh,* killed in the last American war. I am speaking of the Prophet, most faithfully delineated in Catlin's series of Indian Portraits. I could not help shaking hands with him, and addressing to him a few friendly words by an interpreter. He was evidently a conservative of the true water—a sombre, reflective savage of the old times, large, gaunt, square-featured—the able coadjutor of his brother in his scheme of leaguing together all the Indians of North America, to sweep the white men out of the land altogether. In the war of 1813 he assisted the British very effectively, but it is supposed only with the view of weakening his future foes. The Prophet was some time afterwards killed in a fray with those Ishmaelites the backwoodsmen.

It seems unfortunate that the Indians of the

* Tecumseh, the Indian hero, will never be forgotten on the Great Lakes. In 1811, at a council held with the Americans at Vincennes, Tecumseh, having finished his address, showed some displeasure that no seat was kept for him. General Harrison hastened to order one to be brought. "Warrior," said a bystander to him, "your father, the General, presents to you an arm-chair." "He, my father!" cried the chief, fiercely. "The sun is my father, and the earth is my mother. She nourishes me. I sleep upon her bosom." And then the haughty savage sat on the ground, cross-legged.

central parts of North America come in contact generally with outlaws and desperate men, who are not to be called Christians, even for a moment, in courtesy.

Another large body of Indians then present was quite distinct from these. They came from the western prairies on horses, and were slender young men, dressed from head to foot in purple calico; the seams of their little coatees, its cape, and their leggings, edged prettily with a short white fringe.

Close to Amherstburgh there is a grassy common a hundred acres in extent. On this, these young braves were perpetually galloping, and wheeling, and checking in full career their slight horses, in a most absurd and reckless manner, as it seemed to me. One evening the Buffalo-dance was performed by thirty or forty stamping savages, disguised with the horns and portions of the skin of this animal. We were favoured with innumerable frantic bellowings, grimacings, and shufflings here and there.

Three or four days before the expected arrival of our schooner, the Confiance, I went to Détroit, sixteen miles up the river, the capital of the then territory of Michigan. I wished to see for myself the physiognomy and manners of a small frontier town. I embarked in the periodical steamer. The river scenery has been noticed before. The stream is a mile or more broad, and flows, all alive with sloops, canvass, and scows, through a settled country, placid and productive, save on the British side for a few miles above Amherstburgh, where the Huron reserve remains a wilderness.

Détroit now contains (1847) more than 10,000 inhabitants. The territory has become an important state (repudiating). In 1821 it had 1400 inhabitants, scattered over a long straggling street parallel to the river, with a few lanes behind. In the middle of the town was a very singular staring Roman Catholic church, of great size. In the rear was a large common, on which troops of horses were grazing and frolicking.

About nine o'clock on a Saturday morning I landed opposite to a decent inn with two signs—"General Washington," with white tie and black coat with stand-up collar, fronting the river—and an angry eagle, of gilt wood, behind, to face the street. Although this double-facedness did not suit my English notions, I carried my light portmanteau up the bank of twenty to thirty feet, and into the door-way of the inn, where I met with the crummy landlady. On asking her if I could have a bed,—"Oh! yes to be sure."—"And bed-room to myself?"—"Oh! no; but you can have a room with only three beds in it." My eye catching at the moment the sign-board of another large wooden inn, I declined the lady's invitation to walk in, and passed over to the rival house of entertainment under the patronage of "General Winfield Scott," even now a famous and very tall American general, judging from a blue painting of him on the wall.

Presenting myself here meekly, for I had not breakfasted, I was informed that five beds in a room was the smallest allowance they could offer. So humbled was I, and so disinclined to face the "Golden Eagle," that I took my traps up-stairs, and came down to an excellent breakfast.

I shall not carry the reader with me all adown the sweltering, dusty streets of Détroit, empty of every living thing but pigs and poultry. So I left the string of shabby wooden houses, rubbishy stores, full of coarse dry goods, and the loaded gutters, loudly calling for the feathered scavengers of Georgia and Florida. I betook myself home and read the "Détroit Gazette," an out-and-outer, writing boldly and well up to the times.

One o'clock brought dinner, a rough, substantial meal, with at least twenty commensals, in every variety of costume. They were clerks, shopkeepers, lawyers, land-agents, and doctors. Most of these lived in the house; others roosted among their goods. The dinner was soon despatched, and the clatter of plates among the things of the past. The bulk of the diners dispersed, leaving a meditative batch of three or four.

Among these was the editor of the "Gazette," Mr. Sinkler (Sinclair, St. Clair), and Mr. Crittle, the land-agent, shrewd in his own business, but friendly and mild, and very curious about England. To these I must add a very strange personage, who turned out to be a professor of Hebrew, wrapped up in a sort of ample dressing-gown of purple serge or flannel, with trousers of the same. In these places you may dress as you like, provided you are dressed at all. The land-agent wore corduroy cossacks and jacket, as being suitable for his sylvan rambles. The editor and land-agent became great gossips of mine at once. But I must first speak of the professor, as being the greatest original of the three.

As I walked up to the door of the "Winfield Scott," my attention was arrested by the flowing purple of the professor, as he was lounging on the broad bench which ran along the houseside. He was a powerfully made dwarf, high-backed, legs short, and very stout. His head was great and protuberant, and he had large red features, eyes blue, quick, and expressive; his red hair hung over his shoulders in clubs twisted like cables.

This singular being was really a professor of Hebrew, wandering in search of pupils wherever he was least likely to find them. Many such persons there are in the byways of the West. He was swinging his squat person about, and haranguing a small knot of loiterers. For lack of other listeners, he would have lectured to the black cook, as she was splitting a fowl.

The professor was more odd within than without. He was a Scotchman of respectable origin, and a truly learned man; but every word and look of his was so spiced with the extravagant and ludicrous, that there was no listening to his sonorous sounds without a riot of laughter, to the poor man's great loss, grief, and astonishment.

The professors of the university at which he was educated, respecting his attainments, procured for him a private class; but it had only one sitting. After listening to his odd and egotistical discourse for ten minutes, first one foolish student filliped a paper pellet at him, and then another, until the shower was universal; and there was a great row, in which some of the pupils were in danger of being thrown out of the window by the enraged doctor, who although short was extraordinarily strong in the arms.

I sat next to him at breakfast one morning, when he obliged me by some magnifical discourse, of which the following is a faded specimen:—

"So, sir! you are from the good old country, like myself. Why did you leave it? Answer me that! But three-fourths of us professors here are either British, or of the British. Look at Renwick, of Columbia College, Highland Mary's grandson; at Dunglisson; at Pattinson of Glasglow; at myself, a near kinsman of the Gentle Shepherd. One good native teacher I know and honour, Sam Mitchell, of New York. I listened with delight the other day for two good hours while he gave us (quite new to me) the natural history and uses of that admirable esculent the turnip, directing our attention to his diagrams with an African assagai (a dart). Sir, this is an inquiring and an acquiring country. They will know and will have. I shall soon have plenty of pupils. I shall soon be off to the new self-governing and self-supporting college in Ohio, where a man of my calibre is grievously wanted. I have letters to those people, and have sent them my little treatise on the Canaanitish Mysteries. Do you know Professor Parker, of Northland College? Although he is a pupil of mine, I am bound to declare that he has no more brains than a soldier carries in his knapsack. A planet-load of such fellows is not worth a rush. To be sure he would not walk into a well; but as to Hebrew!— Pshaw! I first called on him in the month Chisleu. Certainly he was not sacrificing to Nisroch, his eagle-faced god; but he was with many other fools in his drawing-room, so bewitched with a silly singing-woman, that he told a professor of the Hebrew tongue to call again. But that professor of Andover, with the long name, is of another sort. Yes! with the long name — Longfellow!—'long, long ago,' as somebody used to sing. He is a man of very fair American abilities. When I was at his college, giving a course of Egyptian antiquities, I might have been the noble Asnapper himself, such was his courtesy to the man who is now addressing you. He is good, too, in verse. But, speaking of these poets of the west, I know them all, from Florio of Poughkeepsie, through Percival, 'all purple and gold,' up to Bryant, who chaunts the wild ducks——" &c. &c. till midnight, had I not respectfully called the professor's attention to the cold tea and now solid buttered toast.

I afterwards saw this individual at Quebec, trying to lecture. His money, however, had run out, and he kept his bed three days in despair. Kind words and a subscription revived him. He was grateful. His "subsequents," as the Americans would say, I do not know.

The land-agent, Mr. S. Crittle, and myself, with five others, inhabited at night the same bed-chamber. Mr. Crittle and two friends of his used to keep me awake until twelve at night, by sitting on my bed and asking questions about George the Fourth and George Robins the auctioneer—equally great men in their opinion, as filling up much space in "The Times" newspaper—and about London, Windsor, and Liverpool, &c. In return, I received no little information on the difficult subject of land-sales, private, public, or on military-service tickets. Crittle owned that a smart man might do a good stroke of business at Détroit; that there was a demand for his article; the land, climate, and market, all good; and that the townships were filling up not amiss. He shewed me about the town, saying he could look after trade quite as well in the street as in his little office. I was shewn the Museum, which was very creditable as far as it went; and the library of 1400 well-selected volumes, being one for each inhabitant. Novels I observed were about one-third of the whole collection.*

My little editor was a lively, sharp New Englander, chatty and well-informed. During the extreme heats of the day I twice spent an hour in

* Few towns have made such progress as Détroit since 1821. Its population has increased seven-fold. Among its public build-

his dirt-encrusted printing-office. We talked as he worked off the paper. His leading articles, short and strong, were put into type at once without copy. The paper was of small size, the main part of its contents taken from the latest English arrivals; but the stay and support of the concern were the advertisements, which being duty free were cheap and numerous, and condescended to the smallest imaginable transaction. He did the whole work of the paper, excepting its delivery to the subscribers. In fact, I saw that the Détroiters fared well and worked hard; they were therefore making profit. Many grumbled, but few left.

"Sir," said I to the editor one day, "you told me you were a bookseller. I see some reams of brown and white paper, and a few pieces of paper-hangings. Where is your literature?"

"Oh!" he replied, "I blocked up my windows with books for two years, but they were noticed only by the flies. I did not sell three copies. People have not read through the town library yet. A box in the garret without a lid contains

ings are a state-house, city-hall, state-penitentiary, gaol, eight churches, three markets, a theatre, library, and museum. Country seats stud the environs. Two railroads into the interior are being made. The central railroad is finished to Marshall, one hundred miles; and so is the Erie and the Kalamazoo, thirty-three miles.

my stock of books." So going up-stairs and overhauling the box, I found several American reprints much to my taste.

Men must speak as they find. I have resided for months in various parts of the United States, and have always met with obliging people.

On the Sunday of my stay here I went to the Episcopal church, and was glad to see an attentive and well-dressed congregation. General Macomb, the governor, and his family, were in a neat pew, not differing from those of other people, the general in plain clothes; but his two aide-de-camps in uniform, escorting his lady-like daughters dressed in white. The sermon was good, and the church comfortable.

The following day I visited the prison. It contained a single prisoner, a young Indian, accused of murder. I entered his small round cell. He was squatted on the mud floor, unwashed, unkempt, with an old blanket over his shoulders, and half off. He gave us no glance, but seemed fixed—in an iron dream. Here, indeed, was a soul shut up! I could say nothing. This was one of the most painful sights I had seen in America.

I will change the subject for the following homely but characteristic incident:—

Although I seldom submit to professional shaving, it was indispensable so to do soon after seeing the captive Indian. The operator was a black man, very dressy, self-sufficient, and talkative. During the process I was foolish enough to stiffen my upper lip, to give the razor a firmer surface to work on. He had already cut me twice.

"Now, please, sir," he exclaimed, "do not so—be natural; it will be best for us both. I love nature; with her I know where I am."

Soon afterwards he again drew blood. I held my face then rather low; but he chucked me gently under the chin, crying, "Up, man! up with it." I tell these little things to shew the droll impertinence of free coloured men in the United States. This artist sat down to dinner, I doubt not, without the most distant idea that he had done anything out of the way. In different parts of the world I have come across puppies in dress, but never one, either in Paris or Baden-Baden, at all to be compared to the black man-servant of the celebrated orator Randolph. It was a great treat to see this personage peacocking (*paonisant*) in his flame-coloured waistcoat, frills, &c., before our hotel door at Washington.

I was one evening sitting at tea alone, near the window in the eating-room overlooking the river, after a hard day's work mineral-hunting in some quarries four miles below Détroit. My being served with tea out of the usual course was a great favour. The kindness of the landlady had added the luxuries of preserves, honey, and buck-wheat cakes to the refreshing meal. All the boarders were gone to a rifle-match. I had taken one cup, and was deep in a new-bought book, when I was suddenly awoke by a singular command uttered close to my ear.

"Put down that book, sir! You and I are to pass the evening in this room; and it is not to be spent in reading!"

I looked up at the stranger, and my vexation was at once quieted. I beheld a remarkably good-looking, white-haired old gentleman, smiling kindly upon me out of open, candid eyes, from under a broad-brimmed hat. He was dressed much like a Quaker; and yet he did not belong to that sect of prim faces and noble hearts. He had on a brown single-breasted coat, and pantaloons to match, white neckcloth and white stockings, and—rare to see hereabouts—his shoes were well blacked. As somehow I did not speak, after standing some moments, he said—

"Pray, sir, who are you?"

"Oh! sir," I replied, beginning to be not well pleased at the interruption, "I am a poor, unfortunate, stray Englishman."

I was about to say more, when he broke in upon me, exclaiming, "I am surprised to hear you speak so lightly and untruly. The poverty is not great where there is butter and honey (glancing at the table); and let me tell you that it is an estate to be an Englishman. Never jest with your lofty birthright. You are the countryman of Alfred, Shakspeare, Newton, and Wilberforce. To England and her lineage is committed by the God above us the schooling of the nations. I shall take tea with you." With that he called for a cup and saucer, and a fresh infusion of hyson.

Having sat down, he at once asked me from what part of England I came. Having told him from Nottinghamshire:

"What!" he cried out, "from the county of Byron and Kirk White, of Cranmer and Hartley, of the Savilles, the Willoughbys, and the Parkyns?"

Here I interrupted him in my turn: "Under the circumstances, I am entitled, sir, to ask respectfully to whom I have the honour of addressing myself."

"I am," he answered, "Judge Perkins, by descent a Parkyns of Nottinghamshire, one of the blood of blunt Sir Thomas the wrestler; my grandfather being the first to leave English soil. To-morrow I hold a district court at this place for the despatch of legal business. I reside at Greenfields, about eight miles down the river, where I shall be happy to see you, and shew you my numerous family and pretty place."

I thanked him cordially, but expressed a fear that the shortness of my stay would deprive me of the great pleasure of accepting his friendly invitation.

I had previously heard of Judge Perkins as being popular and much respected in this neighbourhood, and that it was quite impossible for him to *intrude* at Détroit.

I think he occupied full two hours in questions about his dear old county, its present condition in agriculture and manufactures, its nobles and gentry, Merry Sherwood, Thoresby, and the square old tower of Bunny Hall, the seat of the Parkyns. He even knew the quaint motto over the door of the old-world village school-house,—"*Disce vel discede.*" England was still to him the home of ancient days, and in her fortunes he took a deep interest, like most other involuntary exiles.

He then spoke long and well of Europe and America, of their blots and beauties—said that he was satisfied with his adopted country,* but not insensible to its imperfections. He thought that in America both virtue and vice were gigan-

* Neither the Mexican war nor the repudiation of just debts by many of the states had then occurred.

tic—that here, bad men were exceedingly bad, and the good exceedingly good.

He remarked upon the flattering welcome with which Americans are received by all European nations, excepting, perhaps, the British, between whom and the Americans there is a sort of family soreness—the prosperous young nation being too noisy and presuming, and the elder branch too austere.

"But," said he, "it is hardly fair to pass any judgment upon us as yet; we are immature, unripe, formed from a multitude of different races, and hardly coherent—necessarily too busy with the coarser wants of life to attend to the elegancies and refinements of a higher civilization. It is true that the moral sense is low among us—lower than in England. Even there, are you all you ought to be? What says your finest poet?—

'. . . . . Earth is sick,
And Heaven is weary of the hollow words
Which states and kingdoms utter when they talk
Of truth and justice. Turn to private life
And social neighbourhood; look we to ourselves!
A light of duty shines upon every day
For all; and yet how few are warned or cheered!'"

Excurs. p. 204.

Being joined at meals by strangers is common at inns in the country parts of the United States. Besides, in a person of Judge Perkins's age and station, it was an act of condescension to join my tea-table. Far greater liberties are taken in the middle and back districts.

I remember, when the Boundary Commission sat at Utica, in the state of New York, a party of our surveyors were quartered at the second inn of the place (10,000 inhabitants). One of our gentlemen—for such he was by education and by conduct, although a half-caste Indian—was awoke in the middle of the night by the glare of a candle, and the noise of the landlord showing a newly-arrived stranger into bed to him. The stranger had far better have ventured into the lair of a wild cat and her young. My friend lay quiet, and with closed eyes, until the man began to get into bed, when he put his foot to his body with such force and good-will, as to drive him headlong against the door, right across the apartment. Thankful was he to be allowed to pick up his clothes and disappear.

On the evening of my last day at Détroit I crossed the river to a little hedge-inn on the British side, close to Moy, at that time the residence of Mr. Mackintosh, a wealthy and respected merchant. Moy is close to Windsor, a flourishing little village famous for its fine pear-trees.

I had not been long sat, when in stepped a

bold pedlar, with pack and box. He was a broad-chested, short man, with a profusion of sandy whisker. "Well, mistress," said he, "I've had a long tramp this blazing day. I am both dry and hungry. Let us have something comfortable. But of course you know we must trade!" "No, indeed," the landlady replied, "I cannot; I do not want anything in your line." "But, mistress, it is the universal rule of the road." "Except here," says she; "my friend Sugarbutt deals with me, and I with him; and he knows to a day when my thread, soap, and tea are out." "Well, then, mistress," rejoined the pedlar, "at your greatest need may you have a cloudy new moon, your thread break, and your needle want an eye! We don't trade." He shouldered his bundle and departed.

In the meanwhile I was sitting at a little window of one pane, looking up the road. Soon after the pedlar had gone, I descried approaching at an easy pace two strange bearded figures, on large, rough horses, with saddle-bags behind them, and stout over-coats before.

They alighted at the door, in beards to be coveted,—in broad, slouching hats,—long, free-flowing coats, waistcoats, and trowsers of snuff-colour, with strings everywhere instead of buttons.

They were middle-aged men, bulky, erect, deliberate, with large, mild, satisfied faces — elders of the Mennonite persuasion on a tour of inspection among their people, scattered over the upper or western province.

Taking their place among us in the kitchen, they talked unreservedly with every one as they made their simple meal.

I joined them; and after some general conversation, I asked them why they dressed so differently from Christian people in general. The person to whom I addressed myself smiled, and said that dress was not a principal matter, and merely concerned the feelings, &c. For themselves, they bore a love to the Saviour so personal, that they wished to imitate him in outward things as in inward. As He wore a beard and loose garments, so did they. And further, they found this external badge or testimony a great safeguard against the seductions of the world, and any slowly progressive conformity with prevailing practices which might otherwise creep in among them. "Moreover," he added, "I am not sure that bearded Christians are so greatly in the minority throughout the earth as you have taken for granted."

I questioned them as to the great doctrines of revelation, and received correct and sober answers. They certainly differ from us widely in church government, but in little else of importance. As they lead the quiet, godly lives of believers, I could not but indulge them in their harmless peculiarities; and I felt in my heart to love them.

Their people, the elder went on to inform me, at my request, were to be found in many of the western districts, but are most numerous in Gore and Niagara. Many of them are Germans, or of German extraction. German families of Mennonite sentiments are now continually settling in Canada West from Pennsylvania, preferring the stillness and security of the British colony to the racket, worldliness, and most probably the petty persecutions (local), of the United States.

I once met in the woods a migratory family of this kind, reposing on their journey. They had with them two waggon-loads of substantial furniture, drawn by sleek, stout horses. The people themselves were pictures of health and common sense.

During the last war with the United States, when the Canadas were invaded, the British Government wisely permitted the Mennonites to remain at home peaceably, on commuting by money for military service. This was no hardship, because the war had produced high prices, of which the ordinary militia could not avail themselves, as their farms were necessarily neglected.

I afterwards passed through a district of Mennonites, between Fort Erie and Grand River, a swampy country, but with fertile and elevated spots here and there.

Though not a healthy neighbourhood, the Mennonites did not complain. I went into one or two of their houses, which were low, plain, but comfortable. Extreme neatness prevailed everywhere. Their brass vessels were as bright as gold, and their pewter looked like silver. Large pails of milk and cream stood pure and cool in their little dairies; the fatted calf and the home-reared lamb were playing about the homestead and orchard. The owners were a large, fair, calm race, evidently cheerful with Christian hope. I felt glad that there was upon earth such unruffled peace, enduring from childhood to old age—so complete a separation from the temptations and corrosions of ordinary life.

EXCURSION THE FIFTH.

PART II.

THE ST. CLAIR AND LAKE ERIE.

H. M. schooner Confiance — Lake St. Clair — Sickness — Sailor shot — River St. Clair — Belle Rivière Island — The sick Traveller — The banished Lord — The Black River — Fort St. Clair — Thunderstorms — Missionaries — Lake Erie — Boat Voyage — The Settlement — The Governor-General — The Methodist Missionary — Religious Statistics and Observations — Schools — The Storm — The Roman Catholic.

On returning to Détroit from my visit to Moy, as just related in the first part of this excursion, I found that H. M. schooner the Confiance had arrived at Amherstburgh from Penetanguishene, and would next day again mount stream for Lake St. Clair. I therefore early next morning, after a hurried leave-taking, hired a little skiff and two rowers for Amherstburgh, where I had several trifling matters to settle. I had, however, to take another opportunity; for about half-way down we met the Confiance painfully winning her way against the current.

The first thing I saw on deck was the round bald pate of Monsieur Pomainville, our purveyor, and his fine French features, as he was emerging from the hold, where he had been in search of a ham for dinner.

He was full of chat about good looks and a pleasant summer to come, but said no more. Four or five days afterwards, awaking from a siesta on the hot deck, he cried out, "Ah! M. le Docteur, I tell you while I remember, there are two letters from England for you in my cassette." "Then," said I, "had you better fetch them?" which he still seemed slow to do. They were letters from my family, of whom I had not heard for eleven months, through the post-office irregularities of that day. None but such as have been in my place can fully sympathise in my vexation at this tardy delivery of letters.

We were made as comfortable as possible in the gallant little Confiance. Many a happy day did I spend in her. She was commanded by Lieutenant Grant, R.N., the son of a banker of that name at Portsmouth.

Our first surveying operations lay among the many mouths of the River St. Clair. They form a number of large, marshy islands, of course partly in Lake St. Clair. Neither of these, nor of the lake, shall I say much topographically, as they present no striking features.

We were three or four days in working our way from Amherstburgh to a convenient berth in Anchor Bay, near the north-west shore of Lake St. Clair.

When we arrived we found the scenery here very pretty, the borders of the lake, for miles inland, being a savannah of long, bright green grass, with woods in the rear disposed in capes, islands, and devious avenues. I was delighted, and landed for a run; but to my surprise, I stepped into water ankle-deep, and forthwith returned. But a more serious evil was the bad quality of the water, as we were to be here for several days, and the weather sultry and close. It was tainted and discoloured by the dead bodies of a minute pink insect, and was only drinkable after straining and boiling.

Our people spent most of the daylight in the insular channels, and Lieutenant Grant in sounding the lake. The natural result of all this was sickness; but while in the lake the only person seriously ill was my friend the lieutenant. He was attacked by the dangerous fever of the country, with great general excitement, delirium, &c. &c., but bleeding and other appropriate remedies brought him round, first, by conversion of the continued fever into the remittent, and then into common ague, which was driven off by quinine.

Other members of the working party were attacked more slightly a few days afterwards in the River St. Clair, but in such numbers that the survey was discontinued for a fortnight.

From this pestilential spot we removed, in the prosecution of our work, to one of the channels in the island of St. Mary near Baldoon, amid aguish meadows of coarse grass, now (1845) cultivated after a fashion by various remnants of Indian tribes.

As the place looked very likely for game, and the sailors had little to do, permission was given to four or five of them to beat up with fowling-pieces an open marsh of many hundred acres close to us, with clumps of wood on the higher ground.

Towards evening one of the sporting sailors came running to the schooner, to say that a comrade had shot himself; but he was so breathless and frightened, that he could only point in the direction of the body about a mile off. Three or four of us ran off, and, after a little search, we found the unfortunate man quite dead, lying across his discharged gun, on his face, which was in a pool of blood. The cast-off skin of a snake, beautifully perfect, lay near him. As there was nothing to point to foul play, we supposed that he had struck at the seeming snake with the butt-end of his gun, and that the gun had gone off and lodged its contents in the neck, where we found a small round hole close to the jugular vessels.

The seamen—all of us, indeed—were very much affected by this deplorable accident, far more so than I could have anticipated.

His companions carefully prepared for his grave a strong wooden slab, on which they engraved an epitaph of their own composition.

The burial-service was read over the remains, and listened to with unaffected grief, which did not wholly disappear from our countenances until we moved to Belle Rivière Island in the River St. Clair.

There is little to describe in Lake St. Clair. It is a round pond exaggerated into a circumference of ninety miles, extremely shallow, and surrounded by marshes and low woods, with occasionally an unhappy clearance. The ship-channel to Lake Huron is very narrow, and so changeable, that it requires fresh buoying every spring. Its shallowest part has only a depth of 6½ feet.

Its principal rivers are the Thames, the Huron,

and the Bear Creeks. I shall only speak a few words on the first, one of the most important and picturesque of the second-class streams in Canada West.

It is navigable for sloops and steamers to Louisville, thirty miles from its mouth, with an average depth of 16 feet, and a breadth of 200–300 feet. This river passes through some of the finest parts of Canada West, among farming-land of the first quality. Many of the farms here have been under cultivation for fifty years, and have fine orchards.

The flourishing town of London (eighty-five miles from Hamilton in Lake Ontario), with 4000 inhabitants, is situated upon it, as well as Chatham, with a population of nearly 2000, sixty-six miles below London.

We now made our way into the River St. Clair, and cast anchor at the head of Belle Rivière Island, five or six miles from the lake. This river runs a tolerably straight course of thirty miles long, and from three-quarters to a mile and a half broad. Its banks of earth and clay are high along the upper and middle portions, but lower down they gradually sink into marshes.

As before mentioned, the banks of this river are, upon the whole, well settled.

Belle Rivière Island is so called from the considerable creek of that name which enters opposite to it on the south. This island may measure about a hundred acres. It is many feet above the river, and is, for the most part, covered with fine wood.

We soon cleared sufficient space for three or four tents on the bluff at the upper end, commanding a fine reach, with a line of farms on the American side, and on the other a wilderness: the whole settlement on the British shore having, in 1813–14, been clean swept away, burnt, and devastated, in the winter, by the American soldiery, destroying, in its brutality, the means of existence of non-combatants.

A weaker growth of trees, or small, grassy openings, with the gables of ruined houses, still mark the spots.

A beginning was made, in 1821, to re-people this fertile district. Now (1847) the whole north front of the river is occupied; and there are the two cheerful villages of Sutherland and Talfourd, each with its neat Episcopal church smiling upon the wilderness.

We were a week at Belle Rivière. Several little characteristic incidents occurred while we were there.

Not always having a boat at my command, I remained for the most part on the island. On the third day of our stay, scrambling along the tangled margin of the island with the intention of going round it, I saw, some hundred yards from our camp, that the long grass and coppice were beat down and broken into a barely discernible pathway. I mounted by it into the thicket, and fifty yards from the water, hid from all the world, I fell in with a squatter's bark hut, in a clearing of a hundred square feet, on which were planted some potatoes and a few hillocks of Indian corn. The door was open, and on the threshold a couple of neatly-dressed white women were sitting at needle-work, mother and daughter, the younger being the wife of a shoemaker. Their little place was clean and tidy. They showed no alarm: neither did their stout dog attack me. They said that the husband was mending shoes in the vicinity.

I have no doubt but they were in hiding for some unpleasant reason. We had been three days within 400 yards of them without their stirring or approaching us; but now we gave the man a good deal of employment, and the women washed for us.

It was from our present encampment that I watched the first labours of a settler in the woods, as related in the excursion to the Ottawa River.

One very hot day, the sun in mid-heavens, without a friendly cloud to screen us from his fierceness, I observed a canoe, with two men in it, leave the American shore and make for our tents. Their errand was to ask me to visit a young man at their house hard by, ill of the country fever. Of course I went with them.

He was a respectable young American from Oswego, on the south shore of Lake Ontario, on a tour of commercial inquiry, and detained here by this sudden attack.

I found him lying on a hard, uncurtained bed, in a large, low room, with the open window looking into an orchard of apple and peach-trees, then teeming with young fruit.

My patient was passing from the morbid strength of the hot period of a severe remittent fever into the languor of the perspiring stage, and presented a spectacle which few but medical men and clergymen ever see. To use the beautiful expression of an old French writer, he looked like "*le roi déchu* des existences de ce monde" (the discrowned king of nature).

As yet, the pink and white features glowed with most expressive brightness; the liquid eye, vermilion-tinted, was full of painful meaning.*

* In the latter stages of consumption, and in other disturbances of the circulation, when the connexion of soul and body is loosen-

His voice was a whisper, but earnest, and almost spasmodic. The face and heaving chest were beaded by a thousand drops of moisture; and although his feeble arm, when let go, dropped like lead, he was restless, and fought feebly with the flies and mosquitoes which always infest the sick.

I spoke to him encouragingly, told him he should be well attended to, said that I had been at Oswego, and should soon pass through it again. He eagerly interrupted me to beg I would call on his mother and sister, and threw his eyes on his portmanteau, which was near on a chair; but I begged him not to think of business for a day or two; and for some moments he was quiet.

ing, an extraordinary and singularly delicate impress of the new and angelic life is occasionally stamped on the features at certain periods of the day: so, in the hot stage of a severe remittent, the general contour becomes full, and the complexion fervidly brilliant, the most ordinary face is rendered beautiful by some new arrangement of its parts. Arterial blood is evidently accumulated on the surface, and is also stimulating the brain to vivid sensation and thought; so that every part of the frame—every expression, tone, and movement—becomes instinct with unwonted eloquence and force. I have seen this among the humbler classes repeatedly, in persons and places least expected, and in the young of both sexes especially. But when the individual has mixed with pious persons of superior education, the change is still more striking and more lofty. There is then a heavenward tendency, an exalted purity and serene joy, most affecting to contemplate.

He was with kind but ignorant people. The case was similar to that from which our commander was recovering, but the prostration was greater. I had some trouble with him, but he eventually recovered.

As we float over the smooth waters of the St. Clair, having perhaps just escaped from the turbulence of Lake Huron, it is delightful to gaze upon the succession of dwellings, low and roomy, which its western bank presents, embowered in orchards, the children playing under the far-spreading elms, and the cattle grazing in rich meadows; but if you land, the effect is greatly damaged. You are shocked at the meagre, sickly appearance of the inhabitants. They have the thin white face, the feeble, stooping walk of the over-wrought, in-door artizan of an European city. Their minds, you find, are almost as unready and infirm as their bodies. Neither, at the time of my several visits, were they blest with the consolations of religion, except at distant and irregular periods.

The vast tracts of marsh lands around are the cause of all this, bringing upon the settlers the constantly-recurring plague of ague and remittent fever, to be remedied by drainage sooner or later.

It is common for the borders of American rivers to be dry for a mile or so back, and then the land sinks into swampy and rolling country.

The American climate is, at best, changeable, first exciting and afterwards exhausting. Its heat and cold are in extremes, very often most agreeable, exhilarating, from its remarkable dryness, both in winter and summer.

Great portions of the unsettled lands in the United States are extremely unhealthy: such as the south sides of Lakes Ontario and Erie, the states of Illinois, Indiana, and Mississippi; while Canada, except in the extreme south-west, is all but *perfectly* healthy. I would not wish to live in a more salubrious climate than that of the Bay of Quinté, the River Ottawa, the eastern shores of Lake Huron, and many other places; and I am immeasurably astonished at parties from England preferring unwholesome, distant, and often lawless parts of the United States, to regions of plenty and health in this colony, under laws and customs with which they are familiar.

I have reason to believe that the excessive quantity of animal food, which the Americans hurry down, injures them seriously; perhaps bringing on in early life what our Irish recruits call the meat fever, and giving rise to a weakened and too excitable state of the alimentary canal for the rest of their existence. Then come the deleterious agencies of tobacco, ardent spirits, and ill-regulated labour.

Compare the meagre, ill-set frame of the American farmer, and his haggard, uneasy features, with the robust, compact figure of the English yeoman, his open, ruddy, smooth face; and say which of the two is the stronger and happier animal.

In the extensive and fertile districts about Lake Erie, and to the south of Lakes Huron and Michigan, both man and beasts suffer grievously from insects. During the months of June, July, and August, mosquitoes torture thick-skinned animals even more than man. Fires of wet leaves and grass, which give out great volumes of smoke, are made for them to run into; and so anxiously do they thus take shelter there, that many of them are severely burnt. Animals are much troubled here with a fly which I do not see elsewhere. It is of the same shape as the large fly of the butchers' shops, but is black, an inch long and more, and is armed with a long sheathed lance, which enters deep, and brings out the blood in streams. They often attack men, as I have personally experienced. Their incision is not poisonous, like that of the sand or black fly and mosquitoe. We only know that we have been bitten by an effusion of blood, as if a small vein had been opened.

Along the Rivers Détroit and St. Clair you may see in a meadow a number of cattle trying to feed, with their tails in constant motion, when all at once perpendicular up goes the tail, and the whole troop is cantering round the field, in the vain hope of getting rid of the flies. After a time, if possible, they rush into the water, and there remain with nothing but the nostrils and eyes visible. Many a time have I observed the patient eyes of the poor beast watching the progress of my canoe, and the momentary bobbing into the water of their heads to shake off some impudent mosquitoe.

I was sitting about mid-day in the shade near my tent on Belle Isle, the sky on fire, as is usual at that hour, and the gossamer air trembling over the shiny river. Having been immersed in one of Coleridge's rhymed dreams, I happened to raise my eyes, and saw coming down the stream in a canoe a strange-looking person standing upright, with a double-barrelled fowling-piece in his hand, while a boy in the stern was paddling direct for our camp. They landed close to me, and climbed the little bluff on which I was posted. A more singular Robinson Crusoe-like figure I never beheld than the elder stranger.

In the sequel everything was explained. Although seldom seen on the St. Clair, this gentleman was not unknown, and was called by the squatters "the Banished Lord." They knew no other name. His speech and bearing at once revealed that he was an Englishman of distinction. How he came there was another thing. Perhaps he had been *mal-adroit* at Boodle's; or crossed in some darling wish; or else was simply eccentric —who knows? I did not then.

He was a middle-sized, well-made man, slender and sinewy, as erect as at twenty-five, although evidently much on the wrong side of fifty. He had a small, oval, wrinkled face, with the ruddy bloom of out-door life still lingering on it. There had been a time when he was handsome and very fair. His eyes were grey, bold, and uneasy; the nose rather high and well-formed, as well as his lips; and he could not stand steady, on account of a little nervous twitch which was always at work somewhere. He had on a rusty, napless, but well-shaped hat, with some turns of cord round it. His coat was green, single-breasted, built in the year one, and patched with drabs and greens of all hues and shapes, evidently with his own hands, with white thread, most unskilfully. Two or three coils of leather thongs hung in his coat button-holes, as if to carry home game with. The first time I saw him he had no waistcoat; but a coarse clean shirt covered his chest, crossed with a silver watch-guard; but in cooler weather he wore a deer-skin vest up to his throat. His pantaloons were of faded blue calico, fitting loosely, and tightened below the knee with leather straps. His foot-wear was the strong mocassin, the best of all for woods and rocks.

His young scamp of a boy was in corduroy and cap, and was soon lying on the grass looking at the sun through his fingers.

"Sir," said my visitor, when he had made good his footing beside me, "it is very seldom that an Englishman is met with in these waters; we see him pass — that is all. I heard, at my place on the Bear Creek, of your surveyors planting their little red and white flags up and down the St. Clair, so I thought I would take a peep at you, and knock over a turkey on the way; but I have had no sport as yet. Seeing that you are at ease and idle on this bright working-day, what office do you hold in the camp?"

"I have the honour to be, sir," I said, in reply, "*medico* to the Boundary Commission, and British secretary. I may surely say that we are honoured by your visit. I am sorry my friends are out on duty, and that the Commissioners themselves are not with us." He then asked a variety of particulars about our proceedings.

The secluded life of the banished lord seemed to have blunted no faculty. He was not a hollow-eyed misanthrope; but, with a dash of the eccentric, was full of right thoughts; and fitting expressions for them were found at will.

As I was on the wing, and not likely to intrude into his den on the Bear Creek, he was pleased to talk freely with me. He took a gloomy view of the domestic state of Great Britain, and expressed his satisfaction at having escaped from an impending storm, from the great conflict he saw about to arise between the popular will and George the Fourth's camarilla.

"There are," said he, "vast questions, religious, political, and commercial, to be settled, by many destructive oscillations between extremes, and hundreds of thousands will pay in purse or person. Then, sir, I see a very bad sign in great force. Property of all kinds is centring in vast masses, while the millions are in the deepest poverty. In England, destitution will not sit tamely down by the side of repletion. The king cares not to see this; and the great party now at the helm of state will not. The people are silently educating for the struggle; and it will take place in my day. Therefore I fled, as have done many others; but most of them into the United States.* As I have had in my day a good fill of London life, and am passionately fond of field sports, I rushed into the most solitary wild I could find. I was led by mere chance to Bear Creek, in Sombra. It abounds in game of all kinds—the deer, moose, wolf, bear, water-fowl, turkey, and so forth. My patch of land lies high, in a dry section, and we live in health and plenty. It is true, and I confess it, I have been too impetuous. The change was too violent and sudden for my poor wife, who, although she had to suffer much from my relatives, and gladly escaped from them, yet she drooped and wearied in our lone place, and was every day missing some little comfort or other. I could have had all I enjoy here, within fifty miles of Montreal, with easy access to gossip and female fal-lals. She died about four years ago. And now a new and pressing concern has grown up — what to do with two boys and a girl; and, truth to tell, I get stiffer in the joints; so that I am now pondering on a return to civilized life for the education of my children."

The exile had all the talk to himself. He par-

* At this period two or three gentlemen gave me these reasons in nearly the same words for withdrawing themselves and their property from England. They were nervous persons, and liable to act on sudden impulses.

took of some refreshment, and took a courteous leave. His home was six or seven miles into the woods, along a blaze, a little distance lower down the river. I saw him again at Fort St. Clair, our next station on this stream, at the mouth of the Black River, a large affluent from the south.

I had in the meantime obtained some information about him; but his name I did not learn. His reserve and lofty manner, together with some command of money, had procured for him his bye-name.* He had been a good husband. His small farm was in tolerable order. His singular dress must have been a whim. He made no companions, save one or two good shots, who lived ten miles from him; and now and then he had a hurricane tobacco-smoke with a renowned Indian hunter.

At Fort St. Clair he brought me his daughter, ten years old — a handsome, freckled, sunburnt lass, and somewhat delicate in appearance; but full of spirits, as she did not know the object of her visit; which was to have a surplus tooth extracted: this, of course, was done — but re-

* While not very young he had made a *mésalliance* with a beautiful and gentle girl, who joyfully vowed in an English drawing-room to follow the man of her heart anywhere — across the ocean, and into the wilderness; but she sank under the rudeness, the gloom, and strangeness of her new abode.

luctantly. I do not like pulling at ladies' teeth. They never forgive you; but you are to them an executioner for all time.

I suggested to the father the propriety of sending this forest-maid to England, or at least to a good school at Toronto or Kingston; and he took my words in good part.

In the Canadas remarkable persons are continually turning up. The Chevalier and Madame de Brosse are not the only members of the old court of France in the western country. I have repeatedly passed the house (then shut up, and going to ruin) of the Count and Countess of K., persons of high consideration in France before 1790, now long since dead. They had no children, and literally shut themselves up in a Swiss cottage, which they built on the Niagara frontier. It had a heavy roof, and two wooden galleries running round it.

I was extremely pleased (as well as surprised) one Sunday in the woods by a sermon preached by a meek old clergyman, passionless quite, externally, in a little church hid in a wood, and hardly holding thirty persons. I asked an old farmer how it came that such piety and such eloquence were so buried in that out-of-the-world nook? "Mr. Addison," replied he, "is beloved far and wide; but he won't quit his first haven of rest. Thirty years ago he came here from England a broken-hearted widower, with two little daughters. They are married and gone; but he will not go till soul and body part."

I could easily increase this list, if necessary.

The survey having been completed from lake St. Clair up to and beyond Belle Isle, the camp was moved to the mouth of the Black River, ten miles higher up, the British bank being then a forest, and the American occupied by good farms, the brisk and sparkling river running between.

We took possession of a deserted orchard, thirty feet above the St. Clair, and close to the site of an old French fort, on the left bank of the Black River.

The astronomer and all his party left me here for the head of the St. Clair, intending to survey homewards. The bulk of the stores remained with me.

I only saw my friends once in the three weeks of my stay there: company I had none but my servant. There was a large house about three hundred yards off; but it only contained two women and some small shy children. My sight was now and then gladdened by a schooner dropping lazily down the stream, or by the quicker flight of a canoe.

The weather (June 10) was for a week truly

dreadful. For a moment I thought of deserting my charge. Every evening brought its severe thunderstorm and torrents of rain. The lightning every ten minutes during the tempest plunged into the surrounding woods in comparatively thick columns. Trees and cattle were struck; and a woman was so excited by the proximity of one flash, that I bled her with benefit. One dark and stormy night, although my tent was sheltered by trees, the wind blew it down while I was asleep. I thought the wet canvas would have suffocated me; and I was only released after much exertion.

The clouds never left our sky; the mornings were gloomy; but it was in the evening that the tempests occurred. The Black River rose, and brought down an abundance of mud and trees.

One night, a little before dusk, as I stood by its margin, watching the large tree-roots and the entangled masses of turf and stones as they swept down the boiling stream, three men on horseback, with large-caped great-coats, came to the opposite bank, travellers evidently. They shouted for the ferryman; but there was no such official; and my servant had been taken for the survey in place of a boatman laid up with fever. There lay close to me a large pirogue (a hollowed tree-trunk), with a good deal of water in it. But who was to navigate such a ticklish water-machine? —none but myself, utterly inexperienced in that sort of navigation.

I did not like either the vessel or the troubled stream; but, after a little more shouting, I caught the word "Mission!" when the thought struck me — partly jocosely, I fear — that if I was to be drowned it could not be in a better cause. So I fetched a bowl, and baled the rain-water out of the pirogue; and, seizing a broad, heavy paddle, loosed my bark, with no little trepidation, and drove her to the opposite shore. At three trips we then took the men and horses across. By this time it was becoming dusk.

I ran over to the large house, and asked shelter for the dripping horses, and for a little butter; for the party consisted of my friend, Captain Stewart, and two American clergymen, on their way to establish a mission among the Saguina Indians, on the fertile banks of a river of that name in Lake Huron.

I was delighted with my guests, and forthwith covered the two short planks which formed my table with biscuit, chocolate, and some savoury salt pork. Then having placed the large kettle full of water on the fire, I had done my best.

"Captain Stewart," said I, "all the articles that are on the table belong to the King of England. Do you think it right to refresh your republican friends with them?"

"Yes," he answered, "for they are the servants of the King of kings. But," he went on to say, "we have not travelled far to-day; could not Mr. Hudson address a little congregation after supper? The few settlers here are far from church or chapel; it would be a pity to let such an opportunity slip."

As the night was creeping on, I ran again to the house (which I had never approached till that day), and prevailed upon the females to give us the use of their largest room, and to light it up with four home-made candles firmly stuck into the plastered walls. Not only that, but they started off a girl, bareheaded, into the bog for some Irish families, while I ran half-a-mile up the river-side, to tell the people of four huts there that a prayer-meeting would be held at Mrs. Palmer's in twenty minutes.

At half-past nine o'clock we entered the lighted-up room, and were agreeably surprised to find thirty persons assembled — straight-haired, long-faced Yankees, with their wives and children; some shock-headed Irish, all shining with haste, and taking the affair partly as a show, and partly for instruction.

The service was conducted in the Presbyterian

method, almost wholly by the Rev. Mr. Hudson; his brother missionary and Captain Stewart only adding a few sentences; the latter in his usual brief, direct, and soldier-like style.

An easy tune to well-known words enabled most of the assembly to join in the hymn. The sermon was very suitable. The attention was great, and much thankfulness afterwards expressed."

The Irish were such freckled, red-headed, thorough Celts, with the characteristic massy jaws, that I have no doubt but they were Roman Catholics; if so, their presence in that assembly was creditable to them.

Our three friends slept on the floor of the room which they had consecrated, and early next morning they were on their journey.

This seems not an unfitting place for a few desultory remarks on missions to the Indians, suggested by the visit which has been just described.

Are we to be contented with the puny efforts at present in operation towards making this finely-organised and impressible race of red men acquainted with the blessings of the Christian religion? Is it enough to be idly repeating "the wordless mourning of the dove?" Should we not be doing?

In 1848 there were 14,000 Indians in the Canadas, and very many more in the Hudson's Bay territories, while the missionaries were extremely few.

I am persuaded that there is not an inhabited place on the earth's surface where a Christian, with God's blessing, may not convert souls, and raise a church and churches. Nothing can withstand the excellence and loveliness of Gospel principles arrayed in the brightness of a Gospel life. Success is not doubtful. It is simply an affair of time, patience, and prayer.

The following Indian stations should be occupied immediately: — The Rice Lake, on Lake Ontario; the Sheriff Valley, on the Ottawa; the River St. Clair; Penetanguishene; the Falls of St. Mary; the Rainy Lake and River; the Saskatchawine, and its many branches; the Peace River; and many points on the sides of the Rocky Mountains.

These may suffice for the present; for faith is weak, and love is cold. Englishmen have pitched so high the standard of personal comforts and family display, that there is but a small surplus left with which to scatter blessings. Evangelisation is expensive, and requires support from without. The rich will not go; at least none that I know of, since good Dean Berkley went to Bermuda a hundred years ago. It is even difficult to find a suitable *paid* missionary. It is sad to think that the maintenance of the missionary interest at home and the collection of the necessary funds are only accomplished by the super-human exertions of a few, who leave no decent means untried, no argument unpressed, and no corner of England unvisited, in behalf of this best of causes.

I desire chiefly and emphatically to insist upon this great point — that, if possible, missionaries should go out in numbers together, and act upon fixed principles, under the guidance of a responsible local head, to whom you may give any name you please. Missions should not be, as hitherto, established piecemeal and fortuitously, but according to some well-digested plan, taking in the present and future wants of a considerable region. Hitherto, in our schemes, we have not looked into the bright future, but have been confined to the limited prospects of to-day.

It has too frequently been forgotten that conversion from heathenism includes civilization; that therefore conversion brings new wants, new sensations, and new decencies; for all which there should be provision.

In the Indian countries of North America, the missionary should be enabled to show in a striking manner that the practice of Christianity is great gain in this life. He should therefore be accompanied from our shores by a considerable staff of assistants, ready to operate upon the heathen mind in a variety of ways simultaneously — as through the schoolmaster, the medical man, the cultivator, and the various artisans, as well as by his own ministrations, which should fertilize and sanctify the whole.

The permission of the authorities (such as they are) of the district to be operated upon having been obtained, a model village should be established as a palpable object, showing forth all the privileges, comforts, and security of the Christian economy. The Indian should be invited to reside in the village; the young men and women should be taken into the missionary-house as helpers, and as near witnesses to the amenities and graces of a Christian household. They will be the first converts.

Schools, the chief means of conversion for the first twenty years, should be gradually established. The necessity for continuous labour must be cautiously insinuated, because the savage is extremely averse from it. The many simpler arts of agriculture or manufacture should be taught; and, above most things, the weak, aged, and sick should be fed, cured, and cared for.

If these points be kept in view in any tolerable manner, and the Gospel at the same time plainly and affectionately preached, by the blessing of

God, in due season, the result wished for—conversions not only numerous but permanent, will follow; chiefly, however, among the young and very young, rarely among the middle-aged and old, who will have to die off, as a rule, with occasional gratifying exceptions. Their minds are so bricked up with heathen habits and prejudices, that the good news can scarce enter. Meeting with no response in their hearts, it is an unknown sound, and has no significance.

Thus, the grand system of converting the Indians is to provide as many large regions as possible with some such centre of Christian civilization as that just adverted to, with ramifications here and there, as circumstances point out, the branches superintended if possible by natives.

This plan economises labour, and greatly hastens the appearing and ripening of fruit. It is especially adapted to the rude populations of North America, Africa, and the South Seas.

The relief thus brought to the clerical missionary by the division of labour and by the sustaining proximity of friends is enormous; it quadruples his forces.

I speak the more earnestly, inasmuch as I have looked upon the dejected face of the solitary labourer among the heathen, bowed to the earth by weakness and anxiety within; and without, by the perversity and fickleness of his converts, and the active rage of his enemies.

These missionary communities were one great means of propagating the Christianity of the middle ages. St. Bernard planted his Clairvaux among marshes and woods, far away from ordinary society. These deserts he and his companions drained and cultivated; by their kindness and wisdom attracting, in the course of time, a large and prosperous population, untouched by the desolating wars of those dreadful times. There were then many such social and religious asylums in Europe, or man must have been extirpated; and each had its off-sets, sanctuaries of knowledge and help, to which the regions around gratefully resorted.

Something like this has been practised by British missionary societies in modern times, but not fully and systematically. I plead for this as the best and most effectual method.

The Christians of the United States, in their missions to the Osage, Sioux, and other Indians, have long made use of associate groups of labourers, and their success has been proportionate.

One of the most comely spectacles in the world is exhibited in the United States, when one of these missionary bodies is travelling from some city on the shores of the Atlantic westward to the Indian countries. They journey all together.

The time of their arrival being previously known at the towns and principal villages on the route, they are met at convenient distances, and, after a short interval of cordial greetings and prayer, are escorted with singing into the town, where they are entertained by the chief inhabitants. The evangelists depart in the same way, and are often laden with such gifts as are likely to be of use in the wilderness.

This apostolic tribute of respect and sympathy frequently occurs. I wish it were constant.

I have reason to believe that the American Board of Missions will not suffer their agents to accept of or purchase land from the natives under any pretence. This is a point upon which all barbarous people are peculiarly sensitive and jealous. Missionaries are not to pay themselves in this way. Their motives must be beyond suspicion. No policy can be more injurious to the cause of missions than that of grasping or even accepting land. A great English missionary society, otherwise admirably conducted, has made the unhappy mistake of permitting its missionaries to acquire land from the natives; with great reluctance, doubtless.* An association of Quakers at Philadelphia, some years ago, sent a mixed body of preachers and artisans

* *Vide* Report for 1849.

to the Pawnees (or Osages). The Indians granted them permission to occupy from three hundred to four hundred acres of land. They became greatly attached to the wise and patient strangers, fond of their society, and received from them daily benefits in the shape of clothing, medicine, reparation of tools, education, counsel, and especially, what was fast beginning to appear of the most importance, the message of heavenly peace. All was prospering, when enemies to the Gospel from a distance interposed their opinions. "This is the way of the pale faces," said they; "they are enslaving you. Your land they have, and strong houses upon it. They will soon have your hunting-grounds and yourselves. Go into the white country. Have they charmed their own people to be such fools as you are?" The Indians deserted the mission. The Friends immediately perceived the change and the cause of it. They were ordered by their employers at Philadelphia to break up and come home directly. The Pawnees did not hinder them; but in a little time they discovered the loss they had sustained. Some few, from the first, were inconsolable from honest affection; more regretted the lost helps and comforts; the birds ate up their ill-sown and neglected corn; the guns, hoes, and spade were useless. They had begun to delight in the Bible, but there was no interpreter. They were at their wits' end, until they resolved to send a deputation a thousand miles to Philadelphia to bring back their benefactors at any price. The Quakers returned. (*Weyland on Population.*)

If there seem so much ground to be occupied, and the means so scanty as not to permit the planting of large missionary societies, a married missionary, with or without a schoolmaster, is the next best method of conducting this excellent work. Their strength should be principally spent among the young, and in the formation of schools for both sexes. From hence comes the main harvest. Itinerancy, for the purpose of preaching and the distribution of tracts, need not be neglected, but it should be quite a secondary object at a new station. While little impression is thus made upon the older people, a great injury is done to the health of the missionary by the unavoidable exposure to the sun. A room or chapel must be set apart at or near the missionary premises for the regular celebration of Divine service, to which the natives should be kindly and urgently invited.

If missionary societies were to establish a system of periodic inspection by persons of piety, influence, and practical wisdom, the benefit would be great. Mr. Backhouse and his friend were of very considerable service in visiting at their own charges the numerous missionary stations in South Africa, the Mauritius, and elsewhere.

The publication of the report of such tours would pay the greater part of the expense; and, now that steam pervades all lands, the labour and loss of time would not be great. Such publication would stimulate and comfort the distant missionary, and vindicate him when unjustly accused, for evil tales are not wanting in the South Seas, &c. It would rectify mistakes, and stop rising abuses. It is my conviction that our missionaries in the mass are doing their work well, and are thoroughly worthy of our esteem and support.

Missionaries should be adapted to their spheres of action. Send the scholar and the controversialist to the Mahometans, the Chinese, and Hindoos, men of disciplined minds and literary tastes, Send the plain man of God, of a simple character and patient, familiar with the common arts of domestic life, to the uncivilised tribes of North America, &c.

Too much time, I fear, has hitherto been allotted to Latin and Greek in our missionary institutions;—not that they are to be altogether thrown aside, but I am clear that they have greatly usurped the place of more practical things, such as some acquaintance with medicine and surgery (the great recommendation in heathen lands), the management of schools, the use of tools, the reclaiming of wild land. Every missionary should spend a little time at an agricultural college. A great part of the value of a missionary, it should never be forgotten, lies in his being a good administrator, the skilful director of a group of minds not so gifted as his own.

These things will teach the servant of God, among other things, how to provide occupation (so indispensable to the best of us) for his convert, and how to enable that convert to earn his own independent bread,—a power so elevating to the individual, and so carefully insisted on in the Scriptures. The change from the heathen to the Christian often involves a total change in the mode of subsistence, and is one of the greatest obstacles met with in hunting and pastoral countries.

Who have been the most successful missionaries? Not the men of high collegiate attainments. They are invaluable as translators; but the great pioneers, the most eminent cross-bearers, those who have sweetly drawn multitudes into the Gospel net, are Brainerd, Swartz, Moffat, Freeman, Cochran,*

* A schoolmaster in 1825 in a secluded village in Nottinghamshire, and afterwards eminently successful as an ordained minister of the Church of England at the Red River Settlement, Hudson's Bay.

John Williams, who fell at Rarotonga, and the two brothers Williams of New Zealand.* These are a few among many, all full of Bible principles,

* The two Williams' are from the same county as Cochran. Their usefulness has been so great, and their preparation for the work so appropriate, as to be unmistakeably providential.

Their mother was a pious and talented lady. She devoted herself exclusively to the education of her numerous family; first and foremost, doubtless, imbuing them with her own personal interest in the Saviour and his grand designs.

In secular matters her method was that of Pestalozzi, before his day. She familiarized her children with the origin, nature, and uses of every object that met their eye. In a large workroom given up to them, they were taught to delight in the use of tools and how to construct boxes, tables, ships, globes, philosophical instruments, &c. &c. Every child too had his own garden.

Reverses in fortune soon afterwards followed, in which she and hers were blameless victims.

Henry, the elder brother, entered the navy, obtained a lieutenancy, and long bore the buffetings of the sea. Being placed on half-pay, he married wisely, and in no long time sailed as a missionary in the service of the Church Missionary Society, in 1822, to New Zealand, then in the undisturbed possession of the cannibals.

His younger brother William was (and is) of a remarkably mild disposition. He for some years studied medicine at Southwell, &c., but in the end was received into holy orders, and followed his brother Henry. These brothers were from the first unconsciously fitting for hardships and perils under the eye of a Christian mother, who, it is pleasant to record, saw the fruit long waited for.

Hence in New Zealand they were prepared to face the savages, to build houses, a missionary ship, make furniture, and thus, assisted by their Wesleyan missionary brethren, they became the honoured instruments of causing the desolations of heathenism to disappear before the felicities of the Christian religion.

of great practical skill in governing and educating barbarians.

These men have been mostly taken from a rank of life somewhat below that from which the Episcopal clergy are taken. They have not been too delicately brought up, and are ready to meet cheerfully great personal privations.

The class of men especially fitted for this work are farmers' sons of piety, good constitution, and skilled in country labours. A large acquaintance with the Bible, and some knowledge of languages, are also necessary. Such have hitherto been the best Wesleyan missionaries.

I think I see a long line of efficient and pious labourers in this field, about to spring from the new order of schoolmasters and mistresses preparing, by the help of government grants, from among city missionaries, and from the colonies themselves.

The colonies now contain a large and stirring population. I have seen in the Canadas several young men well adapted to American missionary work, but there is great reason to expect difficulties and opposition to any great and liberal effort from the known ultra high-church principles of some of our colonial bishops.

Lest I write a pamphlet, I must now return to the St. Clair and Lake Erie.

Having finished our survey of these waters, we left Fort St. Clair on the 1st or 2d of July; very gladly on my part, for although pretty confident in the powers of my constitution, I did not like the kind of country. Clearances having greatly extended since 1821, it may be more healthy now.

We sailed in the Confiance to Amherstburgh, where for a fortnight or so we took leave of that pleasant vessel.

After a day spent in refitting and revictualling, we left in our own roomy barge for a spot on the shore of Lake Erie, near "The Settlement," in the township of Colchester.

We embarked after an early dinner on a still and sultry day. Gliding gently past the picturesque and not unenvied cottages which stud the Détroit river-side, the last being that of my friends the Chevalier and Madame de Brosse, we entered the broad expanse of Lake Erie;—no land in sight, southerly, except a few specks, called the Sister Isles, and the low mainland, nowhere visible for any distance.

We hugged the north or British shore for twelve miles, with just enough water to float in.

For much of the way it was not easy to point out the actual margin of the lake. There was a curious intermingling of forest, grassy savannahs, and clear water. On narrow ridges of land were growing most august plane-trees in prolonged rows, with a magnificent profusion of leafage. Other trees in drier situations, such as the oak, chestnut, black walnut, were remarkably fine, such as the Huron and other northerly districts cannot boast of.

Upon the long and tortuous roots of trees which jut into the lake, terrapins (fresh-water turtles) were in hundreds, with their little twinkling eyes, sitting as quiet as mice, but plunging by dozens into the water as we approached. They are from six to ten inches long, and prettily marked.

Entangled among these tree-roots, rocked by the waves, we saw a poor dead deer, which, from the freshness of its dapple skin, must have been alive that day.

After a few miles of this low umbrageous country, "a world of leaves, and dews, and summer airs," rises a line of earthy cliffs, from thirty to one hundred and fifty feet high, which continues for many leagues, nay, throughout the principal part of the north shore of Lake Erie.

We pitched our tents about five miles from the north end of these cliffs, on their flat summit, one hundred and fifty feet above the lake, and commanding a very striking range of view.

Standing with my back to the lake, and looking northward from my tent-door, the eye swept over a vast surface—many miles—of low lands and marsh, beginning almost at our feet; an undulating and all but impassable jungle, full of ponds, reeds, alders, vines, willows, and such-like in the hollows, and of the harder woods in the little land that is dry, all of unusual luxuriance, and teeming with animal life, from the panther, the bear, the eagle, and the rattlesnake, down to the smallest insect that plies the wing. This pestiferous morass discharges its surplus waters by the Canard Creek into the River Détroit.

Close to us runs the rarely-trodden Talbot Road, skirting the whole of this side of Lake Erie, more or less practicable, and here overgrown with young trees, among which the graceful foliage of the sumach preponderates,—a sure indication of mosquitoes innumerable.

Turning round and looking south from our tents, we had before us the wide expanse of Lake Erie (for we had cut away the intervening shrubbery to let in the breeze). There was the opposite coast of Ohio, grey in the distance, and the intermediate waters, ornamented with groups of woody isles, from the leafy depths of some of which (the British) the smoke of a free negro hut arose,—an incense grateful to the Almighty Father of all, who hateth oppression.

The whole day after our arrival it had rained

in torrents, but in the evening the weather cleared up, and I ventured out for a walk eastward down the lake.

I had scarcely gone a mile when I met an illustrious group of travellers in most undignified pickle, just where the road was a mere track overgrown with coppice. It was no less than the Governor-General of British North America and suite, part on horseback and part in a country cart, all looking as jaded, and downcast, and saturated with moisture, as if they had been dragged through and through a mill-pond for their misdeeds.

I did not fail to show due reverence, and to offer the poor comforts of my tent; but, after receiving directions as to his route, the Earl of of Dalhousie wisely determined to continue his journey through the bush, sixteen miles more, to Amherstburgh, while there was light; for little had been done to the road further than to fell the trees and border it with a ditch. I do not forget that I was served with more than one ejectment into the raspberry bushes in travelling slowly and doubtingly along this same highway.

I also found my way one day westwards for a couple of miles. There I met with what is called "The Settlement," twelve or fourteen decent cottages, standing apart in a line, each with its cleared land behind. There may be many more, but I did not see them. The inhabitants were evidently decent, industrious people.

Close to the lake, in front of the Settlement, was an Episcopal church, with a tower of white limestone, nearly finished.

There is now a Baptist chapel also.

When I was there the religious wants of the people were differently supplied, and in the manner shown in the following little narrative:—

Towards dusk, on Saturday evening, I was sitting before my tent, thankful for the cool air from the waters, and examining some bright red sand I had found at the foot of the cliff, which proved to be small garnets, when a boy, while he tapped my shoulder, suddenly whispered into my ear, "There will be preaching at Widow Little's of the Settlement, at nine to-morrow morning."

Before I could thank him the boy was gone; and I ought to have mentioned, that a couple of hours before I had been roused by the heavy, measured fall of a horse's foot, an unusual sound; and soon there passed by me, on a well-fed bay mare, a man of about thirty-two years of age, of staid and intelligent features, rather good-looking, dressed in a good coat and waistcoat of dark-grey jane, with drab pantaloons, clean and tidy. He saluted me and rode on. This was the preacher.

At nine o'clock the next morning I was at Widow Little's. She was a respectable cottager, and, besides the willing heart, she had a room rather larger than her neighbours.

I found the place full of people, in their Sunday-clothes, sitting on a few high-backed chairs, and upon very low forms only intended for children.

All was earnest and solemn: every face showed a wish to learn. The missionary stood with his back close to the fire-place, and clearly and unaffectedly he read out entirely the beautiful hymn, which begins

"Yes, we trust the day is breaking!
Joyful times are near at hand!
God, the mighty God, is speaking,
By his word, in every land!"

And then, clasping with both hands the back of a chair, he led the spirited psalmody, in which the little company of about thirty, chiefly women and children, joined loudly and well.

A prayer followed, which I thought too long, but otherwise good; then another hymn, and after that a sermon from the text, "Arise, shine, for thy light is come," (Isa. lx. 1); on the necessity of salvation to all; that it is our first concern to seek for it ourselves, and then to endeavour to communicate it to others.*

The sermon was very striking, but not violent: indeed, except now and then, his tones were low and his manner unusually subdued.

He made many good remarks, and one or two which were called for by the occurrences of the day.

" I was sad and sorry," he said, " to find bro-
" ther Simmons lying on a bed of sickness, and
" some of his children were weakly.

" John has a heart for the work. When well,
" blessed be God, he could and did work both
" for his Redeemer and his neighbour.

" I pray that he may be soon restored to us;
" but now he can do nothing for anybody. He
" has lost that strength and harmony of feelings
" which we call health, and which is absolutely
" necessary either for thinking or doing.

* Although camp-meetings occasionally take place in Canada West, yet for six years I never was within reach of one. They cannot, therefore, be common.

The crazy and wicked scenes said to occur at them I take to be exceptional or exaggerated; though, doubtless, there is often a good deal of religious extravagance and absurdity. This is to be accounted for by the secluded lives of those who attend, the rareness to them of religious addresses, and the effect of sombre woods on the imagination. Simply being in a crowd is sufficient to intoxicate the inhabitant of a back-settlement.

" His fellow-creatures, nay, his dearest friends, " may be on the brink of destruction, but they " can have no help from John Simmons.

" For the present, disease has made him utterly " powerless. He is not to be reckoned upon— " scarcely for a prayer.

" This is very bad, if properly considered; but " let me tell you that there is a far deeper and " blacker pit than this. I mean where a man's " soul is diseased. A man with a diseased soul— " an unconverted man, if I am to speak out— " seeks the chief good, the spiritual good of " none. It is possible that he may desire the " carnal benefit of a few in the things which " perish in the using. Such a soul is dead and " insensible to the mercies of God in heaven and " earth. He is so blinded and infatuated as not " to feel his own misery by nature, and there- " fore seeks for no deliverance. How can such " a man deliver others? He has neither the " wish nor the power. He is the slave of Satan, " and Satan is as strong and cruel as ever; none of " his weapons of war have perished If there be " any answering this description before me now, let " us pray for him or her, until he become one of " the saved; until he call out in triumph, 'I was " ' dead, and now am alive.'

"And it rejoices me to tell you that the sol-"diers of the cross are every day becoming "bolder and more numerous. The baptism of "love is spreading, the kingdom of Christ is fast "enlarging, while that of the devil is dimi-"nishing. Yes, my friends! the kingdom of "Satan is already rim-cracked and centre-"shaken" (in allusion to their household vessels of wood), "and shall be swept away as an un-"clean thing." After a pause he added, "If I "had as many lives as there are stars in the "heavens, I would spend them in the service of "my gracious Redeemer."

After the service I thanked the preacher for his excellent discourse.

We spoke of the state of religion in the parts of Canada West, with which he was acquainted.

He said he was a travelling missionary preacher of the Canadian Wesleyans, and was constantly perambulating a large circuit, embracing a number of half-peopled localities, destitute of religious instruction. A horse was found him, and he received an annual money-payment of 21*l*. He always found a welcome at the various stations in the houses of friends. The number of this class of ministers varies; in 1847 it was seventeen. The

Church of England has (1847) six itinerating missionaries in Canada West.*

He said, that the number of ministers and places of worship was very insufficient; but at the present day (1847) it is ten times greater than in London. He found that while many were indifferent, the bulk of the people heard him gladly, and came from great distances. The new neighbourhoods soon felt the want of a place of worship, and sooner than might have been expected supplied that want. Of whatever denomination the majority happened to be, the minority worshipped with them until they could provide a minister of their own, when all used the same edifice, until each could afford to have its own, which was felt to be a great advantage.

The following is the number of the churches and chapels in Canada West in the year 1847, as far as can be compiled from Smith's "Gazetteer,"

* The Rev. Thomas Green, Episcopal travelling missionary in Canada West, in a letter to the present excellent Bishop of Montreal, describes his duties as very severe. He writes, that since his arrival in his district he has preached nearly a sermon a-day, and has ridden fifteen miles a-day, nearly equal to thirty in England, in every variety of temperature, undergoing constant privations, and frequently resting at night in log-houses, whose unstopped chinks admit the cold air and damps of midnight.

but some, planted in obscure and thin neighbour hoods, must have been omitted :—

Episcopalian.	Baptist.	Methodist.	Presbyterian.	Quakers.	Catholic.	Lutheran.	Free Church of Scotland.	Christian.*	Free to all.	Coloured Persons.	Irvingite.	Moravian.	Unknown.	Disciples.*	Unitarian.	Total.
107	22	114	90	5	48	3	9	5	8	4	1	1	2	1	1	421

The exact amount of the population of Canada West is not known, although a near estimate may be made. It is supposed to be 650,000. In this total is included an undoubted increase since the very imperfect census was taken in 1842. The officers superintending the operation so frightened and confused the enumerators by dividing the information required into 120 heads, that from many of the districts no returns whatever were made.

If, in like manner. we add one-fifth to the number of churches, we shall have one for every 1287 of the population; a result which would be very favourable if the churches were always accessible, which they are not.

No account is taken of the Mennonites, but they are a considerable body.

* Names given to themselves by separatists.

The number of ministers serving these churches is shown in the subjoined table, also compiled from Smith's "Gazetteer" for 1847. The Roman Catholic clergy being omitted, the proportion of ministers to population cannot be given:—

Episcopal.	Wesleyan.	Scotch.	Free Church of Scotland.	Congregational Presbyterian.	Baptist.	Unitarian.	Total.
111	153	40	31	29	38	1	403

The number of the inhabitants of Canada West who are totally or nearly destitute of public worship is not so great as is supposed; but there are, unhappily, too many so situated.

Poverty has driven them into distant wildernesses, where land can be had for little or nothing. They are to be pitied and relieved. Is their conduct to be compared with that of the 80,000 miserable persons in Glasgow who daily hear the church-bell, but systematically for years never obey its holy call? Besides, these lonely settlers know that a few months or years will bring a church or chapel to them.

It seems to me that the Episcopal clergy are taken from too high a class for colonial service. They are usually so dissimilar from their flocks in tastes, habits, and prejudices, that they might almost come from another planet. Their early nurture has been too nice, and their education too academic, to admit of that familiarity, combined with true respect on the part of their people, which gives such well-earned influence to the Roman Catholic clergy in certain parts of Europe, and to the Wesleyan in Great Britain,—an influence which pervades both civil and spiritual life.

English bishops (I speak deferentially) are too well paid, are set up too high above their fellow-clergy, have too much direct patronage, and are placed apart in some distant park or castle, so that they are apt to see only with the eyes of a busy, expectant chaplain or two, and therefore but indifferently.

These and many other crying evils in the Church of England, brought on by the lapse of time and the cupidity of men, are in the course of extinction. The very next generation, it is confidently hoped, will only wonder that such things could have ever been. A thousand influences, open and secret, are at the sure work of their early suppression. As a conscientiously-attached member of the Church of England, I see the necessity for "*nova post lucem lux.*"

The colonial bishops are more active. Many of them are laborious and useful men, but others again are deeply tainted with Puseyism (so worshipful of bishops), and are doing no little harm by frowning down evangelical religion—oppressing it, I ought to say—and encouraging formalism, which is sure to end in Popery.

Greatly as I prefer the constitution and formularies of the Church of England, I am not sorry to see a considerable share of evangelical dissent in Canada West. It shows, that thought is active in the woods upon subjects of extreme importance, and also that many of the settlers are from the independent and meditative classes.

Some say, "Oh, that dissent were altogether swept away from England and her colonies, and that the Established Church held universal and undisputed sway!" But, no; a greater calamity could not befall English Christianity. Despotism in its direst form, the despotism of ecclesiastics, would follow. Freedom of opinion and individual responsibility would be gone. There would soon grow up a small dissentient minority, which would be called heretical, malignant, and then be hunted to the death by an inexorable and all-powerful confederacy. Able and ready instruments for any form of tyranny or cruelty in so sacred and profitable a cause are easily found. I could name them while I write, prompt either to direct or execute.

Differences of opinion among the real children of God on minor points will always prevail. They seem to be part of our intellectual constitution, and are beautifully adapted to our welfare. Among other advantages, they afford a field for the exercise of humility, mutual forbearance, and patient love.

It is delightful to think, that in Canada the State supports equally all the denominations into which true Christians have classed themselves. It has been there conceded that kings and queens are not to be nursing fathers and mothers to a part of the Church of Christ only, but to the whole.

It is well to remember, that "the strength and "glory of a Church consists, not so much in its "temporalities, as in the presence of the Saviour, "the power of the Holy Ghost, the vital godliness "of her ministers and members, and the faith-"fulness, boldness, and evangelical tone of her "ministrations."

All this is undeniably true; but truth, like light, offends the feeble eye, and at first repels: but although, for a time, it may be hid, and hindered in its solemn manifestation, nothing can extinguish its brightness, nor prevent its final triumph upon earth.

There is an elaborate system of schools in

Canada West. I do not undertake to explain it. A book which treats upon all subjects becomes unreadable.

I have reason to think that it works well. The returns, however, are as yet very imperfect; but it can be gathered from Smith's "Gazetteer," that, in Canada West, 353,317 of the population have 1508 schools, called common schools; which is in the proportion of 234 persons to one school. This is independent of many private boarding and day-schools for both sexes. In the thinly peopled districts, 20,000*l.* per annum is paid to the public schools, in addition to small local rates and the weekly payments of the children themselves. The school-houses are built by the districts.

A good system of superintendence has been devised, and tolerably well carried out. Of the details I know nothing.

Besides these means of education, it is the practice of the settlers to form circles of a dozen families each, and engage a young man to teach their children in some centrical situation. He is usually from New England, hired by the year at a moderate salary, and boarding with the parents in turn, for a month at a time. There are serious evils attached to this system. I shall only mention one—the republican principles unconsciously taught and recommended in school histories, &c. &c.

I had personal intercourse with only one of these young schoolmasters, a very interesting person, with whom I resided for three weeks in the same house, on the River Détroit. He was an able and painstaking man, of sound religious principles. He told me a good deal about the plans for self-advancement of young people in the rural parts of New England.

It was the universal custom of the poorer of these to act as schoolmasters in the western settlements of their own country, and of Canada, for a time, in the hope of collecting a little capital for ulterior purposes.

My friend was one of these, a gentle, slight-made, fair-haired young man. He had been four or five years among us, and was on the eve of marriage, and of being settled on a farm in the state of Ohio.

Much might be said on the religious and secular colleges of Kingston, Toronto, and Coburgh—much in commendation, something in reprobation; but, as the passing glance which I can bestow would carry no weight, I prefer being altogether silent.

Our surveyors having only had to complete some triangulations, which sickness had before compelled them to leave unfinished, after a week's stay we left our lofty encampment on the cliffs of Lake Erie, where, by the bye, we had the pleasurable exercise of carrying every drop of the water* we required 150 feet up the steep.

A few hours took us back to Amherstburgh. There we found the Confiance ready to convey us down Lake Erie to the mouth of the River Niagara.

Lieutenant Grant and myself, while walking along the river side the same evening, met a couple of Indians trotting to Amherstburgh, in their usual way when loaded. One had a fine deer across his shoulders, and the other carried four wild turkeys. The latter we bought for a shilling a-piece, and half the deer for four shillings, to be paid for on board our good schooner, where soon afterwards our messmates gave the game a cordial welcome.

The next morning (Aug. 1), we sailed cheerily down the Détroit, and with a favourable but light breeze. So we proceeded at an easy rate, all in high spirits at returning home, down the lake, passing the Sisters, the St. Georges, the three

* One evening the water was at 92° Fahren. in the open lake near the shore. It boiled for our tea all the sooner.

Bass Islands, and lastly, the Island of Pelé,—all looking lovely.

Towards dusk, however, when these isles were dimly seen behind us, the sky became overcast, the wind arose, and by two o'clock A.M. the next morning had become a raging hurricane.

Just before daylight we came far too near the perpendicular rocks of Cleaveland, on the American shore, looming lofty and black in the darkness. These, after great anxiety, we succeeded in avoiding; but I must refrain from a lengthened description of this, the most violent storm on Lake Erie for many years; and it is infamous for them.

We were three nights and two days exposed to its fury, driving from side to side of this narrow lake, but with a general easterly course.

We should have perished, I verily believe, but with God's help for our stout commander and his brave crew. The waves swept away boats, binnacle, deer, turkeys, &c. &c., and strewed the sand of the lake bottom in great quantities upon the deck, and the table-cloth of a sail which we ventured to hoist.

Nobody thought of cooking, and few of eating. I confess to a couple of biscuits. I remained much in my berth, on account of the violent motion of the vessel, with simply a shirt on, white jane trowsers, and light shoes, ready for a jump and a swim. I certainly thought (with the others) that our safety was very problematical. Of course, I felt for myself; but I also regretted the loss of all our surveys, and of our very valuable instruments. The shipwreck would have cost the public very many thousand pounds.

Once only was I nearly on deck to survey the scene; but I had hardly got high enough to see —standing on the companion-ladder—when a large wave, opaque with mud, soused me on the face, and drove me down again, accompanied by not a little water.

Our Canadian *voyageurs* were vastly disturbed. One old fellow with a sharp vinegar face jammed himself into a corner of the hold, and broke his usual silence by giving public notice that, if permitted to land alive, he would burn a candle one pound in weight in the nearest church, in honour of the Virgin—"the mild Mother"—the "Star of the sea."

He had scarcely uttered the vow, when the vessel quivered under a tremendous blow, and was buried for a moment beneath a great wave. Grénier shouted out, that he would pay for six masses. Another shock. The poor man, in an agony, doubled the weight of the candle, set his teeth spasmodically, and never spake more, until the storm had ceased; for he saw all his summer wages a-melting. I have no right to found an argument upon this poor man's ignorance and fright.

Early on the third morning we saw the North Foreland (Long Point) on our north-west. The scud moved quick, and the waves were still high and full of sand, but the force of the storm was broken.

The land on either shore looked most charming. I envied the very cattle which were browsing in the pastures, in gentle contention with the mosquitoes. In due season, to my undisguisable joy, we anchored inside a reef near the Village of Waterloo, our destined haven; and we landed, thankful to our divine Preserver for a new and signal mercy.

One sloop foundered; its crew and passengers all lost. There happened to be but few vessels on the lake. These were much damaged.

We are within about twenty miles of the Falls of Niagara: thither we shall next repair.

END OF VOL. I.

LONDON:
Printed by G. Barclay, Castle St. Leicester Sq.

THE SHOE AND CANOE

OR

PICTURES OF TRAVEL

IN

THE CANADAS.

ILLUSTRATIVE OF

THEIR SCENERY AND OF COLONIAL LIFE

WITH FACTS AND OPINIONS ON EMIGRATION
STATE POLICY, AND OTHER POINTS OF PUBLIC INTEREST

With Numerous Plates and Maps.

By JOHN J. BIGSBY, M.D.

HON. MEM. AMERICAN GEOLOGICAL SOC., LATE SECRETARY TO THE BOUNDARY
COMMISSION UNDER ART. VI. AND VII. TREATY OF GHENT

IN TWO VOLUMES.

VOL. II.

LONDON:
PUBLISHED BY CHAPMAN AND HALL.

MDCCCL.

"There He setteth the poor on high from affliction; and maketh him families like a flock. The righteous shall see it and rejoice."—*Ps.* cvii.

"Make my grave on the banks of the St. Lawrence."—LORD SYDENHAM, *late Governor-Gen. of British North America.*

CONTENTS

OF

THE SECOND VOLUME.

EXCURSION THE SIXTH.

NIAGARA.

EXCURSION THE SEVENTH.

PART I.

LAKES ONTARIO AND SIMCOE, ETC.

APPENDIX.

DIRECTIONS TO THE BINDER.

MAPS.

PLATES.

EXCURSION THE SIXTH.

NIAGARA.

The River—My Friends—The Vicinity of the Falls—Forsyth's Inn—The Indian carried over the Falls—The Stolen Drawings—The Falls—Anecdotes royal and true—Mr. John Vaughan and his Ways—Dr. Franklin—The Chasm and Curtain—Goat Island—Stamford Park—Queenston Heights—Rhodo's Procession—The Deserter.

In this excursion I concern myself with the general features only of the Falls of Niagara, and more particularly with the sayings and doings of the pleasant party with whom I visited them.

I have thought well to separate this light reading from the topographical details and accurate admeasurements which I obtained from the Boundary Surveyors, as being more easily consulted than read. They will be found in the Appendix, together with a small map of this locality, which I hope the reader will glance at before perusing this Excursion.

The River Niagara fully merits its fame. It is magnificent in dimension, beautiful in form, enriched with various and exuberant foliage, and cheered with bright skies.

In 1822 its east bank, a part of the north frontier of the United States, was (and probably is) a scarcely touched forest, while the Canadian shore blooms from end to end with orchards and farms, hamlets and ornamental residences.

The Cataract of Niagara is unrivalled in the impression it makes upon every cultivated mind. Its superiority does not, however, depend so much on its height, or on the accompanying scenery, as on its naked vastness, and its extraordinary beauty of outline and colour.

A cataract as large as that of the Rhine at Schaffhausen might be cut out (so to speak) of that of Niagara, without its being perceived.

In a picture this Fall is tame, formal, and disappointing; but in the living landscape no such effect is produced, and the mind becomes wrapt in solemnised and pleased wonder.

The rapid transition from the placid, lakelike character of the river above to the vehemence and tumult of the Falls, is very striking to the spectator who approaches from Lake Erie, as I did on my first visit, riding jauntily in the spring-waggon of a Seneka Indian well to do, who was dressed, as might be expected in a white man a little eccentric.

Near the village of Chippewa the broad, hurrying stream is seen a couple of miles off to leap into a dark and deep gulf. All between the spectator and the plunge is bright, clear, and verdurous, all beyond is gloomy and grey in the wreathing mists sent up by the shock of waters.

The great chasm which I thus incidentally notice, and its picturesque outlet or gorge at Queenston, are additional features of great interest.

Although it will be described in the Appendix, I may here advert to the singular fact that all the superfluous waters of the great upper lakes pass through it, while in one place it is only 115 yards broad.

I had the good fortune to visit this cataract in very agreeable company. Our travelling party of six represented Philadelphia, Quebec, New York, Paris, and London, very entertainingly. As for me, my youth pinned me down as a listener only. We consisted of an old merchant (or rather philosopher) of Philadelphia, a British colonel on half-pay, a major in the American service, an English barrister, Count Montalembert, an *attaché* to the French Embassy in the Brazils, now a grey-haired Legitimist,* and a young medical man.

Speculators had not then effected the base transmutations of the present day. There were no large clumsy caravansaries, no lines of white-washed lodging-houses, and no vulgar, intrusive bridges to mar the graceful outlines and harmonious colourings of waters, rocks, and sloping woods.

At that time (1822) a visit to Niagara was a great undisturbed sensation. The great Falls were almost in their primeval forests. We came upon the giant river in all its solitariness, rolling its immense wave over jutting rocks, and sepulchred in woods vocal with its roar.

Nothing incongruous met the eye or ear; the picture was perfect and the effect most profound.

In those days there was a small hamlet on the American side of the river, with Judge Porter's handsome house at one end of it; but both hamlet and hall were out of sight.

On the British side there was only one house near it, an inn, kept time out of mind by a family of the name of Forsyth. They were very primi-

* Then all strength, spirits, and gentleness—a *blond*, of rather large and full contours, so rare in Frenchmen, and a most agreeable and highly-educated person.

tive folks, but being careful and shrewd, they passed in the world as rich.

They paid their guests small worship, and could be exceedingly hasty and bitter to the highest; but the gentle and quiet had good entertainment, old-fashioned talk or none, according to the humour, wholesome food and white sheets.

Their place might have been an old farmstead in Worcestershire. The house was low, with little windows and lozenge-shaped panes. It had once been small, but had been added to as the family increased, and therefore shewed a deal of roof. Cowhouses, stables, and pigstyes, hung close around.

There it stood, with an orchard of mossy fruit trees on one side, and large forest trees on the other, the public road being in the rear.

As Newstead Abbey, blackened with the stains of centuries in the days of the poet-lord, was a far more interesting object than in its present elaborate renovation, so Niagara of old was greatly to be preferred to Niagara new and disenchanted.*

For all this old-fashioned still life has been grubbed up; and in its place we have a tall square hotel, encircled with two or three galleries, and

* Many hearty and respectful thanks, nevertheless, to the present owner, the kindly Colonel, who permits free access to this shrine of unhappy genius.

watching the Falls from a hundred windows. On the pillars of these galleries we take a certain kind of lazy interest in scanning quaint devices in pencil, original thoughts and impressions in rhyme and prose, with many newly-married names coupled in love-knots, names of lofty sound sweet to the western ear, such as Adrian and Formosa, Herman and Mariana, &c. &c. Higgs, or Snell, or Smith, usually follows. Other such house-monsters there are hereabouts, and more on the American side.

Instead of the ferry that was wont to cross the billowy current below the cataract with a freight of ladies in a state of safe consternation, we have now two shaky bridges, one above, and the other below the Fall;—the impudence of the mechanician robbing us of the august and natural. It is to be hoped that some April avalanche of ice and trees, rushing at midnight down the rapids, will sweep the upper abomination into the abyss.*

Instead of the seed-royal of prepared worshippers

* Occasionally, from the immense quantity of ice carried over the Falls, the channel becomes choked and blocked up a short distance below the Falls, so as to be passable on foot. This was the case during the winter of 1845–6, when a path was marked out across the ice opposite Clifton House. The Falls are very grand in winter; the rocks at the sides being incrusted with icicles, some of them measuring perhaps fifty or sixty feet in length.—*Smith's Gazetteer*.

(with a few stragglers perhaps), the pilgrimage to the Falls is now performed by swarming crowds of all conditions and ages—Canadians—the sallow Carolinian and his full-blown lady—rich people from Tennessee, Georgia, and Ohio—the Spaniard from hot and hateful Cuba, a spectacled German or two, and occasionally some British officials, in costume without an erring fold, and as impassible to human intercourse as ice to lightning, until warmed up by their favourite Oporto.

The great majority of the visitors only stay a couple of hours, and order their horses for the next stage before they see the show. Those who do stay a little longer treat the patient cataract with the same vulgar, prying contumelies that the public of bygone days did the dragon when the Cappadocian saint had slain him. The Ariel, a little steamer, plying in the chasm for hire, may be almost said to walk into its mouth.

Seclusion, that pleasant nymph, has ran away outright. You are *guided* to death. No sooner has the mind acquired the tension so indispensable to the enjoyment of the wonderful scene, than a man with a bit of spar for sale breaks up the vision; or the angry cries of a sulky child are heard; or a bundle of affectations from one of the interminable streets of New York comes rushing and buzzing up the steep, and effectually cuts short your ecstatics. "Oh, mamma!" I heard a pretty little miss call out, "it is not at all as it's put in my geography-book. Where is the promenade between the curtain and the rock? Where are the bears and the moose struggling in the rapids, and then swept into the abyss? and where are the hundred Iroquois waiting below to receive the wild beasts on their spear-points? I am quite disappointed!"—and so on. If this little lady had been present when the Indian female went over the Falls in 1820, it is hoped that she would have been more than satisfied. It happened thus:—

The poor creature, of middle age, fell asleep in a canoe fastened to a stake in the river-bank, about three miles above the Falls.

During her sleep the cord broke, and the canoe floated gently but swiftly down towards the cataract.

She awoke when within 500 yards of the brink, already amid foaming rapids, and beyond rescue.

Having slowly turned round twice to see if there were any possible escape, she stooped for a large red blanket she had, folded it over her face, and quietly sat down. The woman and the canoe in a few instants were carried over the precipice, and never seen more.

I fear some of the visitors are not honest. My

companion on one of my many visits to the Falls, Captain Vivian, made eight beautiful sketches of them. He had just finished them carefully and left the room for a mere moment—and they were gone. All inquiries were in vain. They were lost, and for ever.

We suspected a very pleasing and talkative young lady in a most becoming green satin dress, who sat next to my friend, a handsome young officer, at dinner that day. She was all "entusy-musy" about cataracts and wildernesses, and above all things wished to take away with her some drawings of Niagara. Is it possible that, with such a happy, open face, she could steal a sketch-book? We never saw her more, and the loss occurred soon after dinner.

Soon after our arrival our whole party walked down the sloping meadow between Forsyth's and the Falls, dipped by a steep bank (adorned with fine tulip-trees of nature's planting) into a narrow slip of wet coppice, and stood on Table Rock, a platform, which, almost yearly diminishing, supports the northern end of the British or Horse-shoe Fall. We could put our feet into the shallow water as it was hurrying to the brink.

The whole scene lay before us. We saw the overwhelming flood, springing in a dense sheet of the tenderest emerald, and of white and grey, into the dark chasm—not in a line uniform and straight, but in a varying and most graceful curve.

We looked around upon the woods, upon Goat, or Iris Island, midway between the Horse-shoe and American Falls,—upwards to the rapids pent in for a couple of miles by high banks,—and then the eye dropped into the grey abyss itself, its dark mossy walls, its masses of displaced rocks, half-buried in the river, and the churning, foamy waters sending a white vapour so high as sometimes to be visible at the distance of twenty miles.

We remained half-an-hour on this spot, and returned to the inn by a little *détour*, which afforded some new points of view.

Very few words were exchanged during the walk home; each was left to the enjoyment of his own sensations. The scene is so simple, so sublime, so full of mingled grace, beauty, and terror, that there is no room for talk, and it is above human commendation.

We went to dinner, not with a hundred strangers at a table very narrow and long, the hot meats cold and the cold warm; but by ourselves, in a snug parlour.

The weather had become sultry, and a thunder-storm was brewing.

The good dinner also disinclined us to leave the

dessert. So we resolved to share a couple of bottles of Forsyth's particular port among us.

There were in our party both good talkers and good listeners; most of us had travelled extensively and in the best company.

Of course the conversation was not on politics; but it became anecdotical. A few of the little stories I recollect to this distant day.

"The last time I was here," said the worthy Colonel, "it was as private secretary to the Duke of Kent. His Royal Highness was greatly interested in the spot. The falling river, the untrodden woods, the prevailing solemnity—all proclaiming the irresistible grandeur of nature and the feebleness of man—went to his heart."

Again, his Royal Highness was brought into the proper frame by a deputation of Delawares and Mohawks, who somehow got scent of his approach, and waylaid him on the heights of Queenston with a soldierlike speech full of woodland tropes.

He greatly admired these broad-chested Redskins, with their measured tread, swart, serious faces, and hooked noses.

The Duke was much taken with the old crone, Forsyth's grandmother—with her simpleness and straightforward oddity. Not knowing clearly at the time the quality of her guests, she was often plainer in her remarks than complimentary. One of the suite had a six-bladed knife, and expected to make at least six uses of it in the west. It had knives, corkscrew, saw, &c. &c. "Well," said she, staring agape at the Sheffield master-piece, "in all my born days I never saw such a knife as that;—no! nor never heard of one. A man with such a wonder as that in his coat-pocket, who comes 500 miles to see our Falls, must be a very uncommon fool!"

As princes sometimes wish to be quiet, especially during the fatigues of a Canadian journey, the Duke of Kent travelled *incog.*, or meant so to do; but the veil was often removed by accident or indiscretion.

"We arrived (the Colonel speaks) rather late " one evening at the little Inn of the Cedars, on " the St. Lawrence.

"The landlord was very attentive, for he saw " that he had under his roof no ordinary personage; " but who, he could not guess for the life of him.

"He repeatedly entered his Royal Highness's " sitting-room. The first time he said, 'I think, " 'Captain, you rang the table-bell. What did " 'you please to want?' The second time he " brought in a plate of fine raspberries, and said, " 'We have found in the woods, Major, a few " 'rasps. Will you please to taste them?'

"He invented a third and fourth excuse for "entering, and saluted his Highness, first as "colonel, and then as general. The last time, "just before leaving the room, he returned from "near the door, fell upon his knees, and cried "out, 'May it please your Majesty to pardon us "'if we don't behave suitable. I know you are "'not to be known. I mean no offence in calling "'you captain and colonel. What must I call "'you? For anything I can tell you may be a "'king's son.'

"To this long speech the Duke would have "given a kind answer, but for an universal and "irrepressible explosion of laughter. If you had "seen the scared old innkeeper on his knees, you "would have laughed too."

The Philadelphia merchant-philosopher was in high talk that evening.

All Philadelphia reveres and loves (or rather did so) Mr. John Vaughan,* old and young, high

* He was an Englishman of good family, who had come to Philadelphia in early life as a merchant; but his affections were too warm, and his anxiety for the advancement of his fellow-creatures in happiness and virtue was too great, to allow his whole energies to be devoted to a selfish object, so that his time, means, and talents, soon became absorbed in schemes of philanthropic, literary, or scientific utility. He did not labour in his calling exclusively. When trade changed its channels, he did not run after it, so that after a time Mr. Vaughan was left nearly high and dry, with but few commissions or correspondents. There was never anything like

and low, for his long life had been a ceaseless current of benevolent acts. Even in the city of Quakers, this Englishman had been before, and beyond all, in good works. I had passed a winter in that delightful town, and was indebted to him for a comfortable home, for introductions to desirable society, and for access to libraries and lectures.

Mr. Vaughan took his proper part in the con-

insolvency. Mr. Vaughan was a bachelor, and I believe had a safe little patrimony. But fifty years before his death, such was his usefulness and special capacity, that he was chosen secretary of the important institution, the American Philosophical Society of Philadelphia, with salary and handsome apartments attached. This mark of the esteem of his fellow-citizens must have been very grateful to Mr. Vaughan.

In 1822 Mr. Vaughan was a little, active, light-hearted old man, with a pleasant, confiding face, wrinkled by hot summers, sharp winters, and a long life in exciting times. I have often seen his open-hearted expression in the countenances of philanthropists and naturalists, but not often in those of professional men and authors.

With all his gentle forgetfulness of self, Mr. Vaughan was ardent and skilful in the prosecution of an object, and few had more irons in the fire than he had at all times. Besides an active share in the business of charitable institutions, he had a multitude of private charges in the shape of widows and orphans. Did a father die early, and leave a scantily-provided family, Mr. Vaughan was accustomed to find himself appointed years before their guardian. He seldom refused the office, and set at once about soothing the bereaved, arguing with or imploring creditors, providing for immediate wants, and so on.

He was always in the fidgets about some one or other of his wards, seeking berths for the boys in ships and counting-houses, and placing out the girls in any proper way he could.

versation, but with the exception of the following characteristic anecdote, I entirely forget what he said.

Although Mr. Vaughan was much Dr. Franklin's junior, he was intimate with him, because there were points of resemblance in their characters, and because public business threw them often together. At the time spoken of, now long ago, Franklin was the editor of a young newspaper,

He had been long in the habit of walking in the morning on the quays of Philadelphia; thus to do good, while taking necessary exercise. If he saw a loiterer with a homeless look, especially if in an English smock-frock, the cheerful little man would enter into talk with him, point out some decent lodging-house, direct him to the St. George's Society for the relief of foreigners, and to other sources of information and help, not omitting to give the stranger his own address in case of need.

The English emigrant has more occasion for this kind of assistance than the Scotch and Irish. The latter have considerable address and readiness, and they meet with more help from their countrymen than the English do.

Mr. Vaughan died at Philadelphia at the age of eighty-six, passing from labour to rest, from hope to recompense. He was honoured by a public funeral. His portrait had hung for thirty years in the City Gallery of Paintings, and now his bust is placed in the hall of the American Philosophical Society, which has so greatly advanced the cultivation of science in the United States.

Mr. Vaughan was an original member of the Wistar Society of Philadelphia, an association of sixteen of the leading persons of the city. Its object was, for each member to hold in his turn a *soirée*, for the purpose of introducing respectable or distinguished strangers to each other, and to the most eminent individuals in the vicinity.

Although this note be rather long, is it not well to pay a deserved tribute to so good a man?

advocating uncompromisingly a certain line of American politics.

In those days men were very earnest. One of Franklin's subscribers disapproved of his proceedings, but forbore for some time, hoping for a change ; but time only made matters worse.

One day the subscriber met Dr. Franklin in the street, and freely told him that his politics would ruin both him and his country. He finished by desiring him to take his name from the list of his subscribers. Dr. Franklin told him he was sorry to lose him, but that his wishes should be obeyed.

A week or two afterwards, not a little to the old subscriber's surprise, he received from Franklin a little note, inviting him to supper on the coming Friday evening.

He accepted, and went. He found the perverse editor in clean, plain lodgings, at a side-table, leaning on some books, in his usual easy humour. Supper was being laid on a round oak table, over which a neat-handed girl had spread a white cloth. She then gradually covered it with a shining, firm cucumber, a pat of butter, a large china jug of water from the spring, a loaf of good bread, three cool lettuces, some leeks, and a piece of ripe cheese, with a little jug of foaming beer, more brisk than strong.

Just as the last article was placed on the table,

a tap at the door brought in that friendly man, Dr. Rush, so well known all over the world for his medical skill. Another knock introduced Mr. Vaughan, most probably then full of young projects, and primed for discussion.

To the subscriber's great surprise, after these two, Washington himself stepped in, his square, grave face relaxing into good fellowship when he saw his company, and the preparations for making a night of it. Hancock, positive, able, and honest, and one more, made up the company.

They disposed themselves round the table, and fell to. So slender a repast, in such a humble room, for such a party, consisting of the first men in America, puzzled the subscriber severely.

All these guests were in their prime, splendidly and variously endowed. Each had passed the day in labour for the good of others — in the senate, the army, or in private life. They now came together for well-earned relaxation. The hours were only too short for the outpourings of their full minds. Twelve o'clock saw them home.

A few days afterwards the subscriber again met Dr. Franklin in the street. "Ah!" said he, "a thousand thanks for that delightful evening. I saw the lesson you were reading me. You meant to shew that a man who can entertain the first and best of our country upon a cucumber and a glass of cold water, can afford to be politically honest."

"Well, friend," Franklin smilingly replied, "something of that sort."

When the thunderstorm had passed over, leaving a delightful freshness behind it, the dinner party strayed up a shady lane near Forsyth's, on the opposite side of the road—up Lundy's Lane, which leads to the round eminence whereon, in 1812, the battle of Lundy's Lane was most severely contested.

I believe we had all forgotten the whole affair, although many brave men fell there in the heroic performance of the duty of the moment, for not a single observation was made on the subject. We simply looked round upon the fertile soil, and upon the signs around us of a daily increasing population. We saw the ready access to markets, and pronounced the easy prophecy that ere long Canada West would be filled with a prosperous people.

The next morning all the party, except Mr. Vaughan and the Colonel, descended into the chasm. They feared the extreme heat then prevailing, and remained at home, amusing themselves with the quaint notions of old Mrs. Forsyth, and with discussing the merits of General Lee, a distinguished revolutionary officer on the American side.

As most of us were young, and out for a holiday, our spirits were at boiling point; practical jokes, frolic, and song, were the order of the day. It was then that I learnt my famous ditty about the farmer's dog, "Little Bingo."

In those days there were no means of descent into the chasm but by long ladders, old and crazy. Two of us, therefore, standing on the summit of the precipice, imitated Henry Navarre at the battle of Ivry, by courageously flinging our hats into the gulf to arouse our courage. We regained them by the merest accident. There was not a wearable hat to be bought within a hundred miles. The count attaché, after we had descended and stood upon the colossal fragments, which, now half buried in the waters, had fallen from above, proposed to bathe in a quiet nook he had espied; but I told him that such trouble was needless, as before he got home he would enjoy a new kind of lavatory.

It was not long before the grandeur of the scene had changed our merriment into repose and thoughtfulness. We sat down upon the rocky slope or talus, nearly on a level with the water.

The upper world of habitations, woods, and broad, shining river, was excluded. On each side, close to us, were mural precipices, 150 feet high, crowned with trees. The eye was filled and fascinated by the wide curtain* of falling waters, whose fair and delicate colour is rendered more marked by the gloom of the surrounding walls of dark limestone.

Colossal fragments in magnificent confusion mount half-way up the precipice, and even obstruct the stream as it rolls impetuously down.

Over the Horse-shoe Fall the water leaps *en masse,* and meets with no obstruction. The same is the case at the small cascade, called the Ribbon or Montmorenci Fall (*vide* map); but at the American or Schlosser's Fall, the descending sheet of water often dashes upon successive ledges of rock, and then, arching gracefully, drops in broken feathery or arrow-like masses.

In the mist which overspreads the front of the Horse-shoe Fall the rainbows are very large and brilliant at times, but they are faint at Schlosser's.

I think I shall better convey to my readers the general impression created by the scenery of the chasm below the Falls, by the following magnificent lines, than by any words of my own :—

" The thoughts are strange which crowd upon my brain
When I look upward to thee. It would seem
As if God pour'd thee from his hollow hand,
And hung his bow upon thy awful front,

* Twelve hundred yards, or two-thirds of a mile broad, including Iris Island.—*Vide* map.

And spoke in that loud voice, which seem'd to him
Who dwelt in Patmos for his Saviour's sake,
The sound of many waters; and thy flood
Had bidden chronicle the ages back,
And notch his centuries in the eternal rocks.
Deep calleth unto deep. And what are we
Who hear this awful questioning? Oh! what
Are all the stirring notes that ever rang
From war's vain trumpet, by thy thundering side?
Yea, what is all the riot man can make
In his short life to thy unceasing roar?
And yet, bold babbler, what art thou to Him
Who drown'd a world, and heap'd the waters far
Above its loftiest mountains?—a light wave
That breaks, and whispers of its Maker's might."

ANON. *U.S. Literary Gazette.*

We scrambled over the fragments lining the foot of the precipice to the north end of the Horse-shoe Fall. Here we observed more nearly its form, colour, and massive thickness.

There is a considerable interval between the descending water and the rock it rushes over.

Into this dark cavern we ventured without a guide, amid a concentrated roar which stunned us, while the whirling hurricane of watery vapour, which filled the place instead of air, beat violently upon our persons, and changed our breathing into a laborious struggle of sighing and gasping.

There we stood, with tottering knees, making dumb shows of astonishment and distress. It was difficult to keep our footing, or to walk over the rough slope of fallen rocks, made slippery by wet mosses, and the slime of the frightened eels we saw darting from stone to stone.

We succeeded in going some ten or twelve feet within the curtain, which was too thick to see through, but its emerald colour was peculiarly clear and soft. We then saw at a little distance a buttress preventing further progress, except at some risk.*

I may almost spare myself the trouble of mentioning that, while in the cavern, every point and angle about our drenched clothes was a water-spout. We were glad to escape and hurry home for a change of clothes at the top of our speed; even the count was satisfied.

It is a fact worth remembering that, although the fields in the vicinity abound in erratic blocks, I only found one in the chasm after an extensive search, a gneis full of garnets. This shews that they had found their present resting-places in the fields around before the chasm was formed.

Not long ago a mastodon was found in a fresh-water deposit, near the Falls, on the right bank of the river.

Our ardour was a good deal cooled by this immersion. We were all for an early dinner,

* I imagine that this has since been removed, and the footing generally been made more secure, because visitors, aided by guides, penetrate farther than we did.

with the intention, some of sauntering to the Burning Springs of Bridgewater, and others of crossing to the American side of the river.

For my part, I went to neither, being occupied the whole evening with a sojourner at Forsyth's, attacked with inflammation of the bowels. The house was full of guests, the few servants, though kind, were busy and little used to extreme suffering; so I had to be nurse as well as physician, and shewed that, besides flourishing a lancet, I could wring a hot fomenting-cloth with any queen of the washing-tub. In a couple of days the patient moved away, weak and grateful.

Our friends were pleased with their evening. Those who had crossed below the falls in the little ferry-boat spoke highly of the view from the middle of the stream.

They mounted the woody American bank by a ladder, similar to that on the Canadian side, but shorter, and crossed by Judge Porter's two bridges into Goat Island. These bridges, of ordinary make, connect Goat Island with the main by means of an intermediate islet. They rest upon triangular buttresses, mere boxes filled with stones, and set with the sharp point opposed to the stream. There are now refreshment-rooms, billiard-tables, and gardens on the island; but the greater part is still in ornamental woods.

The views from Goat Island are very fine, though partial; those from the first bridge of Judge Porter are good. Looking downwards, the white foaming waters are seen among round islets of black fir, hastening to the brink; beyond which, in the distance, and veiled by a thin haze, the Canadian side of the river is seen, a lofty weather-cliff, fringed with coppice, and separated by a green meadow from a range of grassy eminences, sprinkled with tulip and other trees.

The Chippewa or Bridgewater Burning Spring is about a mile and a half from Forsyth's, on the British side of the river, near a cluster of small houses called Bridgewater.

Numerous bubbles of sulphuretted hydrogen gas escape here from the bottom of the shallows near the bank. They are as large as a nut, and smell strongly. A bottomless barrel, full of gravel, is placed over a spot where many bubbles have appeared. To its luted head the hollow trunk of a small tree is fitted, which again receives a short gun-barrel, from whose muzzle the gas arises, and, when set fire to, burns with a broad, flickering flame about eight inches long.

The whole is enclosed in a shed for the purposes of exhibition.

Several shy, little quails, pretty birds, as round as a ball, were met with in this walk to Bridgewater, glancing about among the long grass.

The next morning we left in a body for Queenston, a village at the outlet of the chasm, and at the foot of the heights. We visited the whirlpool on our way, but I shall not notice it now, as it is described in the Appendix.

This is a charming ride through a succession of farms, orchards, village-greens, and woods. The last abounds in the red-headed woodpecker, at least I have seen more of them there than elsewhere. It is a very splendid bird, ever on the wing, and fearless. Its head and neck are of a rich crimson, and the back, wings, and breast divided between the most snowy white and jetty black.

About half-way from Forsyth's, near a cluster of cottages and a school-house, we were shewn a large collection of Indian ornaments, rings and triangular plates of copper, for the nose probably, many beads, and an Indian skull. They had been very recently found under and among the roots of an old tree. Not far from here we had a glimpse of Stamford Park, the country-seat of the Lieutenant-Governor of the Upper

Province, an exceedingly elegant imitation of the Cottage Ornée of the Isle of Wight, surrounded by a broad verandah, and covered with roses.

As we emerged on the brow of Queenston Heights from the rather close scenery we had been riding through, a beautiful and uncommon landscape presented itself.

In the immediate foreground, 300 feet below, are two pretty villages, Queenston and Lewiston, between which the Niagara, escaping from the chasm, expands into a tranquil river, and is traced, winding through a sea of woods, till it loses itself, at Fort George, in Lake Ontario, seven miles off, whose wide waters are represented by a narrow blue line, bounded by the high lands about Toronto. The junction of the river with the lake is marked by the heavy white building on the east bank of the former, called Fort Niagara (in the United States), and the town of Newark, or Niagara, on the west bank, a pleasant place of moderate size.

This panorama could not fail to be suggestive. I see, methought, that the epoch of man is but beginning, that the aspect of the earth, as we now behold it, in its inhabitants and garniture, is in its infancy. A thousand years are a small thing, a portion of the historic time which registers the present moments as they pass, itself a fragment of geological time which may overspread a thousand centuries.

The Almighty and All-wise Being begins nothing in vain, and in the end will leave nothing incomplete. "He appears to work slowly," impatient man may say. How much remains to be done!

Look at the forest-plains below me, idle, vast, and fertile, both in the Canadas and the United States—think of the illimitable and rich countries in every quarter of the globe, hitherto untouched by spade or plough—and yet I must believe destined to be cultivated and enjoyed by countless multitudes.

The physical condition of man—how wretched, how inconsistent with his destinies! and yet how full of promise!

Again, how much has man to learn! How far beneath true, practical Christianity is the civilisation of this day anywhere! Ignorance and perverseness on the part of the weak, and oppression on the part of the strong, are almost universal. The bloody hoof of despotism is still on many kingdoms, and false religions are betraying the bulk of mankind. And yet I both see and hear the footsteps of physical and religious progress. I dare not compare, in number, zeal, and power, the real servants of the Maker of all things, and those who serve him not—the disproportion is enormous.

I repeat, that there seems much to be done before the impending change comes, and that, probably, by ordinary agencies. The millennium may indeed intervene. May it come quickly!

Many good men are expecting the almost immediate end of the present constitution of things; but they have Scripture warrant for nothing beyond uncertainty. They are influenced by temperament, not by reason or inspiration.

We took up our abode at the Queenston Hotel, a humble but clean house of entertainment, and next morning were taken over the rugged, grassy heights, overhanging the village, to see the battle-ground where fell, in 1812, the energetic and gallant Brock. Our friend (Mr. Ridout, of Queenston) had been present in the battle. He shewed us the spot where the victory was won, where the American commander (General Winfield Scott) gave up his sword, and where the British general received his death-wound; neither did he forget to point out the broken precipice, fringed with shrubbery, down which the American soldiers sprang to avoid the English bayonet, and so perished by a death more forlorn, lingering, and painful still, at the bottom of the cliff or in the waters. I hope there is exaggeration in this part of the battle narrative.

We were sorry that a landscape so full of beauty should be connected with so sad a story as a battle always ought to be felt; but so imperfectly Christianised is the world as yet; people and rulers both so ready to invade and oppress, that physical courage and contempt of death itself in the execution of a professional duty must be applauded. Cowardice, crime, and national decay, always go together, as do bravery, virtue, and social progress. We find, in the imperishable pages of Scripture, thirty verses (2 Sam.) dedicated to the names and exploits of valiant men, from Eleazar, who smote the Philistines until his sword clave to his hand, to Benaiah, who went down and slew a lion in a pit in the time of snow.

We returned home to dinner; and afterwards, with great regret, separated for our respective homes.

Here, perhaps, I ought to stop; but I cannot help briefly narrating two incidents which occurred on this same day.

As we were looking out of the inn-window, while the servant-maid (or daughter) laid the cloth for our repast, we saw a female procession moving up the street. We called to Rhoda for an explanation.

"Oh, gentlemen!" said she, with a proud smile, "do you not know? The soldiers' chaplain, who has been here for a couple of years, is leaving us. Well, he has just married one of the Miss Binks', who lives, twelve miles back, behind Short Hills. So the town has determined to present the bride with a new bonnet and a silk dress,—very handsome of course. I have seen them. Yes," she added, after looking into the street, "they are walking to Mr. S.'s house, the white house and green shutters facing the river."

The procession was wholly of prim village ladies, smiling or serious according to their dispositions—about twenty couples—a tidy, happy little girl in hand here and there.

At their heads most solemnly walked, with white wands, two middle-aged men, prosperous churchwardens perhaps. Behind the male leaders came a single female, bearing the bonnet on a tray, but hid from vulgar gaze and from dust in a white muslin napkin; and then followed, covered in like manner, the bulky, but light, silk dress.

It was all methodically done in the true combining spirit of the Saxon race. Some collected the money, others made the purchases, being eminent in such transactions. Several minds were required for the inditing of the address, and two esteemed friends of the bride bore the gifts. So said the voluble Rhoda.

And thus the grateful feelings of the little community made its fitting manifestation; and the hearts of two amiable and diligent servants of God were encouraged. Such a scene could only have occurred in a simple state of society.

The Rev. Mr. B. S. took many ways to win the hearts of the Upper Canadians. One of the most effectual was marrying the tall, fresh-coloured daughter* of a worthy militia colonel, whose ancestors came from Holland.

He thus proclaimed his determination to end his days in Canada. A multitude of new relations and sympathies sprung up at once between him and his flock.

Mr. S. was by birth and education an English gentleman. In his thoughtful, mild face—in his simple and most engaging demeanour—it was instantly seen that all his thoughts were centred in the execution of his high commission. His very uncommon pulpit talents were only secondary in usefulness to the affectionate, holy, and laborious tenor of his life.

* An excellent pastor's wife she made. I spent a happy evening with them afterwards at Montreal, where Mr. S. was of great service in his Master's cause.

Two of us determined to walk to Newark (seven miles) for the purpose of embarking in the Ontario steamer for Kingston.

We were walking steadily along the river-side, among alternate woods and farmsteads, the bank being often hid in shrubbery and fine trees, when a soldier in an undress, and carrying a bundle, and a piece of board a yard long and six inches broad, overtook us. Quickly passing us, he ran down to the water's edge by a little bush-entangled path. In a moment or two he had launched into the stream in a very little skiff. He looked about, wiped his brow, and, kneeling down, began to push eagerly in a slanting course, with his poor board, for the American shore, 700 yards distant.

He was a deserter from the little garrison of Queenston. We sat down on a knoll to see what would happen.

When the man had got half-way across, turning our heads, with a natural curiosity, in search of some pursuers, we saw, with beating hearts, some distance up the river, a boat with four soldiers rowing and a serjeant steering, in full rush, to intercept the runaway.

I own that the regimental triangles,* clotted with gore, came before my eyes, and I earnestly wished the man to escape. He, too, instantly

* A wooden frame to which the soldier to be flogged is tied.

saw his danger, flung a large stone out of the boat into the water, dashed his cap on the floor of his coracle, and coolly, but most stoutly, wrought with his board.

At one time I was sure that he would be caught. I looked momentarily for the uplifted musket, but the serjeant was unarmed—perhaps by order.

The chase, though hot, was short. The whole thing was over in five minutes. The four-oared boat, going (with the current) six or eight miles an hour, pounced upon the man one moment too late.

He had barely beached his cockle, snatched up his cap and bundle, and disappeared, without ceremony, in the foreign bush, when his pursuers swept by him with such force that they could not stop themselves, and so allowed the fugitive to get too far inland for further chase.

My heart was in my mouth all the time, and I was upset for the evening.

Desertion along the whole Canadian frontier is frequent: it is a most dishonourable act; and yet there are strong inducements to be guilty of it. Common soldiers often become thoroughly disgusted with their monotonous, hopeless, and often annoying mode of life. Among no class of men is suicide so frequent, and especially in the British dragoon regiments.

A soldier in debt, or in fear of punishment, sometimes unjustly (for tyranny exists everywhere), rows over the narrow water-line, and secures, he expects, not only liberty, but welcome, and eventually, if industrious, the possession of land, with the sweets of a domestic circle of his own. With such temptations, what wonder if an English peasant soldier often disloyally crosses the border?

But, practically, nine out of ten deserters are driven by want into the American army—a service in bad repute, most irksome in peace, and especially dangerous in war. The soldier has been so long provided for by others, that he usually has lost the faculty of self-maintenance and continuous labour.

I was once present at the roll-call of a company of infantry at Sacket's Harbour on Lake Ontario, and every name was British or German—there was scarcely one American. Their Christian names, Asahel, Ira, Zabulon, &c., are unmistakeable.

EXCURSION THE SEVENTH.

PART I.

LAKES ONTARIO AND SIMCOE, ETC.

Winter Journey from Quebec to Montreal—A Story—To Kingston on melting ice—Disasters—Kingston—To Toronto in a boat along shore—Toronto—Yonge Street—Lake Simcoe—The Johnson Family—Notawasaga Carrying-place, and River.

For the purpose of making my descriptions of each district the more clear, compact, and continuous, it may be remembered that I stopped short in the Second Excursion at the entrance of the French River into Lake Huron; because I then only skirted in a hurried manner a part of the north shore of the latter, and knew but little about the rest of that fresh-water flood.

I shall now be enabled, in an early part of this excursion, to speak fully of Lake Huron, and then to continue my narrative in an orderly manner through Lake Superior to the Lake of the Woods, in South Hudson Bay.

In the summer of 1823, my esteemed friend Col. Delafield,* the American agent of the Boundary Commission, the two astronomers, with their staff and myself, were directed to proceed to the Lake of the Woods, for the purpose of surveying it, and Rainy Lake, another very large body of water. The ground to be passed over on the way thither was mostly new to me.

The British portion of the expedition were ordered to leave Kingston, in Canada West, as early in the year as possible, in a beautiful clinker-built boat for Toronto. From thence we were to transport boat and baggage thirty-seven miles by Yonge Street, in a waggon, to Holland's Landing on Lake Simcoe; then to pass into Lake Huron by the pretty river Notawasaga, and so onwards to Fort William, in Lake Superior. At Fort William we were to find, ready for us, two north canoes, manned by six *voyageurs* each. In these we were to proceed by the Grand Portage, along the old commercial route, to the Lake of the Woods, while the American party were to pursue the new route up the River Kaministigua.

As this excursion is long and diversified, it is naturally divided into four parts, under the heads of—1st, The St. Lawrence, Lakes Ontario and

* Now Commandant of West Point Military Academy, on the Hudson River, state of New York.

Simcoe; 2d, Lake Huron; 3d, Lake Superior; and 4th, The Lake of the Woods, &c.

As the Commission was to meet early in May, for the transaction of business, at Kingston in Upper Canada, I left Quebec, together with Col. Hale, the British agent, in the first week in April, 1823, with the hope of arriving at Montreal at least before the approaching thaws should render the roads impassable.

At two in the morning of the appointed day, therefore, the musical bells of the stage sledge (or cariole, as the Canadian calls it) were sounding adown the street, and then stopped at my door. I forthwith stepped in, abundantly well wrapped up, and with a green veil tied over my heavy fur cap, to protect my eyes from the snow-glare.

We were four in number, exclusive of our civil French driver. Winter travelling in Canada is delightful. When properly clothed, cold is only seen, but not felt. It is probable that the exhilaration universally experienced by persons in health in frosty air, may partly arise from a given bulk of the then condensed air containing more life-giving oxygen than at higher temperatures. We were fortunate in our weather. The snow was well laid, and as crisp as salt; the winds were still; and the stars rode high, and many, in a cloudless sky of raven blue. Our stout Normandy horses felt their task lightly, and made excellent way.

The whole country lay under a white mantle of snow, many feet deep, burying out of sight the fences of the farmer, and often half-hiding his house.

We were soon hurrying through the pine woods of Carouge. The smooth and gently-hissing movement of our sledge produced a dreaminess, which gave strange forms to the snow-loaded underwood, and to the strong lights and shadows sustained high in the air by the tall black stems of the pines; while here and there we had momentary glimpses of a broad, white, sparkling world beyond the wood—either extensive meadows or the ice-bound St. Lawrence itself.

The night appeared long, but at last the intense blue-black of the sky began to pale, and the stars slowly to disappear; the dull grey of the morning in the east slowly overspread the heavens, followed, after a weary interval, by the scarlet, pink, green, and yellow streamers of light which harbinger the glorious winter day-spring of Canada. We shook ourselves, and were glad. So fine was the ice on the St. Lawrence, that at Point aux Trembles, about thirty miles above Quebec, we drove down to it and travelled on the broad bosom of the river for forty or fifty miles, charmingly relieved from the rough joltings of the highway.

The high banks on both sides, the woods and habitations, were all snow-clad and at rest, save that now and then a door would open at the sound of our horses' bells. The day became beautiful;—the sun a ball of fire, making the snow and frost-work glitter almost painfully to the eyes.

The ice was as smooth as glass, and so transparent that we could see the long tangled weeds below, visibly trembling in the current. I leaned over the sides of the sledge to see any fish, if possible, but in vain.

There is danger in very smooth ice, arising from the unsteady traction bringing the sledge round before the horses, on any accidental sharp pull. This occurred to us. Just when least expected, while Jean Baptiste was fumbling in his pocket, with his glove in his mouth, our vehicle swung round, caught on something rough, and over we all went on the hard ice, with some violence.

Great, for a moment or two, were our surprise and confusion; but no one was hurt. Old Judge R—— blackguarded the driver furiously; but as his French was very Scotch, it did no harm. I found myself sitting unhurt on a hat-box, pressed as flat as a pancake. Some broken traces were soon repaired, and we were again under way.

At one o'clock we dined on mutton chops and potatoes, and fancied ourselves warmed with hot rum toddy. In half-an-hour we were pleased to mount and be off. I shall not dwell upon this journey to Montreal, nor in general notice our meals and relays.

At the post-house of Batiscan I thought myself too warm, having on two pairs of pantaloons (as is the habit of the country). Standing beside the sledge, I therefore took off one pair, and got in again, surrounded by a group of idlers waiting to see us start. I had seated myself, and was listlessly making marks on the snow, when I noticed a small round paper package on the ground, and another and another. They proved to be doubloons, worth nearly four pounds each, which had fallen out of my pockets. Just as I picked up the third, the driver's whip set the horses off at a gallop. Another moment lost and I should have been a severe loser. We slept that night at Machiche, two stages beyond Three Rivers. The latter we did not enter, but passed it on the St. Lawrence.

We went 115 miles that day without any fatigue. The horses were always ready, and the drivers skilful and lively. Their activity in managing the sledge is surprising. If they see a difficulty a-head which is not to be overcome with the reins, they jump off at full speed, and by main force wrench the rushing vehicle out of harm's way—a mass of ice, a snow bank, or a deep rut. Laying hold of the sledge, they will run alongside of it for half an hour with frolicking ease.

The next day we were off at four A.M. We quitted the St. Lawrence and followed the high road on its banks, along the street of houses I have noticed before, occasionally crossing a frozen stream. We had four horses for two or three stages, on account of their length. One of the drivers here was a Vermont man. His team, or span, were large bright bays, in first-rate condition and in perfect discipline. Although exceedingly skilful, this man was careless. Now he went at a snail's pace; in a moment afterwards he would whisper "Hist!" and we were galloping at full speed up an ascent, perhaps,—which he called sparing his cattle.

It is quite common in Canada, as elsewhere, for logs of timber to lie on the road-side, and sometimes not a little in the way. We were going at top speed; our driver had turned round to speak to Judge R——, when we struck full against the end of one of these logs. The marvel was this, that all the violence was expended on the traces. They snapped like threads. No one was hurt. The sledge remained motionless, held back by the log, and the liberated horses stood trembling a few yards before us.

We went round the shores of Lake St. Peter — not on it, on account of the roughness of the packed ice.

I was extremely pleased with this portion of Canada, the seigniories of Berthier and St. Elizabeth. The houses were numerous and good, with much land under tillage; and the people looked comfortable and cheerful. I saw that in summer this was a pleasant country, with its winding streams, lanes of willows, wych-elms standing everywhere, solitary and large — and with sheltering hills rising high in the rear. "Here the most fastidious," thought I, "might be well content to dwell."

Early in the day we arrived at Montreal, and took up our abode at the Mansion-House Hotel; the lady-like hostess proving to be an English acquaintance of mine in years past.

While dining there, on the day of our arrival, with certain officers and temporary residents, a commander of the navy, carrying a cloak and small portmanteau, walked into the room.

"Hey!" cried several voices at once, "what has brought you here?"

He looked discomposed and flushed, when he answered, "The same thing that took me away—music: but more and worse. I left because the landlord (Martinnaut) would not stop the flute in the next bed-chamber to mine. I have returned (knife, fork, and plate, waiter!) because my neighbour at Clamp's Coffee-house plays day and night on the key-bugle."

As we did not leave Montreal for ten or twelve days, we accepted several invitations,—one especially to an evening party, at the house of a rich old Canadian. Several officers were there; one of whom, as tall, stiff, and slender as a Polish lance, I thought at the time was exceedingly attentive to a pretty little orphan niece of our entertainer.

One of the ordinary miseries of a garrison town is the propensity of the young and fair to ruin themselves, and break the hearts of their fond friends, by inconsiderate marriages with officers of scanty means.

A week after this evening party saw the niece a bride, to the boundless grief of the worthy old uncle.

The young lady had an useful thousand pounds in her pocket.

It so happened, that two days after the marriage we left Montreal for Kingston, very early in a most bitter morning (April 20), and about seven A.M. we came in sight, at La Chine, of Lake St. Louis, full of ice, floating trees, &c., and the road a quagmire of mud and ice.

We made comparatively rapid progress, because we had good horses; and so we passed, among other people, the new-married couple, on their way to join their regiment at Kingston (200 miles), in a one-horse gig; the tall officer driving, the delicate young creature chatting and laughing under the inclement sky. Two large boxes, voyage-worn, were in front, and a ragamuffin lad was perched behind, to bring the equipage back at the end of the stage. I sighed to see regimental hardships so soon begun; but they are usually borne with light hearts.

My aged and cautious fellow-traveller, Colonel H——, made some very incontrovertible remarks on the transaction, which I omit.

Two years afterwards, I met accidentally the young lady in one of the passages of Kingston Barracks. Although her cheeks were pale, and somewhat hollow, she still smiled; for the Rifleman had proved a good husband. How or when they contrived to reach Kingston I cannot imagine.

During the last day or two of our forced stay at Montreal a sudden thaw set in, which would have prevented our reaching Kingston in time for the Commission Conference, had we not set out on the instant. It is well known that on such occasions the roads in Canada become impassable. Carriages and horses are therefore risked only on exorbitant terms. Only reflect on the immense valley of Upper Canada, overspread with snow and ice, now melting, and drowning all things during their tedious journey down the St. Lawrence and its tributaries, to the ocean. Were it not for a provision of nature, by reason of which the snow and ice of all intensely cold countries melt with great slowness, farms, soil, houses, and people in Canada, would be swept away altogether.

We contrived to cross the head of Lake St. Louis, near the locks of the Cascades, on slushy, honeycomb ice—not very pleasant to move about upon; and pursuing the common road at the rate of one or two miles an hour, we at length arrived at Côteau du Lac, a small cluster of houses at the lower end of the Lake St. Francis, forty-four miles from Montreal.

We slept at the rude-looking, but really civil, old French hedge-inn, not far from the picturesque cross, which we see in Bartlett's truthful sketch of this spot.

I retain a lively remembrance of the mountain of rank feathers which composed our beds, and which all but smothered us.

Starting early next morning, we were pleased to find that Lake St. Francis (25 miles by 5½) would bear a sledge. Along it, therefore, we went at a slapping pace for many miles; but as the day drew on, large rents in the ice began to form, a mile long each, with partial sinkings and overflows. We therefore left the lake a little above the River Raisin.

We then quitted the sledge, and were glad of a common cart to carry us over the half-frozen and deep sludge of the road, and through a cleared flat country, deformed with the ugly Virginia fences and tree-stumps, but dotted with good houses in front of dense woods, all looking blank and dismal enough at this period of the year.

We stopped, weary, cold, and bespattered, at the pretty village of Cornwall, a little above the head of Lake St. Francis, and seventy-eight miles from Montreal. It was the first considerable collection of houses we had seen in Upper Canada.

Good work, considering, we made next day; for we reached Prescott, forty miles from Cornwall, in a spring waggon. Our road, such as the season left it, passed through a productive but marshy country, and ran close to the St. Lawrence—always a quick current, and often a boiling rapid—plunging over ledges of rock, and among islands of maple and oak. Since my visit, gigantic ship-canals have been here constructed, for the transit of produce and goods; and the traffic is already very great.

Through the openings between the islands in the wide river we see the American shore, and the town of Waddington, which, being on a rising bank, appears to advantage.

Colonel Fraser has a good house, twelve miles below Prescott: ten miles below which town we trotted briskly through the battle-field of Chrystler's Farm (1813). It was a very important victory. I looked attentively at the scene, and rejoiced that I was there *after* the fray. The vulgar flatness of the ground, the stagnant ditches, the mossy, rotten fences, the dwarfed leafless trees, and the drowsy creaking of a pot-house sign hard by, indisposed me for a patriot's death,—there, at least.

Four miles below Prescott, a Governor of Upper Canada ordered a town to be built; but Nature said "No," and beat the Governor; there being no convenient harbour. Many houses were erected; but there is nothing left of Johnstown but a few shabby ruins.

I hope that there is at this day a better inn at Prescott (127 miles from Montreal) than we found on this occasion. We met with great civility, but few blankets, with little to eat; and a freer ventilation than was agreeable through the cracks in the wooden walls of our bed-chambers.

A few hundred yards east of Prescott is the finest specimen of a military block-house in Canada. It is called Fort Wellington, and is placed on a flattened mound overlooking the St. Lawrence. It will contain six hundred men at a pinch, I am told. I am sorry I did not sketch its interior, with the ingenious contrivances for stowing away men, ammunition, and provisions. Neither has Mr. Bartlett sketched it, although it would have told well amid the surrounding scenery.*

Half a mile still further east, near one or two windmills, a sharp fight took place in 1837, between the British troops and a party of American Sympathisers. The latter were well worsted, and either killed, taken prisoners, or driven across the river.

* Under the walls of the fort, among large rolled primitive rocks, I found masses of lead ore, mock beryl, anthophyllite, &c. in fine crystals.

Prescott is a lively little place, of 2000 inhabitants (1847), with four churches and chapels. It consists of two principal streets, containing some decent houses, with barracks in the rear, occupied by a company of infantry.

The St. Lawrence is at this spot a mile and a quarter broad, with a steam-ferry to the American town opposite, Ogdensburgh,—a place which exhibits many evidences of prosperity, being planted at the river-outlet of a rich and comparatively populous back-country, famous for its wheat and iron ore; and, perhaps justly, for illicit commerce with Upper Canada (exchanging teas, &c. for broadcloth, &c.)

The next day we proceeded onwards, for the first twenty miles through a country at any other time agreeable, full of river-views and agricultural landscapes, and containing the handsome and showy town of Brockville (population, 2111 in 1847), twelve miles from Prescott, and sixty-two from Kingston. It is chiefly built of stone, and many of its houses would be thought excellent in Europe. It enjoys the commerce of a fertile, well-settled district in the rear.

The immediate vicinity of Brockville is in every direction charming—beautiful hills behind, partly in woods and partly in greensward—while the river-front is a sweet scene of rocky islet and placid stream, with Morris Town, a cluster of white houses on the American shore.

But now we entered a semi-barbarous country of forest, innumerable rocky mounds, little ponds and lakes, with a few miserable clearances, and an uncouth peasantry, hard-to-do—such as we see in Switzerland, when we leave the fat vales and ascend the alpine acclivities. The roads were only passable at a foot's pace, with many a deep slough and knobby rock in the way. We saw scarce a living thing, save a serjeant or two—a bird very like our blackbird, but having scarlet epaulettes.

This rugged tract is a spur, about seventy miles broad, of primitive rocks, going southwards from the vast formations in the north of that class, and connecting them with those of the United States.

We at length arrived at Andrews' Inn, near Mallory's Town, on the high-road to Kingston; and very thankfully.

This family, a fine specimen of the true Yankee, took to us coolly, with none of the agile politeness of our hosts at Côteau du Lac.

Arriving late, and leaving early, we saw nothing of the men; but the womenkind were tall, good-looking, and barely civil. I learnt the very characteristic names of two of the daughters, as

I was dressing in the dark, between five and six next morning, in a sort of lean-to, communicating with the house, and which served as my dormitory.

"Irene," says one of them, "you have not washed up the dishes yet."

"No, Aurely," replied the other; "neither have you scoured the kitchen floor."

My blankets here were again thin and few, and the crannies in the wall wide and many.

A sketch of this inn and its environs is given.

We might be thirty-five miles from Kingston at this inn, and were therefore drawing near our journey's end.

The road, however, only became worse, if possible, and the country, chiefly a forest, more thickly studded with mounds of gneis or of white marble or serpentine. Houses were very rare. We seldom saw the St. Lawrence: when we did, it was black, swollen, and full of moving fields of ice.

There had been during the night a frost after a warmish mist on the preceding day. This had the curious but well-known effect of sheathing the woods in ice a quarter or half an inch thick. The stiff, white-candied limbs of the trees strike the eye very strangely; but the weight of the added matter often breaks the young trees and middle-sized boughs, over very extensive districts.

This whole day was heavy enough. It was principally spent among miry woods, bogs, and rocks, with the exception of two cultivated plains, on one of which we dined, and which were level and fertile, from being based on limestone.

But evening set in again in those disheartening and desolate places. We felt that we were abroad most inauspiciously. A thick, chill fog arose, breathing additional gloom and obscurity upon us. Our pace grew even slacker than before, which to an Englishman would seem impossible.

In fact, we had thick darkness all around. We saw that our horses must fail, although fresh from Brockville and well rested at Andrews'. They could not support the ceaseless strain and the occasional extra effort whipped out of them. We were thinking of humanity and of halting (where?), when we suddenly plunged into a deep hole, and broke our axle-tree, at between seven and eight P.M.

We sent the driver to the next house for help and light. It was a good mile off. He did not return for three hours. As there was no aid to be had at the first house, he had to go further; and there he had met with comfort, if I am to

judge by his renovated looks. But I ought to mention, that when he returned to us I was within an ace of discharging a pistol at him.

Not liking the neighbourhood, so near the frontiers, although in reality there was little danger, I sat on watch, with a loaded pistol, on the driver's seat, which was higher than the body of the waggon, and commanded a long lane or avenue of trees,—not that I could then see up it.

There sitting a very long time, in a half-frozen, dreamy state, I saw a gleam on the more distant trees,—their massy pine branches metamorphosed every moment into some new and ghostly shape by the light and the fog. In the centre of the gleam was a ball of white fire, rather high in the air, which slowly—very slowly—enlarged, quivered, brightened, and glared, until it came quite close to me and filled all things, when I actually screamed out and tried to point the pistol at the advancing object. But fortunately the truth occurred to me that it might be Jonathan, our driver, with his lantern held high over his head that he might see the better.

Jonathan it was, and he brought us good news,—that we must walk some couple of miles to a farm-house, where a spring-waggon, well filled with straw, would be ready to carry us on to Kingston, then eight or nine miles distant.

Having placed our trifling baggage on the horses, we wearily trudged to the promised refuge, and were soon off again. Our carriage was left in the road till morning.

While taking a little refreshment, I could not help smiling at the children and farm-helpers,—half dressed, roused from their beds, peeping at us from behind the elders, with wonderment and pity. We had fallen into the hands of decent people.

By way of climax to the hardships of the day, soon after we got nestled in the straw a gentle rain, mixed with a few soft flakes of snow, began to fall; and this after a time thickened into a continuous soaking shower. This misery, additional to the bad roads and darkness, quite upset us. Umbrellas were vain things; our hats were softened almost into pulp, and our clothes shined in the light of the lantern as if dipped in oil, with the thorough steeping we were undergoing.

I expected a mortal cold, but was disappointed. We sat shivering through the tedious night; now and then faintly smiling at our forlorn estate.

One o'clock in the morning showed us the lights of Kingston—dim and few, and the comfortable old hotel, since deceased.

We were fit for nothing but warm tea and a bed; these we had, and a bath in the morning.

This journey of two persons from Quebec to Kingston (380 miles) cost 90*l.* In the course of last war, Colonel Bonnycastle states that each shell sent from Quebec to Kingston cost the country a guinea.

A talented traveller, speaking of the vicinity of Kingston, says, "the cause which has surrounded Toronto with a desert has done the same for Kingston, otherwise well situated. On the east side of Kingston you may travel for miles together without seeing a human dwelling; the roads accordingly are most abominable to the gates of this the largest town in the province." Not so now.

The cause he refers to is the land being in the hands of absentees and others making no use of it. But the fact is, the land is often not worth cultivation, and the roads themselves are very little used. They are tolerable in summer, and in winter all defects are hid under snow.

The day after our arrival the Commission began its short session, the other members of it having contrived to make their appearance from their several homes.

We were engaged for several days in general conferences, verifying accounts, examining the beautiful maps, which (2½ inches to the geographical mile) had been completed during the past winter, and in laying down instructions for the service of the coming summer.

These things done, the Commissioners despatched the working party already enumerated on their long journey of 1400 miles. Until the month of November they were to lose sight of civilised life.

Kingston appeared to me to be an agreeable residence,—stirring, healthy, and cheap. The environs being elevated, the spectator walks amid an ever-changing panorama, firstly of the comely town itself, and then of the high promontories, Frederic and Henry, crowned with forts and barracks—of dockyards, with men-of-war on the stocks—of large and fertile islands,—and in the south-west, of the open and breezy lake.

Kingston is the principal naval depôt for the Canadas, and is strongly garrisoned. Functionaries in the legal and other branches of the public service are also numerous; so that a large and agreeable society is collected here.

European intelligence is received quickly, *viâ* Sacket's Harbour, the corresponding U. S. naval station. Books are exceedingly cheap.

Kingston is immeasurably improved since my visit. I do not pretend to describe it. Together with its suburbs, it now contains 11,000 inhabitants, with ten churches and chapels, ninety-four taverns!! nine bakers! seven butchers! three booksellers, and two sausage-makers. It has an imposing edifice for various public purposes, entirely of hewn stone, at the cost of 18,000*l*. There is a college, two civil hospitals, a mechanics' institute, and, indeed, the appliances and comforts which in England are only found in much larger towns. The best bridge in Canada is that which Government has built across Cataraqui Bay, to connect Point Henry with Kingston. At the back of the town are large roomy barracks for the soldiery.

On the 14th of May we took our leave and embarked on board a roomy open boat, to coast Lake Ontario as far as Toronto, 181 miles from Kingston, and from thence to proceed in her, *viâ* Yonge Street and Lake Simcoe, to Fort William in Lake Superior, and so on, as already mentioned.

The voyage was commenced with gloomy forebodings of rheumatism and ague; but they were only partially verified. During its course I had innumerable opportunities of admiring the patience and good-humour of my companions under annoyances and privations, severe in their kind, and endured (as I could not endure them) for the hundredth time.

We coasted close in shore by Ernest Town, Bath, Adolphus Town, and Nappannee, twenty miles, to the mouth of the large and singular Bay of Quinté, along a farming country, with a mere glimpse of one or two of the towns, or rather villages, just named.

We encamped in a swamp close to the lake. The rain fell in torrents, and soon went through our one thin tent, giving us a foretaste of good times to come. The tent, I may now observe, barely allowed the three gentlemen who occupied it to lie down side by side in close contact.

The Bay of Quinté is very singularly formed, between the irregular peninsula of Prince Edward's county on the south, and the main land of the midland district on the north. Its length, through its various windings, is fifty miles, and its breadth varies from one to five. It has several arms or sounds in different directions, from two to six miles long. It is very picturesque when the traveller is fairly within it, and so continues to its head, the Carrying-place,—the promontories being often lofty, tree-crowned, and surrounded by broad sheets of water, spotted with islets. Large farm-houses of grey stone, villages, and even towns, such as Belleville and Hallowell, are perpetually showing themselves. The ride from Kingston to Belleville passes through a charming country.

Opposite Capt. Williams's fine farm, near a ferry, is situated the Lake of the Mountain. It discharges into Lake Ontario beautifully, by a cascade shaded by pines, from a height (by guess) of 150 feet.

The Carrying-place, leading from the Bay of Quinté to the open lake, is two-thirds of a mile broad, and has a few houses and stores. A steamer from Kingston visits it every day.

The only instance of rudeness I ever met with in the Canadas, while geologising, took place here, while breaking some fragments of limestone, in a stony field whose fee-simple was not worth ten shillings. The owner came up abruptly to me, and said, "What you are about, thrashing my land with your hammer, I cannot imagine: but I will not suffer it." And he requested me to leave forthwith, which I did. Previously to this gentleman's arrival, I had found many silurian fossils there.

There is little to record respecting this coasting voyage to Toronto. We usually kept close in shore, and thus saw but little of the interior. Where we had a glimpse of it, the land rose slowly to a moderate height, either in flats or hummocks.

The immediate shore (upon which I kept my eyes constantly fixed, in hopes of finding a mammoth) seldom exhibited live rock, but always clay, sand, and gravel, in banks; and beaches, or rushy marshes, lining a succession of bays.

The first remarkable feature westward is Presquisle, a broad, low promontory of woods and grass, at the end of a bay three miles across. It is often used for a harbour.

For many miles west of Presquisle we have only small bays; but we were much interested in observing, at a greater or less distance inland, (100 to 600 yards) well-marked, ancient beaches, either in the shape of rocky walls, of long ridges of clean bowlders, or of sand,—especially ten miles west of Presquisle.

Coburgh, seventy-two miles from Toronto, pleased us much. It stands at the mouth of Jones's Creek, on a high gravelly bank. It is well laid out in good streets, with many excellent buildings, and has a very flourishing appearance. It has a population of 3347 (in 1845), twelve taverns, and three booksellers, six churches and chapels, besides two theological colleges, Episcopal and Wesleyan. It is supported by the Rice Lake country and a tolerably rich vicinity.

Seven miles west of Coburgh we meet with Smith's Creek. Here commences a line (3½ miles long) of clay and sand banks, ten to eighty feet high, with pastures above them, or woods of pine and cedar, and occasionally breaking into picturesque clefts and ravines.

At thirty-five miles east of Toronto we began to pass for many miles very deep bays of shallow water, half grown up with rushes, fit haunt for myriads of wild fowl, and extending far inland, with long spits of shingle here and there,—the back country undulating and showing the mouths of several rivers as they emerge from dense woods.

Fourteen miles from Toronto "the Highlands of York" commence—bold precipices of clay and sand, 80 to 300 feet high, and seven or eight miles long. The angles of some of them are broken into towers and pyramids of considerable grandeur. They are well worth the geologist's minute attention, from the nature of their materials, and the order in which they are deposited. I need say but little here of them, because they are noticed elsewhere. They are useful as landmarks to mariners. Six miles east of Toronto they lower into a woody bank, and retire to a short distance from the lake behind Toronto, and so proceed round the lake.

The reader shall not be fatigued with our encampments. They were usually in some glen near the lake. Perhaps there was occasionally a tavern within half-a-mile of us, but as we were well provided we did not go in quest. Besides, it was best to remain with our men. Our last camp was pitched on Gibraltar Point, on the outer side of Toronto Harbour,—a mere swamp, a breeding-ground for ague. If we had passed the night in the town, all our men would have been intoxicated, with the recklessness of soldiers and sailors going long voyages.

This boat-voyage is now seldom or never made, as both sailing-vessels and steamers pass daily between Kingston and Toronto. We found it rather monotonous. Save the bit of shore we were skirting, neither mainland nor isle was ever visible.

We never saw a human being from Presquisle to Toronto, a hundred miles (save at Coburgh), very few houses, and those miserable ones, partly because we were always under the shadow of alluvial cliffs, or beneath a fringe of woods, left perhaps for shelter. Once or twice we caught sight of the smoke of a distant steamer, or heard in the early morning the loud complaint of the loon, a large and beautiful fowl, as it floated a mile or two out on the quiet waters.

At first there was novelty in the rapid operations of the toilet, conducted wholly in the open air, before a little glass hung on a bush, with cold-water shaving once in five days.

My Toronto and the city of the present day have hardly any relation to each other. Few places in North America have made equal progress. It had in 1817, 1200 inhabitants, and in 1848, 24,000 inhabitants, 91 streets (King Street two miles long), 21 churches and chapels, 10 newspapers, 20 medical men, 5 artists and portrait-painters, 107 taverns, 16 auctioneers, 27 butchers, 19 bakers, and 6 booksellers. The number of taverns observed throughout the Canadas is not altogether indicative of drunkenness, but of the extent of emigration and travelling in general.

Toronto* is a gay place, and in its wealthy shops, stately and crowded churches, paved and gas-lighted streets, public walks, societies, religious, scientific, literary, and social, charitable institutions, is much in advance of British towns of the same size, as was said of Kingston.

The vicinity is liable to ague and its kindred disorders. Rents are very high; some houses of business in good situations are worth from 200*l.* to 250*l.* per annum. The removal to or from Toronto of the seat of government will have no

* Barometric range at Toronto is 1·65 inch, by an average of five years ending with 1844.—CAPT. LEFROY, *Jour. Geog. Soc.* vol. xvi. p. 263.

serious effect upon its prosperity. It has become of fixed commercial importance.

Although it has a pretty bank of pines for a screen behind, Toronto has little local beauty to recommend it.

Glory-loving Americans delight to visit Toronto, because in 1813 General Pike surprised and sacked the place; but his stay was brief. About 260 of the Americans were killed or wounded by the explosion of a mine. Among the former was the General himself, a young officer of great promise.

At Toronto we sent our boat and baggage on stout waggons to Holland's Landing (37 miles), now but a hamlet, and then scarcely more than a single public-house in a marshy country on the river Holland, and seven miles from Lake Simcoe.

We travelled slowly to the same place due north, along an old-established road called Yonge Street, and found the drive rather interesting.

About a mile from Toronto we ascended the woody steep already mentioned, and then soon after another, when we traversed first some uneven ground, then a well-tilled plain, followed by a hilly region nearly to Montgomery's Tavern, ten miles from Toronto, at which, during the late rebellion, Major Moody was brutally murdered. It is to be hoped his poor family have a liberal pension.

A rolling country, often marshy, partially cultivated, took us eight miles to Fleck's Inn, where we plunged into a picturesque and rugged district, mostly wild, with ponds or meres in the various hollows, full of perch, trout, &c.* How they get there I know not, as some of these lakelets are quite isolated. Bond's Lake, one of them, is 783 feet above Lake Ontario, according to the observations of Lieutenant Lefroy, R.A. It is twenty-two miles from Toronto.

A tendency to ascend obtains all the way from Toronto until we reach five and a half miles beyond Fleck's. At that point (thirteen miles from Holland's Landing) we begin to descend towards Lake Simcoe for two miles, among a jumble of oak and pine ridges, called the "Oak Ridges," when we arrive at a level and agricultural district.

Eleven miles from Fleck's we find Gamble's Inn, in a charming country, full of fine large farms on flats, varied by the alluvial terraces and mounds of some now forgotten stream or lake. Woods on high grounds surround the scene, and especially two pine-laden ridges, eight and five miles, respectively, distant from the lake, and running towards its west side.

* Mountain Lake, in the Bay of Quinté, has plenty of fish, without the possibility of receiving any from other waters in the present state of the levels.

This district is occupied principally by Quakers, meekly rigid. Very pleasing it was to look upon their quiet, unwrinkled, well-fed faces on the road, and on their comfortable farm-servants. A few Mennonites or Tunkers are close at hand in the wilder parts, whither they have been tempted by the greater cheapness of the land.

From the Five-mile Ridge, just spoken of, Cook's Bay in Lake Simcoe becomes visible as a narrow belt of water, buried in woods, with high lands in the west.

Where Yonge Street crosses a little rise, four miles from Holland's Landing, we see on our north-east the neat country-town or village of New-market, with six churches and chapels, two ladies' boarding-schools, and 600 inhabitants, in 1846.

We remained as little time as possible at Holland's Landing; and on the 24th of May we floated down the winding river on the edge of an immense morass to the left, and girt with pineries, into Lake Simcoe.

At the point of embarkation* the Holland river is about twenty-five yards across; but it soon

* Among some masses of limestone on the landing-place, brought by the farmers for agricultural purposes from the outlet of the lake, I found one rare bivalve (the *orbicula cancellata* of Mr. G. B. Sowerby), only known in Sweden, some *conularia*, *bellerophones*, and other fossils of the Silurian age.

widens, and receiving four miles lower down a large branch, it becomes 200 yards broad, and opens into Cook's Bay, which is six or seven miles deep, and three miles across.

Lake Simcoe (Shain-eong of the Indians) has pleasing features, clear waters, woody headlands, and islets. It is 498 feet above Lake Huron, according to observations made in 1845 by Lieutenant Younghusband (Director of Toronto Observatory), and therefore 729 feet above the level of the ocean,—a fact which leads us to infer a severe climate.

It is thirty-five miles north of Toronto, and is in length nearly thirty miles, and in its widest part about eighteen. It is a tolerably compact body of water.

There are many islands in the north and east sides of the lake; but only one is inhabited, and this by Indians of the Wesleyan denomination, of whose Christian consistency of life we hear very favourable accounts.

The banks of the lake are generally low, and clothed with wood down to the water's edge; the land, though fertile, is but partially brought under cultivation. In North Gwillimbury and Georgina there are some prettily situated farms, and there is now population enough generally to pay one steamboat.

I only know of six streams of any size which

discharge into the lake. The names of the three greatest of these are the Holland (in Gwillimbury, &c.), the Talbot (in Thorah), and the Brack (in Rama).

Lake Simcoe is remarkable for the vast numbers of wild fowl, ducks, geese, &c. &c., which frequent its marshes.

Its outlet is at the Narrows, at the north end of the lake.

The Narrows lead into a romantic lake (Gougichin), full of limestone islands.* It is twelve miles long by four broad, and on its banks there are two villages, Orillia and Rama. It pours into the Severn or Matchadash river, which, with seven or more portages, runs into Matchadash Bay of Lake Huron.

A large Indian barrow was opened about the year 1820 on the shores of Simcoe lake, and a good many brass and other ornaments and relics found; but I have lost all my notes upon this subject. Captain Skene, R.E., is my authority.

The townships of the Simcoe district are remarkable for the beauty of their names. They were given to them by Sir Peregrine and Lady Maitland. Some of them, I may mention:—In-

* This limestone is of a delicate pale grey colour, very fine in its texture, and in parts filled with organic remains. It has been analysed at my request by Dr. Troost of Philadelphia, and found to be pure carbonate of lime, with a trace of alumina.

nisfil, Medonte, Orillia, Vespra, Tecumseth, Sunnidale, Essa, Rama, Oro, Adjala. They were one day at a loss for another name, when Lady Sarah espying a pretty lap-dog on the rug before the drawing-room fire, suggested that its name, "Tiny," should mark a small part of the wilderness not far from Penetanguishene. The name was adopted.

The surveyors of the state of New York have been most unfortunate in their territorial designations.

This short sketch of a lake but little known to books having been premised, we may pursue our voyage.

We breakfasted in a deserted hut on the Lake Shore, near Holland river. As it rained hard, we rendered it tenantable by flinging a tarpaulin over a rafter at one end.

I speak of this breakfast on account of our having been annoyed there by a singular black fly in countless myriads, which I never saw elsewhere. We could scarcely eat or drink for them. Their black hairy bodies were one-third of an inch long, and their antennæ were armed with beautiful flat brushes, also black. (Bibio. species?)

Other insects, besides the mosquito, sand, black fly, and ants, are sources of great annoyance in the wilderness. On some parts of the plains of the river Saskatchawine (an immense stream which flows from the Rocky Mountains into Hudson's Bay) there are marvellous crowds of wasps, which, although they do not often sting, cluster round the traveller while reposing, and even gather upon the meat he is conveying to his mouth.

Cook's Bay, which we had entered, has low woody shores,* and in my time was only inhabited on its east shore.

Clearing this bay, Lake Simcoe opened to the view as a great expanse, with two islets off the north angle of the bay, and others, larger, in the remote distance easterly.

Towards Kempenfelt Bay, on the west side of the lake, a very gentle rise of land is perceptible, and as we proceed down that beautiful bay it gradually becomes from forty to sixty feet high, chiefly covered with pine groves; now, however, in part, the seat of thriving clearances.

Kempenfelt Bay runs about W.S.W., is from one and a half to two miles broad, by nine miles deep, and distributed as usual into numberless shallow coves.

* Singularly loaded with large primitive bowlders for some distance into the woods. It is not so on the east side of the bay. There is some primitive rock *in situ* on the north and east sides of the lake, and a few ledges of limestone are visible.

The flourishing village of Barrie, with 500 inhabitants, three churches, a mechanics' institute, and cricket club, stands at the extreme end of the bay (1847); in my time an untouched forest.

We took up our abode near the bottom of the bay in a lonely house, occasionally used as an inn by the few travellers going to Penetanguishene (thirty-two miles), or into Lake Huron by the river Notawasaga.

It was then kept by a respectable person named Johnson, who had a numerous family. Here commences the portage of nine miles to a small branch of the Notawasaga; and here we were detained for five days, during very stormy weather for most of the time.

As we stay rather long at Mr. Johnson's, and as it is the last house we shall enter for three hundred miles at least, I will describe it.

It was a clap-boarded* house, square in shape, and rather large, standing upon a gravelly bank, close to the lake. It contained a good kitchen, three or four sleeping-rooms, partly in the roof, two good parlours, and bed-chamber for guests of quality. I have had worse at the best hotel in Washington.

So new was the wood when the house was put together, or so hot are the summers in Kempen-

* A house faced with boards, laid horizontally, and overlapping.

felt Bay, that it had shrunk most grievously. The kitchen and the parlour might almost be called parts of a cage, so well were they ventilated. I also remember a round tub of a boat staked to the lake shore, and a little garden of herbs near a high cleared bank of gravel, behind the house, ranging for an unknown distance parallel to the lake shore.

An hundred yards or so inland begins the forest—a fragrant forest of firs, maple, beech, oak, and iron-wood—many of the trees from fifty to seventy feet high, without a branch. As there is no undergrowth, we may walk at our ease for miles on a soft carpet of last year's leaves, thick as the slain at the battle of the kings whom Chedorlaomer overthrew.

We were soon comfortable here. Good food is essential to persons exposed constantly to wet and cold. So we carried our own supplies, and were not dependent on the split fowl and leathery ham usually presented to travellers in out-of-the-way places like these.

My companions were at their duties in various parts of the portage, hastening the progress of the boat and baggage, while I remained in or about the house.

Towards the evening of our first day I asked our very obliging landlady for candles, and was surprised to learn that they had none. I was much disturbed. What was to be done during the three hours of darkness yet to come before retiring to rest?

She replied that they used a country-made lamp, fed with tallow, but that some candles should be made and placed on table in half an hour; and so they were,—useful, good-looking moulds. After running a thick cotton thread down a candle-mould, they fill it with melted lard, and then sink it deep in the lake for fifteen minutes. Night by night, during my stay, such candles did good service—but not a little blown upon and wasted by the all-pervading wind.

I took some delightful walks in the neighbouring woods, and along the side of the bay; finding a few rare fossils. In one of these perambulations I met with a little wiry old man, who had been a small farmer near Wakefield, and therefore called "Yorkshire Johnny." He had a clearance a mile or two to the north; and we trafficked with him for butter.

"Why, Johnny," says I, "you've got a desperate long way from home. Don't you wish yourself in Yorkshire again?"

"No," replied he; "not a bit on't. In old England we were in a standing fright at four things,—rent and rates, tithes and taxes. Slave we ever so hard, my old woman and me, we could not make ends meet; but now we are putting money into the old stocking:"—and off he went, chuckling. The four things this old farmer stood so much in fear of scarcely exist in the Canadas.

Like the Swiss cheesemakers in their mountain châlets, Johnny had put on a canvass jacket with short sleeves, for coolness. His bare arms had anything but a pleasing look.

Returning from a long ramble, "a silent listener to the stirs of the solitude," I thoughtlessly walked by a back entrance into what may be called the family room of my temporary residence.

It was visible at once that I was an intruder upon an agitating interview.

With his back to me, apparently gazing upon the lake below, was a shapely, but rather short young man, with massy flaxen hair flowing over his velveteen jacket; and before me, standing in the middle of the room, was the most beautiful girl of seventeen I ever beheld. I seemed to look upon an angel unawares. I had not seen her before, perhaps from her being in delicate health.

She was the very ideal of innocence disturbed, and, alas! of fragility. She was small in person, and, as was easily seen through her simple dress, tenderly and elegantly fashioned.

She was too transparently fair for health: her face was perfect—Raphaelesque—and wore the inspired melancholy of certain invalids, with faintly crimson lips and shining ivory brow—the blue, dove-like eye lifted upwards.*

This attitude and play of feeling was but for a moment; for she immediately accosted me with good breeding, and evidently with the hesitation of a half-formed purpose—which now I know.

An elder sister coming in the instant after, opened to me, with affectionate zeal, the secret of the scene. The pair were lovers, and very naturally had their plans.

The young man resided at a fur station, not very distant, and had heard of the approach of our party. He had come to offer himself as guide and huntsman to our party, thereby to make up a little sum for a very important object. But, unfortunately, we were provided months before, so that we could not engage him.

But, "who would die in this bleak world alone?" as the silly song says. They were afterwards happily married; and she lived among the rocks and cranberry-marshes of Lake Huron,

* "Columbinos oculos in coelum porrigens."

astonishing the few wayfarers that crossed their threshold with her modest beauty.

Nature seems to delight in contrasts and surprises: her fairest things are out of sight. Instead of this young person being placed on a barbarous and inclement frontier, it would seem more fitting that she should have been the child of an English baronet; or, better still, of a well-beneficed Devonshire rector, of kind heart and elegant tastes. I am jotting Canadian pictures —accept this as one.

The elder sister, Mary, was almost as remarkable in a different way. She was a strong, tall brunette, full of good-natured energy (she made my candles) —a handsome, broad-faced, happy dame,—one of those self-supporting institutions nobody inquires about. What became of her I do not know, and never shall.* She spoke bravely for her sister's lover, while the poor girl herself could only sit and wish.

A few weeks before our arrival, just when the ice in the bay was breaking up, Mary, looking out of the window, saw a bear swimming across, and about midway. She called to a little sister about eight years of age, seized an axe, and both

* From recent information, I have a fancy that she keeps an excellent hotel at the gay little town of Barrie, hard by, and is as obliging and happy as ever.

jumped into their boat. The child paddled to the animal, now in full retreat, while the Amazon stood forwards, axe in hand, and clove his skull by repeated blows. She showed me the rich, glossy skin, now an useful trophy in sledge and bed-chamber. After this story I had the weakness to be rather afraid of her.

As the father of this fine family was not poor, and as they did not seem uneducated, I suppose he sent them to some neighbouring boarding-school for a year or two, as at Newmarket or Toronto.

At length we left Johnson's, to cross the portage — a broad, sandy opening in the woods, which I shall not further describe, as its features are now totally changed.

Near its lower end we found ourselves overlooking from a lofty bank a vast prospect of marsh and wood, stretching to the south thirty miles or more, and bounded eastward by a long range of blue hills, flat-topped, and running in the direction of Cabot's Head, Lake Huron. This marsh does not go more than three miles northerly, and is succeeded by high forests and occasional lakes towards Penetanguishene.

Not far from this escarpment there was, in 1823, a post for two soldiers, as a guard to any military stores that might pass. An absurd tyranny was practised even here. The stronger soldier was in the daily habit of chastising his comrade for supposed breaches of discipline. Being seldom visited, the weaker man had no present redress.

Into this forbidding marsh, which, in South America, would have been peopled with serpents and alligators, we descended, and near a deserted building embarked in a stagnant creek, twenty feet broad, often quite benighted by trees and creeping plants.

We worked cautiously among fallen trees and loosened masses of earth for eight miles along the perpetual doublings of the creek, among inundated woods of alder, maple, willow, and a few elm and ash. When we drew near to the main river, Notawasaga, the still water was exchanged for a reflux against us.

We entered the Notawasaga gladly from the north: it is large and long; its principal branches rising near the rivers Credit (Ontario) and Grand (Erie Lake), in the townships of Mono and Amaranth.

We struck it, twenty-five miles from Lake Huron, thirty to forty yards broad, and running two miles an hour through grounds for the most part under water, with here and there mounds of slippery shining ooze, weedy mud, or even knolls of grass and trees. It has many sharp turns and long reaches, amid spots of exquisite woodland scenery. Here we often startled the busy wild-fowl. As we descend, the river begins to have, on one or other side, high banks, and it swells out into two pretty but small lakes, dotted with isles of marsh and willows, near the Rapids; the second being one mile above them.

These Rapids are some miles from Lake Huron, and are nine miles long. They only average three miles an hour, and are not rough, except when obstructed by rafts of fallen trees. Their smoothness may, in part, arise from the bed of the river being of white clay or marl, which the soldiers of Penetanguishene use to clean their belts.

Three miles from the head of the Rapids I began to see in the right bank, near the water-mark, two horizontal seams or layers, each four inches thick, of fresh-water shells *closely pressed together*, and lying under from twenty to fifty feet of sand. This was very distinct for three miles down the Rapids, and more or less down to Lake Huron.

These shells are unios,—precisely similar to those found now in the lake. They are large, perfect, friable, with a calcined pearly lustre. Both valves are in juxtaposition, and often contain sand and the smaller fresh-water univalves, &c.; which latter are scattered thinly about these two layers.

This deposit of shells proves that Lake Huron has been much larger than at present, that its waters were then sweet, and that they were laid down during a period of tranquillity.

About the middle of the Rapids the banks run up to the height of 120 feet, and consist of clay, capped with sand and fine gravel.

Below the Rapids the river assumes a steady width of from 150 to 200 yards, with high scarps of sand, bearing groves of fir. It is now for several miles a truly fine river, the land about it dry and fertile, with some magnificent pines. Sunnidale, the township at its mouth, has only 174 inhabitants (1847).

We saw scarcely any living thing in the lower part of the river. Now and then we caught sight of a wild duck or a solitary Indian, and of his canoe gliding under the shadow of high and umbrageous banks.

The Notawasaga discharges into Lake Huron, between banks of drift-sand and shells, which, on the left, shelter the little trading-post of Mr. Robinson, while the other side has a thin grove of pines. There is a bar at the mouth; and, smooth as it was when I passed it (twice), it is the seat of a raging surf when a high north-west wind prevails, and is the dread of all who travel in canoes.

" Huron! chantons, le lac Huron!" cried our steersman, as we swept rapidly between the petty ridges of broken white shells which line the mouth of the river and the strand of the lake.

He then struck up the spirited and original air, which is married to the following simple words; and was well chorused by his comrades:

" Le premier jour de Mai
Je donnerais à m'amie
Une perdrix, oh, là! qui vole, qui vie, qui va là!
Une perdrix, oh, là! volante dans les bois.

Le deuxième jour de Mai
Je donnerais à m'amie
Deux tourterelles, une perdrix, oh, là! qui vole, qui vie, qui va là!
Une perdrix, &c.

Le troisième jour de Mai
Je donnerais à m'amie
Trois rats des bois, deux tourterelles, une perdrix, &c.

Le quatrième jour de Mai," &c. &c. &c.*

---

* Taken from the mouth of the singer.

EXCURSION THE SEVENTH.

PART II. SECT. I.

LAKE HURON.

General Sketch—Canoe-voyage along North Coast of Huron—Giant's Tomb—Indian Fishermen—The Gull's Nest—Crowds of Isles—Stormbound—Indian Grandmother and her Coracle—Indian Home — Parry's Sound — Labrador feldspar — French River—La Cloche—Beautiful Scenery—French Ruin—Sagamuc Rivers—Ojibbeway Indians—Rivers Missassaga and Thessalon—Copper Mines—Indian Sports.—North-west arm of Huron—Lake George—Straits and Villages of St. Mary—Society at St. Mary's—Embark for Drummond Island in Lake Huron.

PRELIMINARY REMARKS.

As we shall feel more at home in our journey through Lake Huron, after a little preface descriptive of its principal features, I shall at once say, that

Lake Huron is the third of the great Canadian lakes from the Atlantic. It is bounded on the north by hills, morasses, forests, and stony barrens; in every other direction by fertile, low, or undulating lands.

It is studded with islands innumerable, some emerging in diminutive mounds of naked rock, or in the gentle swells of inundated woods, so to speak; and others in lofty table-lands, fifty miles long.

Its shape is triangular, but indistinctly, so that its real form can only be learnt by an inspection of the accompanying map.

It is nearly 1000 miles round, and often 1000 feet deep. Bouchette says that its length is 218 miles, and its greatest breadth 180 miles, but, I think, not very correctly.

Its height above the Atlantic is 594 feet.

At the south-western angle of Lake Huron is Lake Michigan,* an enormous gulf, only separated from the former by Mackinaw Straits, four miles broad, but without length, and merely designated by two capes.

By a glance at the map we see that Lake Huron is all but bridged over, lengthwise, by the

* Lake Michigan is 300 miles long, 65 broad, and 730 round. Soundings have given 800 feet in depth, in places. Lake Michigan has the St. Clair for its outlet; but when its waters are unusually high, they flow by the Rivers Des Plaines and Illinois into the Mississippi—a remarkable fact.

Manitouline Islands, which stretch from Cabot's Head to the south-west mainland, and also nearly touch the north main in the La Cloche district.

Of the three portions into which the lake is thus divided the two northern are full of shoals, rocks, and islands. The southern division has scarcely a reef or islet, and is deep and broad; as free to ship or steamer as the mid-Atlantic. It is larger than both the others taken together; but be it remembered that the Georgian Gulf alone is 160 miles long.

Cabot's Head, ninety miles from the mouth of the Notawasaga, is a remarkable headland, evidently once a part of the Manitouline ridge. It is 144 miles almost due north of the outlet the St. Clair, and runs northerly for twenty-five miles. It is not broad; and consists of deeply-indented limestone bluffs, sometimes 300 feet high, skirted by reefs and occasional islets.*

Let us say a few words on the Manitouline Islands.

The appellation of "Manitouline," or "Sacred" Isles, is first observed in Lake Huron, and is constantly met with in the lakes further to the west.

They are four in number, the Fitzwilliam (or

* A little to the north-east of Cape Hurd is a very convenient harbour, a *cul-de-sac*, 800 yards deep by 40 broad, with 7 fathoms water.

Fourth), the Grand, Little Manitou, and Drummond, besides the Isle of Coves, and other fragments, from Cabot's Head to Fitzwilliam Island, the distance being fourteen miles, and almost wholly covered with shoals and islets.

The Fitzwilliam* is small, but its neighbour, the Grand Manitou, is as large as two average English counties, being seventy-five miles long, with an average breadth of eight; the eastern half of it may be safely set down as twenty-five miles across. The old French maps make it a large, very long island. Previous to 1825 the English maps erroneously broke it up into many parts.

Its shores are everywhere deeply indented; singularly so in the middle (Bayfield's Sound) and at the east end, where Heywood's Sound on the north, and the Manitouline Gulf on the south, are only three miles apart, a low ridge of limestone separating them.

The Grand Manitou is often rugged, high, precipitous, looking from a distance like a succession of table-lands. The scenery is sometimes magnificent; and it has large tracts of fertile land.

* On one of the islets close to the Fitzwilliam, Messrs. Thompson and Grant found rattlesnakes. The Flower-Pot Isle is also here, so called from two bare rocks standing together on the long tongue of a high island. The tallest is 47 feet high, with a small base and broad top.

Its summers are hot, and vegetation rapid. Judging from Penetanguishene* (north-east 120 miles), the winters must be very severe.

Indians with their white superintendants alone occupy this island; and these chiefly at the two Government villages of Manitou-wawning (Heywood's Sound) and at Wequemakong (Smyth's Bay), eight miles apart.

They were formed in 1836 by Sir Francis Head, and, all things considered, have done better than might have been expected. In 1840 there were 732 Indian settlers, of whom 437 were Christians.

The Grand Manitou and the isles on its north, both easterly and westerly, are remarkable for dipping on their north side into the lake by a deep wall. Most of their precipices are on their northern side.

An island, called Wall Island by Captain Bayfield, has a submerged wall of this kind on its north side. Two miles out from it in the lake there is bottom at six feet, but move one yard

* At Penetanguishene the thermometer occasionally descends to −32°. Captain Bayfield has seen it at 40°, with rain during the day, and fall to −33° during the night there.—*Quebec Hist. Soc.* vol. iii. p. 49.

In 1825–6 the extreme range was 124°! The extreme range at Madeira is perhaps 40°. Sir J. Richardson found the mean heat of the same year at this place to be 45°.

In June and July the temperature rises to 92°; when the heat is oppressive to the sensations.—*Geog. Soc. Journ.* vol. ix. p. 378.

northerly and you have a depth of 138 feet, with a muddy bottom. A similar instance [Lieutenant Grant] occurs in Pelletau's Narrows, &c.

The Little Manitou and Drummond Island, which continue the chain of islands to the south-west mainland, are comparatively small. Further particulars respecting them will be found in the course of this Excursion.

The large and beautiful island of St. Joseph (British), in the north-west part of Lake Huron, Michilimachinac, the Gulf of Saquina, and the south shore generally, will be treated of in the course of my narrative.

The waters of Lake Huron are clear and transparent, and, according to Dr. Drake of Cincinnati, "so full of carbonic acid gas that they sparkle. "They transmit the rays of light to a great depth, "and consequently having no preponderating "solid matters in suspension, an equalization of "heat occurs." Dr. Drake ascertained that in summer, at the surface, and 200 feet below it, the temperature of the water was 56°.

"One of the most curious things in the shallow "parts of Huron is to sail or row over the sub-"lacune mountains, and to feel giddy from fancy; "for it is like being in a balloon, so pure and "tintless is the water." So far, and perhaps too far, Dr. Drake.

The rivers of Lake Huron are not very numerous; but it has five, as large, or larger, than its outlet, St. Clair. They are the Severn, French, Spanish, Mississaga, and the Straits of St. Mary, all on the barren northern coast. Of the outlet I shall speak in the proper place.

The evaporation must be enormous, but I am not aware of any estimate of it having been made.

The reader must need be patient while voyaging with us along the chill and stormy shores of North Huron. If hard to read, it was harder far to endure; but the great Maker of all things did not disdain to fashion them, and here and there to add an ornament.

Soon after our entrance into this lake our extra provisions failed, and we were content with cocoa, brown sugar, and biscuit, night and morning; salt beef and potatoes for dinner. Our hardy boatmen had their usual Indian country fare, maize-soup thrice a-day, with a glass of whisky after unusual exertions, or in cold weather.

When we issued from the picturesque Notawasaga we found ourselves at the bottom of a vast circular bay, fifty or sixty miles round.

Stormy as the weather very soon afterwards proved, the morning of that day was serene. Everything, lake, sands, and foliage, sparkled under the rays of a burning sun, and looked soft and innocent. In front the eye ranged over waters apparently without a shore, upon whose bright surface the low smooth billows rolled in slow succession to the beach. On our left was a line of woods, having in their rear the "Blue Mountains," before referred to. On our right we had a line of broken heights, usually well timbered, as far as Twenty-mile Point and the Christian Isles, grey and indistinct in the extreme north.

A reperusal of my notes shows that the impression made upon the mind by this inland sea varies with the hour. At one time it is thus written:—
" When the varied shores of these liquid wilder-
" nesses have ceased to attract the eye, and their
" vastness to interest the imagination, all sense of
" pleasure is lost in that of gloom and solitude,
" and in the remembrance of their storms." At another time it is said, " that I am affected even to
" tears to think that I never again shall seek the
" rare insect or fossil, or greet the friendly savage,
" among the shadowy isles, the purple mountains,
" and broad waters of Lake Huron."

Pròceeding northwards from the river, we arrived in due time at the north angle of Notawasaga Bay, and passed the three Christian Islands, once a missionary station of the Roman Catholics.

They are from one to three miles long each, the nearest to the main being three miles distant. They are covered with fine forests.

Four miles and a half further brought us to the Giant's Tomb,* an oval island three miles long. It is a landmark for great distances, from its resemblance to a lofty cairn, and thence its name. It is a high mass of limestone, flat-topped, surrounded by a belt of low land; the whole island, except where there is too much sand, clothed with fine trees.

I was much struck with the state of its shores; that on the north was scraped clean to the rock by the waves, which wash the very roots of the underwood; the east beach is wholly of fine sand, and the south and west sides of the island are covered with vast accumulations of rolled blocks only, of great size, and among others, of Labrador feldspar, which exists some miles to the north-west as a living rock. The ice of winter may have *partly* done this, and dropped its burthens in places of repose.

We now crossed to a naked islet on the direct way to the North Main, holding Gloucester Bay on the east.

Gloucester Bay is large, and very irregular in

* In 1823 there was no magnetic variation at the Giant's Tomb.

its outline.* Its lower end takes the name of Matchedash, and receives the river Severn of Lake Simcoe.

From this point (the barren gneis islet), a sudden change of scenery took place. The deep waters, regular outlines, and fertility of the main (based on limestone before) ceased. The intricate region of islets, of reefs, and marshes, began.

The view from hence, our dining-place (where my compass would not traverse), is very fine. The capacious mouth of Gloucester Bay, partly barred by islands, is on the east, bounded by high woods and headlands. Looking south, past the lofty Giant's Tomb, partly hiding the Christian Isles, we see the successive capes we had just skirted. Northerly, we beheld the thousand rocks of the north shore, backed by ranges of pine forests.

We now made directly north, and encamped for the night on the slippery top of a mound of granite, twenty feet high, some little distance from Rennie's Bay (so named by Captain Bayfield).

Whether we were really on the main or not, I

* Only a few miles from our crossing-place, at the bottom of a very narrow inlet in Gloucester Bay, is the naval and military station of Penetanguishene, one of those dismal places in which the British soldier has so often to vegetate, cut off from the whole world. The winters spent by the officers in low wooden cabins are severe, and tedious beyond measure. Being placed on a narrow isthmus, the station can be attacked front and rear.

cannot tell. We were among a labyrinth of dough-shaped mounds, rushy marshes, and thin groves of stunted cedar, birch, alder, and red oak. We could not see 500 yards into the interior.

Our tent was only secured by laying poles loaded with stones along the bottom of the canvas.

The evening had been lowering, but afterwards became partially clear and starry. I left the tent at about eleven o'clock, and was much struck by the picture before and around me.

Our men were asleep at the fire—all, save the cook on duty, who was feeding it with wood, and stirring the soup. The cool wind was shaking the birch trees, and the waves were whispering and rippling among the reefs below. Looking towards the head of Gloucester Bay I saw several solitary red lights wandering over the surface of the lake, which lay here and there in shadow. These were the canoe-torches of Indians spearing the fish attracted by the flame. When they chanced to draw near, the flare of the light, and the frequent streams of cinders dropping into the water red-hot, were reflected beautifully on the dark men and their craft.

After a time I went and sat on a stone by the side of the cook, and watched his stirrings and tastings.

" Monsieur le Docteur," said he, breaking silence, " these vile rocks and morasses remind me " of a mishap of mine long ago in the Indian " countries, which would have put an end to me, " ' *ici bas,*' had it not been for a tin-pot and a " gull's nest—things very simple, Monsieur le " Docteur."

" Our *bourgeois* (master) took me and an Indian " to look out for a new beaver district on the Black " River, which runs into the Mackenzie.

" Two days from the Fort, while crossing a " pond, I saw a gull's nest, with four little gaping " chicks in it, on a bare rock. I had lifted up " my foot to kick the whole hatch into the water, " according to our notion, that if you kill a bird, " a deer, or what not, ten will come instead, when " the *bourgeois* forbade me.

" Well, one day, three weeks afterwards, our " canoe capsized in a rapid, and we lost all—every " thing, except a tin-pot, which stuck in one of " its ribs. Of course we turned back, and lived " on dead fish, green bilberries, now and then a " young bird, tripe de roche, and Labrador tea, " which fortunately our pot enabled us to boil.

" The cold winds seemed to cut us asunder, and " swept through our very marrow, for we lost " most of our clothes too.

" When we were near spent by many days' weary " travel, the *bourgeois* told us that if we would

" work like gallant men, he would give us a meat-" supper on the morrow's night. We wondered, " but somehow believed the *bon homme*.

" Sure enough, on the next evening, we reached " a pond. I knew it immediately. Above a bare " rock two old gulls hovered and sported in the " air. Trusting the young birds had not flown, " but fearing they had, we rushed to the nest and " found four large plump pullets, which I certainly " think, blessed be God, saved our lives. The " next day we fell in with some friendly Indians."

" So you see," said I, " Baptiste, that mercy is " the best policy."

The next morning early we started for the old trading post of Bourassa. The whole intervening north shore, thirty miles long, is as much cut up, and as full of fiords and inlets, as the coast of Norway. These are sometimes several miles deep, and receive rivers, such as the Muskoka, Moon, and Seguine. It is faced, too, with a multitudinous belt several miles broad, of rocky or tolerably-wooded islands, invested by marshes, rushy basins, and lagoons, so numerous and intricate as to baffle the most experienced guide. Captain Bayfield counted in this part of the lake 7000 islets and islands within forty-five square miles. It was small blame to us, therefore, that we were lost in the deep bay, which is honoured by the name of Franklin, east of Parry's Sound, choked with reedy islets and half-drowned cranberry grounds.*

This happened towards evening. It was then blowing a hurricane in the open lake, where in our boat we did not like to venture. We accordingly crept along under the lee of this and that islet; but although our guide had been on this coast several times, his memory failed him; and we were compelled to encamp, after many weary attempts to find our way.

We were on the outskirts of the island groups. I shall never forget the hoarse raging of the storm, mingled with the whistle of the bowed reed-beds—so different from the crisped smiles of yesterday. We were glad to pitch our little tent in a tolerably dry hole under a bush, fastening it down with double care, and covering it with a few pine-branches to make it warmer; for the low, exposed islet, gave us little shelter from the resistless wind. But when once ensconced within our ingenious defences, it was

* The cranberry grows in shallows, composed of smooth primitive mounds, five yards square, scarcely above water, stagnant ponds full of varied vegetation. Both plant and fruit lie low. The Huron cranberry is far finer than any I ever tasted elsewhere—high-flavoured, full of juice, skin very thin, and of the size of a boy's marble. I boiled up with sugar a good many in October, and found them a delicious addition to our suppers.

right sweet to remember the line of the old poet,—

"Quam juvat immites ventos audire cubantem!"

All the next day we lay wind-bound. At some risk we might have proceeded on the open lake; but it was not thought prudent to expose our valuable instruments to chance of damage.

The surveyors meanwhile prepared their field-books.

On the third day the wind lulled, and we were about to leave, when at two P.M. we perceived a small black object a mile off, in the open and still rough lake. We hoisted a handkerchief upon a pole, when the object drew near, and proved to be an old Indian woman (or witch), in a bobbing corial, travelling on her private affairs (with the wind, be it remembered), her grey hair and brown tatters streaming before her. Our interpreter explained our situation. She promised that her sons should pilot us the next morning into a known part of the lake, joyfully swallowed a glass of whisky, and departed.

Next morning, at nine, two stout young Indians arrived. We were soon ready, and very glad to follow their leading.

Towards the mainland was a basin a mile wide, shut up apparently by tall reeds and islets. This they crossed, breaking through the reeds, and an interval between rocks not more than three or four yards wide, and in like manner traversed basin after basin, with surfaces as unruffled and fair as the open lake was rough and dark.

The Indians now made for a small round island in one of these glassy pools, which was belted round by tall aspen and birch. We landed near a canoe drawn high and dry on shore, and mounting a woody bank we saw before us, to our astonishment, a small oval meadow, in the centre of which was an Indian camp of five wigwams, warm and still within the thick screen of leaves. Men, women, children, and dogs were all about—the men mending nets, the women pounding corn, and the children in busy play until the pale-faces appeared.

I was delighted with the well-fed, good-humoured looks of these red men; and I made favourable comparisons between them and the Glasgow weavers.

They had managed better than us during the last few days—ourselves for shelter embracing a naked rock, they housed in a warm, grassy isle.

> "There's a blossom for the bee;
> The bittern has its brake;
> The Indian too his hiding-place,
> When the storm is on the lake."

The highest compliment that an Indian can pay to a white man is, that he is almost as wise as one of themselves—but this comes not until after an apprenticeship of twenty years.

Having pre-paid our pilots, and bought some fish, we left. After going some three or four miles, our own guide began to espy well-known landmarks, and our new friends took their leave.

The Bourassa Post is on an island in Parry's Sound, and consisted, in 1823, of two long, low, barn-like huts, among sand-hills, mounds, and dwarf-cedars.

Parry's Sound is a magnificent sheet of water, ten or twelve miles broad, and as many in length, containing one very large island, and a countless number of small ones. The River Seguine enters at its bottom. Captain Bayfield found parts of this sound 390 feet deep.

The scenery is truly beautiful. Fir-clad hills all around—rocky islets and open basins. We made the circuit of it close in shore.

Twenty miles north-west from hence we passed in the offing the fur-trading post of La Ronde*

* The district of La Ronde (sixty-five miles from Penetanguishene, according to Mr. Donovan, a respectable Indian trader), so unpromising and desolate, contains a rock formation of great beauty and rarity.

Some little distance into the lake, one or two miles outside the nearer belt of islands, is a cluster (the Indian Isles, perhaps, of (near the Shamenega River), a melancholy-looking log-house, with a cluster of out-houses, sunk for protection behind some sand-heaps and rocks.

Other traders have wintering-houses in this neighbourhood, on the west side of a low promontory, from ten to thirteen miles long. Not far from its bottom there is a very narrow inlet, which runs east two miles or more, and then receives the Muskokony River.

La Ronde is seventy-two miles south-east of the French River.

The features of this long interval are of the same intricate nature as in that from the Giant's Tomb—as full of headlands and deep inlets of marshes and rocky lagoons.

But the islets are usually lower, smaller, and more naked; and they advance further out into the lake, as solitary mounds, hardly emerging above

Bayfield), not very close together, of piny islets, wholly composed, I believe, of Labrador feldspar,—one of the most beautiful of known rocks; and which, as is well known, when polished or merely wetted, assumes a beautiful iridescence. This mineral is rarely found *in situ*. I might not have noticed it; but the heavy rain which occurred as we were rowing by brought out the play of prismatic colours. It is met with at Arendhal, in Norway. The district appeared to be five miles long, and is, I suspect, narrow; as, on my return in the autumn, being obliged by stormy weather to keep close in shore, I did not see it, although I looked for it. I brought away specimens.

water. Being often in line south-westwards, they look at a distance like a shoal of porpoises.

There is little use in minutely describing these monotonous wastes. They are so extensive and uniform, that I think none but a practised Indian could ever find again any given spot—that is, without a large map. Captain Bayfield, R. N. and Mr. Collins have been employed several years in the survey of these and other parts of Lake Huron. Their maps are on a large scale.

We passed along this coast in stormy weather, and had to avail ourselves of the least shelter in endeavouring to make progress. The open lake was often everywhere white with breakers, and therefore not navigable by us. We crept along inside a succession of sea-walls or breakwaters of low rocks, a few feet broad, but each a mile or more long, and such as twenty millions sterling could not build.

While passing through this archipelago, we seldom saw the main; but one fine day (on our return) we stood out into the lake, some miles east of the French River, and saw a considerable way into the interior.

It was an extensive flat covered with pines. It is known that some miles further north the country becomes a fertile table land, 750 feet above the level of Lake Huron.

By way of showing the shifts we were put to in the regions north-west of Parry's Sound, I may mention that, after travelling all day, drenched with rain, we could not on one occasion find a dry place to rest in, and had great difficulty in lighting a fire. From the summits of the mounds we should have been blown away, and their sides were too slippery; so we pitched the tent over a little watercourse created by the rain. We floored it with rough poles cut from the young trees adjacent, and covered them with tarpaulin. On this we laid our little blanket-beds. While staying here wind-bound for forty-eight hours, we heard night and day the ripple of the streamlet beneath our feet.

While in this comfortless abode, our astronomer told me that about twenty years ago a continued and heavy rain occurred about latitude 50° in the Rocky Mountains. The rills and ditches became rivers, the rivers floods and seas. All the low grounds were inundated. The Indians were in great alarm, and thought a second deluge was coming, until one evening a rainbow appeared, which quite appeased them. They call it "the mark of life," or "the sun-strings."

The weather took up when we crossed French River Bay. This bay is three miles broad and two miles and a half deep. Its form is regular, the shores low, but high woody ridges present themselves, from ten to fifteen miles in the rear. Point Grondines, the name of the west angle of the bay, is a mile and a half from the river. It is a headland 1500 yards across. Not far hence there is a group of Indian drawings on a smooth cliff.

The north coast of Lake Huron, from a few miles east of French River, runs a little north of west. It had run north-north-west; and I remarked that a series of high hills which, at the mouth of the French River, was proceeding westwards to join the lake very obliquely, began, in ten or twelve miles, to form its actual margin in slopes and ridges; and it may be said, once for all, that ridge after ridge in succession, in like manner, strike the lake shore nearly to the Falls of St. Mary.

From Point Grondines to the Fox Islands is a distance of twelve miles, principally along an open basin.

The Fox Islands are in thinly-scattered doughy mounds, piled one upon another to 100 or 120 feet, and barren, save a few pines. They are six miles and a half south of Collins' Sound.

The views among the Fox Islands are very picturesque. Twenty or more grotesque high islands of rocks and pines are scattered over a broad expanse of lake. On the north-west is a magnificent circular bay, surrounded by mountains whose base the waters almost bathe. On the south-west, the long blue line of the Grand Manitou is seen passing east and west—grand, indeed, from its height and dimensions. Collins' Sound is full of fine scenery. It is fourteen or fifteen miles broad, and, together with a multitude of smaller islands, has one which is very long, and so narrow in parts, that, being compelled by boisterous weather in autumn to take the inner route between this isle and the mainland, we frequently heard the plash and roar of the waves outside.

This strait is called La Morandière, from having been long the residence of an Indian trader of that name.

Half a mile from a ruined fort is Point Colles,* a low platform of horizontal rocks, jutting a little into the water, and chiefly to be noticed as being the site of observations for longitude and latitude, made by order of the Boundary Commission. Near it is an excellent landmark—a white rock, 350 feet high, rising out of a dense forest.

From the Fox Islands and the contiguous shore

* Point Colles, Latitude 45° 46′ 26″ Longitude 81° 43′ 0″
Hill Island, Latitude 46 5 0 Longitude 82 4 18
according to the astronomers of the Boundary Commission.

the scenery of the lake for thirty miles westwards makes a sudden change. The dreary cranberry marshes, their reeds and mounds, are replaced by the lofty and well-wooded district of La Cloche.

It has been left for Captain Bayfield to lay down these bewildering regions with accuracy in charts; and it has been the work of years.

For my part I only say, that, from the Strait of La Morandière I have passed three times westward, through an apparently endless succession of basins of free water (only recognising at these separate visits a few great features), with the hills of the main on the north—steep eminences of snow-white quartz, from 500 to 700 feet high; and on the south the high slopes and terraces of the Grand Manitouline—almost always a prominent object in Lake Huron. The few islands in the interspaces are of limestone, precipitous and pine-clad. Captain Bayfield's sailors ascended one of these hills, and I took rock specimens from another, one-third of the way to its top. We dined at its foot.

In two places in this neighbourhood, at Cape Peter (the north-west angle of Smyth's Bay), and at the large compact island of La Cloche, the entrance into the north-west arm or wing of Lake Huron is almost blocked up by the near approach to each other of certain capes of the

Manitouline and the main. At Cape Peter the barrage is assisted by islets; and at La Cloche, that island is itself the principal interposed mass. The strait between it and the Manitouline is only a few hundred yards wide; and even part of this is taken up with an islet. It has been passed through by my deceased friend, Lieutenant Grant, in the schooner Confiance. The strait on the side of the mainland is very narrow also; the headland from the north being many miles long, and very indented.

We find Hill Island on the west, and within a few miles of this headland. From a high hill on the main opposite this island, ascended by the crew of the Confiance, the interior appeared level and covered with pines.

The island of La Cloche* is high, compact in shape, and of considerable size. It is uninhabited except by Indians occasionally.

It has some extensive platforms of limestone about it, nearly of the same level as the lake, on which I met with some curious fossils.

We encamped on a low islet for the night, near La Cloche. Its rocks were very full of crevices,

* It is so called from some of its rocks ringing like a bell on being struck. This particularly applies to one loose basaltic mass lying on the shore, fifteen miles below the little Sagamuc, and about three yards square.

which harboured so many long brown snakes (five out of one hole), that it was not until we had killed some, and frightened away the remainder, that we ventured to go to rest.

The same night I had another little fright here. Sitting round a fire at our supper of cocoa, nearly in the dark, just as I was discussing a biscuit rather harder than usual, I happened to turn round, when, behold, a tall figure was stationed on a ledge a little above us, in a strange robe, and holding a long staff in his hand. I nudged my neighbour. After a moment or two's delay, he called out to it, "Nidgé" ("Friend," in Indian). He was an Indian, and then joined us with his usual noiseless tread. He had seen our fire, and had come in hopes of biscuit and perhaps a glass of spirits. Unusual as it is among Indians, he stood waiting for an invitation to join us.

Near the island of La Cloche, on the margin of the lake, almost hidden by young trees, we met with the ruins of a small French fort, at that time only ten feet high, and built a hundred years ago of very large slabs of limestone, for a defence against the Indians.

I can only speak of the district of La Cloche in general terms.

The traveller, from the unsightly north-east shore, comes well prepared to be charmed with it. No part of the great Canadian lakes can be compared with this portion of Lake Huron, as far as my personal experience goes. All at once we find ourselves sailing over calm and clear waters, amid clustering isles of all sizes, some with high cliffs, some lying low, all wooded, and skirting a lofty mainland.

Here and there we pass by little grassy valleys, park-like, with clumps of trees and umbrageous avenues, as if leading to some deserted mansion.

The especial beauty of these places very much arises from deep shadows, and the harmonious tints of the vegetation—from the vivid whiteness of the bald quartz hills, and the quick alternation of open and close scenery. During long journeys on important business we cannot sketch where we most desire to do so. Thus was it here.

So extensive and perplexing is this region of wood, rock, and water, that although some of us were no strangers here, still, by taking a northern direction at the west end of the great sheet of water, either called or near to Le Forêt des Bois,* instead of the proper course, we deviated into a large archipelago of romantic beauty. This error cost us five hours' hard labour.

This style of country, exceeding twenty-five miles in length, terminates westwards a few miles

* North-east of the island of La Cloche.

before we reach Little Sagamuc River, the immediate north shore now becoming lower, and the well-known belt of small islets in-shore being resumed to some extent, while, midway between the main and the Grand Manitouline (plainly seen), are eight large and woody isles, in little groups, spread over the open lake.

The Little Sagamuc enters at the bottom of a shallow bay, under the protection of a belt of trap islands. It is forty feet wide, and at the distance of 600 yards from its mouth is precipitated obliquely over a rock, twenty feet high, buried in woods, and with a very respectable share of foam, fury, &c. It is the outlet of a small lake one mile off.

An Indian trader, of the name of M'Bean, has been here many years, and has given his name to the spot.

On a grassy flat, at the mouth of Little Sagamuc, we found some Indian wigwams, resting in unbroken stillness. The young men were lying lazily about, and the women busy, as their wont is; the younger having their usual good-humoured, chubby faces, their musical voices pouring out multitudinous criticisms upon our manners and appearance.

I ran to gather a specimen of the rock at the waterfall, but such a flock of capering imps attended me that I could scarce perform my task.

I have reason to believe that the Ojibbeway Indians, lately in England, came from this neighbourhood. They were Wesleyan Protestants, and did honour to their profession. There has been a small Wesleyan mission hereabouts.

Near this, to the west, are the rivers Le Serpent and Sand. They are small; but the latter is used to reach Lake Nipissing.

Ten or twelve miles along a hilly mainshore brings us to Spanish Bay, Aird's Bay, or the Bay of Sagamuc. We passed across its mouth, which is many miles wide, and defended by a long line of woody islands, the largest of which is called Aird's. The inner shores of Aird's Bay are altogether out of sight, but we saw that its west side ran northerly, in a series of lofty and partially-wooded bluffs. No map, except the little-known one of Captain Bayfield, gives any idea of this large bay.

That officer told me that it is very large, and receives the finest river of Lake Huron, excepting St. Mary's (from Lake Superior).

The Spanish or Sagamuc River is navigable for boats, without a portage, for thirty-five miles, along a channel averaging 120 yards in breadth, with frequent rapids, some from four to six miles an hour at narrows. The small lakes into which the Sagamuc occasionally expands are full of islets. One of these expanses is called Birchbark Lake. Navigation is stopped by a fall thirty feet high, passing over a shining greenstone. This river communicates with Lake Tematscaming. The name of "Spanish" is given to it from its having been once occupied by Spanish Indians, as I have heard. It has two mouths.

About forty-two miles west from the Little Sagamuc is the River Missassaga, Spanish Bay occurring in this interval. These forty-two miles are distributed into a chain of beautiful and large basins by successive sets of islands, those near the main being of primitive rock, small, various in height (from 20 to 200 feet), and so surrounded by shallows and reefs as to make passing even in boats difficult.

We kept close to the main shcre, and found it well wooded. In the evening many of the trees were enveloped and surmounted by myriads of flies, in a spiral pyramidal wreath, constantly rising and falling. At a distance they looked like a thin smoke. The same may be seen occasionally in England.

The Missassaga is a fine river, and has two entrances, one on each side of a marshy tongue of land 1400 yards across.

The eastern mouth is the largest, and is 120 yards broad, according to Captain Bayfield; and enters the lake in a flat beach, sandy and rocky in places. The falls first met with pass over red granite.

In 1848, Mr. Logan, the provincial geologist, ascended this river for forty miles, one of its tributaries for seven miles, and another for four; as well as two lakes on the Grand Batture Portage.

On another occasion I ascended, with a fur-trader, for five or six miles, to a North-west Company Station, a river of good breadth at the mouth, and widening within, flowing from the interior among large meadows and pineries, into the lake, and this two miles east of the best-known entrance. The Rhine, among the reedy pastures below Strasburg, reminded me of the River Missassaga. We encamped, on this occasion, for the night, on the river side among willows and long dry grass; but the latter took fire, and would have burnt us up, if we had not instantly and vigorously beat it out with large boughs.

In what may be called the Missassaga District, while the edge of the lake is marshy, we have, in the interior, a range of tolerably high hills running parallel to the lake shore.

The space between Missassaga, and the Point, and River, Thessalon (twenty-eight miles along the north shore), is a series of shallow, marshy curvatures, so excessively encumbered with erratic blocks,* that landing is somewhat difficult, especially seventeen miles west of Missassaga.

Along shore we have more sandy beaches than usual, extending a good way into the low and sterile neighbourhood, overgrown with wild vines, and cherries, and dwarf pines.

Scarps of basalt and round-backed mounds, solitary rocks, with glazed surfaces, are sprinkled over our route, but not in the profusion we find east of the French River.

Point Thessalon is a narrow strip of low, wooded land, faced with bowlders and sand, a mile long on its east side. A single tree at the point, in advance of all its brethren, marks the locality well. This was the north-eastern limit of the Boundary Commission's Survey in Lake Huron. It is in this neighbourhood that many orthocera, five and six feet long, have been seen, but not removed on account of their weight and size.

Thessalon Bay (of which the point just mentioned forms the west angle) is three miles across and one deep. It is principally sand-bank, co-

* Among these are masses of beautiful jasper puddingstone; —also seen by Captain Bayfield.

vered with drift-wood. At its bottom the River Thessalon pushes through rugged eminences of trap. It is thirty or forty yards broad at its mouth, and is bordered by willows and other trees. Its size upwards I do not know; but Mr. Logan says, that he met with four falls on it, 13, 18, 8, and 3 feet respectively, affording excellent mill-seats. Some of the land in the valley, he says, is well fitted for cultivation.

The whole region, extending from the River Missassaga, in this lake, to the River Montreal in Lake Superior, in a north-west direction, will eventually be covered with a numerous mining population.

Within the last few years (1849) large deposits of copper ore have been met with at the extremities of the line just indicated.

Considerable grants have been made by Government for mining purposes, after an official survey by the Colonial geologist, whose last Report (made in January 1849) furnishes the following particulars:—

Twenty-two mining locations are claimed of Government on the north shore of this lake, but the Bruce Mines, nine miles west of the Thessalon River, are the farthest advanced and the best known.

All the way from the Falls of St. Mary to

Shenawenahning shows more or less indications of copper.

The copper ore and undressed stuff at the Bruce Mines, in July 1848, was 1475 tons, giving about 118 tons of pure copper. The expectation in September 1848 was, that the lodes would yield 250 tons of such ore monthly. Large quantities have already been sent to Montreal and Boston.

One hundred and sixty-three persons were employed at these mines, which, with their families, gave a population of 250 souls.

Three frame-buildings, thirty log-houses, and two wharfs, had been erected. The harbour was good and timber abundant.

The rocks which compose the Bruce Mines are greenstone, granites, sienitic conglomerate, with its associate slate and quartz rock, whose general strike (and that of the lodes) roughly coincides with the trend of the coast, and therefore west-north-west.

The productiveness of the lodes differs according to the rock they traverse, being greatest in the greenstones.*

* Copper is the most plentiful metal, in the form of vitreous copper, variegated copper, and copper pyrites. Iron pyrites is sometimes associated with them. Copper pyrites, in one instance, was accompanied by rutile, and in another by arsenuretted sulphuret of iron and nickel, with a trace of cobalt.

The lodes vary in breadth from a few inches to thirty feet, and cut through all the rocks. The gangue, or veinstone, in which the copper ores are contained, is in general white quartz.

With these facts before us, it is evident that this part of North America is about to become very important. It is also not a little remarkable that our stock of the metals is receiving increase in proportion to the increased demand, from augmented population and a more extended application of them to the uses of life. Copper is thus prevented from becoming too dear.

Of the interval between Point Thessalon and the Channel of Pelletau I shall say little, as I know little. We sailed at a distance off land, which enabled us to see the successive ranges of hills inland, which we had observed all the way from La Cloche.

Drummond Island, and the other Manitoulines, are in sight, blue from their remoteness; while the fine island of St. Joseph is comparatively near at hand. I never landed here, and therefore perhaps, missed seeing some traces of the fine mineral region on the main.*

* Not far west of Missassaga I met with small fragments both of galena and copper ore.

Pelletau's Channel is so named from a Canadian who long cultivated some rich land on an island at its east end. It is included between the north-east shore of St. Joseph and the contiguous main. Except towards the west end, the channel is an unobstructed sheet of water, ten or twelve miles long, and six broad at the east extremity, but narrowing to a mile and a half in the west.

The two sides of this channel present very different aspects. St. Joseph is a gentle, verdant acclivity, while the north main is a region of half-naked black fastnesses, of trap mounds, swamps, ponds, and ridges.

Near its west end, Pelletau's Channel widens into an expanse twenty-five miles square, and becomes full of islands; one of which is of some size, compact, rather high and woody.* It nearly

* This island has great sylvan beauty. It is in such spots that the Indian makes his home. I think that, unlike the native whites of his country, he has much feeling for the picturesque. His mind is full of metaphor and grand idealities.

On the former voyage in a light canoe with M. de Rocheblave, we had been working our way quietly among the solitudes of the north shore, when we approached this island. We rounded a woody point, and suddenly beheld a hundred half-naked Indians hotly engaged at their game of ball in a meadow which ran down to the water side—their wigwams being under the lee of a steep, and their kinsfolk looking on in groups.

Two parties were contending with infinite heat and clamour to drive a little ball in opposite ways, each to his own goal, casting it blocks up the Narrows (as they are called) at their east entrance.

Two other considerable, nearly naked islands, are close to the main, with which they form an admirable harbour, at one time intended for a military station, under the name of Portlock Harbour. (*Vide* Plate.) It has some very pretty scenery. While in Pelletau's Channel, as you approach this harbour, at the distance of a mile or two, there is perceived an opening or break in

far and high in the air, with long sticks, which had a kind of open cup or ring at the lower end.

Immediately we appeared there was a loud scream of joy and surprise. The game ceased. The Indians rushed to their guns, and filled the air with harmless musketry in our honour.

Canoes forthwith pushed off to us. The north-west trader knew his sad duty.

"Hand out the rum-keg," said he; "give me a couple of quart measures." He half-filled them, secretly, with lake-water from the offside of the canoe, and then ostentatiously poured the coveted liquid into the cans.

By this time the Indians had arrived. Warm greetings were exchanged. The rum was presented:—but how to carry it ashore? The trader could neither wait nor leave his cans.

The savages were at their wits' end; but at length one of them held out a round thing of felt which counted for a hat. Into it went the fire-water. But who shall paint their dismay, their antics, and howlings, when they saw the precious fluid distilling through the well-worn felt in twenty tiny streams! The hat, however, was withdrawn from our canoe—many, many a hand beneath it. In the height of the hubbub, "Down paddle," said the trader; and we escaped. In a few minutes woods, wigwams, and Indian sports were far behind.

a high country, expanding as it is neared, and finally disclosing an extensive haven, interspersed with rocky islets, or girt by heights, starting forth in a series of woody or rocky capes, — the whole supported in the rear by three ridges of hills covered with poplars, birch, and half-consumed pines.

We have now arrived in our tedious, but hitherto undescribed journey (at least, not carefully), to the place where the north-west arm of Lake Huron, communicating with Lake Superior, begins to take shape.

The southern mainland of Huron, having formed the great sound called Lake Michigan, is deflected in latitude 45° 53′ nearly east, to longitude 83° 55′, when suddenly trending northerly and westerly (opposite Drummond Island) it approaches the *north* main to within ten miles, in latitude 46° 20′, and, with it, forms an oblong space, narrowing westwards, 400 square miles in extent, which receives the waters of Lake Superior.

This space is crowded with islands, large and small; the principal one being St. Joseph (sixty-five miles round), which, with the large "Sugar Island" (thus named from its maple woods), is so wedged into the lower end of the channel, or strait, from Lake Superior, as scarcely to give, at the narrowest points, the breadth of a mile to the sum of the four outlets from above.

It is here that, strictly speaking, Lake Huron ceases (or rather begins), and where we find ourselves at the foot of a double set of narrows and currents. The first set (we proceed upwards) consists of three,—namely, those of the "Middle Passage," between Nibish Island and St. Joseph's, the Straits of Pelletau, and the basin below Encampment Douce (a rocky isle at the Nibish).

The Middle Passage is eight or ten miles long, one mile broad above, and a quarter of a mile below, with a southerly run, and emptying into Muddy Lake.

The Straits of Pelletau are formed by the approach of St. Joseph to within two-thirds of a mile of the north main at their west end, and to within a mile and a half at their east end.

The main here is a line of dark lofty cliffs, while the St. Joseph side is a marsh. Narrow as this strait is, it contains eighteen islets—those nearest the main partaking of its forbidding character; sometimes being divided from each other by mural rents, only a few feet across. As the islets approach St. Joseph they lower, and have marshy coves. The current is inconstant—sometimes strong.

From the summit of the adjoining main is presented a truly scenic and striking combination of high and sombre rocks, scantily clad with pine, and overshadowing a labyrinth of waters.

The current of the basin runs among shallows on the north-west side of St. Joseph, at the foot of a still water, into which some of the upper (Nibish) group of rapids pour.

This second or upper group of rapids and narrows forms the outlet of Lake George. This lake is eighteen miles long by five in average breadth. Its west side is formed by Sugar or George Island, which, twenty miles long, stretches from the Straits of St. Mary to within a mile of St. Joseph. It is fertile, but narrow. A shallow water, a mile broad, intervenes between the main on the west and Sugar Island. At its foot, on the south, we have Nibish Island, squeezed in between the main and St. Joseph. It is regular in shape, and ten miles by four and a half in dimensions.

The boundary line under the sixth article terminates in the Nibish (or Neebish) Channel, near Muddy Lake. The seventh article assigns Sugar Island to the United States.

The rapids go under the general name of Nibish. They are three. Their names are,—1st, the Eastern Nibish; 2dly, the Middle; and 3dly, the West Nibish rapid. Their position and size will be best seen on the map.

The Middle Nibish rapid is the ship channel from Détroit to St. Mary's; and even here the ship must be of very small draught, and is unloaded to pass one particularly shallow spot.* A view is given of the encampment of the Boundary Commission, on a pretty isle at the foot of the Eastern Nibish. Passing through Lake George, we reach the river or strait of St. Mary, which connects Lake Superior with Lakes George and Huron.

Almost the whole outlet (now loosely described, in reliance on the map) is of a soft and agreeable aspect, presenting expanses of transparent water, with curving shores of rich woods or successive headlands. Where the rapids occur we have reefs and accumulations of gravel or bowlders, with maple and birch forests, or short pine-clad precipices on either shore.

Where we enter St. Mary's Strait the view is very pleasing.

* The Nibish rapids are sometimes considered to be four: when the East Nibish (the ship channel to St. Mary's) is divided into two, and named the "Little and the East." They are separated by an island a mile or two long.

Encampment Douce, of which a view is given, is at the foot of, and to the west of, this island.

As we pushed up the sparkling current, our boat was surrounded by numbers of white fish (*Coregonus albus*),* whose exquisite flavour, especially when boiled, is renowned over North America, and whose export forms the staple employment at the neighbouring villages.

We had scarcely seen a human being for ten days, when all at once we came in sight of two villages, British and American, on their respective sides of the river, and several canoes passing to and fro, or fishing.

The river itself (seventeen miles long by half a mile to a mile and a quarter wide) is deep, silent, broad: massive woods overhang its banks. Directly before us, at the distance of two miles,† are the boiling rapids, called St. Mary's Falls.

On the British, or left side of the river, an accidental conflagration was raging in the woods. The horizon was considerably darkened by smoke; and every now and then a gleam of fire, faint in the distance, reached us, newly fed by some resinous trees.

Anxious to see the devastating process, as soon as we landed at the North-west Company's station I walked as far as I could into the burning woods. The fire was running about on the

* It is allied to the salmon family.

† There is excellent clay for brick-making here.

ground, wherever there was a sufficiency of dry matted grass or undergrowth of any kind. The tongues of fire crept up the hot pines, which were perspiring turpentine, and sometimes burst suddenly into broad sheets of flame. The crackling, flare, and rapid combustion of leaves, branches, and grass, were all new to me, and grand; but the smoke, driven about in gusts, was so loaded with acridity, that I was glad to escape with burnt shoes into a respirable air. When the fire reached any little plot occupied by diseased or old pines, whose boughs are always heavily loaded with Spanish moss, the whole started into an atmosphere of flame. This conflagration was considered small; but it had embraced, from first to last, an area of several square miles.

The surveying party of the Boundary Commission, with whom I was now travelling, passed rapidly through St. Mary's into Lake Superior. This journal ought to be continuous with their movements; but I beg the reader's permission to delay for a little our excursion into Lake Superior, in order to assemble in one chapter all our proceedings in, and remarks upon, Lake Huron.

We shall be glad enough to rejoin our friends.

At the time of this visit St. Mary's was a very modest settlement. I imagine it remains so.

The Canadian village is, or was, a straggling

line of fifteen log-huts on marshy ground, with, at its lower end, the comfortable dwelling of Mr. Ermatinger, whose daughter's acquaintance I had unexpectedly made on the western branch of the Ottawa.

The North-west Company of fur-traders have an important post near the head of this village, close to the rapids, on the broad tongue of lowland full of little watercourses, which is the British portage. This post consists of a good resident's house, large storehouse, stables, labourers' dwellings, garden, fields, and a jetty for their schooner. The cattle were in a remarkably good condition.

The American village is but small: it has, however, two or three houses of a better class, and is on higher ground, with a few Indian wigwams interspersed.

The Americans have a stout barrack here, called Fort Brady, and two companies of infantry.

Mr. Johnson, a much-respected Indian trader, lives here most hospitably in a house, whose neatness is in striking contrast with the careless dilapidation reigning around.

A few potatoes and some Indian corn are raised on either side of the river, and there is a little pasture land.

Mr. Ermatinger built a windmill, in a vain

attempt to induce the people to grow wheat. It is said that the cold mists and draughts from Lake Superior check the growth of corn.

St. Mary's is healthy. I did not hear of ague there. Our party enjoyed excellent health in Lake Huron.

But in point of agricultural improvements there is both room and opportunity, by the drainage of swamps and shallow lakes. It is now in these countries as it was in the early times of Britain. * Early Britain A great part of England was then taken up by unwholesome marshes and woods, so that the lower levels were but little inhabited. Many of the towns, villages, and Druidical remains, were on the hill tops. Now our valleys are healthy, warm, and productive. We therefore inhabit them.

The white and red inhabitants of St. Mary's live chiefly on white fish caught in hand-nets at the foot of the rapids, and they, as before said, are salted in very large quantities.

The rapids rush tumultuously in a white mass of eddying, billowy, foamy surge, through a strait only half the usual breadth, and half a mile long, bordered on both sides by almost inaccessible swamps and dense woods, where the lowness of the banks has permitted a number of petty channels to form. Looking up from the middle of the river the scene is full of life, and stir, and strong con-

* See a book, "Before London", by Richard Geoffreys — if he spells his name that way — for a notable retrospect of early Britain

trasts. We see dark woods and dazzling waters, often crowded with Indian canoes. One reef, or ledge, very visible from the shore, is supposed to cause a drop of six feet. An American surveyor has calculated their total descent to be twenty-two feet ten inches. The underlying rock is a horizontal sandstone, mottled red and brown, belonging to the Silurian age. Father Hennessin (edit. 1696, p. 34) describes St. Mary's Falls exactly as they are now.

In 1824 I remained three weeks a guest at the North-west Company's post, enjoying the great kindness of Mr. Sivewright, the superintendent, an old officer in the fur trade, familiar with the most remote regions of the north-west, and very communicative.

Every place has its own peculiarity, I suppose. Here it was the correct thing to live almost solely upon white fish morning, noon, and night. Rich and delicately-flavoured as this food was at first, in the end I loathed it, and for ten years afterwards could not see fish on the dinner-table without a shudder. White fish here varies from three to six pounds in weight. In Athabasca Lake they run to twenty pounds.

I was much pleased by my visits to Messrs. Ermatinger and Johnson. The former was every inch a trader, public-spirited, skilful, sanguine, and indefatigable. Save two rooms, his whole dwelling was a warehouse. My shepherdess was quite at home among the Indians and the white fish. Her *boudoir* was full of little tokens of Atlantic city education. She seemed mosquito-proof, and did the honours of her home with kindness and grace.

Mr. Johnson was a merchant, with the generous and social qualities of the old Irish gentleman. He had been plundered and burnt out by the Americans in the war of 1814, in one of the many unchristian ravages which both parties committed on the unoffending citizens on the frontiers. Up to the time of my visit (ten years afterwards) Mr. Johnson had received no compensation from his own Government, although his loss was very heavy, and his claims respectfully urged in the appointed manner.

I was surprised at the value and extent of this gentleman's library; a thousand well-bound and well-selected volumes, French and English, evidently much in use, in winter especially; and not gathered together in these days of cheap literature.

Mr. Johnson was an Irishman of good family, and died in 1828.

He was so kind as to invite some of his few neighbours to meet me at a good dinner, and produced a bottle of crusted port of an especial vintage—a sort of good thing of which I was utterly unworthy.

Mr. Johnson had married the daughter of a powerful Indian chief, residing on the south shore of Lake Superior, which, of course, brought him the friendship and trade of all his tribe. She was a portly, bustling, happy-looking creature, and had imbibed all her husband's notions; and she united to the open-handedness of the Indian the method and notableness of the Englishwoman.

They had several children, the eldest at that time a gay half-pay lieutenant of a Canadian corps. His eldest daughter has since married Mr. Schoolcraft, formerly an Indian agent, but now at Washington at the head of the Indian department; a gentleman in every way worthy of his advancement, and to whom I am considerably indebted both for information and attentions. She then strongly reminded me of Walter Scott's Jeanie Deans by her quiet, modest ways, by her sweet round-oval features, expressive of the thankful and meek devotedness so universal in Indian women. The style, manners, and conversational topics, both here and at Mr. Ermatinger's, were remarkable, and quite distinct from those of the cities we had left behind us.

I shall not be so ungallant as to describe the dress of the ladies. No lady likes to be described in a fashion ten years old, although no obsoleteness in dress can hide goodness and intelligence.

I could not help inwardly smiling at the garb of our male company in their vast coat-collars "*à la régent*," and waists so high that the coats were all skirt. Their pantaloons were slit up outside, and adorned with a profusion of bullet-headed brass buttons; while, in imitation of the Mexican *rancheros* and the English dragoons in Spain, these good people, who never crossed a horse, made the inner parts of this nameless garment almost wholly of leather.

I envied the masses of long black hair which rested upon the shoulders of my friends. They had enough hair to make perukes for twenty duchesses.

The unsettled postures, dark hue, and wandering black eye of the Indian, were well marked in some of the guests, and the perfect gipsy face. Their English was good, and without the disagreeable nasality of the American.

It is true that we ate fast and in silence, but this being over we were very merry, in spite of an abundance of mosquitoes. Each took up his own easy position, uncourtly but not uncourteous, and talk became plentiful. We wasted no words upon civilised man. We dilated upon the prospects of the fishery, of the wild-rice harvest, the furs of the last winter's hunt, the rumoured incursions of the Sioux and other Indians upon the quieter tribes, the massacre of the whites at Red River, then recent, while I obtained from one or another descriptions of the adjacent regions.

All this made me feel that I was near the wild man's land; and I was confirmed in the idea by one day meeting in the village a handsome white woman, who wore a broad silver plate on her head on account of having been scalped.

The young men of this neighbourhood were brave fellows, who could steer the canoe and point the rifle, and would ask nothing better than a roving war-commission at the head of their Indian friends to kill and be killed at ten shillings a-day for all time.

Their principal occupation in winter was to follow the Indians to their hunting-grounds to the south and west of Lake Superior, for the purpose of taking their furs almost as soon as ready, to ensure repayment of the usual autumnal advances made to the Indians.

In summer my friends performed the functions of country gentlemen. They farmed, fished, and sported.

The great defect in colonial life is the lower civilisation which characterises it; where the inferior appetites, the animal instincts, prevail, and are exclusively gratified; where a man's thoughts seldom go further than himself, his shop, farm, bottle, horse, and rifle.

In the country parts of Canada few young men get above the class of "gents.," and the elders seldom rise higher in their notions than the second-rate retired tradesmen at home. There are here and there some few loftier minds, driven into hiding-places by misfortune; but they only mark, and so thicken, the general gloom. There is not enough of the fine gold of English society to make a public impression. In England the female gentry, in their respective rural neighbourhoods, do a large amount of good, as living examples of wisdom, generosity, and gentleness.

I advise only the uneasy classes of Great Britain to live in Canada; the easy classes, however, I strenuously advise to visit it.

I did not find my time heavy at St. Mary's. Opportunities of leaving are rare, and must be made; so my friends contracted with two very young Indians to take my old travelling companion, Mr. Tabeau (on a second missionary tour), and myself to Collier's Harbour, on Drummond Island, in Lake Huron, forty-five miles from St. Mary's. It was 1100 miles from Quebec, and the most westerly British post.

EXCURSION THE SEVENTH.

PART II. SECT. II.

LAKE HURON CONTINUED.

Canoe-voyage to Drummond Isle — Mosquitoes — Muddy Lake — St. Joseph — Indian Widow full of trust — Night-storm on a Shingle Bank — Arrival — Port Collier — Garrison Life — Heads in a Sack — Indian War Party — Mackinaw, Town, Island — Mr. and Mrs. Macvicar — Indian Chiefs — Lady and Ring — Voyage with Indians to Drummond Isle — Their kindness — American Officer killed — Arrival in state — Boundary Commission — H. M. schooner Confiance — Entomology — Little and Grand Manitoulines — Thunder-storm — Voyage down Southern Huron to River St. Clair.

About the middle of a calm, sultry day, we embarked in a small crampy canoe, with a little tea, biscuit, and ham.

It was again my lot to leave kind hearts. With many a good wish expressed, and many a wave of the hat, we glided down the gentle current of the strait, more borne along by its friendly force than by Indian diligence, for we soon found that of those who ply the paddle between Mackinaw and the Yellow Stone River we had picked up th veriest idlers of all. But they were civil, merry and talkative. Reproof or encouragement were difficult, as they only spoke the Chippewa tongue.

Time, however, stole on, and — thanks to the current aforesaid — evening found us twelve or fourteen miles from St. Mary's, towards the bottom of Lake George. Twilight coming on, we pushed into a creek, or rather stagnant ditch, for a hundred yards, and found a little greensward, which pleased us at first with its coolness,

"Under the blossom that hangs on the bough."

But our operations preparatory for the night aroused the mosquitoes, which rushed in clouds upon us, ravenous for the prey. While taking a little tea, I had only to open and shut my hand to crush half-a-dozen ; but they were in the air, the grass, the trees, in billions. This is the case all over the Indian countries at certain seasons, and is a plague only to be moderated by mosquitoe-nets, and by encamping, if possible, on a rock free to every wind. Our Indians did not seem much annoyed by them.

I shall not describe the night we passed. The

hired beggars in the Hindoo flea-hospitals do not fare worse. I quite lost my temper under the persecutions of my innumerable foes and the clammy, stifling heat of the place; always a great mistake, but I am bound by the Christian verity to confess it, as I now do.

We were early risers, most anxious for the open waters, and sped along at a goodly pace down the West Nibish Rapid into Muddy Lake, the vicinity being rendered very picturesque by sparkling rapids, islets, and verdant uplands, in every direction.

Muddy Lake, a part of Lake Huron, is so named from the nature of its bottom. It is nine miles across from east to west, and about the same length. Its boundaries may be seen by a glance at the map. The shores run into deep and often grassy bays.

There is a series of small streams and lakes which lead from Lake George to Goose Islands, near Michilimackinac, which furnishes a short and quiet way thither from St. Mary's. Brine springs are common upon this route, and Goose Islands have a considerable deposit of gypsum.

St. Joseph belongs to Canada, and is a compact island, seventeen miles by twelve in general dimensions, its length running south-east.

Its interior rises to the height of 500 feet by

three tiers of rich woods, which are called the "Highlands of St. Joseph."

At its south-eastern extremity there had been for thirty-five years a small British post, until about the year 1820.

It is fertile. Its coasts are broken into bays with a few islands about them. It has at least two creeks. They are on the south and east sides. One is at the south-east cape, near an excellent harbour.

Our surveyors, rowing a mile or two up this stream, were surprised one day to find a neat log-house far up in the woods, with a patch of Indian corn and other vegetables. It was inhabited by an Indian widow and her daughter. Nothing could exceed the cleanliness of this lodge in the wilderness. They were not alarmed at our visit, and came to our camp for needles and such-like little matters. They were Roman Catholics, and pleasing, well-conducted people. We had not been aware of any one being upon St. Joseph; it is a jungle containing only bears and other wild animals. We did not afterwards meet with any one who knew them. Two lone women in such a desert in the howlings of a Canadian winter! —what resignation and trust in a presiding Being!!

But to return to our voyage of two days and two

nights to Collier's Harbour. We loitered through the second day in Indian fashion; life being with our red friends not a task but a holiday.

By the middle of the day we had passed the narrow part of Muddy Lake, through the strait (a mile broad), had skirted the ascending shores of Isle à la Crosse, and were leaving behind us the ruined fort at the south point of St. Joseph, when we saw a black cloud arise on the north, the lake growing dark in that direction, with a rough brown scud driving towards us.

As we were within five miles of Collier's Harbour, with the wind, though gustful and muttering, in our favour, we held on, and were approaching the first of the three little islets which spot the route between St. Joseph and our destination, when a blast of wind came suddenly upon us, and almost lifted our tiny craft out of the water, bodily. There was distant thunder, and lightning was flashing behind us: single drops of rain began to splash heavily in the water.

The Indians immediately paddled to the islet at hand, a mere morsel of shingle, of an acre perhaps, with a young birch-tree and a few bushes on it.

A few minutes sufficed (for we worked in haste) to drag the canoe ashore, turn it keel upwards to shelter the Indians, and fling our little sail over two poles and some bushes for ourselves, with some ham and biscuit, if we chose to eat; which, however, we did not.

Scarcely were we under our poor covering when the coming storm assailed us, not with its mere fringes, but in its full fury. I thought the wind would have swept us into the lake; it clipt off the crests of the foaming surf, and drove them right across the little beach.

The waves swept by us, that dark and moonless night, in line after line, of tall, white breakers; and in reality threatened rather unpleasantly to swallow up our bit of shingle. All this while our thin sail at intervals shook vehemently with the tempest, and shielded us very imperfectly from the occasional bursts of heavy rain.

The lightning was quite blinding; each flash (and they were many) revealed, as clear as day, leagues of stormy waters and scattered isles; and then left us for several minutes in utter inky darkness.

My brows began to ache; and the brightness was so painfully intense that I wrapped my head in a boat-cloak, and committed myself to a merciful Providence.

The Roman Catholic priest sat quietly by my side, now and then endeavouring to read his breviary by the light of a taper, which the storm put out every three or four minutes, and which he re-lit by help of his tinder-box. Fire we had none, of course. He afterwards gave up the attempt, and laid himself down to listen to "luctantes ventos, tempestatesque sonoras."

The storm lasted several hours. Towards midnight it moderated, and we fell asleep.

Next morning, as is usual after such passionate outbreaks, every thing looked fresh and gay; and the sun was shining upon a smiling world.

Of the Indians under the canoes, and how they fared, we knew nothing, save that the eddies of the wind from time to time brought to us a strong odour of tobacco; so that to them that ugly night may have been a season of luxurious enjoyment.

We put off, and passing on our left the snug little village of Portoganess, on the crescent-shaped island of that name, we arrived, by seven o'clock or so, at the north portage of Port Collier, where we found some officers of the garrison awaiting our arrival (or anybody's, for they knew us not). They had seen our canoe from the eminence behind the barracks, and made many kind inquiries how we passed the tempestuous night.

I shall say but little topographically about the British post on Drummond Island, because it is deserted, having been assigned to the United States.

But I may mention that both the barracks and the village ranged along the front of the harbour. Behind is a slope loaded with rounded white rocks, called "Drummond's Lambs" (at a distance they look like sheep), and surmounted by a natural terrace of rock.

Drummond Island is twenty-four miles long; its greatest breadth twelve miles, and its least two and a half miles. It is separated from the American main by a strait of about a mile across.

This post was established by General Drummond about the year 1812. It is healthy, but most dismal,—a mere heap of rocks on the edge of an impenetrable medley of morass, ponds, and matted woods.

I observed in two or three of the houses, in the village of Indian traders and their half-breed children, that some of the rooms were lined with moss and birch-bark,—a very good contrivance in so cold a climate.

In 1823, the garrison consisted of two companies of infantry. It may be well to put down a few notes on garrison life on the frontier of a British colony.

The friendly and intelligent gentlemen of the garrison had little to do save read, hunt for fossils, fish, shoot, cut down trees, and plant potatoes. Their military duties took up little of their time. Now and then they made an excursion to Michilimackinac, or they rowed over to St. Joseph's to inspect the government herd of cattle grazing there.

They had few or no visitors,—a few Indian traders, and an inspecting-officer once a-year. They were more than 200 miles from the nearest British military station.

Their shooting was either utterly unproductive, or so abundant as to cease to be sport. Pigeons and ducks at certain seasons are so plentiful that it is said (I do not vouch for the fact) that you have only to fire up the chimney and a couple of ducks will fall into the pot.

Judging from my experience, the officers fared hard and yet did not save money. Every pound of fresh meat came from a distance, and therefore was dear. The island grows little else than potatoes.

I quartered myself upon the excellent medical officer, Mr. White, "candidus" by name and by nature.

I dined at the officers' mess. At my first appearance there, we were nine sharp-set young fellows. A small square lump of highly-salted beef, a fowl (perhaps two), a suet-dumpling, and two dishes of potatoes, were both dinner and dessert. I was astonished. This was followed by a poor Sicilian wine. It appeared that contrary winds had retarded their usual supplies.

Such is military life on detached service.

The men were employed as much as possible at one kind of work or other; but both drunkenness and desertion were too common. They obtained whisky from the village in spite of strict regulations to the contrary, and had no notion of saving their surplus pay. As a less demoralising mode of getting rid of the soldier's money than buying whisky, the commandant in my time sent to Détroit, 300 miles, for a small company of players, into whose pockets the men joyfully poured their money. Among these strollers there was a modest and very pretty young woman, the daughter of the manager, Blanchard by name,—one or two of the officers went crazy about her; but, in the midst of the excitement, the commandant suddenly shipped off the whole party, and the flame went out.

Desertion is scarcely to be prevented when soldiers are placed so near the frontier of the United States. There is, at least, a change for them, and they expect for the better.

While I was there, an order came from Quebec to the post, forbidding the employment of

Indians in capturing deserters; for during the preceding summer five soldiers started early in the morning across the strait to the American main, and made by the Indian path for Michilimackinac. On arriving there they would be safe.

The commandant sent half-a-dozen Indians after them, who in a couple of days returned with the men's heads in a bag.

The Indians knew a short cut and got a-head of their prey, and lay in ambush behind a rock in the track. When the soldiers came within a few feet of them, the Indians fired, and in the end killed every one of them.

During my stay at Collier's Harbour a war-party (forty-five) of the Pottawattomies, from Wisconsin, accompanied by three women, paid a visit to the post. They were as grim as red and black paint, red moose-hair, spears, clubs, and guns could make them.

The commandant caused a large bower to be built on the beach; and, surrounded by his officers in full dress, there received his guests.

The chief, a fine dauntless fellow, made a long and animated speech on the occasion, in brief but picturesque sentences, with the usual pauses and gesticulations with his spear.

'I remember that he began by begging Major F. to clear out his ear with a feather from an eagle's wing, that the way to his heart might be free. The jist of the speech was, that they had been out on a war excursion, and had killed three pale-faces (Americans).

The British officer replied, that he was extremely grieved to hear this, and that they must abide, unassisted, the wrath of the people they had injured.

The Indians professed themselves greatly surprised. They thought it was with us as with them,—once a foe, and always.

Except three or four, these Indians were much inferior to the European average in size, weight, and strength. Where they had picked up the women I know not, being a war-party.

After the conference they danced a war-dance with great solemnity to the drums and songs of their three women; a remarkable sight, and often well described.

Rations were given to these mistaken, but very self-satisfied people, for a few days, when they departed. They received no presents.

Drummond Island is celebrated for abounding in beautiful and new fossils, some of which are figured in the London "Geological Transactions." Its orthocera, a many-chambered fossil mollusc, are sometimes five and six feet long.

Awaking one bright and fragrant morning, the

window being open, I was surprised to hear a chorus of voices coming off the water. Having asked what it meant, I was told that it signalled the approach of a canoe with despatches and newspapers.

"They are full six miles off yet." So I lay and listened.

As long as the music was distant it was charming, like—

> "Voices of soft proclaim,
> And silver stir of strings in hollow shells."

but when it came near, its delicacy ceased.

Humming-birds are both large and numerous at this place. How often have I sat at the open window of Mr. White's cottage, whose light was tempered by a trellis of scarlet-beans, and watched these graceful little beings, while they tremblingly sipped on the wing the honey from the flowers!

After remaining on this occasion a week or more at Drummond Island, together with my friendly priest I again started for Michilimackinac (forty-two miles west), a small but important island at the entrance of Lake Michigan.

Leaving in the early morn, and having willing and stout canoe-men, we arrived late on the same night without any adventure.

Our course was straight, holding on our right

the south-west mainland, a series of points and shallow bays.

The lake is here pretty clear of islands, and is shallow; its floor of limestone being very visible far from shore, huge slabs sometimes rising to the surface.

Twenty-five miles off, Michilimackinac (Mackinaw) is a long, low cloud on the edge of the horizon.

It is an oval, nine miles in circumference, lying nearly north-west, a few miles to the east of the imaginary line separating Lakes Huron and Michigan.

The short sides of the island are pebbled beaches, the long sides picturesquely-wooded cliffs of white limestone.

The view into Lake Michigan from the Indian path, which winds among the shrubbery on the summit of the south-west precipice, is particularly pleasing. The land, at first closing on the water at the pretty hamlet of St. Ignatius and its opposite cape, at once dilates into a capacious sound with curving woody shores, and sprinkled with islands in the distance.

The projecting point, 150 feet high, near the south-east angle of the island, is perforated by two large windowlike openings, close together. The height of this rock, its whiteness contrasting with the dark investiture of cedar, and the light of the blue sky streaming through the apertures, make a striking composition for the painter.

Excepting three small farms, little had been done agriculturally when I was there. The heavy timber had been felled, and was replaced by flourishing shrubbery. I ran hastily over the higher parts of the island, and found them rough and often marshy. In the middle, near an oblong mound, is a singular mass of limestone shaped like a sugar-loaf, fifty or sixty feet high, and so steep as to have only a few cedar-bushes upon it.

The town is at the south-east end of the island, on the narrow beach, and under a high cliff. It then consisted of from 100 to 120 wooden houses in two parallel streets, that in the rear being the best.

The church in the middle of the town was a disgraceful wooden ruin, standing among the neat white habitations of the citizens.

I did not go into the fort. It overlooks the town in a broken line of officers' houses (white, with green verandahs), with strong white picketing in the gaps, and ornamentally terminated at each end by square white towers. A narrow walled road leads up the crumbling precipice from the town.

There is neither harbour nor pier. Vessels lie out far from land.

A friend was prepared for me at Mackinaw in the following manner.

Forty-five years before my visit to Drummond Island, a Scotch youth, tolerably well educated, of the name of Macvicar, ran away from his parents at Banff, and entered as a common sailor on board a merchant vessel bound to Quebec. There he left the ship, and made his way into the extreme west of Canada, and his parents never heard of him more. But it was known that he had sailed for Quebec.

About this time, a nephew of the runaway, a military medical officer, arrived at Quebec on duty, and was charged to inquire after his lost relative. At length he heard that there was an Indian trader of the name of Macvicar in Lake Huron. The officer was an old friend of mine, and gave me a letter of introduction to his uncle, if he should prove such.

I found a Mr. Macvicar at Collier's Harbour, and he proved to be the very man.

He was nearer seventy than sixty, built large and bony, with broad rugged features, crowned with tangled masses of grizzled hair. He had early married the daughter of a chief of the semi-civilised tribe of the Ottawas, and by her he had large family. His businesslike habits, a smattering of medicine, his tried bravery, and his matrimonial connexion, soon enabled him to accumulate property in the fur-trade.

In 1823 he had a valuable establishment on Drummond Island, and a still more important one at Mackinaw, which latter Mrs. Macvicar conducted.

I dined once or twice with Mr. Macvicar at Collier's Harbour, found him very companionable, and inquisitive about Scotland and his nephew, to whom, by the bye, he wrote a letter of thanks.

He was not annoyed at all by what occurred at dinner, and throughout the evening at each of my visits—the perpetual straying in and out of our room of dirty Indians, women and men, in ragged blankets.

Down they squatted in the corners, puffing their abominable weed-smoke into our faces, and joining freely in the conversation.

I told Mr. Macvicar my English notions of this. "Such is our custom," said he. "They are all respectable people. If I denied them, my trade would stop; and I might soon have between my ribs a knife-thrust, sharp and sufficient." I said no more.

He was so kind as to give me a letter to his wife, good for comfortable board and lodging as long as it suited me. To her, therefore, I went on arriving at Mackinaw.

She gave me a nice clean bed, in a large empty granary; cool and airy in the summer heats then prevailing. She told me the hours of the family meals, and gave me the escort of one of her sons in my various excursions.

I would not mind seeking a lost uncle for any other of my friends, if he had such a wife as Mrs. Macvicar.

She was both kind and sagacious. She saw in a moment my wants, and supplied them.

Many Indians speak French excellently. Mrs. Macvicar understood both English and French, but only spoke Indian. She was stout, a little taller than most Indian females. She was of a right genial nature. Her swart countenance was written all over with benevolence; it was one great symbol of love and help; and yet all her numerous household obeyed "the mother" at a look. Nothing could be moro orderly than her establishment. She superintended everything, from the merchant-store to the scullery.

Her brother and his two sons, of pure Indian blood, were the handsomest men of any nation I ever saw.

Having been thoroughly wearied by clambering

about in the island the day before, I slept rather late one morning—to between six and seven; and was then aroused by a massive but elastic footstep in my spacious bedroom.

On opening my eyes I beheld, to my astonishment, and with some little nervous thrill, a magnificent Indian, with shaven crown, in the splendid attire of his people—six feet high, moulded in the perfection of beauty and strength. He was pacing to and fro, like a High Admiral on his deck of state—a living portrait of force in repose—and filling the air with white curling volumes of smoke from a long feathered calumet.

He was one of Nature's gentlemen, and smiled slightly at my awaking, and then left the granary, as I suppose, that I might dress.

If he had remained, I fear he would have thought it his duty to fling my poor corpuscle through the ample window into the lake below, as a certain Harry L. was served—and as is said to be done with the weakly infants of these regions.

In the course of the morning I made the acquaintance of the chief in due form, and that of his son, eighteen years old, a youth of remarkable beauty—without his father's muscular developement, and his face, with the pride of the Indian eye, retaining the delicacy of the child. He was also dressed in rich materials, silver armlets, breastplate, dyed moose-hair, bead-embroidered leather, as soft as a lady's glove.

An elder brother was with them, about twenty-one—a remarkably fine Indian—symmetry itself; but entirely differing in general expression from his relatives. It is well known that family peculiarities pass over one or more generations and reappear. Accordingly, this youth had a dangerous bird-of-prey beauty, the eagle-nose, the lowering, implacable eye of some forgotten ancestor. He seemed to have been bred, not under the dove, but the vulture. I instinctively avoided this young gentleman.*

The fact was that these kinsmen had arrived over-night at Mackinaw, on their way with their tribe to Drummond Island, to receive their annual presents from the British Government.

Although actually residing at L'Arbre Croche in Lake Michigan, and in the United States, they considered themselves British subjects, and some years afterwards migrated to the Grand Manitouline of Lake Huron.

Indian notions of honour and obligation differ sometimes from ours.

* Some may say, "The Ottawas are semi-civilised; you are colouring too highly." No; the sketch is exact. Clive, the conqueror of India, was bred in a parsonage.

These comparatively opulent persons saw no wrong in going a hundred miles for a few small presents. They looked upon them as a retaining fee, and the journey as a holiday just before maize-harvest.

During the summer of 1822 a very large and splendid steamer* (I have seen none equal to it in Europe, 1849) made her appearance in the Huron waters—the first vessel of the kind that had been seen there.

Red men and white flocked to see her from great distances; and among others the three Ottawas I have been slightly describing.

The steam-ship arrived at the appointed day, crowded with fashionables from the Atlantic shores of the United States, eager to penetrate so safely and agreeably into the far Indian solitudes.

Among the numerous passengers was an uncomfortable looking, shaky old gentleman, from the sweet village-town of Geneva on Lake Seneca, evidently a rich man, laden with silly jewellery, and with a much weightier burthen in a romantic and very fair wife, one-third his own age, as eager and impressible as he was stark and torpid.

When the Ottawa tribe appeared on the waters, each canoe carrying its own red pennon—when

* The Walk in the Water, Job Fish commander. These names are genuine.

the warriors stood on the deck, resplendent in silver and scarlet, in a costume of which the Mexican cacique of old would have been proud, the American lady was almost beside herself.

Forgetting her displeased husband, who tottered anxiously after her, her nimble and glowing imagination filled with unreal visions of sylvan life, she wandered in ecstasies from group to group, and at length stood transfixed before our youngest Ottawa friend, Mrs. Macvicar's nephew, as he was gazing in one of his picturesque attitudes at the new monster, its strange entrails, wreathing vapours, and great white wings.

In a little time the lady awoke from her trance, and asked for an interpreter. One was easily procured. Through him, standing in the midst of a large wondering circle, she asked the young Indian to permit her to place upon his finger a richly enchased gold ring, as a remembrance of their meeting on the bright waters of Huron.

The young man was at first mute with surprise —looking at the sky, the ring on his finger, and the lady; when at length, in a few slowly-spoken and scarcely-audible words, he said, "Tell the "pale sister with the blue eyes, that Mahkiouta "accepts her ring as the emblem of love. Tell "her that she has poured sunbeams into his soul, "and made him strong in the forest.

"Tell the pale sister, that as my belt of scented "grass* reminds me of my wide savannahs, so for "ever shall her ring of this happy meeting."

This incident suited the American taste, and went the round of the newspapers. I joined the steamer (being then on an excursion) at Détroit on her return voyage, and descended Lake Erie together with Mrs. G., the lady of the ring, a three days' trip. I found her an interesting person, fanciful, and clever—much to be pitied, and the victim probably of sordid parents.

Having been sufficiently long at Mackinaw, Mrs. Macvicar, my good genius, engaged a seat for me in the canoe of an Ottawa chief, going to Drummond Island with his people for presents—not with her splendid brother, but with the Blackbird† (I do not mean our soprano of the woods).

The price of my conveyance, I am sorry to say, was a couple of bottles of rum.

When introduced to this great warrior, as I had heard him described to be, I was surprised to find before me a small man, with a knowing little face,

* There is a grass, abundant here, of a strong and agreeable perfume, and called Indian grass. It is often made into ornaments for sale.

† So named from the device painted on the right side of his face. The eye of the bird was represented by one of his, while the head and beak spread over his forehead and temple.

which would have fitted a country shoemaker. There was no melo-dramatic nonsense about him.

I was provided with a lump of ham, a large loaf, and a bottle of whisky, stoppered, for want of a cork, with half of one of Miss Edgeworth's novels (doubtless originally from the garrison), and then was told that the Indians had embarked.

Running down to the beach with my knapsack and provision-bag, I found a little fleet of twenty-five canoes on the point of starting; and was bidden by signs to jump into the canoe nearest me, but seeing no room, I hesitated.

The craft was not large. On the prow, where there is a little shelf, there sat an unquiet young bear, tied with a cord,—two smoking Indians and three children sitting on the canoe-bottom next to him. Then came four women-rowers, among whom I was to squat, or nowhere. The stern-half of the canoe was occupied by the Blackbird and a friend, with three more young imps and a steersman. Two or three dogs kept constantly circulating among our legs in search of dropped eatables, who so approved of my ham that I was fain to keep it on my knees.

But we all settled down into a sort of stiff comfort.

The water was as smooth as glass. The strong unclouded sun was in mid-heavens. We moved away with many an uncouth antic and shriek, both on land and lake, and I was once more abandoned to the happy-go-lucky do-nothings of the Indian race.

They certainly never intended to go further that day than a well-known point fifteen miles distant, on the south-west main; for seeing that there was the gentlest possible of all airs in our favour, when they had gained the open lake, the ladies dipped paddle into water, but seldom and most delicately, falling into that murmuring musical gossip we hear in an aviary. And thus it was all the fleet through.

We proceeded, therefore, lazily and irregularly, greeting by turns every canoe as we passed or were passed. The heat was intense, but I saw no Indian drink; sufficient for him was the pipe—that brought the complacent reverie.

I employed myself in a variety of ways—in watching my neighbours, and especially the bear, who knew the others, but not me. I counted the 240 circular buckles of silver on the back of one of the women, fastened close together like the links of chain armour, each worth about tenpence. Her neck was hid under blue and white beads, and she wore broad anklets and armlets of silver plate. She had also slung over her back, by a white cord, from her neck, a massive silver cross, eight or nine inches long. The other women, likewise, had on similar visiting finery.

The men were grandly dressed with chamois leather leggings, ornamented with fanciful traceries in porcupine quills, and fringed on the outer seam with red moose-hair. They wore broad breast-plates of silver, with their name or device engraved on it, and armlets and fore-armlets of the same metal three or four inches broad.

Some had European hats, with broad bands of solid silver, silver cord running here and there, and an ostrich feather. Others wore a stiff, high round cap, covered with red moose-hair which streamed over their shoulders.

It must be remarked, that although the general effect was very fine, the details were often defective; for instance, their many-coloured or red shirt of stiffened calico, made very full, was not always of the newest.

To the great delight of my cramped limbs, at six in the afternoon we put on shore on a shingle point, with a few bushes, and some drift-wood ready for burning.

As soon as we landed, two or three men started with a net into a little bay close by, and in less than a couple of hours returned with a good catch of salmon-trout for general distribution.

Meantime the Indian women built the wigwams,

—a simple process—made the fires, pounded the maize, walked up to the knees into the lake, and there scoured their noisy children well all over.

The men lounged about, playing at duck and drake with the taller boys, all screaming most triumphantly at a capital throw.

I saw, indeed, nothing but good feeling among these people, and was very pleased in the course of the evening to observe the great tenderness bestowed upon a paralytic young Indian. He had lost the use of his left side. He had a bed, with blankets, in one of the canoes; his head was so raised that he could look about. All his braveries were on, and his hat was decorated with gold cord. His face was flushed, and looked rather irritable, but was intelligent. His friends carried him carefully to a wigwam.

I believe they took him to receive his present as an amusement to him, although it may be necessary for every Indian to appear personally. This is not the only instance of kindness towards the helpless that I have seen among the savages.

For a long time nobody took any notice of me, so I begged a blazing stick and made myself a fire, with which I roasted and smoked a slice of ham (cut with a penknife). Of this, with some bread, I was making a sorry supper, when, seeing a bottle by my side, five or six Indians joined me, and were, as far as signs went, very civil, but cast longing looks at my whisky-bottle, with words, among which I recognised, "Nidgé—skittewabo" ("Friend—fire-water").

Eventually—you must imagine the process—they drank all my store, with my perfect good-will, and left me.

Some may ask, Whether it was safe to be alone with a large body of Indians? Yes!—because I was known to be a king's officer, and this band was going for presents. Had I been an American, the case might possibly in these days have been different.

That same summer a young medical officer in the American service, stationed at Mackinaw, having obtained leave of absence to fetch his wife, was crossing a portage near Greenbay, Lake Michigan, when he engaged an Indian, he met with on the road, to carry his portmanteau. So the Indian walked after the medical officer, with his load upon his head, and his gun under his arm.

All at once the Indian said to himself, "This is a Big-knife! The Big-knives shot my father—I will shoot this Big-knife!" and did so instantly, through the back, and killed him.

The poor officer had left his wife, on service, a few days after marriage, and had been away a year.

While I was sitting alone after supper, the Blackbird and another man brought out of the woods some long supple boughs, and planted them in the ground as the skeleton of a bower — for some sick woman, I supposed. Over them they flung an old sail, and smoothing the floor within, they lined it with fragrant fir-tops, then with a mat, and finally with green baize cloth.

The good Blackbird, to my surprise, put my little baggage into the back part of the bower, and then led me by the hand to it, with many gentle but unintelligible words, and made me take possession. I gave him the thanks of the eyes, having no other.

Tied to a bush just behind my bower was friend Bruin, restless and strange, every now and then twitching and dragging at his tether. This I did not like.

As I sat upon the ground in front of my new home (I had thought for once to have slept in a wigwam with the family!), watching the scene, a young man brought me a large middle cut of a salmon trout, boiled and smoking hot, enough for a whole dinner-party in London, on a clean board, with a bone-handled knife and fork. My previous supper did not prevent my relishing this present highly; there was but little left.

Now would I have gone to rest, for the moon

was rising, and the air was chill; but the Blackbird, and six or seven elders of the tribe, sat down round the mouth of my bower to talk over the news—not with me, for I could speak no Chippewa, and they no French.

The chief brought with him a case of spirit-bottles, and at long intervals handed round, with polite gravity, little thimble-like glasses of whisky to the circle. In an hour they retired, each to his dormitory.

I covered the upper half of my doorway, made a pillow of my provision-bag, threw my greatcoat over me, and soon slept, in spite of the rippling waters, and the grunts of the restless bear behind.

I must have been asleep two or three hours when, suddenly, down fell my head to the ground. I thought of savages, wolves, and bears; but on opening my eyes, I saw my pillow, with its ham, &c. moving quickly out of the bower, between the teeth of a foxy Indian dog, whose green-red eyes glared frightfully on me.

He had companions, but they all fled at my shout, leaving the pillow. I had the good fortune to settle soon again to sleep, and did not awake until five in the morning, when it was time to arise.

I sallied forth, and found the Nidgés loading the canoes, drest in their best. But a dense fog, caused by the cold night air, put everything out of sight—the woods, the lake itself, and our little fleet. We saw nothing but the rimy bushes and stones, and the dim waters that crept along the bank of shingle.

We set off partly with paddles, partly pretending to sail at every momentary puff of wind ; and thus we glided slowly through the thick mist, guided, I doubt not, by the land on our left, of which I saw nothing.

I began to prepare my mind moodily for another day and night with the friendly Redskins ; but a gentle breeze sprang up, dispersing, in some degree, the fog, and pushing us on at the rate of five miles an hour — every eye gladdening his neighbour ; for the dancing motion of the canoes, and the relief from labour, had put us all in spirits.

We continued thus for several hours, and then, to my disappointment, turned into a bay three miles from Collier's Harbour, and there landed— not to breakfast, but for the Indians to don new ornaments, repaint their faces, and hoist the British flag at the stern of the two canoes belonging to chiefs, while the others had small red banners flying over them.

The whole fleet at length drew up in line, and started for the British post.

When, to my unspeakable content, we arrived just outside of the harbour, the sun burst forth most opportunely, and lighted up the pretty capes and isles, the white houses and uplands of the port. There was quite a forest or town of wigwams (from one hundred to a hundred and twenty) on the beach, and a crowd of soldiers, Indians, and white settlers, at the edge of the water, to greet and criticise our *entrée*.

The moment we were embayed, and therefore without wind, the women struck out vigorously, gazing with modest joy upon their lords and brothers, as they silently arose in grim and glittering array, and so stood until we landed.

Looking round me at the time, I thought I had never seen a gayer pageant—a fleet of fine canoes, pennons flying, full of athletic savages clothed in silver, and coming peacefully, without a shot being fired even in compliment.

The red spectators were mute; the white men cheered.

I parted with the Blackbird and his nation in the most gracious manner, and frequently met the chief in the village afterwards with his device in full force on his face.

Many of these Indians had brought furs for sale, which were paid for, against law, in rum.

There were, on our arrival, 700 Indians encamped on the beach, and many more were expected. The same night showed us the Indian character in very unpleasing colours.

A grand drinking-bout then took place according to custom. It began early in the afternoon. Soon after dark, voices began to be loud among the wigwams. Indians were rushing about, the women after them, with lights, in great agitation, hurrying to hide guns and knives. An uproar now and then rose higher than usual; one or two were stabbed, and the garrison interfered. To go among these infuriated people was not very pleasant; but as the doctor had to do so, I went with him on one of his calls; but all was quiet, the conflict was over, the combatants gone—asleep, perhaps. We had only to deal with a wounded man and a few grateful women.*

I believe that drunkenness from cheap spirits has a demoniacal energy of its own, quite distinct from the drowsy exaltation produced by beer or porter.

* The greater part of the Ottawa nation now reside on the Grand Manitouline. Whether their removal was wise I doubt much, but they may have had strong political reasons. They have moved into a severer climate, to an insular position, and probably to a worse soil. But they are increasing in numbers. They have become stationary, and subsist on a rude husbandry and fishing. In 1845 they sent our schooner loads of fine maple sugar for sale at Détroit. The occupation of making maple sugar exactly suits an Indian.

Confluence Harbour at S. E. Point of St. Joseph.
Carver Mounts of N. Mainland in the distance.

I did not stay long at Collier's Harbour, but embarked in a merchant-sloop for Détroit, in the strait of that name, which connects Lakes Huron and Erie.

As it is desirable to place in a connected whole all my observations on Lake Huron, allow me to state, that in the summer previous to this I found myself in his Majesty's schooner Confiance, then employed in transporting from place to place the officers of the British Boundary Commission.

Our two astronomers and their staffs were directed to make a trigonometrical survey of the north-west arm of Lake Huron. In the performance of this duty we spent the summer, encamped in various places,—at Encampment Douce, at the foot of the East Nibish Rapids, on the south point of St. Joseph and the islets on its east, in Portlock Harbour on the north main, in the Pelletau Narrows, and on the Little Manitou.

Our surveyors being numerous and able, the work proceeded at a rapid rate.

I shall not enter into any further details merely geographical. The accompanying map and sketches render this unnecessary.

With correct maps, soundings, and information as to the agricultural or public value of the islands, there was no difficulty in determining the boundary line, or in giving for such determination a satisfactory reason.

I employed my leisure in the examination of the geology of the country, and in the collection of insects. I met with ninety new species of insects and two new genera. They have been described, and some of them figured, by the Rev. W. Kirby, F.R.S., in the "Fauna Boreali-Americana" of Sir John Richardson. A list of them will be found in the Appendix.

It was remarkable, that when I had to all appearance exhausted any given locality, the insect population of the next station, ten or fifteen miles distant, consisted one half of new species, and so on from place to place,—and this, perhaps, from a difference in the vegetation and in the season of the year.

Compassion—deep and irresistible—has made me forswear the occupation of the entomologist, whose very mercies are the cruelties of other men, whether he kill by scalding water or the red-hot iron wire.

I glued to a tray, in a dark charnel-house of 1200 dead insects, a large and beautiful butterfly, of a sky-blue colour, supposed to be dead. There it was during six months of travel. When I examined my treasures at Quebec, on my return, this imprisoned Peri slowly raised and gently

B. del — R. Young sc

Encampment [illegible] below the Nibish Rapids Lake Huron

shook its wings to [illegible]. [illegible] not this a torture to [illegible]

We remained for [illegible] Douce, where our [illegible] on a sandy point, near a [illegible] heat was intense [illegible] two occasions, but the [illegible]

We were devoured with [illegible] scenery was open, [illegible] Plate.)

As I was [illegible] skirts of a small [illegible] was suddenly [illegible] the underwood [illegible] into the lake. [illegible] dangerous, except [illegible] This reminded me of [illegible] on the St. Lawrence, among the [illegible] Islands, where I was [illegible] ning hastily [illegible] seen a bear. "[illegible] Tommy?" said his [illegible] leavings," replied the boy.

We were [illegible] the South Point, [illegible] the neighbouring [illegible] to the east of the point [illegible] of olivine in [illegible] surrounded with flourishing young woods, the insect harvest was plentiful.

An odd incident partly occurred here.

A little river runs for a mile or so on the edge of this marsh. Lieut. Grant and myself were entomologising near our tents when a splendid and quite new butterfly sprang up. We pursued it eagerly for a good way along the river-side, making many an useless dash at the prize, when the insect darted across the stream and escaped.

Casting our eyes to the ground, we saw the olivine, and instantly fell to work in taking specimens. All this time, unknown to us, there were Indians in the woods on the other side of the river, following our every step in perfect amazement, persuaded that we were mad. And why? Because we chased a poor insect,—lost it,—and in our impotent rage were smiting the dumb rocks. They intended to seize and convey us to our friends; but seeing that we afterwards became calm, they refrained.

Of these kind people, and their intentions, I only heard accidentally two years afterwards in a public stage-coach in the state of New York, 700 miles to the south-east! A gentleman was entertaining his fellow-passengers very cleverly with the little story, and was greatly amazed by my telling him that I was one of the butterfly-hunters.

Bottled Harbour N. W. Shore of Lake Huron

Near the Old Fort we built a large and handsome bower, as a living and work room, as well as for a temporary church on Sundays,—the congregation consisting of five or six gentlemen, eight or ten blue-jackets, our servants, and some boatmen, among whom were Roman Catholics.

The sacred day was always kept with great propriety, and the services gladly attended.

I am of opinion that our sequestered and contemplative mode of life was more favourable (for a time) to the growth of the Christian dispositions than the formal attendance on church duties in cities (by no means, however, to be lightly spoken of), surrounded by the temptations, distractions, and anxieties of civilised life. David's most spiritual psalms were written in the desert.

If a man have any, the least, religious tendencies, they will be awakened in an American wilderness. The Creator and the Preserver feel wonderfully near in the thunder, the gale, and the snow-storm.

Of the scenery about Portlock Harbour and the south-east point of St. Joseph, the plates are specimens.

We disturbed a bear at each of these places, and endeavoured with great zeal, but unsuccessfully, to catch and eat them.

The little island on which I was encamped alone, off the south-east point, was singularly infested with red ants. There was hardly a spot free. They swarmed in my tent and bed. But out-door fatigue enabled me to sleep in spite of this crawling annoyance. The ants of Lake Huron are of various kinds,—some very large.

Our encampment on the Little Manitou Island was characteristic and snug. It was on the north side, nearly in the middle, on a dry, sheltered knoll, eight or ten feet high, overlooking a boat-cove, itself within a small round bay, where a schooner or two might anchor.

Here we passed three happy and busy weeks,—the surveyors at their field-work,—myself scaling every accessible precipice, and wandering from beach to beach.

We cleared a sufficient site for tents, formed other habitations, more fragrant, from branches of pine—squaring huge seats from their trunks for fireside seats,—and such fires! The untravelled English cannot conceive their wasteful immensity.

Although it was only September, the lake now was stormy and cold; we were therefore glad, as evening drew in, to have so comfortable a nook,—the Confiance, with her amiable commander, in the little haven, and we listening to the gusty winds and labouring trees in pleasurable security.

The smoke from our fires, our white tents, and the various movements, one day brought to us a bald-headed eagle, who inspected us long from the highest bough of a fine oak—in fact until observed by our idle purveyor, a Canadian of sporting propensities.

He and I crept round the cove and got under the tree. Twice we fired without even disturbing the bird's steady gaze; but the third shot brought him down dead. It was a barbarous act. He was large, richly-plumaged,—how broad from tip to tip of his wings we will not say; but we greatly admired and then ate him.

During our stay here I accompanied the surveyors to the Grand Manitouline Island, eight miles from our encampment. It is separated from the Little Manitou by the strait called the Third Détour, eight miles long by four broad, an open water, with a clear and unobstructed lake at either outlet.

The west end of the Grand Manitou is of a different and more majestic character than any part of Lake Huron that I have seen.

At the north end of the strait the shores sweep in easy curves, lined with stairs of shingle, supported behind by ascending woods.

Towards its centre, ledges and low precipices begin to appear along the beaches, which at length rise to the elevation of 200 feet and more, crowned with cedar and pine. Their height is either strictly perpendicular, or is attained by piles of displaced masses, each from twenty to thirty feet in diameter, resting pell-mell upon each other. These great blocks advance into the water, and with the help of the pebbles, which gather round them, afford a hazardous and toilsome path over their slippery faces, under arches, and through winding passages. The woods here are impassable from fallen trees, fissures, and narrow ravines, mantled over with an enormous growth of mosses and creeping plants.

Within half a mile of the south-east angle of the Détour these great masses lie horizontally one upon another, fitting in pretty accurately, and extend far into the interior, as a naked platform intersected and surrounded by luxuriant woods.

The extreme neatness and regularity of these natural terraces, their isolated tufts of flowering shrubs, their waving borders of foliage, and their gloomy alleys, seem to realise the fairy scenes of old romance, and produce a feeling of unwonted awe and expectation.

I ventured among them, in search of fossils, as far as I dared. There was a sort of old-fashioned, prim decay about them, which reminded me of the gardens of Haddon Hall.

On the morning of the 27th of September we left our pleasant cove for the River St. Clair, having completed the Lake Huron surveys.

During the day we lay off the Third Détour waiting for a breeze. There had been heavy rain. A thick white mist was curling in patches over the woody slopes close to us. About three P.M. came the desired wind, and we set forth to pass down the Détour, but scarcely were we half-way through, when we perceived very foul weather a-head, in the south, with occasional gleams of lightning. We immediately put about, and ran behind the Little Manitou for security.

This thunder-storm did not, as far as I saw, like those under the equator, first appear at the edge of the horizon, a small sooty cloud, and gradually cover the heavens, with driving rain and incessant discharges of electricity; but it was formed by the meeting, from several quarters of the sky, of clouds, piled and voluminous,—one being much the largest. They descended low, with a flat under-surface, just cutting off (out of sight) the tops of the pines on the heights near us.

The clouds themselves moved slowly, but occasionally we saw in them a rapid internal wreathing and rolling, with a continual building up, for a instants, of new shapes and structures.

The thunder came, but in prolonged reverberations, traversing and retraversing great distances.

It was near sunset, a patch of sky in the west

being clear. Each flash of sheet lightning, as it descended from the upper sky, enriched and brightened the momentarily translucent clouds with the most lovely colours imaginable, principally yellow, red, and bistre.

The lightning was seldom forked, but both in sheets and in straight columns, striking upon the woods and waters perpendicularly.

Although I could not always look upon this interesting scene, for now and then the flashes were overpoweringly vivid, I noticed that they only silvered the outer leafy surface of the trees, without going deeper, as the light of day does.

As our little vessel was under good cover, we only saw the hurricane blackening the lake at a safe distance. Some little rocking we had; and the rain fell heavily and straight down, rebounding from the water in grey spikes six inches high.

We were in the thick of the storm about dusk, and it lasted two or three hours.* I went to bed, and on rising next morning found that we were

* Lake Huron is celebrated for its terrific thunder-storms (Bouchette, "Topog. of the Canadas"). They are generally far more formidable in North America than in England. It is for this reason that the chief private houses and public buildings in the United States and elsewhere are armed with lightning-rods.

In August 1821, Quebec was visited by an electric storm of great violence. This city stands high and exposed, and its houses and churches have metallic roofs and window-shutters. On this occasion the lightning was incessant, and ran in thin through the Détour, and some miles on our way to the River St. Clair, distant 160 miles almost due south.

The weather was yet threatening and the lake sullen. The waves were short and high, so that not a few of us were miserably sea-sick.

sheets about the roofs from corner to corner, as if desiring to leap down, but dared not. The needles of some ladies, in the act of sewing, were pointed with pencils of electricity. Several lives were lost, besides much damage done. Great numbers were seized with vomitings during the storm.

As might have been expected from the greater heat in the summers of the Canadas, and other meteorological conditions, thunder-storms are violent and frequent. Col. Sabine, F.R.S., in his Report on the Meteorological and Terrestrial Magnetism of Toronto, U.C., has noted many particulars respecting the thunder-storms of that place during the years 1841, 1842. These I have consolidated into two tables, to be found in the Appendix.

From them it appears that in 1841 there were twenty-two of what we mean by thunder-storms; and that of these ten were very violent. Sheet lightning also occurred five times alone.

In 1842 there were eighteen thunder-storms, of which nine were very severe; besides sheet lightning once, and two distant but audible thunder-storms.

The following little table will show the monthly distribution of the storms:—

Year	Jan.	Feb.	Mar.	Apr.	May.	June.	July.	Aug.	Sept.	Oct.	Nov.	Dec.
1841	—	—	1	—	—	7	6	3	5	1	—	—
1842	1	1	3	1	2	1	3	3	3	1	—	—

I am not aware that any similar tables for Lower Canada or the United States exist.

We were in a great expanse of fresh water, without reef, shoal, or island in our path. On our left was the long, high terrace of the Grand Manitouline, with a few islands (the Ducks) close to them. But we soon left that fine island astern, and obliquely neared the southern or United States' shore of the lake, sighting it a little west of Thunder Bay. We scudded alongside its low forests, its sand-beaches and ledges of limestone, until we again lost sight of land for a short time as we crossed the mouth of the great bay of Saguenay, twenty-five miles across and forty-five miles deep, and off which Colonel Bonnycastle says, that leads have been sunk 1800 feet without finding bottom, that is, 1200 feet below the level of the sea. The fine river Saguenay enters Lake Huron at the bottom of this bay. It is 180 yards broad for twenty-four miles (Rev. Mr. Hudson, missionary to the Saguenay Indians), flowing through a level and heavily-timbered district. It then divides into three small, winding branches, one of which is called Flint River. The River Saguenay is 120 miles from Détroit by land, and more than 200 by the lake.*

We neared the south angle of this bay, Point aux Barques; and as we ran down the sandy, low

* Sir John Richardson informs me, that very recently extensive coal-fields have been discovered in Saguenay Bay.

coast, to the mouth of the River St. Clair, we did not omit to notice, half-way down, the well-known "White Rock," a large, erratic block.

We were delighted to enter the smooth and transparent St. Clair, the American Fort Gratiot, low, white, and trim, on our right hand, and the marshes of Port Sarnia on the left, now (1849) occupied by a busy population.

Storm-tossed as we had been in Huron, the still waters of St. Clair were most grateful.

After a parting look at the angry surges of the lake, and having again, for a moment, listened to its rough music, we forthwith began those reparations in cleanliness, costume, and creature-comforts, which our tortured heads and stomachs did not previously permit.

EXCURSION THE SEVENTH.

PART III.

LAKE SUPERIOR.

Brief Description — Boat-voyage from St. Mary to Grand Portage by the North Shore — River St. Mary — Gros Cap — Maple Islands — Disaster recorded — Marmoaze — River Montreal — Copper Mines — Haggeweng Bay — Point Gargantua — The Prairies — Michipicoton Bay, River, Fort — The Goat — Fine Scenery — Gloomy River — Indians, Otter's Head — Indian Road-marks — A Run on Shore — The Ravine — Curious Fresh-water Animals — Basalt Dykes — Peek River and Isles — The Julia — Mist — Wind-bound at the Black River — Written Rocks — Snow again — Nipigon Bay and Islands — Mammelle Hills — Black Bay — Thunder Mountain — Count Andriani — Fortwilliam — To Grand Portage among fine Scenery.

PRELIMINARY OBSERVATIONS.

Lake Superior, also called "Keetcheegahmi" and "Mississawgaiegon" in certain Indian districts, and "Bourbon" formerly by the French, is contained by west longitude 84° 18′ and 92° 19′; and by the north latitude 46° 26′ and 49° 1′.

It is placed to the south of, and near to the ridge of high lands which, stretching from the Rocky

Mountains to Lake Superior in broad plains and undulations, divides the waters flowing into the Mexican Gulf from those of Hudson's Bay; and which proceeds from near Lake Superior eastward to the coast of Labrador in a continuous range of shattered and often denuded hills; then constituting the northern dividing ridge of the valley of the St. Lawrence.

From near the west end of the lake this ridge (no longer an undulating plain) is lost on the south and east in the elevations of the United States; but still affords a connected series of successively descending levels for the St. Lawrence, its chain of lakes and magnificent tributaries, Lake Champlain and the Ottawa and Saguenay Rivers.

Lake Superior occupies an irregularly oblong basin, whose length lies east and west, and amounts on its south side to 541 statute miles, as ascertained by Mr. Astronomer Thompson by a patent log. This measurement commences from Point Iroquois at the mouth of the River St. Mary (communicating with Lake Huron), passes the outskirts of all bays, except when their breadth renders the crossing unadvisable, and, rounding Point Keewawoonan, terminates at the mouth of the River St. Louis at the Fond du Lac.

The sum of the canoe-courses round the lake is

1155 miles, always avoiding the bays, and especially Black Bay (north coast), which is itself ninety miles round.

Captain Bayfield, R.N., following the sinuosities of the coasts more closely, makes the circumference of Lake Superior to be 1750 miles, and its length in a curved line through its centre 420 miles, its extreme breadth opposite the River Peek being 163 miles. It does not appear so broad in his map as in mine. It is thus by far the largest collection of fresh water on the earth. Lake Baikal, in Asia, although 410 miles long, is only forty in average breadth.

Of the south shore thus measured a few words must be said. It is divided by the promontory of Keewawoonan* into two nearly equal parts, the eastern of which is chiefly a concave shore, 176 miles long (Schoolcraft), the remainder consisting of a large bay at each end of this gentle but extensive curve. The most remarkable localities are the Pictured Rocks and Grand Isle, which abound in singular and beautiful scenery.

The Huron group and others near Granite Point are almost the only islands on this side of Point

* This word is written after the manner of Mr. Astronomer Thompson, whose residence for twenty-seven years among the Indians, acute ear, and good general education, make him an excellent authority in the orthography of Indian words.

Keewawoonan. There are 139 rivers and creeks on the whole south shore, but fewer in this the eastern division than in the western.

Keewawoonan is a rocky promontory, with three principal summits, from forty to forty-five miles long, and from fifteen to seventeen miles in its greatest breadth, which is at the Portage. Its length lies north-east, and it tapers almost to a point at its extremity.

This great headland is, in fact, a peninsula connected with the mainland by a portage 2000 yards long. The waters giving it this character are a small river and lake.

Vast deposits of copper ore are in the neighbourhood, of which we need only say in this place that, according to a Wisconsin newspaper, a million and a half pounds of nearly pure copper were shipped from hence in the first eight months of 1848.

From Point Keewawoonan, westwards, the shore passes nearly W. S. W. with a waving outline to the strongly-marked headland immediately north of Point Cheguimegon, and fronted by the little-known cluster of islands named after the Twelve Apostles. Here the Fond du Lac commences.

Rivers are very numerous in this part of the lake; but the shore is of moderate height, except where the Porcupine Hills approach the lake in longitude 90°. Travellers make these hills from 1000 to 1800 feet high.*

Of the north shore of Lake Superior we need say nothing here, as it is sketched with sufficient minuteness in the course of this Excursion.

* 593½ now 600

Lake Superior may be considered to be 593½ feet above the surface of the Atlantic.

I cannot learn that any gradual diminution is taking place in the quantity of its water. The contrary might be presumed, from its receiving the contents of 220 rivers and brooks, some of them of great size, and from its having only one outlet.† Ninety years, however, have produced no change at the Grand Portage, where such an event would have been readily detected.

90 yrs Grand Portage

The appearances on the coasts indicating recent drainage are owing to temporary and local changes of level caused by storms, or to events anterior to historic time.

The effects of tempests in raising the level of certain parts of the lake are considerable. In

* I acknowledge with great pleasure the personal attentions of Mr. Schoolcraft, now at the head of the Indian department at Washington, and his obliging liberality in the communication of information.

† American lakes very rarely have more than one outlet; neither, if the matter be considered, is more than one necessary. Lake Wollaston, however, in longitude 112° west, placed on the summit level between the waters of Hudson's Bay and of the Arctic Seas, has two. I know of no other case.

Lake Temagami is said to mean five outlets in the Chippewa language according to Mike Ristoul, half breed autumn, a westerly gale lasting more than a day will sometimes inundate the site of the Hudson's Bay storehouses at the Falls of St. Mary.

Respecting the depth of Lake Superior I have little to offer. It is doubtless very deep, judging from its steady and uniform coldness. Captain Bayfield found 300 and 400 feet a common depth. Some distance into the lake he found bottom at 600 feet.

The body of the lake never freezes, although there is always much firm ice near shore and among islands.

Colonel Delafield found the temperature of the water to be 44° Fahr., from an average of many observations in June and July, 1823.

Its depth cools down the water, and this acts upon the air, so that Lake Superior is not hot for many days together. Captain Bayfield made the mean temperature of the air at noon for July and August, the two hottest months of the year, to be 58°.* This was in Pays Plat, on the north shore.

Colonel Delafield found ice on the lake on the 28th of June, and so did the sailing-master of Captain Bayfield near the same time the previous year.

The climate and vegetation of Lake Superior

* At five A.M. in July, Captain B. found the air at 33°.

are almost arctic, although in 47° of north latitude, and but little to the north of Milan, in Italy. It is considerably colder than Sikla, in 57° north latitude, the Russian post on the north-west coast of America. The reason of this seems to be that there are, as far as I know, no high mountains running east and west to screen this lake from the polar winds. The hills on its north for 300 or 400 miles, which I have seen, are short and low, never exceeding 1500 feet in height, and their trend and that of their numerous valleys is more or less north and south.

The vegetation on the great grey granite and gneiss districts of the north shore of Lake Superior is extremely scanty, there being scarcely any soil, while that of the basaltic and amygdaloidal regions is diseased and very small, though dense.

A few observations have been made on the height of the basin containing Lake Superior.

The lowest point of the barrier is, of course, at its outlet, St. Mary's.

For several miles north and south of Point Iroquois and Gros Cap the land at the present day is much lower than elsewhere, and does not reach 400 feet in elevation, while the dividing ridge (the summit-level) on the north shore is always much higher; as also are certain parts of the south shore, if not all.

The height of land between Lakes Superior and Winnepeg (Hudson's Bay) is supposed by Captain Lefroy, R.A., to be about 1500 feet, from a mean of several barometrical observations* made at Coldwater Lake, on the new route to the Lake of the Woods, fifty miles direct from Lake Superior.

The summit level of *water* at the source of the West Savannah River, between the waters of St. Louis (Superior) and those of the Mississippi, has been estimated at 550 feet in Mr. Schoolcraft's narrative, and therefore 1143 feet above the sea, seventy miles direct from Lake Superior.

The highest water-level on the old route to the Lake of the Woods is at the portage of the East Lake of the height of land, twenty-four miles direct from Lake Superior, and about 1207 feet above the sea by estimate.

The height of land is seldom very distant from the lake, and the remark may be extended to the lower lakes, Huron, &c.

Making use of the best accessible map of the vicinity of the Lake Superior, that of Major Long (James's "Expedition to the Rocky Mountains"), the sources of all the rivers on the south shore are within sixty miles of the lake, measured in a straight line. On the north shore, the interval

* Journal of Geographical Society, London, vol. xvi. p. 263.

between the lake and the summit-level is very variable.

We now return to the astronomer of the Boundary Commission and his party of surveyors at the Falls of St. Mary.

We left him on his voyage to the Lake of the Woods; but, having now returned, we shall not leave him again until the end of the Excursion.

Having had our boat carted by oxen across the British Portage, we commenced on the 10th of June, 1823, our coasting voyage, so rarely made now, along the north shores of Lake Superior as far as the Grand Portage, a distance of 445 miles.

The River St. Mary is a truly American stream in size and aspect. The banks, from one mile to one and a third apart, consist of marshes and fine woods of pine, maple, elm, &c.

We had to stem a moderate current for the first two miles upwards, when it ceased to be perceptible, and we were soon at our sleeping-place, Pine Point, six miles and a half from St. Mary's. It shelters a rather deep bay and convenient harbour for schooners.

Pine Point is broad and low, and the neighbourhood sandy, wet, and much overgrown with aquatic plants.

Standing on this point, thinly clad with pines,

and looking down the river back upon the country just left, we have before us a striking landscape—a broad sheet of water flowing through woods, and disappearing at St. Mary's in a sunken forest rendered grey by distance. On the left we have a long line of blue hills stretching towards the north shore of Lake Huron. On the right nothing is seen but the woods of the river-side.

We were sorely mosquito-bitten at Pine Point. The whole party heard the shout of "*Alerte!*" our usual morning *reveillez*, with vast content.

Above this point the River St. Mary suddenly widens, and seven and a half miles westerly brings us to its head, guarded on the north by Gros Cap, and on the south by Point Iroquois.

Banks and beaches of reddish sand frequently line the shore, derived from the sub-rock.

Point Iroquois is a somewhat lofty and commanding promontory densely covered with trees. It is several miles apart from its fellow, Gros Cap.

We breakfasted under Gros Cap, among its *débris*, using a large fallen mass of rock for our table.

If I am to speak of my own feelings, they were greatly excited by having realised the wish of many a year, to sail on the waters of Lake Superior. The prospect is in itself beautifully wild; but it becomes magnificent when we reflect on the size, celebrity, and remoteness of this body of fresh water.

The spectator stands under shattered crags more than 300 feet high, with an apparently boundless flood before him. A low island is in front. Point Iroquois is on the south, a terraced hill; while on the north and north-west a picturesque and high country is somewhat faintly visible.

Lake Superior differs widely from Lake Huron, in having a more regular outline, in having but few islands, in the grander features of its coasts, and in its geological structure, which, as far as I know, have no parallel in America. We have here the advantage of plenty of named localities.

Gros Cap includes the rocky hills constituting the east shore of the lake for four miles from the River St. Mary, which then sinks into a rugged slope enveloped in shrubbery. Both ends are well marked.

* These hills are of silicious porphyry, in knolls and crags, piled upon each other to the height of from 400 to 700 feet, a mile from the south end or headland, but are lower elsewhere, and usually dip into the lake by advanced ledges or scarps.

These hills are often bare, but mostly they are covered with dwarf pine, aspen, coppice, and

* Porphyry, purple; there are red, purple and green varieties (quite?)

Goulais Bay, from old protean French?

Goulée, a large mouthful, gulp.

Goulet, the narrow or strait entrance of a harbour.

Goulot, the neck or gullet of a bottle or vessel.

Goulotte [t d'Archit.] a little channel.

Goulu, glutton, guttler, greedy-gut.

Goulu, [animal sauvage; hyène des anciens; glouton] glutton; a wild and greedy animal bred in Lapland and Muscovy (Wolverine)

Goulu, a tamed cormorant.

Gueule sf. mouth; from Lat. gula

Gueules sm. pl. gules (heraldry). Of oriental origin; from Persian ghul, a rose (red

Gui, sm. mistletoe (sometimes on oak trees — does the mistletoe grow about "Oak Bay"? They have a socalled Spanish moss in the Lake Superior country — do they also have a pseudo mistletoe?)

The word gulé may suggest a color — do the purple, red (or yellow) rocks (porphyry) appear about the Bay?

Did time permit, these notes could be expanded into an essay — perhaps it is not worth the powder.

E. L. C.

"Goël or Goule * * * is clearly Guelph or Whelp, the wolf-cub, of which Lovel or Lupus is the Norman-French equivalent"—A. S. Ellis—quted in "Battle Abbey Roll", Vol. 2, p 188.

Goulais, or Gulé Bay of the Voyageurs:

By Kelham's Dictionary of the Norman or Old French Langauge, 8vo, Lon. 1779, a law dictionary: "Gule, the beginning or first day of the month". It would be a farfetched assumption that the spring voyages usually started up the North Shore about June 1 and that the first night's camping place was called Gule Bay for that reason.

Travels and Adventure in Canada, etc by Alexander Henry, Fur Trader (New Edition by James Bain, p198): During the famine winter of 1767, Henry went to "Oak-bay, called by the French, Anse a la Pêche, or Fishing-cove, which is on the north side of Lake Superior, at a distance of twelve leagues from the Sault", now known as Goulais Bay (Anse, a creek, a little bay, cove, bight) At another encampment "an hour's fishing procured us seven trout, each of from ten pounds weight to twenty."

The Grand Dictionnaire, Par Fleming et Tibbins: Gull, a sea bird; a fish. Gull [in sea-langauge; strait, narrow between shoals], détroit, passage entre des bancs, goulet. Goulet, the narrow or strait entrance of a harbour. Goulot, the neck or gullet of a bottle, etc.

By Jamieson's Scottish Dict. 4 vol. 4to, 1840: Gull, A large trout; called also, a Boddom-lier. Boddum. Bottom. 3 The seat of the human body; hips. Boddum-lyer. A designation given to a large trout because it keeps to the bottom.

Gule, adj. yellow. V Gool

Gule, Gules s. Corn-marigold.

flowers. Near the north end there is a small but showy cascade dashing over the rocks.

The general course of this, the east coast of the lake, from Gros Cap to the River Michipicotou (125 miles by canoe route) is about a point to the west of north.

The most conspicuous promontories in this interval are Marmoaze,* forty-one miles from St. Mary's River, and Gargantua, ninety-three miles from St. Mary's. These are the outer points of great curvatures, which contain subordinate bays of considerable size. Just within the most southern of these, the Goulais, or Gulé Bay of the *voyageurs*, we passed the night of June 11.†

Early next morning we crossed the mouth of the bay, and made for the lesser Maple Islands, leaving behind us the greater island of this name, sometimes called "Parisien," loaded with timber. The last-mentioned is three miles north-west of Gros Cap. The three others (with Green Island) resemble it, and are based upon horizontal sandstone.

We breakfasted on one of the lesser Maple Islands.

* A Chippewa word, signifying "an assemblage," and here referring to islets and reefs. It is the Memince of the *voyageurs*.

† At 5 A.M., June 8, the thermometer stood at 30° Fahr., so that we had no fear of mosquitoes.

Everything looked innocent and pretty: the transparent shallows washed the very tree-roots, and extended far into the lake. Any thought of danger seemed absurd; and yet it was here that two well-manned canoes of the North-west Company were cast ashore about the year 1815, and nine persons drowned. Among the saved were Mr. W. M'Gillvray (my Amphytrion at Montreal) and Dr. M'Loghlin, many years Governor of Fort Vancouver.

We must suppose that the disaster commenced some distance from land, and that the winds drove the canoes upon this strand.

We next come to the Batchewine Bay, deep and large, with a flat island, called Green Island, on its north side, and lofty hills overhanging it; but the interior on the south and west is low and woody.

In September, on our return, we were glad of a couple of pigeons shot here on the main in the bay succeeding that of Batchewine.

The south-east arm of Batchewine Bay is lined with horizontal white sandstone in low ledges at the various points, but elsewhere by sand-banks, extending into dense woods of poplar and spruce, which are backed by hills of imposing outlines, from 700 to 900 feet high. A winding river, fifty feet broad, enters at the bottom.

I observed on the sides of the nearer hills three patches of winter-snow not yet melted; and at our dining-place, near the north angle of this bay (the first south of Marmoaze), we met with a singular but not unprecedented freak of Nature—a solitary pine growing upon the upper surface of a large cubic block of Marmoaze pudding-stone, which itself rested upon four granite bowlders. The block must have weighed forty tons, and was from twelve to fifteen feet square.

From near this place the main continues for four miles and a half, rocky, and tolerably straight to Point Marmoaze; the interior being woody and rather low.

There are three or four islets surrounded by reefs and scattered rocks near the point.

Gros Cap, and even Whitefish Point, on the south-east shore of the lake, are visible from hence, with Point Iroquois between them, looking like an island.

Point Marmoaze* is an interesting spot, and yields indications of copper. With little search on my part I found several small masses of copper pyrites, and of the green carbonate; and we know that, many years ago, an English Company worked

* The minerals I met with at Marmoaze are interesting. They are apophyllite, zeolite, cornelian, agate, laumonite, calcedony, stilbite, amethyst, rock crystal, prehnite, calcspar.

some deposits of copper ore on the neighbouring river Montreal.*

Point Marmoaze, and its vicinity for seven miles northerly, consists of trap, vesicular, amygdaloidal and compact in parts; all interleaved with pudding-stone, of rounded masses of granite, trap,

* A mining company has been formed at Montreal, with Sir G. Simpson for its Governor, Hon. G. Moffat, Hon. P. M'Gill, W. C. Meredith, Esq., and J. Cringan, Esq., Directors, to work the copper mines on the north shore of Lake Superior, of which Marmoaze is one district.

This Company (the Montreal Mining Company) held their first general meeting of shareholders on the 16th of November, 1847, Sir G. Simpson in the chair.

Mr. Forest Shepherd, practical geologist, and mineral explorer of the Company, who had just returned from Lake Superior, presented to the trustees "a systematic and minute geological diagram of the coast of Lake Superior, from St. Mary's to Pigeon's River, a distance of more than 500 miles." Upon this work of labour and science a party of seventeen men, with competent geologists and surveyors, had been employed all the season, from the opening of the navigation until the month of November.

Specimens of the ore from separate localities belonging to the Montreal Mining Company were examined at the Assay Office, Gresham Street, London, September 2, 1846:—

No. 1,	Copper,	85	per cent.
2,	do.	73	,,
3,	do.	61	,,
4,	do.	16	,,

and about 44 per cent of silver.

The Quebec and Lake Superior Mining Company (Johnson and Sons) have also copper mines on the north shore, whose ores yield about 33 per cent of copper.

Sixteen or seventeen locations for copper mining, each consisting of a tract two miles by ten, have been made.

amygdaloid, and sandstone, from a size invisible to the naked eye, to that of some square feet. The shore, therefore, assumes a peculiar aspect. It is iron-bound, from ten to one hundred feet high, and scooped into windowlike holes, arches, and shallow caves.

A considerable way into the lake are rugged islets, with short jagged needles of rock here and there. In two places on the main the pudding-stone breaks into right-angled blocks, thirty feet square, mounted one upon another. The effect upon the eye, with its dark tawny colour, and large differently-coloured bowlders, is new and grotesque.

From Point Marmoaze we crossed a shallow bay, seven miles wide. Its rocky shores are only high on the north side, and there they are of granite. Its north cape (with an isle in front) is a massive and lofty bluff. It is followed, northerly, by a second bay, three miles and a half across, with very high angles, and an elevated interior; —the margin of the bay being sand and gravel.

This is now called Mica Bay; the picturesque village of that name being just within the northern headland, called Pont aux Mines, about ten miles south of Montreal River.

About 100 people were employed at the mines here in September last. There is another mining establishment in the Pays Plat, and a third near Pigeon River or Grand Portage, exclusive of several on the American shores of the lake. I am indebted for this recent information to Sir John Richardson, the distinguished Arctic traveller, who passed through these districts in September 1849.

We next approach the Bay of Huggewong (or Hoguart of the French maps). It is from ten to twelve miles across at its mouth, the south side being eight miles long, and the northern about three.

Off the entrance of this romantic bay lies the flat and woody Island of Montreal, from three to four miles long.

The immediate shores of this bay rise for the most part suddenly, in steep, round-backed hills, precipitous towards the lake, from 400 to 500 feet high, and with woody ravines between them.

Along the outer half of the south side, shingle beaches are common, from ten to thirty feet high; with extensive deposits behind them of large and small bowlders of the granite of the district, imbedded in sand, both confusedly and in horizontal layers.

The Montreal River, celebrated for its copper ore, enters Huggewong Bay in the middle of its south side, in a cove guarded by dark-coloured bluffs. It is 150 feet broad at its mouth, with a current of three miles and a half an hour among beds of sand and gravel. Six hundred yards from the lake there is a cascade, ten feet high, in a hollow between two conical hills.

The bottom of Huggewong Bay is faced with sand-banks, which retire in successive stairs a mile or two inland. Here the River Huggewong, with two others (smaller), enters the lake. The Huggewong is large, and near Lake Superior runs through low woods; but farther off, occupies the defiles of a rugged country.

At the south and inner end of the bay there is a cliff, 500 feet high, overlooking a terrace of white sand, thirty feet high, and half a mile long. Circumstances made this spot, with its sparkling, hospitable beach, its silver birches, and smooth-faced precipice, a most welcome haven to us in the midst of unapproachable shores and tempestuous waves. In September, on our return home, early in the grey of the morning, we boldly started to cros from the north side of Huggewong direct to Montreal River, on the south, a distance of nine miles of open and nearly shelterless water. We had made two-thirds of our way, and were expecting soon to reach the river, when suddenly the sky and waters darkened, the winds arose, and raised such waves that we must have gone to the bottom in a canoe. As it was, the danger was considerable; and we were glad to run some miles out of our course into the fair nook just noticed. We breakfasted there, and waited until the storm had passed by.

Point Huggewong (sixty-six and a-half miles from St. Mary's River) is round, and consists of bluffs and cliffs, dipping from shattered and round-topped eminences 400 to 600 feet in height.

There are four rocky islets with high, sloping sides, off this point, besides several smaller ones around an indentation, an excellent harbour half-a-mile from the extreme point at the entrance of the bay. We here saw on a little cape an Indian signal or guide-post—a stick fastened to the rock, and holding a bunch of grass in its cleft end. It pointed in the direction which the Indian's friends had taken.

From this conspicuous point to Gargantua, the next remarkable headland, the distance is twenty-seven miles. The first fifteen of these are slightly concave, and are almost entirely of silicious sand. The interior is high. I ascended a hill near the lake, 600 feet high, as a panoramic point, I hoped; but the prospect inland was closed in by a barrier of similar elevations.

The streams are numerous here, the principal being the Charon, six miles from Point Huggewong, and Gravel River, five miles further north-west. Gravel River is sixty yards wide at the mouth, with a woody isle close by, and a cascade not far distant among the rocks of the main.

A mile south-east from Gravel River the lofty hills of the interior come to the lake, and dip into the water for three miles in slopes and scarps.

The remainder of the twenty-seven-mile route to Point Gargantua is a naked and rugged coast, the outskirts of a high, granitic region.

Point Gargantua is a prominent feature on the east side of Lake Superior. It has a very indented front, being composed of parallel ridges of black amygdaloid, rising one above another in retreating succession to the height of from thirty to eighty feet, from time to time much dilapidated; and with little coves of black sand.

The granite region, a mile inland, is nearly destitute of any vegetation but burnt pines, looking most desolate; but the point itself, and the parts adjacent, being of amygdaloid, a fertilising rock, is clothed with fir, birch, poplar, &c., and a profusion of mosses.

The River Gargantua issues at the bottom of a small bay beset with isles, south of, and contiguous to the point.

Gargantua Point has numerous islets scattered along its south side, for two or three miles close in shore, low and woody; one, however, having a cliff 100 feet high.

Intermixed with these islets, and especially lakewards, small detached pointed rocks and solitary ridges rise out of the water naked. One of these, a few hundred yards from the point, is a rude pyramid from fifty to sixty feet high. Its strange shape, dark colour, and the surrounding gloom, have induced the Indians to worship it as an idol. It has given to the place the name of Gargantua.

Point Gargantua may be considered the south angle of the great bay of Michipicotou.

The two sides of the bay, together with a line drawn across its mouth, form something like an equilateral triangle, the north side and base being twenty-seven miles long direct, and the south twenty-five miles long, while the bottom is four miles in length.

The south side, along which we first travel, is broken into several important bays, Capes Choyyé and Maurepas being the most remarkable headlands.

We were stopped at Gargantua for a day by a heavy gale of wind and rain on our return home, rather late in the season.

Our astronomer was sitting in the tent, over a map, when he suddenly dropped his pencil on the paper. Looking up, I saw that the dim curtain of reverie had fallen before his eyes, and the lights and shadows of former years were playing over his hard features.

After a time I broke into his trance, by asking him what he was thinking of, and where he had got to? "Got to!" repeated he, mechanically, and then said, "Why, if you must know, I was once more on the east flanks of the Rocky Mountains, in my old pursuits, with my old companions,—scenes and friends I shall never more see. People may fancy and may say what they like, but give me a gallop into the natural meadows, the glorious hunting-grounds of Central America, with their clear skies and bracing airs. Let me wander over parks of bison, deer, and moose feeding promiscuously. Let me listen at the close of the day to the cries of the wild creatures, as I sit at the door of my skin-tent—to the loud whistle of the stag, the sullen, gong-like boom of the elk, the bellow of the bison, or the wolf-howl.

"Then comes the buffalo-hunt! and the well-trained Indian horse! How beautiful to watch his motions, prepared for the chase, as he stands on a gentle rise, in full view of a herd of bison! His frame erects and stiffens. He paws the turf, with his eyes on fire, and his ears pointing to the game; but when put at speed the ears fall back and seem lost in the head. He is directed to a cow-bison; away she scampers blowing and snorting, swaying from side to side, and changing leg from time to time, as her manner is. Sooner or later the fatal shot is fired. The animal is disabled, and left for inferior hands to slaughter.

"The moment a shot is fired a curious scene takes place.

"Up to that instant, nothing but the dun bulks of the bison had been visible; but now a bear or two may be seen stealing away; deer arouse themselves in the grassy hollows and flee; wolves become numerous, standing on their hind-legs, snuffing and peering about. Ravens, eagles, and vultures, take wing and hover about, awaiting their portion.

"It is dangerous to attack a bison on foot," continued my friend. "I had to do it once, and paid very dearly for it. It was in the time of snow. I crept up to the animal on all fours and fired, wounding him desperately; but still he was able to reach me. I did not run,—that the hunter never does,—as it would be almost certain destruction.

"I laid down motionless; and the bull seemed to doubt whether the death-like object which lay before him was his enemy. So, after staring about a bit he laid down, with his bleeding mouth and deep-sunk, glaring eyes, close to mine, breath to breath, eye to eye, — aye, and for some hours.

"At length, feeling that my limbs were freezing and stiffening, I was meditating the desperate step of making a run for it, when an Indian boy came in sight, dancing and carolling on a snowy knoll. The bull saw him, got up, and staggered and floundered to him, as well as he could, as his true enemy. The boy, perceiving his danger, jumped into a snow-drift, and the bull could not find him, although he searched diligently, and with many a groan. There the boy remained till night. For myself, I could not move at first, so thoroughly was I benumbed; but in the end I managed to crawl to the fort. Next morning the bull was found dead 300 yards from the snow-drift." * * * * * *

A lofty style of country prevails in this part of Lake Superior; the hills rising in steps or ledges, or in slopes covered with foliage, or again in vertically-fissured precipices. The immediate shores are rocky, and often high.

At Cape Choyyé (where we saw, on the 14th of June, two masses of hard snow at water-mark) the rocks are vertical, and cut up into ravines; but within the lesser curvatures there are extensive beds of sand and bowlders.

All this region is very picturesque, but especially the bay south of Cape Maurepas. Its shores are a confused and steep assemblage of high rocks. A beautiful cascade near the bottom pours a ribbon-like stream from height to height, and so into the lake. This spot reminded me of some scenes in the Cape de Verd Islands, where we have the same bare red crumbling rocks.

Michipicoton River

The inner third of this side of Michipicotou Bay is comparatively straight, often in scarps, and very lofty in the interior. Three or four miles from the bottom there is a cape, from which canoes usually cross to Point Perquaquia, on the north side of the bay, a headland projecting a mile into the lake, and about 400 feet high. We did not make this traverse.

The sandy bottom of this bay receives the River Michipicotou, which is large and long, and is the nearest way from hence to Moose Fort, in Hudson's Bay. We went a short distance up the river to the Hudson's Bay Company's fort there.

We found the neighbourhood flat, but dark hills were discernible in the distance; and among them, from the lake, we distinctly saw a ridge of sugar-maple trees many miles long. It goes, with breaks, as far as St. Mary's River, at the distance of ten, fifteen, twenty miles from the lake. There is another, which stretches from the Perdrix Falls, near the Grand Portage, to the

Fond du Lac. Those extensive groves of sugar-maple are highly prized by the Indians.

I was glad to see a fur-trading establishment. This consists of a low wooden house, substantially built, for the officer in charge, a storehouse or two, a line of low dwellings for the servants and their families, put together in a hollow square, so * as to be defensible in case of need. There are often a few lodges of Indians on the sand-drifts close by, with furs for sale.

To my young servant and myself the important duty of setting up our tent was intrusted; and it had been left on the sand-bank for that purpose; but, on leaving the fort to do it, we found a very large he-goat in full possession, standing on it and stamping defiance at all intruders. When we came near, he ran full butt at us, and we were more than once near being much injured. But he was merciful, and after his plunge upon us always returned triumphant, to pace over our prostrate tent. I was much ashamed; but thought it best to lay the case before the superintendant, who sent a man to bring Taffy to his senses, which was speedily done.

I need not say that we were made very welcome by Mr. Macintosh. He gratified us with some good milk. The cows here, as in Lower Canada, are frequently fed upon fish.

Cows fed on fish?

* This must have been the earlier H.B. Post across the river near the Magpie Falls.

Visitors are very rare, and domestic comforts on a modest scale, as people come to Michipicotou to acquire, and not to spend. On this occasion, Mr. M. did us the honour of dining with us, and on our only dainty,—Donkin's preserved meat; which we had for dinner occasionally in Lake Superior, but in the close hot forests on the old route to the Lake of the Woods, we had it twice a-week as long as our supply lasted.*

Mr. Macintosh showed me near his fort some shingle banks twenty to thirty feet above the common level of the lake, which are reached, he says, by the surf in the long and severe storms of early winter. [Very doubtful.] These ranges or stairs of shingle are met with all over Lake Superior.

We were never able to make accurate observations on this subject.

One night, however, having pitched our tent on a sand-bank on the edge of the adjacent wood, we were awoke in the dark night by the sound of high winds and approaching waves. The waters

* This article of diet is an admirable substitute for the recently-killed animal. A transport between the tropics, full of soldiers and their families, under my medical charge, became generally attacked with dysentery, against which medicine seemed powerless. In the course of three or four days I distributed among the soldiery 750 pounds of Donkin's preserved meat, and the disease ceased. We landed six weeks afterwards at the Cape of Good Hope, a healthy ship.

had risen four feet in a very few hours, and would soon have been in our beds had we not removed in the midst of storm and darkness to a higher position.

The next morning (Sunday, June 15) we left Fort Michipicotou; but a high wind with rain prevented us from proceeding further on our route than two miles south-east of Point Perquaquia.

We obtained pleasant shelter in a cove among mounds of trap.

We never found detention by storms to be tedious. If it occurred on a week-day, we had journals to correct and transcribe, surveying field-books to prepare, and personal matters to attend to. If, as on this occasion, we were weather-bound on Sunday, we had the special comfort of the day. We never failed to celebrate Divine service every Sabbath, and read a portion of Bickersteth on Prayer, or some such book, as a sermon.

Our astronomer, Mr. Thompson, was a firm churchman; while most of our men were Roman Catholics. Many a time have I seen these uneducated Canadians most attentively and thankfully listen, as they sat upon some bank of shingle, to Mr. Thompson, while he read to them in most extraordinarily pronounced French, three chapters out of the Old Testament, and as many out of the New, adding such explanations as seemed to him suitable.

Our treatment of these men had convinced them that in all things we meant them well.

The Irish, on the contrary, think the English mean ill towards them, but most falsely, at least in the present day; and hence the few conversions among them to the simple faith of the Bible.

The next morning at daybreak saw us once more progressing by the north side of Michipicotou Bay. We found it to maintain a tolerably straight western course, but full of petty indents. Its hills do not differ from those already noticed hereabouts, except that they are fewer and not so steep.

From Port Perquaquia to the Dog River (about fourteen miles) the shore is frequently faced by deep and extensive sand-banks, and near this river is gravelly, and forty feet high.

The Dog River is thirty feet broad at its mouth, but immediately widens within. Six hundred yards from the lake it undergoes a descent of twenty-five feet by two ledges in a chine or gorge of greenstone slate, whose dark colour, and some recent conflagrations, invest this scene with peculiar wildness and gloom.*

From this river to the crags of Michipicotou (eight miles) the shore is wholly ledges of rock, gradually ascending inland.

These crags are four miles long. They begin and end abruptly, and are bald, shattered rocks, steep or precipitous, dipping into the water from the height of 150 to 400 feet, the hills, of which they are the flanks, being 800 feet, according to Captain Bayfield. At their west end, these hills, turning northwards, slowly leave the lake shore.

Here the north side of Michipicotou Bay may be said to end.

Not far west of these crags, in a dell of considerable beauty, which permits the escape of a noisy stream, we found some Indian families successfully engaged in fishing. We not only exchanged with these civil people many kind words, but some tobacco for a very acceptable supply of fish. I can readily imagine what passed through the minds of these ragged Indians, the natural proprietors of the West, when they traced, in the pale-faced stranger, the ill-concealed confidence of mastership, and saw him laden with a thousand things most enviable to *them*.

* The Indians burn large tracts of pine barrens in order to favour the growth of very useful autumnal fruits.

As Lake Superior is not under the exclusive control of the Hudson's Bay Company, its Indians can exchange their furs for ardent spirits whenever they please. Their drunken bouts, therefore, are but too frequent. On these occasions, when quarrels arise, they all, men and women, have a strange propensity to bite each other's noses off, and particularly when the passion of jealousy is concerned. One of our surveyors at this place saw an Indian with a fresh leaf stuck on the small remains of his nose. This had been recently done.

In another part of the country I saw a similar case, but of some years' standing.

I must not forget to say that, a few miles outside of this great bay, and twelve miles from the nearest main (on the north), lies the large island of Michipicotou or Maurepas.

At Gargantua we saw it in the distant horizon, about twenty-five miles on our west. It is from fifteen to twenty miles long. Several high ranges of hills are distinguishable on it, 800 feet high in places. It is only visited by Indian hunters. The telescope showed that it is primitive, geologically speaking.

The interval of seventy-five miles between the crags and the River Peek presents but two localities known by name, viz. the Otter's Head, thirty-four miles; and the Smaller Written Rocks, sixty-one miles from the crags.

From the crags to Otter's Head the coast rounds gradually to the north-west, in a chain of steep, bluff hills, scantily clothed, and having aspen in the damp hollows. The immediate beach is sand or shingle, with here and there a steep islet, and reefs in front of a small cape. On more than one of these points* we observed the Indian road-marks which we noticed at Gargantua.

We cannot particularise the numerous lesser curvatures in this part of the lake. Their sand-beds are very large, and extend into the interior for a mile or more, especially from seven to eleven miles south-east of Otter's Head, where they are 150 feet thick, and in two or more terraces.

The Otter's Head we passed on the 17th of June. It is an upright slab, from thirty to thirty-five feet high, placed on some scantily-clad rocks, 120 feet above the lake, and at an interval from it, which, though looking small, is much greater than it appears. These rocks guard a deep cove, with islets in front, one of which is well wooded.

Soon after leaving the crags, I thought it possible to run along the shore and keep abreast of

* Here we saw a piece of birch bark in the cleft of an upright stick, with four white fish drawn on it, and some marks I could not make out.

our boat. I therefore landed, my object being to see the rocks better; but smooth as the coast seemed from the boat, my utmost exertions were required to keep pace with it. I rushed through water-runs, or over patches of sand; I skipped from rock to rock, like an angry Sicilian shepherd in chase of his goats; but after an hour thus spent, I was fain to embark, beaten by the little wrinklings of the rough coast.

We had made but little way this morning (June 17), before the wind became so violent, and raised such a boiling sea, that, to my secret content, we were obliged to put ashore.

Seeing that I had the day before me, I set off, hammer in hand, and ink-bottle on button-hole, determined on a long stroll.

The country consisted of bare ridges of white granite (you may see the same, but darker, in Merioneth, Wales), increasing in height as we leave the lake. I first scrambled a mile or two directly into the rear, among white hills, dotted with knotty pines. A wide expanse of waters was beneath me, darkened with surcharged clouds, and the great island of Michipicotou in the remote south.

From this point I changed my course, and proceeded with speed over the rugged and slippery rocks for four or five miles parallel with the coast.

I was then suddenly brought up by a ravine 400 or 500 feet deep; its shelving and shattered sides feathered with young shrubs, and its bottom a receptacle of great blocks, which had fallen from above. The lake was white with foam, the few stunted trees bent before the gale. I held my hat on with both hands. What did I see in the depths of the chasm, but an European figure, kneeling, bare-headed, on a flat rock! His back was to the wind—his long, iron-grey locks streamed before his face. On getting nearer, I saw that it was our astronomer, who, like Moses in the wilderness of Sinai, had escaped from the camp to worship the Lord.

I thought I had been swift, but here was one swifter, and on a better errand. It is in such utter wastes as Lake Superior, as I have said before, that the inner life—the devotional spirit—often awakes and labours. Thousands, in solitary places, have discovered that none need cry in vain, with aching heart, "Oh, that the Comforter would come!" The sacred and secret hand of God is everywhere.

Near our sleeping-place, a few miles north of Otter's Head, I found some very curious animals resembling molluscs, from one-third to half an inch long, and broadish. They are peculiar in having no shell, but are studded very closely all over with a single layer of very small pebbles, each the third of a line perhaps in diameter, always of a hard rock, such as quartz, feldspar, jasper, bits of granite, &c. The twisted form of the animals is closely followed by the mosaic of the pebbles, and the effect is pretty and singular, especially when shining in the water. I brought away six specimens, and showed them to the Philadelphia naturalists, who said that, although rare, these animals were not unique. In my various removals I have lost them. I found them nowhere else. They have been named *Thelidomi* by Mr. Swainson, F.R.S., from two Brazilian specimens; and Mr. Lea, of Philadelphia, has described them as a new shell, which he named *Valvata Arenifera;* but Mr. J. E. Gray, the eminent British naturalist, says, that they are only the cases of a caddis-worm, common in the Brazils and the United States, but they differ from the European form in the cases being spiral.—*Annals of Nat. Hist.* vol. v.*

The coast between Otter's Head and the River Peek (forty-one miles) is more deeply indented than that between the former place and the crags. Its hills are higher, more massive, and

* For this information I am indebted to Mr. Sylvanus Hanley, who possesses, I am informed, the finest collection of fresh-water shells in London.

often dip precipitously into woody dells. The water-margin is lined with low, jagged rocks, while the interior is very barren, the whole vegetation being a few small Canada pines, apparently dead, save a little pencil of leaves at the top.

About twenty-one miles from the Peek River there is a broad sand-bed, 120 feet high, and passing inland out of sight. It is cut through by a river from a level and rather fertile country of granite hills.

A similar deposit, extensive, but low, is in the bay south-east of this river. These are usually in regular horizontal layers.

The Smaller Written Rocks are, in a sandy cove, defended by islets fourteen miles south-east from the Peek River. They here are smooth and coated with tripe de roche and other lichens. Various names and figures of animals have been traced on them, both long ago and recently.

The basalt dykes, which form such a peculiar feature in the geology of the north shore of Lake Superior, are particularly abundant in this region. They are from one to sixty feet broad, and they cut through all the primitive rocks indifferently, proceeding without the slightest change of size, texture, or direction, from one to another. In a district of white granite their appearance is very striking, and resembles a ruined staircase, cleav-

* Perhaps like the banks of the Michipocoten R. below junction with Hawk R out of the sand country below Hawk L.

ing and mounting acclivities of all heights. As they are broken into transverse pillars or steps, more or less perfect, they are the best road up the hills—a kind of staircase. Near the Written Rocks, an eminence 800 feet high is thus traversed. I saw the same dyke on both sides.

The rivers of this interval are not remarkable.

About three miles and a half from Otter's Head, a moderately large river descends into the lake by three slanting falls, into which the stream is divided, close to the lake, by two high crags.

Above these three channels is a small basin, into which the river falls from a still higher level, the whole dip being about ninety feet. The scene is interesting: its beautifully-grouped cascades, the heavy masses of water, the high-ascending spray, and the wild accompaniments, would have told well in a sketch, but the King's business was urgent, and away we went.

The River Peek takes its name from an Indian word, signifying mud, as it pours out an ash-coloured, and, when swollen, a reddish-yellow water, tinging the lake for a mile or two round its mouth, and derived from beds of yellow and white clay some distance up the river.

Eighty yards wide at its mouth, but wider within the bar, it issues with a gentle current at the south-east corner of Peek Bay, among sand-drifts, tufted with pines. For ninety miles inland this river flows quietly from the north, with little change of dimension, and having banks of sand and clay, with greenstone heights a little way off. The first fall occurs ninety miles from Lake Superior, and, of the two others, the third is thirty miles further on, and passes through a sandhill 200 feet high, having worn its way to the primitive rock beneath.

The Peek River leads to Long Lake, 180 to 200 miles from Lake Superior by canoe route. Long Lake is seventy-five miles long, but is narrow. It is on or near to the height of land.

At the mouth of the Peek River the Hudson's Bay Company have a fort—a picketed square, formed by the superintendant's house, other dwellings, and storehouses.

Peek Bay is of moderate size; its north arm is a line of woody steeps, with several thickly-timbered islets at its west end.

The country here is of a softer aspect than has been the case latterly. The hills swell in gentle, egg-shaped slopes, and are freely wooded with spruce and birch. At a distance from the lake they become loftier, and are seen in retiring series.

Seventeen miles and a half by canoe route, north-west from the River Peek, is Peek Island, opposite a lofty and broad promontory of fissured, dull-red rock. It is several miles round, and has three naked summits. One of these, 760 feet high, I ascended, while our astronomer trafficked for fish with an Indian canoe lying under its lee. Bargaining with savages is always lengthy and ceremonious; so that I had plenty of time. The view from that elevation was beautiful and wide.

Lakewards, the pure blue waters extended shoreless as far as the eye could reach. As I turned towards the land, tall casque-shaped islands* were seen here and there, bordering the north shore, full of sinuosities, and overlooked by pleasingly-grouped hills of conical or waved outline, from 600 to 800 feet high. I was well repaid for the trouble of the ascent.

The bay north-west of Peek Island is deep, and nine miles across at its mouth. A round islet of greenstone, near its middle, is of great use in rough weather to canoes. Its hills are in broad, imposing flanks, from 800 to 1000 feet high.

* If I mistake not, it was under the lee of one of these islands that we espied the trim schooner, the Julia, in which Captain Bayfield, R.N. was surveying Lake Superior. We exchanged news and civilities for a few moments, and passed on. Captain Bayfield had been employed on this service for three or four years, without a sick man among his crew; but that summer Government supplied him with a medical officer, and half the ship's company were shortly laid up with illness.

A convenient cove, with a narrow entrance, a little within its western cape, has given to that angle the name of Bottle Cove Cape.

The previous night we had passed in a nook east of this bay; and we started in a foggy morning; but, until breakfast, not so densely as to prevent travelling. We took that useful meal inside the great bay just spoken of, on the slimy beach, our clothes and faces shining with cold rime.

By this time the mist was so thick that we could hardly see objects at the boat's length.

We nevertheless started, and rowed heartily for full four hours, until we suspected something was wrong, because we ought to have struck shore. Putting, therefore, our boat direct north-east, after half-an-hour's rowing the shore loomed in sight—first the high trees, then the rocks, and last the breakers. We had been working in a circle, and in four hours had not made two miles of good way.

The wall of rock constituting Bottle Cove Cape rather exceeds two miles in length. It is crowned with pine-woods, and backed by a range of heights. It ends westwards in a second cove, darkened with high cliffs, and receiving at its bottom a slanting cascade.

Two more irregular and large bays succeed

westwards (the direction of the coast from Peek to Gravel Point in the Mammelles being west). They are remarkable for their high and extensive sand-banks, unmixed, as is usual here, with lime or clay; and hence their comparative barrenness.

The Black River is now at hand. * Slate Isl. Of the islands a little to the east, and seven miles from this river, named "the Slate Islands," from their being of greenstone slate, I only know further that they are rather large and high. Captain Bayfield has visited them.

Black Riv. We were enabled to examine the Black River for five or six miles inland, as the fog of the morning was succeeded by a storm of wind and rain, which kept us for two days near its mouth: into which, in fact, we ran our boat. On the sudden occurrence of a storm, landing is a delicate affair in the large lakes of the interior, such as Superior, Winnepeg, &c.

The very approach to the land is dangerous, as a loaded canoe must not touch earth or rock.

When a brigade of fur-trading canoes, ten, twenty, or thirty in number, are compelled to land suddenly, it is done one by one in rapid succession. The first makes a dash at the beach. Just as the last wave is carrying the canoe on dry ground, all her men jump out at once and support her; while her gentlemen or clerks hurry out her

Good trout fishing here. Hardy.

lading. During this time the other canoes are, if possible, heading out into the lake; but now one approaches, and is seized by the crew of the canoe first beached, who meet her up to the middle in water, and who, assisted by her own people, lift her up high and dry: and so on with the rest. If the loading gets wet, a hindrance of two or three days' duration is necessary, in order to dry it. Every brigade of canoes has a well-paid guide. If he permit his goods to be thus injured, he loses his place, which is worth from 70*l.* to 90*l.* per annum.

Our canoe was never suffered to touch ground, except when turned upwards.

Close to the calm basin into which we had pushed our boat, and close also to the lake, was a flourishing wood of pines. In the midst of this we pitched our tent, and set up the tripod for the *voyageurs'* fire, after having with our axes cleared a sufficient space of ground.

We were quietly at work, when one of the men informed us that the wood we were in was a mere belt, 300 yards across, and that there were extensive open plains beyond, with lofty hills in the distance. We threw away pencil and pen, and set off to explore.

The Black River, rising near Long Lake, enters Lake Superior on the west side of a small bay, with a rocky islet or two on its outskirts.

A hill of bleached granite, a mile and a half from the lake, overhanging the river, showed us the environs to advantage. From hence we see, five or six miles inland, a line of hills, bare, high, and hoary, ranging parallel with the lake shore; the space between them and it, east and west, as far as the eye can reach, being a flat of gravelly sand,* bearing mosses, with a few small firs, and now and then pierced with a knoll of granite. I found a deer's antlers lying on it.

This deposit is 170 feet thick near the lake, and there lowers in a succession of banks, six in number, except where occasional coalescence makes them fewer. But close to the river, on the east, all the lower levels have been swept away, lost in one great concave steep, facing both lake and river, of 1300 yards' chord. It is the shore of a deserted bay. I mention these particulars to point out that, in these regions, the same land-lift has taken place as in Europe, &c.

The Black River, fifty feet broad, passes through the gritty plain between three regular terraces, makes an elbow round the granite hill from which we take our survey, and then under-

* Very small pebbles of greenstone, granite, and quartz, in a dark brown coarse sand.

goes a series of descents, until it arrives at the lake, with accumulations of erratic block at every obstructed point.

The first fall is sixty feet high (*vide* Plate), pitching into a deep funnel-shaped chasm, 250 yards long, at the lower end of which several other jets of great beauty take place. The river then escapes into Lake Superior from a pretty basin, amid islets tufted with cedar, spruce, and alder.*

I found many traces of copper pyrites about the mouth of this river.

The Written Rocks, chiefly deserving notice as a point of reference, are seven miles west of the Black River. They occur in a cluster of islets close to a large headland of glaring red colour, like all this vicinity, and which are separated from the main by a narrow, not quite a mile long, and called "The Détroit."

The drawings which have given a name to this place are made by simply detaching the dark lichens from the flat red surface of the rock. At their west end there is a good representation of

* "How divine the liberty for mortal man
To roam at large among unpeopled glens
And mountainous retirements, only trod
By devious footsteps;—regions consecrate
To oldest time; and reckless of the storm
That keeps the raven quiet in her nest!"

an Indian firing at two animals; and not far off is a cross set up by some pious traveller, in memory of a drowned comrade. Here we saw snow again.

From the west angle of a picturesque, but small bay, close to the Written Rocks, commences a line of iron-bound coast a mile long, a dangerous pass for canoes in particular winds. It ends abruptly at Cape Verd, to form the important and picturesque bay of Nipigon.

Cape Verd is so called from the fine woods with which it is crowned. Its rocks are basalt. Wherever this rock or any of its congeners prevail, such as amygdaloid, porphyry, &c., there vegetation becomes luxuriant, and the trees numerous, but not large.

Both here and at Marmoaze I found the woods completely impassable. For several hundred yards inland the ground is buried in blocks of stone, carpeted with moss a foot thick. Fallen trees are rotting in every direction, matted with briers and wild roses. Every step hazards the breaking of a limb in some unsuspected crevice. The prostrate trees are often mere forms; in treading on them we plunge into a green mass up to the middle. I cannot but think, from the flourishing state of the cryptogamia here, that some new species might be discovered.

From Cape Verd westward to Fort William (ninety to ninety-five miles by canoe) the north shore of Lake Superior is divided into three very large bays — Nipigon, Black, and Thunder Bays. They require separate notice.

The first of these, Nipigon proper, extends to Gravel Point, on the great peninsula of the Mammelles, a distance of forty-six miles, outside of the islands soon to be mentioned.

Nipigon Bay may be roughly stated as thirty-six miles across from east to west, four to six miles deep at its east end, and sixteen on its west end. Its wide mouth (or outer face) is closed up with a dense belt of large and small islands, which, taken together, are denominated "The Pays Plat," a translation from the Chippewa language, and refers only to the shallow black or red floor * of the lake hereabouts. It is true that there is one, a large island, very level in parts, and covered with shingle and loose rocks; but, generally speaking, it is an elevated region. I cannot describe this splendid bay and archipelago with any minuteness. Mine was only a *reconnoissance*. The surveyor and naturalist will follow.

The islands are numerous. I made the circuit of the whole by going outside in June, and inside

* According to the colour of the amygdaloid or porphyries subjacent. The lake, too, is remarkably transparent here: for miles from land we see its bottom.

in the ruder month of September. St. Ignatius, the most westerly island save one, is much the largest. There are three or four others, extending from it to Cape Verd, girded with some that are smaller.

The island of St. Ignatius, according to Captain Bayfield's map, is twenty-six miles long by twelve broad. It is oblong in shape. Its centre is table land, sometimes 1300 feet high, and dipping on all sides in rough declivities and precipices, whose features change with the component rock. If this be porphyry (common here), we have long pilasters, beginning at the crest of some sterile height, and ending below on a slope of ruins, thinly wooded. This we see on the south side of the island, in Fluor Island,* at the west end of Ignatius, and in Stag's-home, Détroit. The high black cliffs of the latter are very impressive and gloomy. If the cliffs be of red sandstone (often as hard as jasper, and fissured horizontally), they are only in patches at the very summits of lofty flanks buried in woods.

The islands east of St. Ignatius are often very high: their sandstone precipices are occasionally formed nearer the level of the lake, and then they are worn by watercourses into singular shapes,

* See plate, taken from the west-south-west. Fluor Island is in hummocks, and rises to the height of 1000 feet. It is very picturesque.

J. T. B del. [illegible]

[illegible] Island [illegible] Nipigon Bay, from the [illegible]

such as pillars, arches, recesses (for statues!) and window-like apertures, which not a little resemble a street of ruined chapels and chantries shrouded by mosses, vines, and forest trees. We have this fissured state of the rock both in the inner and outer route.

Wherever the sandstone or red porphyry is found all the beaches and bare places are red; but as much of the Pays Plat is of black trap and amygdaloid, the colour there is rusty black.

On one of the islets at the west end of the Pays Plat we have a beautiful display of true basaltic columns. A sketch was given me by Captain Bayfield.

The island called La Grange is in a fine open basin not far from Nipigon River, with a few others about it having flat tops. It is a naked mass of trap rock, springing high and perpendicular out of a slope of coppice. It is exactly like one of the long barns of Lower Canada, and thence its name. We passed it on a lovely evening towards sunset. Not far from this island I took as a memorial, perhaps unwisely, from off a jutting point, the skull of a bear placed on a pole. It was as white as snow, and must have been there many years as a land-mark.

The trappose and amygdaloidal districts are here thickly wooded, but the trees—mountains ash (very common), spruce, pitch pine, birch, &c.—are hide-bound and small, sheathed in the trailing moss called goat's-beard.

The region around Nipigon Bay is full of enchanting scenery. As we journey up this great water we have the ever-changing pictures presented by the belt of islands on our left; while on our right we have the Nipigon mainland, an assemblage of bold mountains from 900 to 1200 feet high, tabular, rounded, or in hummocks, or sugar-loaf, and only separated by very narrow clefts or gorges.

My sketches give a poor idea of all this, as I could only draw where I had opportunity, not in the finest situations.

The bay is a beautiful lake of itself, so transparent that we can, for miles together, see its red pavement, and the living and dead things there inhabiting. It is sprinkled with a few isles of conical or tabular rocks, each with its girdle of verdure, in which are little coves, inviting to repose, with bright red beaches, reminding one of the Ægean Sea, or the Friendly Isles.

The Nipigon, Alempigon, or Redstone River, enters the bay at its west end. It is from 80 to 100 yards broad at its mouth, and discharges a muddy grey water. Its length is ninety miles, and on it are seven cascades and three rapids. It comes from Lake Nipigon (or St. Anne), which is sixty miles round, and in a barren country.*

The Mammelles Hills are 21½ miles from Gravel Point, a well-known resting-place. There are several, but the two most conspicuous are cones of soft and beautiful outlines, at least 800 feet high, and close together at the south-west corner of the great promontory between Black and Nipigon Bays, being the southern extremity of a long ridge coming from the north.

The Mammelles district consists of this headland and the multitudinous islands which are in front of it. It bears a strong resemblance to the Nipigon country. Space forbids our entering into a detailed description of it.

We slept, on the 23d of June, on the edge of a beautiful basin, two miles and a half south-east of the Mammelles Hills, and next morning plunged into a charming labyrinth of porphyritic, amygdaloidal, and sandstone islands, sheltered even from a hurricane. From time to time we saw the free lake at the bottom of a long vista of pine-clad islands; and we were glad, for the sake of change,

* From Mr. Mackenzie of Fort Nipigon, who told me a singular story of the momentary resurrection of an Indian about to be buried without his arrows and medicine bag, &c., some years before Beckford's Italian legend of a similar kind was in English print. It shows that human nature repeats itself all over the world, with modifications.

to come suddenly (nine miles from camp) into open water, opposite Thunder Mountain (see Plate), seven miles from us, at Point Porphyry.

This magnificent headland is a principal feature in Lake Superior, and forms the north-west end of Black Bay. This bay, I am informed by Captain Bayfield, is forty-six miles deep, and extremely woody. It receives a large river. The mouth of the bay is partially guarded by a great assemblage of woody, and for the most part low islands.

The high hills at the bottom of Black Bay are visible from its mouth, of course much depressed below the horizon. Several islands occupy the centre of the bay.

It is not always that a boat can cross from the Mammelles to Thunder Mountain; but on the 24th of June the lake was as smooth as glass. We greatly enjoyed the gradual unfolding, as we approached, of the various parts of the great basaltic cape.

Thunder Mountain is several miles long, and of considerable breadth, except at the point, where it descends into the lake in three shelves. The west half of its summit (1350 feet, Captain Bayfield; 1400, Count Andriani*) appears to be

* Count Andriani, an Italian nobleman, about the year 1800 fitted out a light canoe at Montreal, through the agency of Messrs.

J J B del. R. Young sc.

Thunder Mountain, from the East L. Superior

table land; but the eastern half is hummocky. About the middle of its south side an immense crater-like cavity, with steep woody acclivities, is scooped out of the body of the mountain. The precipices are largest and finest on the north-north-west, and extend in rude colonnades over two-fifths of the whole height, terminating in naked taluses, 300 to 400 feet high, which, however, do not reach the water, but are succeeded downwards by three woody terraces, the lowest of which touches the lake.

On the side of Thunder Bay I saw no precipices.

At and about the water-level, under Thunder Mountain, I saw a good deal of fixed limestone (without fossils), the only place where it is known to exist on the north shore of this lake.

Thunder Bay, to which we have now arrived, under the shadow of its great promontory, is round, and from ten to twelve miles across. Grand Point is its western angle; its margin is

Forsyth and Richardson, and circumnavigated Lake Superior. He occupied himself in astronomical observations and the admeasurement of heights, mingling also freely with the Indians.

Mr. Astronomer Thompson furnished me with the above fact respecting Thunder Mountain. Lord Selkirk quotes him in a pamphlet on the late disputes in the north-west territories; but I cannot find any publication of the Count's, although I have made diligent search.

swampy on the west, but its bottom is here and there bold and precipitous.

The only islands in Thunder Bay are Welcome, Hare, and Sheep Islands, opposite the mouths of the River Kaministigua, or Dog River, where Fort William is placed.

Pursuing our journey, we made for Welcome Island, and were soon afterwards safe in the fort.

On our return from the Lake of the Woods, as we passed Sheep Island in September, we were agreeably surprised to see lines of haycocks, and four haymakers in white shirt sleeves and straw hats. This sudden coming upon one of the prettiest sights of Christendom, which we had left far away, and long ago, made us quite tender, as the Indians say.

* Fort Will. p 240

Fort William, once the depôt at which every year were assembled the wintering partners of the North-west Company, with the proceeds of their trade with the Indians, is placed on the northern of the three channels of the Kaministigua River ("River of the Isles,"—Chippewa), 800 yards from the lake. It is a large picketted square of dwellings, offices, and stores, all now in comparative neglect. It is 403 miles from the Falls of St. Mary, and forty-two miles north-east of the Grand Portage, as measured on the ice by Mr. Astronomer Ferguson (Boundary Commission).

* For William M. Gilvray, fur trader Vol. I p.108

I was much pleased at Fort William. Although its palmy days were gone, when the rich furs of the Arctic circle and the Rocky Mountains were brought here by the adventurous men who alone, in those days, could conduct a distant commerce with savages, attended by a crowd of clerks, trappers, and voyageurs, still some interesting remnants of these people were at the fort during my visit.

We all took our meals together in a plainly-furnished, low-roofed hall, capable of seating a hundred persons. We were placed a good deal according to rank, the seniors and leaders at the head of the table, and the clerks and guides, &c. of respectable but humbler grade, ranged down the table in order due.

The conversation was wholly north-west and Indian.

My *vis-à-vis* was a handsome young gentleman, but pale and wasted, who told me that he had been living upon his parchment windows, and a little tripe de roche, for three or four weeks, the fish and fowl having failed at his winter quarters.

I asked him how the Company fed their fur collectors during the idle time of summer. "We give," said he, "to each family, if in the great plains, six bullets and a quart of powder, with * which to kill the buffalo. If in the lake country,

* 6 bullets + quart of powder! — do they retrieve the bullets?

they subsist upon geese and fish, and receive a net and some shot, instead of bullets, with their gunpowder."

I saw at Fort William several fine specimens of the Cree and other tribes of the plains.

We engaged an active young Indian, born in Lake Lapluie, as our guide to the Lake of the Woods, by the old route. The treaty for his services was quite a scene — his apparent indifference, his solemn looks, and evident resolution to sell dear, and, above all, the endless, enormous volumes of white smoke he emitted from nose and mouth, were past belief.

When the bargain was completed he shook hands with his new masters, suffered his features to relax, and proved a most useful fellow. Like the rest of his tribe he wore his hair long, and plaited into twenty or thirty slender strings, which were weighted with bits of white metal interwoven at regular distances.

As some of these hung over his face (poodle fashion), when he wanted a clear sight he somehow, in an instant, shook them all behind him.

We left Fort William* for the Grand Portage on one of the last days of June.

* The Dog River, on which this post is placed, issues from a considerable lake of the same name, on the new route to the Lake of the Woods, in longitude 84° 40′, and latitude 48° 45′.

We found the shore of Lake Superior swampy as far as Grand Point, but there the hills, which in lofty slopes and scarps for some way inland skirt the Kaministigua (and are perhaps the highest—1000 feet—at Mackay's Mountain, near the south fork), join the lake, and line it in precipices from 300 to 800 feet high, south-westwards, to near Pigeon Bay. They are flat-topped, cut up by ravines, and clad with pines. A slope of ruins, clothed with birch and aspen, creeps up their sides.

The shores of the two bays east of Pigeon Bay are also frequently escarped, but being low, disclose a barren interior of broad rock ridges, attaining an elevation of from 600 to 900 feet, and affecting a rough parallelism with the coast.

Pigeon Bay is supposed to be the "Long Lake" of French geographers, and to have been intended in the treaty of 1783, between Great Britain and the United States, as the point of departure from

In the first half of its course it runs south, and east during the second half. It has numerous rapids, and some splendid cataracts, especially those of Du Chien and La Montagne. The soil at its lower end is fertile — sand, clay, and vegetable mould.

It enters Lake Superior, amid extensive morasses, by three channels, of which the southern is the longest, and the middle much the smallest, being also obstructed by fallen trees. There is another smaller river in Thunder Bay, a few miles north-east of the River Dog or Kaministigua.

Lake Superior of the boundary line passing to the Lake of the Woods, therein ordered to be designated.

It may seem odd to call so small a bay by the name of Long Lake; but in a very old French map in my possession, Pigeon Bay is made to run fifty or sixty miles into the interior, westerly, very narrow, and especially at the mouth.

Pigeon Bay is three miles across its mouth by four in depth. In one of its coves, sheltered by an islet, a schooner belonging to the North-west Company usually winters. Its worthy commander bears the singular name of Maccargo.

Pigeon River enters at the south corner of the Bay. It has a beautiful cascade, 120 feet high, a mile and a half from the lake.

From Pigeon Point, a rocky coast for a few miles brings us to the bay of the Grand Portage. Anxiously we looked into it as a celebrated spot, by which we were to enter the northern interior.

Grand Portage Bay is two miles and three-quarters wide by one and a third deep, with a margin of sand and shingle.

The North-west Company formerly had an important post here, of warehouses, stables, gardens, &c., which occupied a grassy flat, backed by high hills.

A small island (Mouton) is near the east angle of the bay, which is called Point Chapeau, rising in the rear to the height of 840 feet by our astronomer's geometrical admeasurement.

The whole voyage from Fort William to this place has been full of scenic beauty. The very lofty and broken interior is nearly naked; but where there are woods, we have the tender green of the aspen and birch down below, while sombre pines crown the black precipices.

The large and broad island called the Pâté, near Thunder Bay, is a prominent feature from every part of this region.

It is everywhere lofty, and at its west end an immense square rock, like a raised pie, rises perpendicular from a woody flat to the height of 850 feet. It gives name to the whole island, and is joined to it by a low isthmus. This pilastered and tower-like eminence may be half a mile in diameter.*

Isle Royale is forty-five miles long and nine

* On our return in September we breakfasted opposite the Pâté, in a cove, on a raw, misty morning. All our provisions were gone, except the men's soup, and of that there was little. We were then glad to share a hawk (shot by Mr. Thompson, junior) between four. I roasted it. We had had nothing but salt meat, cocoa, and a very little biscuit dust, for nearly three weeks. We dined the same day, however, at Fort William, distant sixteen miles.

broad in the middle by admeasurement (in the winter). It extends from near Thunder Mountain to the Grand Portage, and is about fifteen miles from both. Its general direction is north-east, as is that of its several ranges of hills. The north-eastern half of its shores is fringed with narrow islets or reefs.

Isle Royale is lofty, and particularly at its west end. I am indebted for this information to Mr. Astronomer Ferguson.

Father Boucher, in his account of New France (Canada), dated 1663, announces the presence of copper ores in Isle Royale, and the fact has been fully confirmed within the last twelve months.

The numerous islands between Thunder Bay and the Grand Portage, running along shore, in addition to the two large ones just noticed, have the fine bold features of those of Nipigon Bay. They assisted to embellish a delightful sail in our canoe.* Their position is best seen on the accompanying map. They are rocky, in hummocks, cliffs, and ledges, not often a hundred feet high; but for this, Isle Royale and the Pâté compensate fully.

* We had exchanged at Fort William our boat for stout north canoes, manned by six *voyageurs* each.

See Vol. 1 p 131-2 for "light canoe" 36'x6' manned by 15 paddlemen + 4 passengers

The remainder of the north shore of Lake Superior, to its western extremity at the River St. Louis, is almost wholly bold and iron-bound. The hills on the immediate coast range from 900 to 1200 feet above the level of the sea, and are principally basalt. *

* See the U.S. Geol. Rep 4to 1852?
By Robert Dale Owen.

EXCURSION THE SEVENTH.

PART IV. SECT. I.

OLD ROUTE TO THE LAKE OF THE WOODS.

The Fur-traders — Grand Portage — Pigeon River — Mosquitoes — Outard Lake — Migration of Dragon-flies — Moose, Mountain, &c. Lakes — Wild Rice — Lakes of the height of land — Hudson's Bay — Gunflint and Keseganaga Lakes — Sick voyageur — Indian Family — Bears — More Lakes — Indians — Watch-tower — Crooked Lake — Sioux Arrows — La Croix and other Lakes and Rivers — Rainy Lake circumnavigated — Scenery — Natives.

In my sketches of the north shore of Lake Superior I have been as brief as is consistent with the fact that, in addition to its natural claims as a remarkable and but little known region, its mineral riches are attractiug a large population, who have a right to look for information to those who preceded them in this new seat of human enterprise; and I may at the same time add that a new and flourishing state, that of Wisconsin, has been established within the last few years on its southern borders.

Although the wilderness now to be entered upon be almost certainly metalliferous, a party of miners being now at work close to it, we shall only mark the leading points in the journey of 431* miles from the Grand Portage to the north end of the Lake of the Woods.

The country between Lake Superior and the Lake of the Woods is, like the whole watershed between Hudson's Bay and the Valley of the St. Lawrence, a rugged assemblage of hills, with lakes, rivers, and morasses, of all sizes and shapes, in their intervals. It is, in fact, a drowned land, whose waters have assumed their permanent features by a balance of receipt and discharge.

They all communicate practically with each other, either by water or by portages, so that the traveller may reach the Lake of the Woods by many routes, differing only in danger, labour, and directness. Thus nineteen of the rivers which enter into Lake Superior west of the Grand Portage rise near Lake Boisblanc, the tenth lake on our route. All these are used from time to time

* We actually passed over 1000 miles of the waters north of Lake Superior, if we include our circumnavigation of Lakes Lapluie and of the Woods.

by the Indians to get to Lake Lapluie, &c., and so is a chain of lakes leading westward from the Nipigon country to Lake Boisblanc.

During great part of the eighteenth century, before the union of the Indian traders into one company, the North-west, the Lake Superior end of the Grand Portage was a pent-up hornets' nest of conflicting factions intrenched in rival forts.

The traders first coalesced into two companies; one called the "X Y Company," from a mark placed on their packs, and consisting of Sir Alexander M'Kenzie, and Messrs. Ogilvy, Richardson, and Forsyth; and of the North-west Company, at whose head were Messrs. W. and S. M'Gillvray, M'Tavish, and others. Latterly both these firms united to contend with the old Hudson's Bay Company, acting under the charter of Charles the Second and later parliamentary sanction.

The American Government, properly conceiving that the Grand Portage, the centre of so much commercial activity, was within their territory, signified, about the year 1802, to the amalgamated company, now called the North-west Company, their intention of imposing a duty of from twenty to twenty-five per cent on all goods landed there.

After having in vain offered a composition of five per cent, the North-west Company abandoned the place, but not before they had well examined the Pigeon River from the north end of the Grand Portage down to Lake Superior. Sir Alexander M'Kenzie occupied a long day in this task, accompanied by two Indians; but they found that high falls, rapids, and shelving precipices, rendered the river utterly impracticable for commercial purposes.

The company then built their Fort William, and made the Dog River and other streams and lakes their road into the north-west fur countries, although this is inferior in every respect to the old route; so much so, that the *voyageurs* had to be coaxed and bribed into the use of it.

I am obliged to Mr. Astronomer Thompson for this information.

The direction of the old route is nearly west as far as the mouth of the River Lapluie. From Lake Lacroix westward the two routes unite.

We left Lake Superior on the 29th of June, and walked over woody hills and waded through swampy bottoms to the west end of the portage (eight miles and one-sixth), greatly annoyed by mosquitoes and the closeness of the air, the path, such as it was, being overgrown by briers and coppice. The trees were sometimes large, and fruits were in blossom.

We were visited here by two of the birds called "Whistling John." It has a long bill, and is almost all feathers. Its back is brown, and breast white. It is extremely familiar, and goes about whistling a little note of its own, seeking small objects, which it hoards. It is of the size of an English blackbird.

We encamped on the banks of the Pigeon River several days, waiting for our canoes and baggage. It was here from 120 to 130 feet broad, with a gentle current and muddy bottom.

One mile east of us, towards Lake Superior, begins a long and most picturesque series of cascades and rapids, one of the former plunging into a mural chasm 200 feet deep with a gloomy desperation worthy of the Handeck in Switzerland. The sides of the river hereabouts are rocky terraces, naked and high, or are ravines choked with huge *débris* overspread with underwood, wild roses, and raspberries. Its left bank rises to the height of 800 or 900 feet, and has only a few tufts of pines growing in the fissures. It is a very savage place, and will repay a visit. I was almost a whole day in scrambling two miles below the first fall, and returned to camp in a very tattered state.

The mosquitoes were ferocious, their bites being also much envenomed by our salt diet. Although the heat was very great in these close woods, we wore gloves, veils, and caps over the ears. My pantaloons were tied close down to the boots, or the creatures would have crept up the legs.

I could not help wishing them to leave me alone, and with Bryant begged them to

> "Try some plump alderman, and suck the blood
> Enriched with generous wine and costly meat:
> On well-filled skins fix thy light pump,
> And press thy freckled feet."

We had at this place a curious instance of the boldness and endurance of the mosquito.

My servant, a very handy lad, was lining a waistcoat with a prepared deer-skin which I had just bought of some Indians, and which I thought would be warm on our return voyage. A mosquito settled on his hand, and filled itself with his blood. Calling my attention to what he was about to do, he cut off (wholly, I think) the hinder part of the animal, a mere bag of blood, with his scissors; but the insect continued to suck and the blood to drop out from behind. The young man now struck at the mosquito, but it escaped; soon returning, however, to the same hand, and there again fastened, when his two wings were deliberately cut off without disturbing the drinker. Another blow killed him.

We hear at our camp the roar of an upper set

of falls a mile and a third up the river. They are fine, the largest being forty-nine feet high.

We travelled up the Pigeon River eighteen miles, partly through meadows,* with occasional rapids, to Outard, or Fowl Lake (six miles long by two where broadest). It is so called from an Indian tradition that the hens and chickens of white men have been heard to clack and scream there.

This lake may in some sense be considered as an expansion of the Pigeon River, as this river enters high up, near the narrows, and leaves at the bottom.

We enter it by a long portage, woody like the rest of the environs, and overlooked at its west end by a basaltic precipice not less than 600 feet high. The view from the summit is beautiful. A strong north-west gale was blowing across a clear sky successive companies of clouds, which mapped the sea of woods before me with fugitive shadows. Looking to the north-west, Lake Outard lay below, nearly bisected by a rushy narrow. Beyond it we have hilly ranges of woods, running

* We slept, or tried to do so, in these meadows. The mosquitoes were in billions. As soon as the tread of man gave notice of his approach, I saw them rising to the feast in clouds out of the coarse grass around. We burnt the grass after watering it, and lived in the smoke.

W.N.W., with long valleys between. To the south and south-east we see the valley of Pigeon River buried in dark pines, among which we still discern short silvery traces of the stream itself.

The loose stones on the eastern shore of this lake were, for several hundred yards together, covered over with myriads of bright sky-blue dragon-flies, their long bodies crossed by three or four bars of black. They were doubtless preparing for migration,—a proceeding, I think, not common among insects.

Two similar facts are recorded in the 'Magazine of Natural History" (iii. 516, 1839), as having occurred in Germany in 1816 and 1838. Vast numbers of *Libellulæ depressæ* and *Quadri maculatæ* went from Weimar, Halle, and other places, into the Netherlands, following the course of the rivers.

Lord Selkirk attempted to form an agricultural establishment on the low lands about this lake; but it failed, and is deserted. A short carrying-place now took us into Moose Lake (three miles and a quarter by one-half to two-thirds of a mile). Like Outard, it is hid in pines, cypress, spruce, and aspen. Its length runs west. I shall never forget the numbers and activity of its mosquitoes.

A short series of portages and ponds of rushes

* I have see dr-flies migrating in autum but not in June-July

and wild rice brought us into Mountain Lake (six miles and one-third by half a mile).

This picturesque lake in one place shows six distinct distances in lofty basaltic headlands.

In the vicinity, but away from the lake, we see large, naked, solitary, barrow-like hills,—high, and often precipitous.

Our astronomer says that he has not discovered the feeders to this lake, and our Indian guide, "the little Englishman," says there are none.

As we float over its transparent waters, we notice below us very large blocks of basalt reposing on fine mud.

A short carrying-place conveyed us hence into the fine irregular sheet of water called the Entre-deux (three miles and one-fifth long).

Its scenery, of open basins and narrows, ample groves, hills, and cliffs, is very striking. (*Vide* Plate.)

The new Grand Portage (2200 yards long), low and swampy, now leads into Rose Lake, another delightful *morceau* of lake solitudes.

It is heavily wooded down to watermark, with high precipices of trap, jutting capes, brightened by the delicate green of the young aspen. It runs nearly west for six miles, being very narrow two-thirds of its length.

In the middle, this lake is very shallow (deep

elsewhere), the bottom smooth and level. The *voyageurs* are convinced that the mud, without touching the canoe, attracts and retards it. It is almost liquid to the depth of ten or twelve feet below the apparent bottom.

Sir Alexander M'Kenzie is inclined to think so too; and certainly, though it seems impossible, we thought our canoes dragged slowly and heavily over this ground.

A couple of moderate portages and some ponds now bring us to the East Lake of the Height of Land, a narrow basin about three miles long, westerly, and pouring its waters into Rose Lake.

It was here that we saw the Indians, even at this early period of the year, gathering their rice harvest. Several canoes were at work (men and women) in a flooded marsh. The men cut off the green heads of the rice-plant, and let them fall into the canoe, while the women stowed them away. Great was the merriment. We looked on for a few minutes.

We next passed into the West Lake of the Height of Land, by a carrying-place (468 yards long) profusely loaded with trees, shrubs, and grass. We are now in waters tributary to Hudson's Bay, and seventy-eight miles from Lake Superior.

The West Lake is five miles and a half long, but

its principal part lies to the east of our route, and is surrounded by very high hills. We therefore cross it obliquely towards the north (one mile and a third), passing by porphyry of silicious base *in situ* on a point close to our route on the east.

We now gain access to Gunflint Lake (six miles and a third by two miles) by two sets of narrows and rapids, altogether three miles long.

Gunflint Lake often takes the name of Red-ground Lake, from the ochrey red gravel with which it abounds, and the ferruginous colour of its basalt. We find on it greenstone porphyry in lofty hills, with fine olivine or feldspar crystals; most likely a part of the basaltic and cupriferous rocks of Lake Superior.*

Leaving this lake we descended to the still larger lake, Keseganaga, by a series of five small basins (or lakes) and narrows; the whole twelve miles long, and often the seat of rough rapids,—the scenery of hills, shattered rocks, and turbulent waters being savage in the extreme, especially at the portage of the Wooden Horse.

The moment we entered this chain of waters, the high table-lands, the cliffs, the rich vegetation of a basaltic district, the regular outlines of the lakes, the absence of islands, were exchanged for

* We found puddingstone on the Grand Portage, and the silicious porphyry of Gros Cap, Lake Superior, in West Lake.

a naked country of granite, in mounds, either piled one upon another or single (low, perhaps), and surrounded by wide marshes; the prevailing tints of the country being red and dark grey; the former from the granite or gneiss, and the latter from the admixture of scorched pines and young poplars everywhere filling the eye.

There are several very fine cascades in these twelve miles, almost rivalling the best in the Canadas. The occasional rapids were so strong and billowy as to shake the canoe severely.

On the Height of Land one of our *voyageurs* was seized with inflammation of the bowels, which bleeding, &c. subdued only for a time,—being reproduced by the roughness of the waters. The man's agony and exhaustion were extreme. We were, therefore, exceedingly glad to see, on entering Lake Keseganaga, a large wigwam, on a marshy point, belonging to a well-known old Indian named Frisée. He had two or three strong sons and three or four daughters and daughters-in-law, and their children, all looking brown and fat, although said to be starving.

Frisée willingly received the sick man, but said that both hunting and fishing had failed them; that his young men had been out four days and had only killed two rabbits. The *voyageur*, he said, must be content with family fare.

And on landing I was not a little disturbed by seeing two men and a woman, at the entrance of the wigwam, feeding with their fingers, out of a tub, on the unwashed entrails of a rabbit, and wiping their hands, when they had done, on their own heads or on the back of a dog.

There was no help for it—stay our man must; so Mr. Astronomer Thompson prepaid Frisée one-half of the proposed reward in tobacco and coarse blue cloth, promising the remainder on our return to receive our man again. I gave some yards of tape and of scarlet and yellow riband to the girls, who are very fond of such things.

To our friend we gave tobacco and biscuit. He was content to stay, and nodded languidly to his comrades as they stepped into the canoe. When we had begun to move through the water I looked back, and saw behind the wigwam the children with my riband, cut into short pieces, tied in their hair. They were scampering and screaming with joy like little furies. Indian children are treated with great indulgence.

Lake Keseganaga, down which we are now moving, is much larger than any we have yet seen; and pass along its length (fourteen miles). It is very irregular in shape, and derives its name from being full of islands. Its south shore displays three ranges of heights;—first, the green slopes at the water's edge; secondly, a thinly-wooded purplish-red ridge; and thirdly, behind it, a blue line of hills, still higher, and visible along all this side of the lake.

Its outlet is a river of the same name, which flows into Hudson's Bay by Lake Sturgeon of the New Route.

Here we saw two bears (where the Indians had seen none); one was sitting at gaze on a high rock. As soon as he perceived us, he wheeled about, and hurried into the interior.

We met with the other on our return home. What I took to be an old hat floating in a wide expanse of water was declared to be a bear. Bears swim low. Both canoes made for him as fast as we could paddle, and we soon came up with poor Bruin.

Our astronomer took his stand at the bow, and quietly discharged his piece into his neck. The animal gave a loud howl, and rolled about in the bloody water violently, while we struck at him with poles and an axe. So great was the hubbub that I thought we should all have been drowned, for a small birch canoe is the last place to make war in; but the bear being soon stunned and quiet, a *voyageur* laid hold of him by the neck, and we slowly drew him to the shore.

When on dry land, and the water had ran off a little, the bear suddenly revived, stood up and showed fight, but he was so weakened by loss of blood that a few more blows on the head laid him low for ever. He was skinned that evening, and we made three good meals of him. Fresh meat is a luxury those only can estimate who have been living on salt provisions for some time in hot, steaming woods.

We saw but few bears this summer, but in that of 1824 the party met with nearly twenty, owing probably to a new distribution of food making fruit or fish more plentiful here than elsewhere.

Leaving Lake Keseganaga, we again found ourselves among basaltic hills and marshes; and after a couple of carrying-places, passing down Cypress Lake (five? miles long), and its near neighbour, Knife Lake (nine miles and a half long).

The soil of these portages is two-thirds primitive gravel, the rest sand and brown clay.

On Knife Lake I saw a cypress whose bark had been stripped by lightning from top to bottom, in a spiral three inches broad. I have seen other trees so treated.

A succession of rapids, closely shrouded in foliage, sometimes violent (and an expanse, some-

Outlet of Lake Brisbane South Hervey's Bay

times called Carp Lake), bring us into Boisblanc Lake (fifteen miles long—Mackenzie), so called from its producing bass-wood.

Its many islands, high and well-wooded shores, with pretty beaches of yellow sand, render it very picturesque. We passed a wintering-post of the Hudson's Bay Company, consisting of two or three comfortable huts on a cape.

Boisblanc Lake is very crooked, and resembles the letter Z in shape. I found here the *Etheria exitiosa*, the destroyer of peach-trees, as determined by Say of Philadelphia; but I saw no peach-trees.

On our return home in autumn through this lake we espied a canoe rounding a point to enter one of its deep bays. Being then very short of provisions we hastened after it, and found it in company with four others, all filled with Indians. They could only sell us some strips of dried deer's flesh, each a yard long and four or five inches broad. It looked like thick, red leather; but our men were glad of it to thicken their soup. While this purchase was going on, the gentle breeze drove a canoe full of women alongside of mine. As we rocked on the wave, the women fixed their eyes with wonderment upon me sewing on a button. The needle having an eye, and carrying the thread along with it, caused many a low, soft note of surprise; but when I presented a needle and some thread to each of the dark ladies, they were delighted. Although their prattle was unintelligible to me, not so their thankful eyes.

A series of violent rapids and cascades, from three to five miles long, now follow, with their portages. Of the first, the reader is presented with a view. At the lower end of one of these rapids there is an interesting relic of ancient Indian warfare in a hollow pile of stones, five feet broad by six long. It is now only three feet high, and has an aperture in the side, by which the rapids below may be watched. Each stone of the ground-tier (granite and gneiss) would require the united strength of three or four men to move it. Under this shelter, in days now gone by, the Chippewas, or Wood Indians, used to watch for their invaders, the Sioux of the plains,—a race of horsemen and warriors living principally on buffalo.

We next came to a narrow of still water, the entrance in fact of Lake Croche (crooked), about twenty miles long. This narrow is walled in by high precipices of shattered granite, beautifully striped downwards by broad bands of white, yellow, red, green, and black stains (vegetable). Until lately, the arrows shot by the Sioux, during a conflict at this spot, might be seen, sticking in the clefts of the rocks.

Seven miles from the upper end of the lake, the passage is almost closed by large blocks and bowlders; but not far from thence, westerly, the lake widens, and becomes diversified by fine islands, and an occasional high white hummock on the main. Some square masses of bleached rock dotting the shore made me think I beheld a Canadian village.

In the middle of the lake, where the islands were thickest, we shot past a pretty and unexpected sight.

We saw, sitting before a conical wigwam, a handsome, comfortably-dressed young Indian and his wife at work, a child playing with pebbles on the shore, and a fox-like dog keeping watch. There they sat, fearless and secure. When they saw us they only nodded and laughed. It occurred to me that many an Englishman might envy them.

Heathen though they be, the greatest affection often obtains between husband and wife. An Indian and his wife, I was informed, hunting alone on the plains, were met by a war-party of the Sioux. They endeavoured to escape, but the poor woman was overtaken, struck to the ground, and scalped.

Seeing this, the husband, although at this

time beyond either the balls or arrows of the Sioux, turned, and, drawing his knife, rushed furiously upon them, to revenge the death of his wife, even at the inevitable sacrifice of his own life; but he was shot before he reached the foe. This occurred not long ago.

After some sharp currents along narrows, and the picturesque Iron Lake (three miles and two-thirds across), we arrive at the Pewarbic, or Bottle Portage, and Lake Lacroix. (See Plate.)

The Lake of the Cross is thirty-four miles long by eighteen wide, according to Mackenzie. According to our survey, it contains 260 islands, often pine-tufted with rushy sides, besides rocks innumerable.

Its shores are extremely capricious in their outlines, and often bare and high. The Indians have names for most of the localities, but we could seldom procure them.

Wild rice grows so abundantly and fine on the south shore of Lake Lacroix that we sometimes could hardly push our canoes through it. Its water-lilies are superb, much the finest I have seen. They are about the size of a dahlia, for which they might be taken. They are double throughout, every row of petals diminishing by degrees, and passing gradually from the purest white to the highest lemon-colour. There is in

R. Young sc

Lake [illegible] from the [illegible] Portage

the neighbouring lakes a variety, wholly bright yellow.

A few miles from the Pewarbic Portage, on an island near the south main, there are the remains of a round tower, or defensive building of some sort, twenty-seven feet in diameter. It was erected by the Indians, and commands a wide view of expanses and woody isles.

The new or Dog-River route, from Lake Superior to the Lake of the Woods, enters Lake Lacroix on its north-east side by the River Maligne, and thenceforwards is the same as the old route.

The large River Lacroix (the outlet) leaves the lake on its north-west side, and finds its way into Lake Namaycan. We ascended it on our return home, entering from a small, quiet bay in Lake Namaycan, full of reeds and water-lilies, its shores lined with long grass and fine young oaks: but when once in the river all is romantic—that is, beautiful and dangerous.

This stream is a chain of vehement rapids and still waters; the former pent up in high walls of black basalt, from thirty to sixty yards apart, and crowned with pines; the latter, wide, full of marshy islets, rushes, and lilies. It is twelve or fifteen miles long—more, perhaps—and leaves

Lake Lacroix by a series of pretty cascades and rapids.

Two miles up the river from Namaycan the rapids were hardly practicable. We therefore unloaded, and scrambled over the tangled cliffs for a considerable distance, using the tow-rope to the canoes. But good and new as the tow-rope was, the strain was too great; it broke, and away went the first canoe down the heaving, foaming rapid, ten miles an hour, our two men in her escaping by miracle almost.

Just as a bend of the river took our distressed people out of sight, looking up the stream, we saw a long spear erect in the water, and riding rapidly towards us. This I could not at all understand; but in a moment or two there darted down the current, from an upper bend, a canoe in full pursuit, one Indian at the bow, standing aloft on the thwarts, spear in hand; another was guiding. In striking a large fish, it had wrenched the weapon from the hand of the spearsman.

This river is unfit for commercial purposes, a fact we had to verify, because other formidable rapids, as well as cascades, are met with beside this. The falls near Lake Lacroix are pleasing.

We slept on the lake-shore, just above the portage, and had to complain of the singular cry of the whip-poor-will all night, in a tree close to us, screaming into our ears his unhappy, reproachful notes, without a moment's cessation. This bird, the *Caprimulgus vociferus* of naturalists, is not often seen so far north as this. It breeds in Louisiana, and is noctarnal in its habits. Its food consists of winged insects.

In a wood close by, which had lately been fired, I found a beautiful tomahawk-hatchet. I took it in return for many little valuables left behind in our twilight morning starts.

But we must return to our outward journey. We entered Lake Namaycan by the Loon's Narrow (Mangshe-pawnac), by Vermillion Lake (so named from a paint found there), and finally by subsequent channel choked with aquatic plants.

There is a fur-collecting post on Lake Vermillion, where the scenery, though sometimes bold, is on the whole softer and more fertile than is common in gneiss districts. Encamping on a greensward, we were glad to catch a few fish for supper.

Of Lake Namaycan, I shall only say that it is about twenty miles long in a north-west direction, singularly broken up into bays and inlets. It resembles in its general aspects the granite lakes of the old route. We were cheered by noticing five wigwams at an open, pleasant-looking spot.

* There are no trout in these waters and the black bass are in minority. There are rumors of grayling in the

We gained admittance into the much larger lake Lapluie (or Rainy), by a short portage near the mouth of the River Namaycan. This stream is short, and runs through a wild rice country.

We had here the pleasure of shaking hands with our friends the American portion of the Commission. They had surveyed along the new route up to that point from Fort William.

We spent fourteen days in Rainy Lake, and had fine weather all the time, two days excepted.

As neither map nor description of Rainy Lake has been as yet published, a few pages will now be devoted to its topography. (*Vide* Map of Route, vol. i.)

We went carefully round it, and found the sum of our courses to be 294 miles, in which measurement small curvatures are not taken into account. We also counted 516 islands, small and great, besides mere rocks, and others which we did not see.

Its length along the south shore from the River Namaycan to the River Lapluie, taken direct by compass from the map we constructed (one inch to one geographical mile), is thirty-eight and a half statute miles. The traveller would of course find it longer.

From the same river Namaycan to the bottom of either of the two gulfs, horns, or arms, the distance, similarly marked off, is fifty statute miles.

Its breadth varies from three to thirty-one miles, the former occurring about the middle of the south shore, and the latter being taken from Black Bay (south shore) to Spawning River in the north-east arm.

Captain Lefroy, R.A., of the Toronto Observatory, makes this lake to be 1160 feet above the level of the sea, from a mean of many observations by barometer and boiling water. Of its depth I know nothing.

The south shore of this lake, compared with the others, is straight. It has one large promontory, and three principal bays — Wapes-kartoo, Cranberry, and Black.

Wapes-kartoo is the first on the east; it does not call for any remark.

Cranberry Bay takes its name from the delicious fruit which it affords. Rather more than half a mile from its east angle and near the main lies Maypole Island, a favourite sleeping-place of *voyageurs*. It may be distinguished by a tall pine-tree trimmed into a Maypole.

Black Bay is a shallow, swampy water, from three to four miles in diameter, with a narrow entrance, and full of rice, rushes, and water-lilies.

The Grand Détroit on the south shore, called by the Indians Wabash-gaundaga, is formed by a lengthened group of islands and the main. It is nine miles long; its east end being near and east of Black Bay. It is part of the canoe route to the Lake of the Woods. One of these islands, on which we encamped, abounded in wild onions, which, although small and hard, were excellent in the long-boiled soup of our *voyageurs.*

Close to Black Bay, on a pebble beach, we saw a lynx standing to look at us. It looked like a tall, gaunt shepherd dog, with dirty white fur and prick ears, with pretty tufts at their ends. Our interpreter fired at it, but missed. The prudent beast did not wait for a second shot. Near Perch River, on this shore, five or six miles west of the River Namaycan, we were preparing our night-camp, when a black and white animal, with a rich fur, called a skunk (*Mephitis Americana*), rushed by not far from us. "In a few minutes," one of the men said to me, "you will know more about that handsome fellow:" and so it was. A most abominable stench gradually infected the air, and lasted about an hour.

The east shore of the lake from the River Namaycan is tolerably straight (for this lake) for eighteen miles, when we meet with a bay seven miles across at its mouth, and nine miles deep, in a north-eastern direction. I have called it Seine Bay, from the name of a large river at its bottom.*

The north-east horn or arm commences in the centre of the north shore of the lake, with which it communicates by a pass only a few yards broad. The main shores are not a thousand yards apart, and the interval is greatly lessened by islands.

It is a labyrinth, twenty-two miles long, of sounds, bays, and coves—here in broad sheets of water—there thickly studded with islands, woody, but seldom high.

The main shores approach very closely in four or five places. One of these, at the foot of an expansion called Otterberry Lake, and about three miles from the entrance, is noted for the passage of bears. The Indians kill many here; but after a time the bears pass by some of the other narrows, having, without doubt, by some means learnt their danger. The bears subsist on berries, bilberries, bears' grapes, &c. which are

* Dining in a strait where the flow of water seems to have always been free, between the rivers Cormorant and Wahschusk, I observed an oval hole (kettle) in the rock, three feet deep, twenty-three inches by sixteen at the top, but gradually narrowing towards the flattened concave bottom. A crack in the side admitted the water of the lake and a few fresh-water shells. There is another on the River Namaycan, which has vase-like sloping lips.

extraordinarily abundant, and in finest flavour when they have passed a winter under snow. Fish is another great resource. One of our men, while strolling up a shallow brook, on a former journey, came upon a bear sitting upon his haunches in the water. Every now and then he landed a fish on the bank, by striking the water sharply with his paw.

I have nowhere seen or read of shores so wrinkled and devious, so full of unexpected bifurcations, closures, and openings, as in this and the neighbouring horn.

The (north-east) horn is remarkable for the pure, smooth, porcelain whiteness of its granite hills, which are often very high, and gleam through their scanty clothing of pine in a beautiful and singular manner, while the dark forests of cypress at their feet greatly heighten the general effect.

At a place where a lofty cascade falls into the lake with a loud roar, this kind of scenery is quite melodramatic. It presents a somewhat new combination of colours in landscape—white rocks, black foliage, and blue lake.

The vegetation in the bottoms is rich in oak, pine, cypress, poplar, and various useful fruits.

In the evening I ascended the hills near this fall, to obtain specimens of the white granite before-mentioned, as well as to sup upon the large juicy bilberries, which lay on the ground so thick as to be crushed at every step.

On my return, I found a small party of Indians at our camp, with whom we bartered a supper of fine fish for some tobacco and biscuit.

From their leader, "Le Grand Coquin" by name, we procured a rude but very useful map of the adjacent parts of the lake; for every Indian has an accurate knowledge of the district he frequents, together with great facility in map-making. These Indians were too familiar and lengthy in their visit, and more civil than was agreeable.

On the west side of this horn, ten miles from its north end, in a narrow side-bay, four miles long, I found well-characterised prisms of beryl, and in two spots; but I had no time for a careful search for more.

A tempest of wind and rain overtook us in this neighbourhood, and detained us for two days in a pleasant little islet. Our camp was pitched in a dry grove of large cypress-trees, where the time passed agreeably and profitably.

Rainy Lake being near a principal post of the North-west Company, and possessing in itself a variety of resources, we met with more Indians here than in any other lake.

At the eastern angle of the mouth of the north-

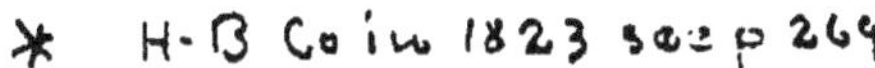

east born, three or four days afterwards, we fell in with a numerous band of Indians, men, women, and children, under a chief with the sinister name of " Two-hearts." They were occupying a quiet cove. As it would have been offensive to pass them by without notice, we landed and exchanged the pipe of peace. Our astronomer, well accustomed to the manners of the Indians, always made a point of treating them with that punctilious decorum they so much love.

After having received a little present of tobacco, and while sitting in friendly conference, Two-hearts said that his people had seen us frequently (we had not seen them), as well as other canoes of pale-faces, holding up pieces of shining metal to the sun.—" Have you suffered wrong from any red man? What is your purpose in rambling over our waters, and putting them into your books?"

Mr. Thompson replied, that we had met with no molestation whatever; that our purpose was to find how far north the shadow of the United States extended, and how far south the shadow of their great father, King George. He added, that the Indians would not be disturbed in any way.

Two-hearts expressed content.

I could not help wishing that the intrusive white might permit this almost extinguished race to hunt undisturbed, over these bleak wilds, for some time to come; for I am not sure that any change, apart from Christianity, would add to the sum of human happiness.

We have now to speak of the north-west horn.

It occupies the north and north-west side of the lake. It is 21½ miles deep, and is distinguished by the same extreme irregularity of outline, and the same prolonged and devious curvatures, as the north-east horn; but it is usually broader from main shore to main shore, and therefore of greater area. It runs west of, and behind, Fort and River Lapluie.

The land around is lower than that of the north-east horn, is often naked, or has aspens and willows at the water's edge—the interior showing great wastes of grey granite, over which the desolation of fire has passed. It is full of islands.

In this portion of the lake Mr. Astronomer Thompson was taken ill. We rested under a granite hill, while the proper remedies were successfully employed. The weather had been close and sultry in no common degree; the heavens above seemed brass, and the blue lake beneath shone into our faces like a sheet of hot steel.*

* Having broken my thermometer, I do not know the temperature of the water during these days. In shallows it was very

At the mouth of this horn (1500 yards broad), near the part of the lake called Peché, nine miles from Fort Lapluie, we met a merry band of Indian women, alone, gathering early berries from the rocks. We bought some for our men, for the prevention of scurvy.

The islands of Lake Lapluie are counted by thousands—few more than two or three miles long: the mere rough-tracing of their shores would be a great and profitless labour. They do not call for further remark.

It has twelve principal rivers, including Rainy River, besides others, small, and without names.

They are, on the east shore, the Namaycan, Wahschusk, Cormorant (antlers as a guide-post near it), and Seine River (seventy yards wide at

warm. Colonel Delafield favoured me with the following table of temperature, taken in deep waters, two feet below the surface:—

Day of Month.	Place.	Temp. Fahr.
1823. June 26	Lake Superior . .	44°
July 4	Pigeon River . . .	69
16	Outard Lake . . .	72
17	Mountain	72
20	Boisblanc	74
24	Crooked	72
25	Lacroix	72
25	Vermillion Lake . .	75
26	Namaycan	73
28	Lapluie River . . .	70
31	Ditto	72
Aug. 2	Lake Lapluie . . .	72

the mouth). In the north-east horn, Turtle and Spawning Rivers. In the north-west horn, Manitou-saugee (fine falls), Nah-katchiwon (from near White-fish Lake). On the west shore, Little Peché and Lapluie Rivers; and on the south shore, Wah-chusk-wateep-pear, Wapeskartookow, and Perch Rivers. These are of good size, and navigable by canoes.

Mr. Thompson found the magnetic variation to be 11° east, both at the upper parts of the north-east horn (August 5th, 1823), and on the south shore, near Rainy River (August 11). It was 10° east at the mouth of the River Namaycan.

Every one of the series of lakes we have been passing through has its own set of water-levels, from one to five horizontal lines, usually green or yellow, and formed of the surface-scum of the waters, which, by the bye, are almost always of the most excellent quality. The larger the lake, the greater the range of water-lines.

The highest line or level in Lake Lapluie was five feet above that of the time of my visit. This was well seen on the north shore, opposite the Grand Détroit, and in the Peché district.

The Rainy Lake and its vicinity is naturally a good fur country; but its proximity to the United States keeps the stock low, as its commerce cannot be confined to the Hudson's Bay Company.

EXCURSION THE SEVENTH.

PART IV. SECT II.

THE RIVER LAPLUIE AND THE LAKE OF THE WOODS.

Fort and River Lapluie—Hudson's Bay Company—Indian Massacre — Lake of the Woods — Murder Rock — War-road River — Driftwood Point — Monument Bay — North-west Corner of the Lake — The Rat Portage — The Nectam — River Winnepeg — Red Cliff Bay — Whitefish Lake — Isle of the Yellow Girl — Portage des Bois — Turtle Portage — The Thunder Bird — River Lapluie.

A THOUSAND years ago, while yet our England was a wolfish den, the silver Trent of the midland counties must have greatly resembled the Lapluie of the present day. I am not sure that the fur trader, an Italian perhaps, had not a hut on its banks; but certainly, at the time we are speaking of, both these streams flowed smoothly and freely in a succession of lovely and sequestered reaches, and through terraced meadows, alternating with rich woods and reedy marshes.

The Lapluie seems made for a pleasure excursion; all is serenity and beauty. The winds can seldom come near, in summer at least; and as to rocks beneath, there are none, save in a very few places, and easily avoided. At the mouth of any of the tributary streams, during most of the open season, a net will secure a supper—nay, I am told that sometimes the canoe can hardly get along from the number of fish. In the autumn the gun will bring down a score of pigeons, a wild duck, or a swan.

Rainy R
some fish

We entered the River Lapluie on the 14th day of July by the rapids at its head (120 yards broad) in two sets, the upper caused by a low, rocky isle, the lower by a greenstone ledge. Having passed these without difficulty, we arrived in a basin 1300 yards wide, but soon contracting again.

14 July 1823

Two miles and a half then brought us to the Cataracts. These are two, a higher and a lower. * The first descends ten feet, and the second twenty feet, with a boisterous interval of fifty yards.

A few hundred yards below this last cascade, within the hearing of its roar, is the Hudson's Bay fort, Lapluie. It is on the north bank of the river, a cleared, alluvial terrace, fifty feet above the water.

H B Co

* The Chaudier Falls near Fort Frances named for wife of Sir George Simpson. now site of water power development.

The fort is a set of timber dwelling-houses, stores, stabling, &c., forming a hollow square, protected by strong picketing and heavy gates. Near to these last is a small hole in the picket, through which to pass articles in unsafe times. High above all is a wooden platform, ascended by a ladder, and used as a look-out.

The fort is quite safe from a coup-de-main of the Indians, but at present there is no fear of any such event.

We were cordially received by Dr. M'Loughlin, the Governor, a chief factor of great energy and experience. He has since been several years Governor of Fort Vancouver, on the River Columbia, and has taken a leading part in founding the city of Oregon. He is the same gentleman whose narrow escape from drowning in Lake Superior I have noticed.

Our fare in the Fort was primitive — chiefly damper (scorched balls of dough), potatoes, and fish, wine, coffee, and tea. We partook of the same food as our hosts, and were thankful; but I was rather surprised that the fat meadows about did not produce beef and mutton. I well remember, gourmands as we were, that we left the fort purposely before twelve o'clock, on our way down the river, and dined on our own more substantial fare on an island out of sight, some hundred yards below. Our life-errant in the open air for months had given us ravenous appetites.

Walking out, the morning after our arrival, with Mr. W. M'Gillivray, the Lieut.-Governor, I saw on the opposite side of the river some buildings, and a tall, shabby-looking man, angling near the falls. I asked my companion what all that meant. He replied, "The two or three houses you see form a fur-trading post of John Jacob Astor, the great merchant of New York. The man is one of his agents. He is fishing for a dinner. If he catch nothing he will not dine. He and his party are contending with us for the Indian trade. We are starving them out, and have nearly succeeded."

The expedients for preventing a rival from entering a rich fur country are sometimes decisive. Every animal is advisedly exterminated, and the district is ruined for years.

Permit me here, as perhaps the most proper place, to state the conclusion I came to respecting the treatment of the Indians by the Hudson's Bay Company.

They are based upon the personal knowledge (limited, indeed) which I acquired at the several stations we passed through, and still more upon extensive inquiries made of persons acquainted with the distant stations.

Where I state what I saw I expect to be believed, whatever others may have seen at other times and in other places. My opinions and inferences must be taken for what they are worth.

I have no connexion with the Hudson's Bay Company, and do not know by sight any individual belonging to it.

My conviction is, that their sway is a great blessing to the Indians. True it is, however, that it might readily be made more so, because there are important errors of detail capable of removal. The whole, almost boundless, region under their management, five millions of square miles, is at peace. None of those slaughters *en masse*, or solitary murders, that are now of daily occurrence along the western border of the United States, from the Valley of the Saskatchawine to the frontiers of Mexico, take place within the territories of this Company, or with extreme rareness.

Within their dominions every man's life, family, and goods, are safe. Order and ready obedience everywhere prevail.

A man's ability in the occupations peculiar to the country is known, and he is treated, I have every reason to believe, with tolerable fairness. He knows that his reward is at hand, and certain, though small, for the Company are prompt paymasters.

When distress from famine, sickness, inundations, or any other public calamity, arises, the Company steps forth to assist, and expects no return. When its hunters are worn out, they and their young families are provided for as a recompense for past services. It is the interest as well as the duty of this corporate body of merchants so to treat the natives, but this cannot be done by private traders in the midst of competition, and only thinking of the gain of the day.

The result is, that the Indians of Hudson's Bay are not decreasing, although they are, and rapidly, in the southern latitudes, under much more favourable natural circumstances. To be stout, or even fat, and in good humour, was the rule among the Indians we met with. The ravening, meagre figures, who loiter about the sea-board towns of America, the modern representatives of the "masterless man" of the middle ages, we rarely or never saw.

These are great facts. My feeling, therefore, is, that the Hudson's Bay Company ought to possess the exclusive privilege of trading with the Indians dwelling in this portion of North America now under consideration, and that to deprive them of it would be, on the part of Parliament, a step most impolitic, and followed instantaneously by disorder, crime, and misery.

I am confirmed in this opinion by the nature of

these territories, their distance from human inspection and authority, by the ignorance inconsequence, irritability and waywardness of the Indians, ever the victim and sport of their own wild passions.

I hardly need here observe that it is the duty of the Company, as speedily as possible, to remove this state of pupillage, and not to allow it to subsist as an excuse for keeping these aborigines in bondage.

To throw open the fur trade would inevitably do away with every present advantage, and would render impossible all attempts at religious and social improvement.

This vast region, hidden from all eyes, would be filled with unprincipled and daring adventurers, looking only to the gain of the moment, and rivalling each other in violence and libertinism.

A few years would see the extermination both of the fur-bearing animals and of the natives themselves.

The murderous contentions, which have not been put down many years,* would be renewed

* It was only in 1848 that the Cree Indians residing near Fort Pitt, on a branch of the Saskatchawine in the Hudson's Bay territories, massacred a party of nineteen Blackfeet Indians, who happened to approach too near their camp.—*Ch. Miss. Record, Feb.* 1850.

This must be a very unusual event, and, it is hoped, has met with due punishment.

under new captains, with the Indian onslaught,—"fear in front and death in the rear,"—as of old; scenes of which I took many notes from the lips of the traders: but man was not created to furnish incidents for the novelist, nor a gallery of battles for Versailles.

One such story, I think, may not be out of place here.

In picturesque barbarity, it is such as Walter Scott might have told of a clan of Scottish Highlanders in the fourteenth century. It only happened in 1810, and exemplified the misrule then prevailing in the Indian countries.

I was dining one day as usual in the canoe, on Lake Superior, when an old *voyageur* began to tell the tale to his next neighbour; but hearing it imperfectly, I asked the astronomer about it. He said it was all true, and happened when he was in the vicinity.

Twenty Iroquois and four white men had hunted unsuccessfully the Lake of the Woods, the Winnepeg River and Lake, and high up the River Saskatchawine.

They then heard that there was game on the Bow River, a southern feeder of the Saskatchawine.

Mr. Hughes and other traders, living at a fort some fifty miles from the Bow country, entreated these hunters not to go there; but they were all brave, experienced, *and poor;* so they went.

Soon after they appeared on the rolling meadows (with here and there a patch of poplars or alders), of which the district consists, the lawful occupants residing near a cascade, and therefore called the Fall Indians, fell in with the newcomers.

After counsel taken, it was resolved either to make the strangers pay tribute for their hunt, or drive them away. "This," said they, "may be only the first of many such bands. We shall be devoured."

They now sent two spies to the Iroquois camp, who reported twenty-four determined men, armed to the teeth.

A week or two afterwards, no offence in the interval having been given or taken, twenty-five or thirty Falls entered the camp of the newcomers, which was pitched on a creek bordered with balsam-poplars, with their muskets charged with powder only—*not with ball,* be it remembered.

They came with professions of amity, and had a long talk—whether payment for their trespass was agreed upon, or what other proffers and promises were made—is not known, but all parties became so kindly and confidential, that the Fall Indians ventured to remind the Iroquois, that it was an old custom in the plains for friends to change guns. All started to their feet; and the exchange was instantly made, when the Falls stepping back a pace or two, each shot his man. All fell dead or mortally wounded, except two whites and an Iroquois.

The latter ran off, but was followed and killed.

A chief tried hard to save the whites—to make a present of them to Bras Croche (the *nom de guerre* of Mr. Alexander M'Donald, a favourite trader), at a fort some miles distant.

He obtained a reluctant and imperfect consent to their lives being spared, and the party set off for the fort.

But the chief made the whites walk immediately before him, and close behind some of his young men.

One of the whites, an elderly man, as they were trudging on, wished to go aside for some temporary purpose. "No," said his protector; "if you do, you die." The man, however, perhaps from not knowing exactly what was said to him, stepped out of the line of march, and was in a moment shot dead.

The chief then wrapped his blanket closer about him and called out, "Young men, it is not worth while going to the fort with one white; the shriek of the Blackfeet may perhaps be even now heard in our village, and the scalps of our wives already borne away." The last of the twenty-four did not live five minutes more. The Indians wheeled round, and went full trot home.

In 1815 the unauthorised and wicked subordinates of the North-west Company shot down like carrion birds seventeen unarmed men (one an officer of Scotch Fencibles), belonging to Lord Selkirk, in a grass-field at the Red River Settlement.

The best endeavours of the Government of the United States are now put forth in vain to prevent the robberies and wholesale murders resulting from unrestrained intercourse between the white and red races of men; and this because they employ troops and diplomatic agents instead of an exclusive trading company under the inspection of public officers.

I must now state, that at the Hudson's Bay posts I visited rum did not appear to be the staple article of exchange, neither was it used as a means of throwing the Indian off his guard.

Some was given, perhaps, because the southern boundary line was near, on which less scrupulous rivals had stations. Doubtless, too, rum is distributed in the Rocky Mountains, because the neighbouring distilleries of Oregon within the limits of the United States are ready to supply ardent spirits to all comers.

The great bulk of the trade lay in necessaries, blankets, gunpowder, lead, knives, guns, cooking-pots, pomatum,* &c.

Lord Lincoln, in the parliamentary session of 1849, made a speech (most probably a mere party speech), in which he complained that 7000 gallons of rum were consumed here in 1847. But what is this in so rigorous a climate, and in so vast a region? A single London gin-shop distributes as much in the same time (18 gallons a-day). There are 200 fur-stations and their outposts to be supplied, and not only natives, but the Company's servants.

I am aware, as Col. Crofton (lately resident at the Red River Settlement) has said, that the sale of spirits was at one time totally prohibited by a general order. The circumstances which have led to its partial resumption I do not know.

So earnest in the cause of temperance have the Hudson's Bay Company been, that they stipulated, in a recent treaty with the Russian Association of Fur Traders, for the total disuse in trade of ardent spirits in their territories.

I am persuaded that the influence of this Com-

* Pomatum is, or was lately, a favourite medicine among the Indians, taken in scruple doses, and sovereign in many cases. Why not?

pany is actively used on the side of morality. At the forts I observed great order, sobriety, and economy, with a marked cheerfulness in the faces of all, save in those, perhaps, of one or two old clerks, who thought they had not met with due preferment.

There were no outward and visible improprieties. As in India, a better social tone has arisen in these wastes, and it will soon receive a new impulse.

Little or nothing has been done until lately by the Hudson's Bay Company, as a body, for the Christian instruction of the Indians, but some of their servants have made isolated efforts. The East India and New Zealand Companies have done as little.

What has been effected is almost wholly due to the Church and Wesleyan Missionary Societies of England. But a fairer prospect is now opening upon these countries in the enlightened labours of the excellent Bishop Anderson, who has just arrived at the Red River Settlement, which may be called the capital of Rupert's Land. It is to be hoped that he will be the vigilant and fearless protector of the red race in their best interests, temporal and spiritual. But I fear he can do but little with a flock sprinkled in scores on spots in an arctic climate from 100 to 500 miles apart, and whose subsistence requires continual change of abode.

A nomade population like that of the Plains and Rocky Mountains require at present less a principal shepherd than a number of under-pastors, to watch over the Indians with that incessant and minute personal care which they especially need—a care which must descend to the smallest details of general life.

It seems to me that the will of the testator who provided the funds for this new bishopric (a great boon) would have been more truly and beneficially carried out, if one of the clergymen now at the Red River—such as the Rev. Mr. Cockran, an experienced and able labourer in this mission—had been made an archdeacon, with an increased salary for travelling expenses; and the rest of the noble legacy had been expended, for twenty years to come, on one or two additional missionaries, and on schoolmasters and catechists. At present a solitary bishop absorbs the whole, living in a small group of villages with a population of perhaps 3000—Wesleyans and Roman Catholics in great numbers, as well as Episcopalians, and 1000 and 2000 miles apart from important portions of his charge.

The inhabitants of Rupert's Land certainly

submit to many grievances, but to none without remedy, or of sufficient moment to call for a withdrawal of the charter.

Of these I will only mention the exorbitant and almost incredible price of European goods, of which the Company, directly or indirectly, has the monopoly. A cotton handkerchief, perhaps worth a shilling in England, costs in Hudson's Bay 1*l.* 12*s.* 6*d.*; and all other articles in proportion, according to the tariff furnished by the Company to Mr. Murray for his account of British North America; thirty-three per cent on the prime cost being at the same time sufficient to cover the expenses of transit.

The Company is accused of being averse to colonization: and it may be so, any further than is necessary to support their stations. Their business is to buy and sell furs — not to promote emigration. As for colonizing their territories east of the Rocky Mountains at present, the idea is preposterous. A large part is irremediably barren, consisting of vast deserts of sand, gravel, and bowlders, of rocky, moss-covered barrens, immense lakes and morasses. Most of it is from 2000 to 3000 feet above the level of the sea, and exposed to the full force of the arctic cold. Within the last three years Fahrenheit's thermometer has stood at 50° below zero at the Red River settlement, close to the south frontier, where, nevertheless, the short, hot summer, sometimes abundantly rewards the cultivator ofthe rich soil around.

Let the fertile lands of New Brunswick and Upper Canada, &c., first be occupied and subdued.

To proceed with our voyage down the River Lapluie.

Its descent took up two delightfully placid days, although aided by its always sensible and often strong current.

It is estimated to be eighty-five miles long, and runs westerly, with considerable bends, however, north and south, through a level country. Nothing like a hill is ever seen, but one, where there is a small hummock of sienite.

Vegetation is everywhere abundant; the trees —elm, basswood, oak, pine, birch, and poplar— are often large and healthy. Usually they are mixed; but we often sail by a single species of tree for a mile together, according to the nature of the soil.

I am informed that these fine woods do not extend far back from the river, the land generally sinking into swamps.

The meadows (sometimes deserted clearances)* are loaded profusely with strong tall grasses and

* As to settling on this river, many things are desirable besides fertility. The drawbacks here are overpowering. They are, a long

flowers. I had difficulty in making my way for a mile through one of these, near the Long Sault Rapids. I was sometimes up to my shoulders in grass.

About nine miles above the entrance of the river into the Lake of the Woods willows begin to abound, and then we enter extensive marshes of tall reeds and rushes, which gradually become broader, until the dry banks of the river and their hard wood are out of sight, and we finally are sailing over the shallows of the lake.

Excepting the marshy districts just mentioned, the banks of the Lapluie are alluvial, with one or two terraces behind, from twenty to fifty feet high.

Although there is some black loam, the soil in general is a mixture of grey clay, sand, yellow limestone grit, and decomposed vegetation, well seen opposite Little Fork River.

We just see enough of the rocks of this district to show that it is most probably (or certainly) underlaid by horizontal yellow limestone (Silurian), resting on sienite and greenstone.

During the first four miles below Fort Lapluie

and severe winter, total want of society, and of the means of education, dearness of many necessaries, and insecurity of life and property. The Lapluie is a frontier river, and therefore liable to devastation in the time of war.

the north shore is lined with a breccia of primitive pebbles in a calcareous cement. The beaches and banks are everywhere strewn with masses of limestone, some of them more than a ton in weight; and this especially near the Lake of the Woods. They must be *in situ*, or very near, and have been split up by the thaws and frosts of spring.

The water of the River Lapluie is excellent, and very clear, except near the mouths of tributary streams, where it is discoloured by the clays or ferruginous matters over which the latter have flowed.

The river ranges in breadth from 200 to 400 yards, until we come to within fifteen miles of its mouth, when the width gradually increases, until we come down to the marshes already spoken of.

Contractions, however, take place at the only two rapids which occur below the fort.

The first is the Manitou Rapid, from thirty to thirty-five miles below the Hudson's Bay post, at a rocky narrow. They are not long, but violent, and include one short slant of from eighteen to twenty-four inches perpendicular, succeeded by billows, eddies, and back-water. Our tow-rope broke on our return at the sharpest spot, and the canoe with her men were all but lost (*timor—pallor*).

The Long Sault Rapid is seven or eight miles lower down, and is two miles and a half long—

powerful but variable. They are caused in one part by an island; in others, by a narrowing of the river-bed, by shallows, and drift-wood.

There are twelve islands—small, woody, single, or in pairs.

Sable Island, at the mouth, is five and a half miles long, and made up of sand-hillocks and granite-mounds. It bears willows and aquatic plants.

The rivers entering the Lapluie are large, and often very long.

The principal are eight in number. The first from above enters from the south, and is called the Little Fork. A Canadian named Roy has cleared the east side of its mouth, and built a house. An extensive meadow is all the farm I saw; but I did not land.

I understand that the Wesleyan Missionary Society has established a mission here under Mr. Peter Jones, a converted Indian.

Judging from what I saw of him in England a few years ago, he is well qualified for the work. As the number of tractable Indians within reach is here great, and as the means of support are easily obtained, I am sorry that excellent society did not send to this place a regular mission-staff, as explained in p. 322, vol. i.

Such is the only true method of doing extensive

and permanent good; but I suppose they desired to proceed cautiously.

The next is the Valley River, coming in from the north (?), hemmed in by very high banks, but which, as we proceed up it, subside into marshes filled with diminutive spruce. The mosquitoes were unusually distressing at this place.

Three miles lower down we come to the Great Fork. It enters from the south, and comes from near Lake Cassina, once supposed to be the source of the Mississippi, and six or eight days' journey from hence. This stream is one hundred yards wide at its mouth, with high woody banks on one side and swamps on the other. Three miles further down we meet, on the south bank, with the Black River, both large and long.

Near the head of the Long Sault Meadows, seven miles below the rapid of that name, the Oak River enters amid a grove of oaks growing on high banks.

Next we have Rapid River, on the south bank, flowing in from a circular basin edged with grass. The river leaps into the basin by a cascade, beyond which we see high walls bounding a fierce rapid.

A few miles downwards bring us to Steep Bank River; and then, at an interval of two miles, we come to the River Baudet, called by the Indians, "The River of the Bitter Side of the Ribs." It is at the mouth from 100 to 130 yards broad, much choked with rushes and grass. I have been induced to set down these topographical details so fully, because I do not know where else they can be had.

We now enter the Lake of the Woods with pleased and inquisitive eyes; but before proceeding further it will be well to make a few brief observations on its leading features.

The Lake of the Woods is not so much one body of water as three, connected by short straits, through which either ships or canoes can freely pass. They are very different in size, shape, and aspect. The southern division is aptly named by the Indians "The Lake of the Sand Hills," or "Parpequa-wungar;" the northern is called by them the "Lake of the Woods," or "Kaminitik;" and the eastern, "Whitefish Lake." With its Indian appellation I am not acquainted.

The two first-named, taken together, run northerly, and are 400 miles in circumference. We made their circuit in ten long, laborious summer days.

The Lake of the Sand Hills, from which Rainy River proceeds, is by far the largest, being seventy-seven statute miles wide, from east to west, near the parallel of Reed River; its greatest length from Rainy River to Lake Kaminitik, at the narrows, being fifty-one miles; and it is thirty-two miles across from Rainy River to its northern shore,—a great promontory soon to be mentioned.

It is extremely irregular in shape. Four-fifths of its surface is wholly, or nearly, free from islands; but it has very many on the east and north. Other particulars will come out in the course of our voyage.

It is divided on the north from the Lake of the Woods, as named by the Indians, by a very large, oblong promontory, but which is so hemmed in by Whitefish Lake that it is nearly an island. This promontory is thirty miles long from its base near Whitefish Lake, and advances westward to within six miles of the western shore of the lake, there meeting two large islands, which occupy most of the interval. It is twenty miles broad near Whitefish Lake, and fourteen near its west end, a few miles east of Portage des Bois, a carrying-place, created by a singular meeting of two deep, narrow cul-de-sacs, one on each side of the promontory; which makes the commercial route from the Rainy River to the north end of the Lake only seventy-five or eighty miles.

The northern and upper division of the Lake of the Woods, called Kaminitik, is an irregular oblong twenty-four miles in length northerly. Its greatest breadth of twenty-eight miles occurs at the deep inlet called Dryberry Bay; but its average breadth is from ten to twelve miles.

Of Whitefish Lake, the little we know is found a few pages onwards.

These bodies of water are interesting in their characters, but very dissimilar.

The Lake of the Sand Hills resembles a lagoon in Holland, in its shallow waters and low, sandy shores of regular outline, belted with pines, willows, reeds, and rice plants.

The Lake Kaminitik is a maze of rocky islets and deep sounds, like the gneiss lakes we have passed through; while Whitefish Lake wears the general features of the basalt lakes of the old route.

Map of the Bound. Com. 2 m. to 1 inch

The map which accompanies these pages has been reduced from the large one (one inch to two geographical miles), constructed by order of the Boundary Commission, the present Secretary for Foreign Affairs having very liberally allowed me access to it in the archives of the Foreign Office.

It is not from trigonometrical survey, but made by fixing fifteen principal points on the lake at about equal distances from each other, by observations for latitude and longitude, and then filling * up the intervals by compass and log or estimate, —our rate of going having been found to be 120 yards per minute, or rather less than four miles per hour. A degree of accuracy is thus attained,

* Compass and log — David Thompson's patent log — see p. 179

quite sufficient for practical purposes. To have attempted more would have incurred useless delay and expense.

As the Lake of the Woods is of importance in a national point of view, as the point of departure westward of a great boundary line, and is a portion of the route from the Canadas to the Red River settlement, the Buffalo Plains, and the regions beyond, and as it has never been circumnavigated either before or since, it may be well to bestow a few pages on its topography.

Having advanced a few hundred yards out of the River Lapluie, if we look into the Lake of the Sand Hills we have on the west open waters, with a few black spots marking so many emerged rocks; no shore is visible in that direction;—it has sunk under the horizon. In front (north) there is a compact belt of woody islands from fifty to a hundred feet high, and five or six miles off. On the north-east and east the islands are continued, and there is seen a low mainland of sand and hummocks of rock.

We did not pursue the usual commercial route, which runs directly north from the River Lapluie. We were ordered to go round the lake, to discover, if possible, its most north-western corner, and therefore turned off to the west, and kept as close to the south shore as the shallow waters permitted.

Once fairly launched into the lake, it was perceived that we were in a new region. Two fine fishing-eagles were soaring over our heads, with white bodies and black wings. Hitherto, throughout our whole journeyings, we had noticed very few birds. An hour or two afterwards were observed flights of geese, swans, and a solitary crane or two winging their way to the marshes. Hundreds of small grey gulls were hovering about the solitary mounds that dotted the lake shore. On one of these we landed, and found it so covered with their eggs that we unavoidably crushed them at every step. They proved very acceptable to our men; neither were we too nice to partake of them.

In sailing along, we found the south and southwest borders of the lake to be mere sand-flats and dunes,—the latter capped with small poplars and other stunted trees. All around, landwards and lakewards, were lagoons and marshes.

The lake is extremely shallow,—not more than from eighteen to twenty-four inches deep a mile or more from shore, with a bottom of white clay, sand, or weeds.

Four or five miles from the River Lapluie, the

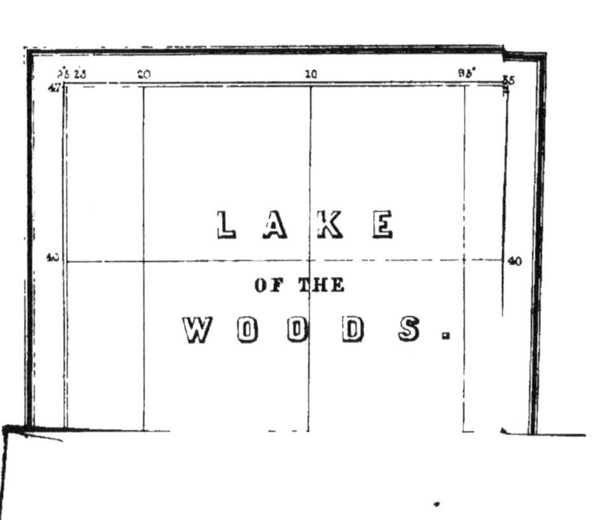
LAKE
OF THE
WOODS.

Muskeg Bay

noted that it gave passage to the Muskeg, or War-road River, — names sufficiently indicative of its character and uses, "muskeg" being the Indian word for "morass."

We then proceeded to encamp near Buffalo Head (see map), the north-west angle of this great bay; and so called from a tradition that a buffalo, or rather a bison, was once killed there, which had strayed from its companions in the great plains, seventy or eighty miles distant.

The War-road River is fifty yards broad at its mouth, and drains the marshes which occupy the interval between this and the Red River of the great plains. It rises in or near Reed Lake (a large and shallow lake communicating with Red River); but although this is the direct route to the settlement on the last-named river, it is only used by the Indians on account of a long and troublesome portage.

The water of the lake had always been greenish from within seven miles of the River Lapluie; but in Muskeg Bay and its neighbourhood, for miles from land, it was filled with dead shad flies and rotting marsh-plants. The paddles moved heavily through it, and it could not be drunk until strained, and then it was turbid and disagreeable.

marsh-plants

We slept near Buffalo Head, where the land is

Coues in note, p 23, "Henry-Thompson's Journal" says: Buffalo Pt. is historically interesting as the site of Verandrye's old Fort St. Charles., 1732 rather higher and drier than elsewhere, and bears some young hardwood trees.

Within a few yards of our encamping-ground was a wintering-house of the Hudson's Bay Company, in which I had great hopes of residing during the coming winter; but as the work was finished sooner than was expected, I was disappointed.

It ought to be mentioned, that red, fawn-coloured, and white limestone, abounding in fine Silurian fossils, are in such large sharp-edged blocks that it must be *in situ* close by, and most probably underlies all this western portion of Sand-hill Lake.

In the Lake Kaminitik we saw no calcareous *débris;* every fragment of rock was primitive.

The next day we proceeded northerly along the skirts of three or four bays, passing Reed River in the first of them, to Driftwood Point, or Cape Embarras, on this west shore; the style of country remaining much the same as in Muskeg Bay.

Driftwood Point is thirty miles direct from the River Lapluie, and is a broad tongue of marsh and shingle, so heaped up with snow-white driftwood as to have received its name from the fact.

Our Indian guide and myself landed, and ran along this beach for two or three miles. He was a little before me, and disturbed a wolf smelling at a dead fish; and soon after we came upon a lynx standing still, all a-drip with water. My companion fired at him and missed. We heard a plunge into a cove and saw it no more.

Nearly opposite Driftwood Point, and five miles in the offing, is a considerable island, which we call Cornfield Island, for we observed there a little plot of potatoes and beans, about a quarter of an acre, planted by Indians. Upon the whole, these people are discouraged from agricultural efforts, as, while they are necessarily away at some hunting or fishing-ground, the produce is liable to be taken by strangers on travel.

Seven or eight miles north of this, among savannahs, grassy shores, and groups of small larch, we enter a strait between the main and an archipelago of islands, leaving henceforth the shallow expanses of a limestone district for the wrinkled shores and crowds of islands always met with in a primitive district.

We are, in fact, at the south angle of what may be called Monument Bay (three miles across and opposite Shebashca), on whose north-west side is the most north-western corner of the Lake of the Woods, sought for as the termination of the water-line under the seventh article of the Treaty of Ghent, and so determined in 1842 by Lord

Ashburton and Mr. Webster, aided by Dr. Tiarks and other astronomers.*

I am informed at the Foreign Office that a satisfactory conclusion was arrived at by passing an imaginary north-east line (on paper) westwards over the face of the lake, touching and leaving, successively, the curvatures and indentures of the west main-shore, the last touched and most westerly being then assumed to be the most north-western, and the point desired.

This takes place at the bottom of a narrow, marshy cul-de-sac, eight miles and a half deep, at the northern part of the bay across whose mouth we are now passing. It is in north latitude 49° 23′ 55″, and west longitude 95° 14′ 38″. It is 3′ south of the parallel of the Portage des Bois, and 32′ on its west.

A stone monument has been erected to mark the place, two-thirds of a mile from the end of the inlet; perhaps on account of the wetness of the ground at the exact spot.

From this point, according to treaty, a line is carried due south to the 49th parallel of

* Upon this point the original commissioners, Mr. Barclay and General Porter, could not agree. The matter, not being of immediate and pressing importance, was suffered to remain in suspense. It was thought advisable by the British Government, about 1841, that Dr. Tiarks should make a personal inspection of the Lake of the Woods, which he accordingly did.

north latitude, which parallel, from thence to the Rocky Mountains westwards, is the boundary between the two nations concerned.

The boundary-line from the great lakes, and eastward, meanwhile, has been advanced directly hitherwards from Rainy River, and passes at the mouth of and within Monument Bay certain islands, which are numbered on the official list.

Great advantages arise from the adoption of this parallel of latitude, as, with more or less exactness, it runs along the dividing-ridge, the water-shed of the two great hydrographic systems of the Mississippi and of Hudson's Bay. It, therefore, takes away from Great Britain any pretence for entering the waters of the Mexican Gulf from its tributaries, while it excludes the United States from Rupert's Land and its streams. The height of land thus felicitously selected is a natural geographical boundary.

Doubtless in 1783 a better bargain might have been made, which would have placed under British sway the feeders of the Missouri and the rich prairies of Iowa. But have we not as much as we can manage?

Any deviation from this line might have been productive of serious misunderstandings. If removed a few miles to the north, it would have given to the United States the Red River Settlement, while a parallel a little more southerly would have placed a British fort on the Missouri.

Besides the advantages just hinted at, this boundary gives to the United States access to the more valuable furs of the north.

New and arbitrary arrangements were made to obtain this boundary for Central North America, which bear evident marks of the far-sightedness of Dr. Franklin, one of the four American diplomatists employed in concluding the treaty of 1783.

We see that the treaty of 1783 ordered, first, that the water-boundary should end at the north-west corner of the Lake of the Woods. Secondly, that from that point a line should drop south on the 49th parallel; and, thirdly, that this intersecting point should be the starting-place of the boundary westwards to the Rocky Mountains.

Now, in the sixth article, the line always pursued the shortest course from the outlet to the head of each lake, leaving, in Lake Huron, the lion's share to Great Britain; but, in the seventh article, this principle is departed from as to Lake Superior, in order that the boundary should leave at the Pigeon River, and so to move along the old route to the north-west corner of the Lake of the Woods. This assigns to the United States Isle Royale, a fine island, now the seat of prosperous copper mining, and all the west end of Lake Superior, with a full quarter of its north shore.

To return to our coasting voyage. From Monument Bay, on our route to the Rat Portage, we skirted every bay, and entered sufficiently within them to keep the true main in view.

I have no doubt but that we passed unnoticed several small rivers, because, in a low, woody country, it is not easy to see an entering stream, unless we catch sight of it when fully opposite, or are very near.

We encamped, on the 18th of July, on an islet near the mouth of the River La Platte, from fourteen to sixteen miles south-west of the Rat Portage. It comes from a very large and shallow lake of the same name.

I refer the reader to the map for details respecting this part of the lake. It is full of low islands, usually set thickly together, but sometimes allowing of extensive views around. The main is low, rushy, and grassy, densely planted with oak, spruce, poplar, and larch.

Towards the Rat Portage the country rises, and the scene becomes precisely that of the Thousand Isles on the St. Lawrence below Kingston, so exquisitely beautiful when seen on a calm evening when the shadows are long. We

have the same low cliffs and morsels of rock, the same pines and birch in artistic groupings, the same deep and transparent waters.

In one place, while our canoe was moving through the water rapidly, it received a sudden and startling shock. We had struck upon a sleeping sturgeon, which we traced in the troubled waters making off with all speed.

The Rat Portage, in north latitude 49° 46′ 22″ and west longitude 94° 39′, which leads from the Lake of the Woods into the River Winnepeg, its outlet, we reach by a narrow cul-de-sac, 600 yards long, ending in a grassy swamp, the portage lying between two eminences, naked but for burnt pines, a few cypress trees, and poplars.

This cul-de-sac is 120 yards broad at the portage, and is made offensive and foul by dead insects, the croaking of frogs, and the plague of mosquitoes.

The hill east of the cul-de-sac, 200 feet high, gives an excellent idea of the environs. It embraces the Lake of the Woods and the waters of the Winnepeg. We see from hence that the Portage is a neck of land fifty paces across, between the dirty cove in the lake and a magnificent sheet of water formed by the junction of the Winnepeg with a large river, whose name I could not learn, coming from the west; and the united stream flowing down a prolonged woody valley. Wild islands of granite stud the west side of this basin, whose shores are high and naked, and backed by three ranges of lofty hills, either bare or covered with bright young verdure.

We were honoured at this place with a visit from the Nectam* of all the Algonquins, the still-acknowledged chief of that wide-spread Indian tribe.

We were at dinner when he was announced as being near. It was thought proper to show him due respect, although he was now only the faded head of a fading race, and in a very different state from that in which the Five Nations demolished every habitation in the island of Montreal, killed a thousand men, and burnt twenty-six alive at a public festival.

The Nectam was almost alone. As he was long in appearing, I could not help going to see what was the matter. After some search I found him in a thick coppice, in the act of being adorned by his wife—a hearty, middle-aged Indian—in the needful braveries, out of a wooden box, the royal wardrobe. Being ashamed of my intrusive tendencies, I retired hastily, and, it is to be hoped, unobserved.

* An Indian word, signifying personal pre-eminence.

In a few minutes the chief slowly and meekly approached us. He had on a good English hat, with broad silver edging round the brim, gold strings around the crown, and black ostrich feathers. His coat was of coarse blue cloth, with here and there a bit of tinsel; and his leggings and mocassins were of fine leather, richly worked in porcupine quills.

We arose at his coming, did obeisance, and received in our turns his proffered hand.

Our astronomer pointed out a box for his seat and presented him, after the exchange of some further courtesies, with a plate of salt beef and biscuit,—great dainties to him, and the only ones we possessed. We gave another plateful to his faithful spouse, who then retired to a stone and a bush hard by.

The Nectam had seen forty years, was well made, and middle-sized. His face was ruddy and comparatively fair, regular and pleasing, but far too mild and unresisting for one of his race. His whole person was utterly destitute of the prompt watchfulness of the Indian—all touch, all eye, all ear,—whose every faculty is ready to spring into instant and violent action.

He asked none of the jealous, uneasy questions, of the wiry savage of Rainy Lake. He merely ate his dinner, drank his glass of rum, received some little presents, and after a few whiffs of the peaceful pipe, took his leave, gratefully observing, "Tapoue nih-kispoun" ("Verily I am satisfied").

Other Indians visited us here, partly from curiosity, and partly in hope of presents. A company of six remained about us for some time,—Indians of the olden days,—broad-chested, powerful bronzed statues, with serious and rather fierce physiognomies. They were nearly naked, wearing only the breech-cloth and a buffalo-skin or a blanket loosely across their shoulders, and a string, it must be added, of bears' claws about their necks.

We had no fear of them, and never carried arms. The Englishman's foot is on the Indian's neck. If an Indian had robbed or offered us violence, the Hudson's Bay Company could, and most probably would, have stopped the subsistence of all the tribe until the evil doer had been brought in for judgment.

The summer before our visit to this lake, a factor of the Hudson's Bay Company was encamped for the night near some wigwams on Lake Namaycan, and next morning missed a keg of gunpowder. His Indian neighbours disclaimed all knowledge of the theft; when, after a long parley, the white man seized a woman and child, and hurried off.

Very shortly a canoe was perceived following in double quick time; and with many explanations and apologies the missing keg was exchanged for the living hostages. The powder was much wanted, or perhaps instant redress would not have been sought.

I spent three pleasant days in sketching and geologising about the Rat Portage. The weather was charming, but had been sultry.

We left it on the 22d of July, and made an earnest but vain attempt, on the west of the portage, to find out any well-marked spot entitled to be called, in the language of the treaty, "the most north-western point of the Lake of the Woods." An idea then prevailed that this locality lay hereabouts; but the decision of 1842 has properly placed it many miles to the S.S.W. of Rat Portage. It is a matter of very inferior moment to the adoption of the 49th parallel as the great central boundary line.

We now returned eastwards to complete the circumnavigation of the lake.

A mile to the east of the Rat Portage cul-de-sac I noticed one of the outlets by which the Winnepeg* escapes from the lake,—a rough rapid

* To the mouth of the River Winnepeg, in a light canoe, is a journey of from two and a half to three days. Its general course is N. or N.N.E., among naked primitive rocks, from ten feet to one

flowing down a rocky narrow ; and a mile further east we come upon another channel, terminating in a cascade.

hundred or five hundred feet high ; but at its mouth it passes over white limestone. It is a large and as yet uninvestigated river. It receives many tributaries, and divides into numerous channels, broad and unknown, among islands. It has twenty-five cascades, some of them high and picturesque, besides frequent rapids,—three so strong as to become carrying-places. It forms into lakes, communicating with each other by falls and rapids in straits, of which few, however, are less than 400 yards wide. This information I gathered from traders frequenting this region. One of these, a friend of mine, Mr. J. Mackenzie, met with an awkward adventure on this river a few years ago.

He and his wife were left intentionally by his men at a carrying-place. It was at a rocky spot, in a labyrinth of morass, forest, and river expanses. Together with his wife, Mr. Mackenzie had gone a little aside to gather the pleasant berries which there load the ground in August, while the men were passing the goods over the portage.

They were but a short time away, and then walked to the place of embarkation, from whence, to their great astonishment and dismay, they saw their six canoes smoothly proceeding down a long reach. Signals were made of all possible sorts, but in vain ; not a face turned in the canoes ; and soon all were out of sight.

Two hundred miles of impassable country lay between the forlorn pair and a house. The wife sat down to weep ; but soon started up, and said she thought she knew the country, having been there more than once with her tribe. The river just there performed a circuit of thirty or forty miles in length. She said, that by going straight through the woods for fifteen miles, with hard walking and wading, they perhaps might be able to reach a certain portage before their men. So off they set ; and by most severe labour, and with many anxieties about the proper direction, they gained the portage in time, and saved their lives.

On questioning the *voyageurs*, only frivolous excuses were offered. Some thought their master and his wife had walked on ;

As to the northern and eastern side of the Lake of the Woods proper, I can only speak of its topography in general. The reader is referred to the accompanying map.

The whole east shore, as far as the great Promontory, is distributed into bays and sounds, usually filled with islands.*

Sixteen miles of coasting brought us through various groups of islands, often bristling with young pines, to the River Auogoyahmé (Spawning River). It enters by a fine fall, over granite, at the bottom of a deep bay. The coast had been rocky, but not high, and well covered with small trees of hard wood.

The lake was almost always polluted with green scum and dead insects. It is not shallow here. There is in all lakes a sort of rough proportion between their depth and the height of the neighbouring land.

others, that they had changed their canoe, and were with the party, &c. &c. I do not know that they were punished.

* A thousand and nineteen islands were counted, and more or less fully laid down, in Lakes Kaminitik and Parpequa-wungar. There are very many more. Those we saw rarely attained the length of eight miles, and these are near Shebashca. Mere rocks are not noticed.

None of the islands on the Old Route and in this great lake, embracing a line 430 miles long, are as yet appropriated to the United States or Great Britain. Some of them must very speedily become valuable mining property, as on Gunflint Lake, Iron Lake, &c.

Continuing our southerly course along the east shore, we come to Red Cliff Bay, so called from its many greenstone (basaltic) cliffs, from thirty to one hundred feet high, coated with red moss, and having perpendicular abutments, such as we see propping the walls of old churches. The new colouring gives a singular effect to the scenery.

Erratic blocks of great size are common here. I saw a large one on a mound thirty feet high. Any alluvial deposits or embankments which may exist in this portion of the lake are hid under foliage.

Six miles further south bring us (in crowds of isles) to the marshes called "Sucker Fishing-place" by the Indians, from the abundance of that fish found there. Near this the main was hilly; and here we slept.

Next day, hugging the shore, we breakfasted near Yellow Girl Island, eight miles south of our sleeping-place. It is small, woody, and rather high. It takes its name from a young girl in a yellow dress having been seen standing on one of its cliffs. She disappeared on being searched for.

Islands are fewer in these parts. We again met with a pair of fishing-eagles.

About two miles south of Yellow Girl Island is a narrow inlet in the east main nine miles long. It receives Dryberry River. In this cul-de-sac my young servant carelessly dropped my indispensable hammer into the lake. As the weather was warm, the waters clear though deep, and as he was an excellent swimmer, I requested him to recover it, which he gladly did.

On our return towards the mouth of this inlet we perceived an opening in the main, which we found to lead into White-fish Lake, the third portion of this great body of water.

We did not enter here, but by another channel a few miles to the south-west. From this part of White-fish Lake to the Turtle Portage, which connects it with the south-east side of the Lake of the Sand Hills, the direct distance is thirty-five miles. White-fish Lake must therefore be of considerable size, as it extends also northward and eastward from this spot.

We only went a couple of miles into it. I saw a large expanse of clear waters, with two or three lofty islands. The scenery resembled that of the basalt lakes of the Old Route, or of Lake Superior about Pigeon Bay. Dark heights and pine-crested headlands were all around; and the lake was as blue and unruffled as the lagoon of a coral island.

We returned to the Lake of the Woods by a third channel, guided by our Indian, and proceeded west, having on our left (to the south) the great promontory which, with one principal island, and some others, cuts the lake into the two parts, so well named by the Indians, and which the commercial route from Lake Superior to the Red River crosses at the Portage des Bois.

Along this part of the route a pouring rain and endless changes in our course (" wandering in vain about bewildered shores") prevented accurate notes being taken.

The shape and dimensions of the promontory have been already given, but I must add that the outline of its shores is irregular on the west, and its end broad. Its average height is under one hundred feet. It is well wooded, but burnt in patches. Islands abound in its vicinity, as almost everywhere else. One of these near its east end is called Pipestone Island, from its having in its sienitic greenstone a vein of hard chlorite earth, about eight inches thick, of which the Indians, far and near, make their pipe-bowls. There is another place in the lake where this substance may be procured.

The Portage des Bois, ten miles from the west end of the promontory, enables the traveller to avoid going round it and its islands. It is a grassy swamp, one hundred paces across, at the bottom (on the north) of a fissure or cul-de-sac, about ten miles deep, and full of small islands.

We rounded the promontory by Point aux Chênes, through the narrow on the eastern side of the long island adjacent, and entered once more the Lake of the Sand Hills. We paid a passing visit to the south end of the Portage des Bois, and found it in a moderate-sized bay. From thence we skirted the promontory eastwards, eight miles (?) to Gravel Point, a cape surrounded by gravel, sand, and bowlders.

The view into the lake from Gravel Point presents in every direction islands of gneiss and granite, large and small (from one to five miles long), either naked or topped with pines and poplar; but in front, or southerly, they are fewer, and very small, so that far in the distance, through isles, whose trees loomed high in the haze, we saw the open lake.

Proceeding eastwards, along the southern and straighter side of the promontory, we met for a time with open waters, islets (small and few) chequering the foreground, and larger beyond.

Here we found a party of Indians gathering black bilberries (*Vaccinium. Canadense*). This fruit is incredibly abundant all over these countries. For miles we cannot tread without crushing them under our feet; and we owed much of our health and strength to the free use of them. The berries are very dark purple, as large as the out-door English grape, and they grow on a low creeping shrub. Their flavour is sweet and agreeable; most so in the spring, when they have lain a winter under snow. At that period of the year they are a very important resource to birds, bears, and other animals.

While we were purchasing bilberries, I noticed a sulky old Indian sitting apart on a somewhat high rock, with his arms round his legs, and his head on his knees.

I asked "the little Englishman" who that woe-stricken man was; when he gave me the following statement.

Some years ago this Indian had strangled his lunatic son—his only son and favourite child.

The youth, eighteen years old, for a year or more had refused to hunt, became abstracted, melancholy, and at times frenzied.

When his paroxysms were coming on he would warn his family to protect a particular sister from his unwilling violence, as he had an irresistible propensity to kill and devour her; and, in fact, he made several attempts upon her life.

After a time, his lunacy, for such it was, changed its object; and he declared that he must murder and eat the first Indian he could master in the woods or elsewhere.

He now daily begged his father to put him to death; and so end his miseries.

The surrounding Indians took alarm at all this.

The father, as is usual in great emergencies, called a council. It sat several times, and after much deliberation ordered the lunatic to be strangled by his own father, the *giver* of his life.

The father obeyed. The youth, after listening to a long speech, and assenting aloud to every separate observation, bared his neck to the cord, and soon ceased to breathe. His body was burnt, lest he should rise again.

The parent never looked up more.

We slept that night on a small, flat, well-timbered island, not far from the east end of the promontory. In my geological ardour I determined to run round it, though cautioned not to do so. Away I went as fast as I could go; but such were its innumerable little wrinkles, among deep waters, the night also soon setting in, that I did not reach the camp until past eleven o'clock, thoroughly worn out, and thankful for a supper of cocoa and bilberries. Had not the moon arisen at about ten o'clock, I must have slept in the woods.

Although the west end of the promontory is well wooded, towards its middle it becomes naked, and is often purposely fired by the Indians.

Going still eastwards, we soon exchange the

comparatively open lake for a vast belt of low islands, pretty well covered with young trees, and girt with white granite mounds barely appearing above water.

Beaches and hillocks of sand are now almost universal on the main, and from time to time we see the same great collections of erratic blocks which encumbered the west shores of the Lake of the Sand Hills; but here they were on the heights 120 feet above the lake, among tall straight cypress-trees.

Being now about thirty miles from the west end of the promontory, we leave it, and from going east we gradually turn to the south.

We have in this vicinity access twice to White-fish Lake, at places ten or twelve miles apart.

The northern of these points is at Turtle Portage, across eighty yards of swamp and rock. The other is at the Falls of the Pine River (twenty feet high), at the extreme east end of the lake, at the bottom of a deep bay, and thirty-five miles direct from the nearest part of Rainy Lake. This river, however, does not actually communicate with White-fish Lake, but only passes near it. It is much the shortest way to Fort Lapluie from White-fish Lake, assisted by a chain of streamlets and lakes.

It was remarkable that at Turtle Portage we

found among some long grass a turtle, from twelve to fifteen inches long, of a very dark colour, and its markings, if it had any, obscured by dirt.*

The shape and direction of the east and south shore of Sand-hill Lake are best seen on the map. It is very long, and sweeps in large, easy, low, sinuosities of sand, in ridges and flats, with frequent marshes and productive rice-grounds. Thousands of foreign rocks of large dimensions crowd the sands and shallows, which extend very far into the lake.

There are very few islets; one of these is named Elm Island.

Twelve miles E.N.E. from Windy Point on Sable Island there is a remarkable spot, Point Brûlé, a striking landmark.

It is a sloping headland of white gneiss, sprinkled with small pines. On its summit, once doubtless hidden by trees, is an ancient round look-out against the hereditary enemy, the Sioux, and of the same size as that near Lake Croche; but here, all the stones are thrown down in circles outwards. The Indian imagination of the present day has found out a meaning for it. They call it the nest of the Thunder Bird.

Three miles west of Point Brûlé is Rice River,

* It was probably the wood terrapin (*Emys insculpta*), but larger than is common.

one of three in the lake of the same name. It looks large and flows through low lands.

A course of eight miles from this river, along a mainland of sand-banks, bushes, with small burnt trees in the rear, brings us to Windy Point, a spot five miles north-east of Sable Island, at the mouth of the River Lapluie.

A violent thunder-storm, followed by a gale of wind, drove us into the narrow pass between the main and Sable Island, among tall rushes and grass. We then reached the River Lapluie, and completed the circuit of this distant but interesting lake.*

I shall spare the reader our homeward journey of nearly two thousand miles. But for aught I know, he may have long ago left us engulfed in suffocating woods, or on the waters, which, unlike those of Siloam, do not go softly.

We were greatly indebted under Providence to the care and skill of Mr. Astronomer Thompson.

* Highest water-mark in the Lake of the Woods proper was five feet above its level in July 1823.

Magnetic Variation:—

1823.		
July 17,	Near Driftwood Point	7° E.
18,	N.W Coast, 30 miles from Rat Portage, mid-day	14° E.
24,	South side of Portage des Bois	13° 14′ E.
26,	Mid-day. Sandhill Lake. On Promontory .	12° E.
28,	East angle of mouth of Rainy River . .	12° E.

There was a good deal of wear and tear in our life of little ease, constant exposure, and unsuitable food.

The ill effects were only temporary; and we soon remembered only the pleasurable part of our wanderings.

Great was the enjoyment of returning to the comforts and amenities of civilised life. Milk was a luxurious novelty. The Indians call the land of the pale-faces "the cow-country." The use of money was strange, and so was access to letters, newspapers, and large assemblies of people. Few things, however, struck us so much as the happy eyes, carmine lips, and pleasant voice of childhood.

APPENDIX.

(A).

As there are very few, if any, of the *Voyageurs* songs in print, it would be desirable to insert a few of those which are sung in the Indian countries, but the want of space forbids the insertion of more than one. It was taken by the author from the lips of the singer, and is evidently ancient Norman, in the Canadian *patois* :—

CHANSON.

Quand j'étais chez mon père,
  Petite et jeune étant,
M'envoyait à la fontaine } *bis*
  Pour pêcher des poissons. }
    La violette dandine, la violette dondé.

La fontaine est profonde,
  Moi de couler au fond ;
Par-ici ils passent
  Trois cavaliers barons.
    La violette dandine, la violette dondé.

" Que donneriez vous, belle,
  Pour vous tirer du fond ?"
" Tirez, tirez," dit-elle :
" Après-ça nous verrons."
    La violette dandine, la violette dondé.

Quand la belle fut tirée
  S'en va à la maison;
S'assied sur la fenêtre
  Et commence une chanson.
    La violette dandine, la violette dondé.

"Ce n'est pas, ma belle,
  Ce que nous demandons;
C'est votre cœur en gage,
  Savoir si nous l'aurons."
    La violette dandine, la violette dondé.

"Mon petit cœur," dit-elle,
  "N'est pas pour un baron;
C'est pour un gentil-homme,
  Qui à la barbe au menton."
    La violette dandine, la violette dondé.

"Oh! dites-nous, ma belle,
  Où est-il, votre mignon?"
"Il est à la fontaine
  Qu'il pêche la poisson."
    La violette dandine, la violette dondé.

"Oh! dites-nous, ma belle,
  Quel poisson y prend-t-on?
On y prend la carpe,
  Aussi l'esturgeon."
    La violette dandine, la violette dondé.

"On y prend la carpe,
  Aussi l'esturgeon,
Aussi des écrevisses
  Qui vont à reculons."
    La violette dandine, la violette dondé.

&c. &c. &c.

Mrs. Henry Malan has very kindly favoured me with the following pretty but free translation of the above ballad:—

With heart as wild
As joyous child,
Lived Rhoda of the mountain,
Her only wish
To seek the fish
In the waters of the fountain.
Oh, the violet, white and blue!

The stream is deep,
The banks are steep,
Down in the flood fell she,
When there rode by
Right gallantly
Three barons of high degree.
Oh, the violet, white and blue!

"Oh, tell us, fair maid,"
They each one said,
"Your reward to the venturing knight
Who shall save your life
From the water's strife
By his arm's unflinching might."
Oh, the violet, white and blue!

"Oh! haste to my side,"
The maiden replied,
"Nor ask of a recompense now;
When safe on land
Again I stand
For such matters is time enow."
Oh, the violet, white and blue!

But when all free
Upon the lea
She found herself once more,
She would not stay,
And sped away
Till she reached her cottage door.
Oh, the violet, white and blue!

Her casement by,
That maiden shy
Began so sweet to sing;
Her lute and voice
Did e'en rejoice
The early flowers of spring.
Oh, the violet, white and blue!

But the barons proud
Then spoke aloud,
"This is not the boon we desire;
Your heart and love,
My pretty dove,
Is the free gift we require."
Oh, the violet, white and blue

"Oh, my heart so true
Is not for you,
Nor for any of high degree;
I have pledged my truth
To an honest youth,
With a beard so comely to see."
Oh, the violet, white and blue!

&c. &c. &c.

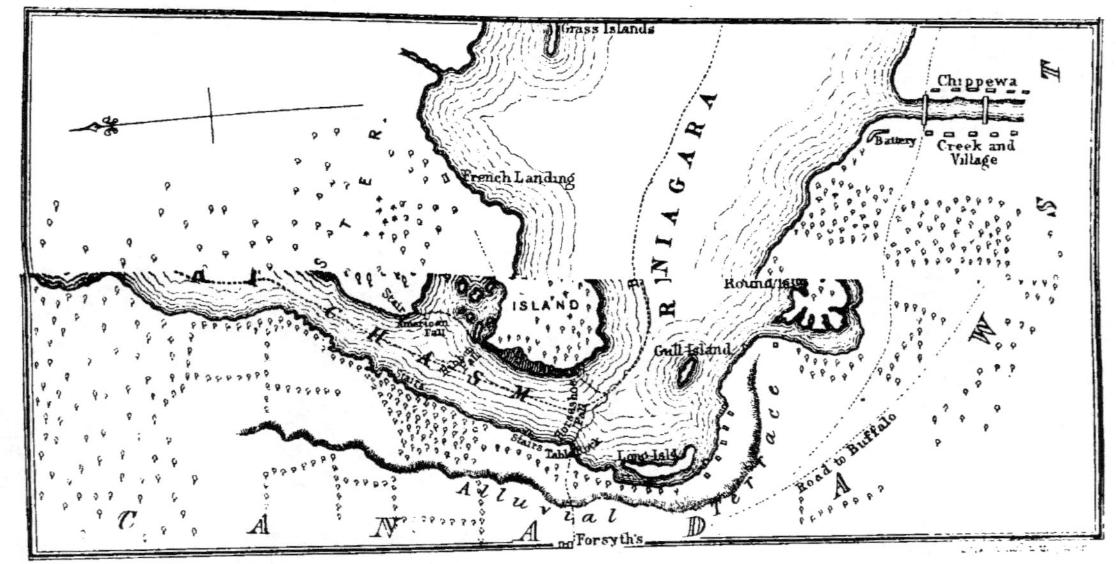

Grass Islands
French Landing
Chippewa
Creek and Village
Battery
NIAGARA
R
ISLAND
American Fall
Horseshoe Fall
Stairs
Table
Gull Island
Long Isld
Round Isld
Alluvial Terrace
Road to Buffalo
Forsyth's
C A N A D A

APPENDIX (B).

BRIEF NOTES ON THE TOPOGRAPHY OF THE RIVER NIAGARA.

(WITH ADMEASUREMENTS.)

THE River Niagara issues from the north-east end of Lake Erie, and enters Lake Ontario on the south-west side, forty-six miles from its head, after having crossed, with a general north-by-west course, the intervening neck of land, at that point 26½ miles broad.

This isthmus is here divided into two levels, the upper (to be noticed first) advancing from Lake Erie to within seven miles of Lake Ontario; but at that distance (at Queenston), it lowers 370½ feet at once, by a steep slope, which skirts, at various heights, the whole south and west shores of Lake Ontario, under the name of the "Parallel Ridge."

During the first twenty miles of the upper level, from Lake Erie, the land on both sides of the Niagara is so moist and flat as scarcely to assign a direction to its streams. It is raised but little above Lake Erie, and would be flooded in spring were the vernal rise of water as great as in the Rivers Ottawa and St. Lawrence.

On the Canadian side of the Niagara, and probably on the American also, there is close to it a border of raised ground, varying in breadth from half a mile to two miles, or more. The banks show that it is composed of brown loam, clay, and small angular fragments of the black geodiferous limestone of Niagara.

The direction of the Niagara for three miles from Lake Erie is north, and then bends round to the north-west for two miles, when it is divided into two narrow and distant channels to within 3¾ miles of the Falls by a very large island, from the foot of which the river runs west by north.

The current for the first three or four miles from the head of the river is swift, especially about and below Black Rock, where it is seven miles an hour, smooth on the surface, but violently agitated within. From thence to near the Falls the rate is uniform and moderate. The decline in level from the head of the river to Chippewa is said to be fifteen feet.

Its depth is by no means great, especially at the lower end, where the shores, &c., are often marshy. Opposite Black Rock it is thirty-two feet deep all the way across, according to the careful soundings of Mr. Allen. General Porter has there constructed a large basin for shipping, whose walls rest upon horizontal rock.

The breadth of the Niagara varies much, as is seen from the following statements, which are taken from the large maps of the Boundary Commission :—

	Miles.	Yards.
At Bird Island, 1070 yards above the head of the river	1	220
At the exact commencement of the river	-	733
Opposite General Porter's House, at Black Rock	-	462
At the middle of Squaw Island, below Black Rock	-	1320
At Strawberry Island, one mile below	1	440
At the head of Grand Island	1	880
At Tonnewanta Island	2	230
At the lower end of Grand Island	2	1313
Ditto Navy Island	1	430
At Chippewa River	1	220
At the head of Goat Island	-	1310

This river has islands only on its upper level, and these are twenty-eight in number, for the most part low and swampy, and finely wooded with sugar-maple, elm, oak, and linden trees, when a few feet above water-mark. Their length usually runs parallel to the river.

Bird Island, opposite Fort Erie, is a mere ledge of rock 220 yards long. Squaw Island, 1¾ mile below, is 1880 yards long, and close to the east shore. The next, Strawberry Island, is 1¼ mile long.

Grand Island is five miles from Lake Erie, 7½ miles long by 6½ miles in greatest breadth. It is an irregular oval, and chiefly in a state of nature, the interior being a morass, and often a group of ponds. Where dry it is heavily timbered. It contains 17,924 acres.

The channels on each side of Grand Island are not broad, that on the American shore being 513 yards wide where narrowest, and 660 yards on the Canadian where narrowest, three-quarters of a mile below Beaver Island.

Beaver Island is small, and 350 yards from Grand Island.

Rattlesnake Island is a strip of marsh 2000 yards long, near the head of Grand Island. Tonnewanta Island is close to the east main, and rather exceeds half a mile in length. Cayuga is the next, also near the east main, and 2060 yards long.

Buckhorn Island follows, on the east of, and very near to, Grand Island. It is marshy, 2000 yards long, and tapers to a point below.

Navy Island is the only island in this river belonging to Great Britain. It is semi-circular, and contains 304 acres.

The size and position of other very small islets may be seen on the plan of the Falls, placed in the Sixth Excursion.

Iris, or Goat Island, is somewhat triangular in shape; its base, 400 yards long, being on the same line with the cataract. It is half a mile long: its soil is of light brown clay, supporting a gravel of rolled limestones and primitive pebbles, of the tertiary age, according to Professor Hall. The island is flat, and mostly covered with fine clumps of beech. Between it and the American shore there is a round islet, which, by two bridges, connects Iris Island with the main. A little below it are seven other patches of rock, bearing a few pines.

The streams which enter the Niagara along its upper level are a few sluggish creeks, the discharges of extensive swamps. I shall simply name them. They are, French, Black, Chippewa, Ellicott, and Tonnewanta creeks.

At Chippewa commences the more disturbed portion

of the river, preluding the Falls, now 2¼ miles distant. Its ample breadth sensibly diminishes.

On the British shore the accelerated current begins here to ripple; and at Bridgewater, one mile lower down, it dashes and foams over a succession of ledges, which are most conspicuous opposite the head of Iris Island. Below this the water moves with equal swiftness, but smoothly, over pebbly shallows, until it is precipitated into the great chasm.

On the American shore the same is going on, but with still greater fury.

Together with these changes in the state of the river, the banks, from Chippewa to Bridgewater, very gradually attain the height of forty feet, in scarps and grassy slopes. This apparent rise is caused by the sinking of the bed of the river;* but from hence for the remaining mile and a quarter a real elevation of the bank and adjacent country takes place. The united effect of this is the formation on the Canadian shore of slopes and terraces, which have been carefully measured and laid down by Professor Hall, of Albany, New York. They skirt the river from the late Colonel Clarke's, at Bridgewater, to and beyond the cataract, in grassy knolls, highly ornamented here and there with fine trees, among which are well-grown tulip trees. The American banks ascend from the water in a richly-wooded slope.

In this interesting locality, twenty-one miles from Lake Erie, and at the foot of what we must call the

* Philadelphia Museum, vol. viii. p. 215; fifty-eight feet between Chippewa and the Falls.

remains of Iris Island, the Niagara plunges at once into a rocky chasm 156½ feet deep, 960* yards broad along the chord, and prolonged for seven miles east-north-east, almost at right angles, with the former course of the river.

This descent or leap takes place obliquely to the direction of the river, and is divided into three parts by Iris Island, and the islet on its right. These are named the Horse-shoe, the Ribbon or Montmorenci, and the American or Schlosser, Falls, respectively.

The whole line of subsidence is 1200 yards long. Of this the Horse-shoe Fall occupies about one-half, and the American Fall, with the base of Iris Island, each a quarter, while the Ribbon Fall and an adjoining islet take up twenty yards of the line.

The Horse-shoe Fall is on the Canadian side. Its name no longer describes its form, a correct idea of which, indeed, is not easily obtained, owing to certain perspective deceptions. The sketch accompanying these pages gives its shape in 1822, as laid down in the charts of the Boundary Commission, with great care and exactitude.

A naked, flat ledge, called the Table Rock, at the northern angle of this fall, permits the visitor to dip his feet into the water as it passes over the precipice.

It is this fall which presents the unbroken curtain of emerald edged with white or brown. The stream beneath the pitch is smooth, but white with intestine commotion. A little way down it forms into billows, and maintains a great velocity through the whole chasm to Queenston.

* Boundary Survey—as always.

At the foot of the Horse-shoe Fall the gusts of a tempestuous day permitted me to see some very large fragments of rock, by having driven away the spray and broken water which usually conceal them.

The Ribbon Fall is aptly named. It springs from its dark channel with great force and beauty.

The American Fall is 162 feet deep (" Philadelphia Museum"). Its face, although on the whole pretty straight, is in several places jagged or serrated, so that the line of descent is varied and picturesque.

The cataract has beyond all doubt excavated, by solution and fracture, the whole chasm from Queenston heights, during a period of time which we cannot measure, having been directed, according to Professor Hall, into that channel by a slight natural hollow pre-existing.

The inhabitants of the vicinity now testify to the reality of the process ; indeed it is self-evident. Together with a slow retrocession and change of form from smaller losses, large masses of rock are dropping from the line of subsidence into the gulf below from time to time. A portion of the Table Rock, weighing many tons, fell a few months before my first visit.

It would degrade and fall away much faster were not the upper rock a hard limestone, while the lower half of the cataract-wall consists of a crumbling shale.

From the varying nature of the rocks over which it has flowed from Queenston to its present site, it must have changed its form very often ; and never was so imposing and diversified in its features as at this time.

There is little doubt but that in some parts of its course it was a long slanting fall, as when it passed over shaly sandstone; in others it was in two or more parts, dropping down in great steps, as when it reached the grey quartzy sandstone, and separated from each other by distances more or less great according to the resistance of the underlying stratum to its powers of erosion.

When this process began we know not. Of its rate of proceeding, either by years or centuries, we know very little; but, judging from the hard nature of the rocks between the present cataract and Lake Erie, some thousands of years must elapse before it reach the latter. It will have more or less effect in draining Lake Erie, according to the breadth of the rocky lip over which the water falls, and the depth of the passing wave. The lip, at Lake Erie, is 733 yards broad, instead of 900 at the Falls; but the depth of water is greater. These two being considered together, little drainage will probably take place until the cataract shall have worked still further back into the lake.

The Niagara group of sandstones and limestones is, according to the state geologists of New York, the equivalents of a part of the Wenlock series of the British Isles. The indefatigable labours of these highly qualified gentlemen have left little to be desired as to our acquaintance with the geology of these districts.

We now proceed to bestow a few words on the lower division of the River Niagara.

The chasm is 6¼ miles long, and for two miles from the Falls runs east-north-east, when it turns to the north-west, a mile further, to the whirlpool. It there changes suddenly to the north-east, and so continues, or with slight variation, for two miles, to a little beyond the Devil's Hole, on the American side. From thence a northern course is slowly assumed, and, with a few jutting elbows, is continued to Lake Ontario.

The whirlpool just alluded to is a circular basin 500 yards in diameter, on the Canadian shore, created by the sudden change in the direction of the river. Its violence has been somewhat exaggerated. The water rushes into it in billows from the pent channel above, and then, with eddies here and there, courses round the basin in a swift smooth current, and slowly flows off—so slowly, indeed, that on one occasion a dead body was observed in it for two or three days.

The side of the chasm may be described in general terms to be precipitous; often, as near the Falls and elsewhere, mural in the upper half of its height or more; and terminated below by slopes of fragments, naked or overgrown with vines and other creeping plants: but more commonly the stream is flanked by ledges and enormous displaced masses, numerous or few, high or low, in places; and being interspersed with patches of soil, are clothed with underwood and fine trees.

The average breadth of the river in the chasm is 300 yards; but a mile below the whirlpool it contracts to 115 yards, near the ruins of a saw-mill. Here the bottom is seen, nearly in mid-channel, to consist of large fragments of rock, over which the water passes with inconceivable fury. The precipice on the Canadian side is so shattered here that, with some ingenuity, an indifferent cart-road has been made down it. Two miles and a half below the whirlpool the breadth of the river is 135 yards. Half a mile above the gorge of Queenston it is 130 yards broad, and at the gorge 212 yards.

Of the depth of the water in the chasm I know very little. Mr. Forsyth, the proprietor of the two British hotels at the Falls, told me that in the middle of the basin, in front of the Falls, the depth is 160 feet.

The bed of the river makes a gradual descent of 67 feet* from the foot of the Falls to Queenston Gorge. At this last place the sides of the chasm are higher than at the former. Mr. Gourlay states the elevation of Queenston Heights to be 370½ feet, and, I believe, correctly.

The depression at Queenston of the upper or Erie plateau is sudden; but the subsequent widening of the stream is slow, and seldom varies from 700 yards.

The course of the river is henceforth rather west of north, its current averaging two miles per hour. The banks are of slaty clay and argillaceous sandstone at Queenston, supporting a gravelly loam, and are from fifty to eighty feet high; but from thence to the river mouth they are of a rich red clayey soil, and rather high.

At the contiguous shore of Lake Ontario the banks are from twelve to fifteen feet high, of pure clay below, covered with large primitive bowlders and a mixed soil. The river expands but little on meeting with the lake; its width between the American Fort Niagara, at the confluence, and the British town of Newark, being from 800 to 1000 yards. There is a considerable bar of sand and mud off the mouth.

* Philadelphia Museum, *ut ante*.

APPENDIX (C).

As the climate of Canada is extreme both in heat and cold, we find there some new genera and many new species of insects.

The following list, collected by the author principally in Lake Huron, has been drawn up by the Rev. W. Kirby, F.R.S. He has fully described them in the "Fauna Boreali-Americana" of Sir John Richardson, with figures of the most interesting.

The new species are distinguished by the letters appended (K.N.S.).

Order .. Coleoptera.
Section.. Pentamera.
Tribe .. Carnivora.
Sub-tribe Terrestria.
Family .. Cicindelidæ.

Genus Cicindelidæ, Linn.
—— Marshamii, K.N.S.
—— marginalis, Fabr.
—— Canadensis, K.N.S.
—— albi-labris, K.N.S.

Family .. Carabidæ.

Genus Brachinus, Fabr.
—— crepitans, Var. Br.
Genus Chlœnius, Bonelli.
—— pulchellus, K.N.S.
Genus Chlœnius.
—— dimidiatus, K.N.S.
—— obscurior, K.N.S.
Genus Agonum, Bonelli.
—— parampunctatum, F. Br.
Genus Calosoma, Fabr.
—— angulatum, K.N.S.
Genus Carabus, Linn.
—— obscuratus, K.N.S.
Genus Omophron, Latreille.
—— Canadense, K.N.S.
Genus Elaphrus, Fabr.
—— intermedius, K.N.S.
Genus Bembidium, Latreille.
—— littorale, Eur.

Subtribe .. Aquatica.
Family .... Gyrinidæ.

Genus Gyrinus, Linn.
—— æneus, Leach. Br.
—— impressicollis, K.N.S.

Tribe .. Brachelytra.
Family .. Staphylinidæ.

Genus Creophilus, Kirby.
—— Villosus, Br.
Genus Lathrobium, Gravenhorst.
—— bicolor, Grav.

Tribe .. Serricornia.
Family .. Buprestidæ.

Genus Buprestis, Linn.
—— fasciatus, L.
—— acuminata, F.
—— strigata, K.N.S.
Genus Trachys, Fabr.
—— aurulenta, K.N.S.

Family .. Elateridæ.

Genus Elater, Linn.
—— castanipes, F. Br.
—— flavilabris, K.N.S.

Family .. Lampyridæ.

Genus Lycus, Fabr.
—— reticulatus, F.
Genus Lampyris, Linn.
—— corrusca, L.
—— pectoralis, K.N.S.
Genus Telephorus, Geoffr.
—— marginellus, K.N.S.

Tribe .. Clavicornia.
Family.. Silphidæ.

Genus Silpha, Linn., ichthyophaga, K.N.S. (found in dead fish.)
—— lapponica, L. Var. Eur.

Family .. Dermestidæ.

Genus Dermestes, Linn.
—— murinus, L. Br.

Tribe .. Lamellicornia.
Family .. Scarabæidæ.

Genus Onthophagus, Latreille.
—— scabricollis, K.N.S.

Family .. Rutelidæ.

Genus Pelidnota, W. S. Macleay.
—— punctata, Lake St. Clair.

Family .. Melolonthidæ.

Genus Melolontha, Fabr.
—— rufipes, K.N.S.
—— angustata, K.N.S. } Var.?
—— assimilis, K.N.S. }
N.B.—On willows.
Genus Serica, W. S. Macleay.
—— subsulcata, K.N.S.

Family .. Cetoniadæ.

Genus Trichius, Fabr.
—— Bigsbii, K.N.S. L. St. Clair.
—— viridulus, Var. ?
Genus Cetonia, Fabr.
——fulgida, Ft. St. Clair.

Section .. Heteromera.
Tribe .. Melasoma.
Family .. Tenebrionidæ.

Genus Upis, Fabr.
—— ceramboides, F. Eur.

Tribe .. Taxicornia.
Family .. Diaperidæ.

Genus Bolitophagus, Illiger.
—— cristatus, K.N.S.
N.B.—On the boletus of the birch.

Tribe .. Stenelytra.
Family .. Helopidæ.

Genus Meracantha, Kirby, N. G.
—— Canadensis, K.N.S.

N.B.—I have another species of this *genus* from Georgia, which seems synonymous with Blaps Metallica, F.

Genus Arthromacer, Kirby, N. G.
—— denacioides, K.N.S. L. St. Clair.

Genus Xylita, Paykull.
—— buprestoides, Paykull, Br.

Genus Cistela, Fabr.
—— erythropus, K.N.S.

Tribe .. Trachelida.
Family .. Cantharidæ.

Genus Cantharis, Geoffr.
—— antennata, K.N.S.

Section .. Tetramera.
Tribe .. Rhyncophora.
Family .. Bruchidæ.

Genus Anthribus, Geoffr.
—— fasciatus, Oliv.

Family .. Attelabidæ.

Genus Opoderus, Oliv.
—— bipustulatus, L. St. Clair.

Genus Attelabris, Linn.
—— curculionoides, L. Br.

Genus Rhynchites, Herbst.
—— ovatus, Oliv., L. St. Clair.

Family .. Curculionidæ.

Genus Calandra, Clairv.
—— pertinax, Oliv.

Genus Hylobius, Germar.
—— confusus, K.N.S.

Genus Lepyrus, Germar.
—— colon, Eur.

Family .. Brachyrhinidæ.

Genus Brachyrhinus, Latreille. (Sitona Germar.)
—— melanostichus, K.N.S.

Tribe .. Longicornia.
Family .. Lamiadæ.

Genus Lamia, Fabr.
—— Canadensis, K.N.S.

Genus Saperda, Fabr.
—— sexnotata, K.N.S.
—— miniata, K.N.S.
—— concolor, K.N.S.

Family .. Cerambycidæ.

Genus Clytus, Fabr.
—— lunulatus, K.N.S.

Family .. Necydalidæ.

Genus Getniaca, Kirby, N. G.
—— lepturiodes, K.N.S.

Family .. Lepturidæ.

Genus Leptura, Linn.
—— tormentosa, F. Eur.
—— ventralis, K.N.S.
—— tricolor, K.N.S.

Tribe .. Eupoda.
Family .. Crioceridæ.

Genus Denacia, Fabr.
—— crassipes, F. var. } Br.
—— micans, Marsh } Br.
—— cuprea, K.N.S.

Genus Macroplea, Hoffmans.
—— nigricornis, K.N.S.

Tribe .. Cyclica.
Family .. Hispidæ.

Genus Hispa, Linn.
—— bicolor, Oliv.

Family [illegible]

Genus [illegible]

Family [illegible]

Genus [illegible]

Family [illegible]

Genus [illegible]

Family [illegible]

Genus [illegible]

Family [illegible]

Genus [illegible]

Family [illegible]

Genus [illegible]

Genus [illegible] Latreille. [illegible]

Family [illegible]

Genus [illegible] Latreille.
—— [illegible]
—— [illegible]
[illegible]

CPSIA information can be obtained
at www.ICGtesting.com
Printed in the USA
BVHW041324271019
562107BV00003B/3/P

9 781298 590817